Richard Troward

A Collection of the Statutes in Force Relative to Elections down to the Present Time

Richard Troward

A Collection of the Statutes in Force Relative to Elections down to the Present Time

ISBN/EAN: 9783337778354

Printed in Europe, USA, Canada, Australia, Japan

Cover: Foto ©Suzi / pixelio.de

More available books at **www.hansebooks.com**

A COLLECTION

OF THE

STATUTES

IN FORCE RELATIVE TO

ELECTIONS

DOWN TO THE PRESENT TIME,

WITH

A COPIOUS INDEX:

ALSO,

AN APPENDIX,

Containing the Orders of the Houfe of Commons concerning Elections, the Acts regulating the Elections of Peers and Members for Scotland from the Time of the Union, and, an Abftract of all Controverted Elections, as well upon the Right as otherwife, determined by Select Committees; with References to the Journals of the Houfe for the Proceedings thereon, and to the printed Reports where the Cafes have been reported.

By RICHARD TROWARD,

OF NORFOLK STREET.

SECOND EDITION.

LONDON:

SOLD BY J. BUTTERWORTH, FLEET-STREET; E. BROOK, BELL-YARD; AND J. DEBRETT, PICCADILLY.

M DCC XCVI.

ADVERTISEMENT.

The extraordinary demand for this book, has been the moſt ſatisfactory proof to the Editor, that he has not failed in his object of producing a work of real utility. As a General Election is preſumed to be approaching, a new edition thereof is offered to the public, with ſuch additional acts, and orders of the Houſe, relative to Elections, as have been made ſince its firſt publication.

PREFACE.

This volume will be found to contain every statute in force, from the 5th year of Richard the Second to the present time, on the regulation of Elections,—the qualification of electors and of persons capable of being elected,—the duty of sheriffs and returning officers,—the forming of select committees, their duty and authority,—and the privilege and protection of the persons of members; and the Appendix will shew all the orders of the house, now in force, which are supposed to have relation to the writ, the execution and return thereof, and proceedings respecting controversies, before committees, as well with respect to the *right* of Election as otherwise. The different acts and resolutions are indexed under such heads or titles as have appeared to be most convenient and easy of reference.

The three acts of 7 Ed. 1. stat. 1,—4 Ed. 3. cap. 14,—and 46 Ed. 3.—are not printed, as they are conceived to be obsolete and virtually repealed by subsequent acts; nor has notice been taken of the acts to regulate the Scotch parliament previous to the union

union of the two kingdoms, these having already been collected and published.

The acts regulating the election of the sixteen peers for Scotland, and the forty-five members of the house of commons for that part of the kingdom, are also here given. They are thrown together in the Appendix; because they could not have been incorporated with the English acts in one general Index, without much obvious inconvenience.

Short abstracts are also inserted of all causes which have been determined by select committees, referring by dates to the Journals of the House; and, where the cases have been reported, distinguishing the name of the reporter and the volume in which such case is to be found. This addition, it is hoped, will prove of considerable utility in practice.

On the whole, no endeavour has been spared to make this publication as complete as possible for every purpose, and nothing has been omitted which was thought likely to be instructive to returning officers in the execution of the writ, and to candidates themselves, when they may happen not to be within the reach of legal advice; or which might be convenient to gentlemen of the profession, particularly at the poll and before committees.

CONTENTS.

TITLES OF THE ACTS.

1382. 5 *Rich.* II. *cap.* 4.
"Every one to whom it belongeth fhall upon fummons come to the parliament," page 1 and 2.

1405. 7 *Hen.* IV. *cap.* 15.
"Manner of electing knights of fhires," p. 2 and 3.

1409. 11 *Hen.* IV. *cap.* 1.
"Penalty on fheriff for making an undue return of the election of the knights of parliament," p. 4.

1413. 1 *Hen.* V. *cap.* 1.
"What fort of people fhall be chofen, and who fhall be the choofers of knights and burgeffes," p. 5.

1427. 6 *Hen.* VI. *cap.* 4.
"The fheriffs traverfe to an inqueft found, touching returning knights," from p. 5 to 7.

1429. 8 *Hen.* VI. *cap.* 7.
"What fort of men fhall be choofers, and who fhall be chofen knights," p. 8 and 9.

1432. 10 *Hen.* VI. *cap.* 2.
"Certain things required in him who fhall be a choofer of knights," p. 10.

1444. 23 *Hen.* VI. *cap.* 10.
"The order of levying the wages of knights," from p. 11 to 13.

1444. 23 *Hen.* VI. *cap.* 14.
"Who shall be knights—manner of their election — remedy where one is chosen and another returned," from p. 13 to 19.

1514. 6 *Hen.* VIII. *cap.* 16.
"An act that no knights nor burgesses depart before the end of parliament," p. 19 and 20.

1535. 27 *Hen.* VIII. *cap.* 26.
"Concerning the laws to be used in *Wales*," p. 21 and 22.

1542. 34 and 35 *Hen.* VIII. *cap.* 13.
"An act for making of knights and burgesses within the county and city of *Chester*," from p. 22 to 24.

1543. 35 *Hen.* VIII. *cap.* 11.
"The bill for knights and burgesses in *Wales*, concerning the payment of their fees and wages," from p. 24 to 29.

1672. 25 *Car.* II. *cap.* 9.
"An act to enable the County Palatine of *Durham* to send knights and burgesses," from p. 29 to 31.

1677. 30 *Car.* II. *cap.* 1.
"An act for the more effectual preserving the King's person and government, by disabling papists from sitting in either House," from p. 31 to 37.

1690. 2 *Will.* & *Mary*, *cap.* 7.
"An act to declare the right and freedom of election of members for the *Cinque Ports*," from p. 37 to 38.

1694.

1694. 5 *Will. & Mary, cap.* 7.
"An act for granting to their majesties certain rates and duties upon salt, and upon beer, ale, and other liquors, for securing certain recompences and advantages in the said act mentioned to such persons as shall voluntarily advance the sum of *ten hundred thousand pounds* towards carrying on the war against *France*," [commissioners not to be members], from p. 38 to 39.

1694. 5 *Will. & Mary, cap.* 20.
"An act for granting to their majesties several rates and duties upon tonnage of ships and vessels, and upon beer, ale, and other liquors, for securing certain recompences and advantages in the said act mentioned to such persons as shall voluntarily advance the sum of *one million five hundred thousand pounds* towards carrying on the war against *France*," [members enabled to be of the corporation erected by this act], from p. 39 to 41.

1694 6 *Will. & Mary, cap.* 2.
"An act for the frequent meeting and calling of parliaments," [triennial act], from p. 41 to 43.

1696. 7 *Will.* III. *cap.* 4.
"An act for preventing charge and expence in elections of members," from p. 43 to 45.

1696. 7 & 8 *Will.* III. *cap.* 7.
"An act to prevent false and double returns of members," from p. 45 to 48.

1696. 7 & 8 *Will.* III. *cap.* 25.
"An act for the further regulating elections of members, and for preventing irregular pro-

ceedings of sheriffs and other officers in the electing and returning such members," from p. 49 to 56.

1699. 10 & 11 *Will.* III. *cap.* 7.
"An act for preventing irregular proceedings of sheriffs and other officers in making the returns of members," from p. 56 to 58.

1700. 11 & 12 *Will.* III. *cap.* 2.
"An act for granting an aid to his majesty, by sale of forfeited and other estates in *Ireland*, and by a land-tax in *England*, for the several purposes therein mentioned," [members disabled from being commissioners or farmers], p. 59 and 60.

1700. 12 & 13 *Will.* III. *cap.* 3.
"An act for preventing any inconveniences that may happen by privilege of parliament," from p. 60 to 65.

1700. 12 & 13 *Will.* III. *cap.* 10.
"An act for granting an aid to his majesty for defraying the expence of his navy, guards and garrisons for one year, and for other necessary occasions," from p. 65 to 67.

1703. 2 & 3 *Annæ*, *cap.* 18.
"An act for the further explanation and regulation of privilege of parliament, in relation to persons in public offices," from p. 67 to 69.

1707. 6 *Annæ*, *cap.* 7.
"An act for the security of her majesty's person and government, and of the succession to the crown of *Great-Britain* in the protestant line," from p. 69 to 75.

1710. 9 *Annæ, cap.* 5.
"An act for securing the freedom of parliaments, by the farther qualifying the members to sit in the House of Commons," from p. 75 to 79.

1710. 9 *Annæ, cap.* 10.
"An act for establishing a general post-office for all her majesty's dominions, and for settling a weekly sum out of the revenues thereof for the service of the war, and other her majesty's occasions," [no officer of the Post-office to interfere in elections], from p. 80 to 81.

1710. 9 *Annæ, cap.* 11.
"An act for levying certain duties upon hides and skins, &c. for prosecuting the war and other her majesty's most pressing occasions," p. 81 and 82.

1710. 9 *Annæ, cap.* 20.
"An act for rendering the proceedings upon writs of *mandamus* and informations in the nature of a *quo warranto* more speedy and effectual; and for the more easy trying and determining the rights of offices and franchises in corporations and boroughs," p. 82, 83.

1711. 10 *Annæ, cap.* 19.
"An act for laying several duties upon all soap, &c. &c." [commissioners not to intermeddle with elections], p. 84.

1711. 10 *Annæ, cap.* 23.
"An act for the more effectual preventing fraudulent conveyances in order to multiply votes for electing knights of shires to serve in parliament," from p. 85 to 92.

1713. 12 *Annæ, cap.* 5.
"An act to explain the last act, as far as relates

lates to the afcertaining the value of freeholds of forty fhillings per annum" from p. 92 to 94.

1713. 12 *Annæ*, cap. 15.
"An act for making perpetual an act to prevent falfe and double returns of members to ferve in parliament," p. 94 and 95.

1715. 1 *Geo.* 1. cap. 38.
"An act for enlarging the time of continuance of parliaments appointed by an act made the 6*th W.* & *M.* for the frequent meeting and calling of parliaments," [the feptennial act], p. 95 and 96.

1715. 1 *Geo.* I. cap. 56.
"An act to difable any perfon from being chofen a member of, or from fitting and voting in the Houfe of Commons, who has any penfion for any number of years from the crown," p. 97 and 98.

1724. 11 *Geo.* I. cap. 18.
"An act for regulating elections within the city of *London*," from p. 98 to 108.

1729. 2 *Geo.* II. cap. 24.
"An act for the more effectual preventing bribery and corruption in the elections of members," from p. 108 to 115.

1730. 3 *Geo.* II. cap. 8.
"An act for the better regulating elections in the city of *Norwich*," p. 115 and 116.

1733. 6 *Geo.* II. cap. 23.
"An act to explain and amend an act made the 7*th* and 8*th W. III.* fo far as the fame relates to the holding of county courts," from p. 116 to 118.

1735. 8 Geo. II. cap. 30.
"An act for regulating the quartering of soldiers during the time of the elections of members," from p. 119 to 122.

1736. 9 Geo. II. cap. 38.
"An act to explain and amend so much of an act made in the 2d year of the then king, as relates to the commencing and carrying on of prosecutions grounded upon the said act," from p. 122 to 124.

1738. 11 Geo. II. cap. 24.
"An act to amend an act passed in the 12th and 13th *W. III.* for preventing any inconveniences that may happen by privilege of parliament," from p. 124 to 128.

1740. 13 Geo. II. cap. 20.
"An act for the more effectually preventing fraudulent qualifications of persons to vote as freeholders in the election of members to serve in parliament for such cities and towns as are counties of themselves," from p. 129 to 133.

1742. 15 Geo. II. cap. 13.
"An act for establishing an agreement with the governor and company of the Bank of *England* for advancing the sum of *one million six hundred thousand pounds* towards the supply for the service of the year 1742." [The governor of the Bank not disabled from sitting in parliament], p. 133 and 134.

1742. 15 Geo. II. cap. 22.
"An act to exclude certain officers from being members of parliament," from p. 134 to 137.

1745. 18 Geo. II. cap. 18.
"An act to explain and amend the laws touching

ing the elections of knights of the shires to serve in parliament," from p. 137 to 149.

1746. 19 *Geo.* II. *cap.* 28.
"An act for the better regulating of elections of members to serve in parliament for such cities and towns in *England* as are counties of themselves," from p. 149 to 160.

1757. 31 *Geo.* II. *cap.* 14.
"An act for further explaining the laws touching the electors of knights of the shire to serve in parliament," from p. 160 to 162.

1759. 33 *Geo.* II. *cap.* 20.
"An act to enforce and render more effectual the laws relating to the qualifications of members to sit in the House of Commons," from p. 162 to 166.

1762. 3 *Geo.* III. *cap.* 15.
"An act to prevent occasional freemen from voting at elections of members to serve in parliament for cities and boroughs," from p. 166 to 169.

1762. 3 *Geo.* III. *cap.* 24.
"An act to prevent fraudulent and occasional votes in the elections of knights of the shire, and of members for cities and towns which are counties of themselves, so far as relates to the right of voting by virtue of annuity or rent charge," from p. 170 to 177.

1770. 10 *Geo.* III. *cap.* 16.
"An act to regulate the trials of controverted elections or returns of members to serve in parliament," from p. 178 to 190.

1770. 10 *Geo.* III. *cap.* 41.
"An act to enable the *Speaker* of the House

to issue his warrants to make out new writs for the choice of members to serve in parliament in the room of such members as shall die during the recess of parliament," p. 191 and 192.

1770. 10 *Geo*. III. *cap*. 50.
" An act for further preventing delays of justice by reason of privilege of parliament," from p. 192 to 195.

1771. 11 *Geo*. III. *cap*. 42.
" An act to explain and amend an act made to regulate the trials of controverted elections, or returns of members to serve in parliament," from p. 195 to 199.

1771. 11 *Geo*. III. *cap*. 55.
" An act to incapacitate *John Burnett*, &c. and others, from voting at elections of members to serve in parliament, and for preventing bribery and corruption in the election of members to serve in parliament for the borough of New *Shoreham* in the county of *Sussex*," from p. 199 to 203.

1772. 12 *Geo*. III. *cap*. 21.
" An act for giving relief in proceedings upon writs of *mandamus* for the admission of freemen into corporations; and for other purposes therein mentioned," from p. 204 to 207.

1774. 14 *Geo*. III. *cap*. 15.
" An act for making perpetual two acts passed in the 10*th and* 11*th* of the present king, for regulating the trials of controverted elections, or returns of members to serve in parliament," from p. 207 to 208.

1774. 14 *Geo*. III. *cap*. 58.
" An act for repealing an act made in the

1st *Hen. III.* and so much of several acts of the 8th, 10th, and 23d *Hen. VI.* as relates to the residence of persons to be elected members to serve in parliament, or of the persons by whom they are to be chosen," p. 208 and 209.

1775. 15 *Geo.* III. *cap.* 36.
" An act to explain and amend an act made in the 10th year of the present king, to enable the *Speaker* to issue his warrants to make out new writs for the choice of members to serve in parliament in the room of such members as shall die during the recess of parliament, and for enabling the *Speaker* to make out new writs for the choice of members to serve in parliament in the room of such members as shall during the recess of parliament become peers of *Great-Britain*, and be summoned to parliament; and for suspending the execution of the said act with respect to the borough of *Shaftesbury*, in the county of *Dorset*, during the next recess of parliament," from p. 210 to 214.

1780. 20 *Geo.* III. *cap.* 1.
" An act for holding the ensuing election of a knight of the shire for the county of *Southampton*, at the town of *New Alresford* in the said county," from p. 214 to 216.

1780. 20 *Geo.* III. *cap.* 17.
" An act to remove certain difficulties relative to voters at county elections," from p. 217 to 231.

1780. 21 *Geo.* III. *cap.* 43.
" An act for continuing an act made in the 20th year of the present king, so far as the

same

same relates to the removal of troops during the elections of members to serve in parliament for a limited time," p. 232 and 233.

1780. 21 *Geo.* III. *cap.* 54.
" An act for the better regulating elections of citizens to serve in parliament for the city of *Coventry*," from p. 233 to 240.

1781. 22 *Geo.* III. *cap.* 29.
" An act for further continuing an act made in the 20*th* year of the present king, so far as the same relates to the removal of troops during the elections of members to serve in parliament, for a limited time," p. 240 and 241.

1781. 22 *Geo.* III. *cap.* 31.
" An act for the preventing bribery and corruption in the election of members to serve in parliament for the borough of *Cricklade*, in the county of *Wilts*," from p. 242 to 246.

1781. 22 *Geo.* III. *cap.* 41.
" An act for better securing the freedom of elections of members to serve in parliament, by disabling certain officers employed in the collection or management of his majesty's revenues from giving their votes at such elections," from p. 246 to 249.

1781. 22 *Geo.* III. *cap.* 45.
" An act for restraining any person concerned in any contract, commission, or agreement, made for the public service, from being elected, or sitting and voting as a member of the House of Commons," from p. 250 to 255.

1784. 24 *Geo.* III. *cap.* 26.
" An act to repeal so much of two acts made

in the 10*th* and 15*th* years of the prefent king, as authorifes the *Speaker* to iffue his warrant to the clerk of the crown for making out writs for the election of members to ferve in parliament, in the manner therein mentioned; and for fubftituting other provifions for the like purpofes," from p. 255 to 261.

1785. 25 *Geo.* III. *cap.* 17.
" An act to enable the Houfe to authorife the felect committee appointed to try the merits of the petition of the *Hon. Saint Andrew Saint John*, complaining of an undue election for the county of *Bedford*, to proceed in cafe the faid felect committee fhall be reduced to a lefs number than is prefcribed by an act made in the 10*th* year of the prefent king to regulate the trials of controverted elections, or returns of members to ferve in parliament," p. 262 and 263.

1785. 25 *Geo.* III. *cap.* 84.
" An act to limit the duration of polls and fcrutinies, and for making other regulations touching the election of members, and alfo for removing difficulties which may arife for want of returns being made of members to ferve in parliament," from p. 263 to 274.

1786. 26 *Geo.* III. *cap.* 100.
" An act to prevent occafional inhabitants from voting in the election of members," from p. 275 to 277.

1787. 28 *Geo.* III. *cap.* 52.
" An act for the further regulation of the trials of controverted elections, or returns of members to parliament," from p. 277 to 301.

1790.

1790. 30 Geo. III. cap. 35.
"An act to explain and amend an act passed in the 20*th* year of the present king, touching the election for knights of the shire," from p. 301 to 304.

1790. 31 Geo. III. cap. 3.
"An act to give further time to *John Macbride, Esq.* and his sureties, for entering into their recognizance, in respect of his petition presented to the House of Commons, complaining of an undue election and return for the borough of *Plymouth*, in the county of *Devon*," from p. 305 to 307.

1792. 32 Geo. III. cap. 1.
"An act to extend the provisions of certain acts of parliament made to regulate the trials of controverted elections, or returns of members to serve in parliament," from p. 307 to 309.

1793. 33 Geo. III. cap. 64.
"An act to explain and amend an act passed in the 7*th* and 8*th William III.* so far as relates to the publication of notices of the time and place of election," from p. 309 to 311.

1794. 34 Geo. III. cap. 73.
"An act for directing the appointment of commissioners to administer certain oaths and declarations required by law to be taken and made by persons offering to vote at the election of members to serve in parliament," from p. 311 to 320.

1794. 34 Geo. III. cap. 83.
"An act to explain so much of an act made in the 28*th* year of his present majesty's reign, intitled,

titled, " An act for the further regulation of the trials of controverted elections, or returns of members to serve in parliament, as relates to the time of presenting certain renewed petitions, and taking the same into consideration," from p. 320 to 323.

1796. 36 *Geo.* III. *cap.* 59.

" An act for the more effectual execution of several acts of parliament made for the trials of controverted elections or returns of members," from p. 323 to 327.

CONTENTS OF THE APPENDIX.

PART I.

Resolutions and Orders of the House of Commons.

Issuing the writ, and delivery thereof to the proper officer, p. ii.

Interference at elections, and qualifications of electors, p. iii.

Bribery, p. v.

Evidence at the poll and before the House, p. vii.

Qualification of candidates, p. ix.

Jurisdiction of the House, p. xi.

Petitions, proceedings on petitions, and soliciting the attendance of members, p. xii.

Exchange of lists, p. xxi.

False evidence and tampering with witnesses, p. xxi.

Amending returns, p. xxii.

PART II.

Elections of Peers and Members for Scotland.

1706. 5 *Annæ,* cap. 8.
"An act settling the manner of electing the sixteen peers and forty-five commoners," from p. xxiii to xxix.

1707. 6 *Annæ,* cap. 6.
"An act for rendering the union of the two kingdoms more entire and complete," from p. xxx to xxxii.

1707. 6 *Annæ,* cap. 23.
"An act to make further provision for electing and summoning the sixteen peers, and for trying peers for offences committed in *Scotland*; and for further regulating of voters in election of members to serve in parliament," from p. xxxii to xlvi.

1713. 12 *Annæ,* cap. 6.
"An act to better regulate the elections of the forty-five commoners," from p. xlvi to l.

1714. 1 *Geo.* I. *cap.* 13.
"An act for the security of his majesty's person and the succession, and for extinguishing the hopes of the pretended *Prince of Wales*," from p. l to liii.

1734.

1734. 7 *Geo.* II. *cap.* 16.
"An act for better regulating elections of members for *Scotland*, and for incapacitating the judges and barons of the courts of session, justiciary, and exchequer there, to be elected, sit, or vote," from p. liii to lx.

1743. 16 *Geo.* II. *cap.* 11.
"An act to explain and amend the laws touching the elections of members for *Scotland*, and to restrain the partiality, and regulate the conduct, of returning officers at such elections," from p. lxi to xciii.

1774. 14 *Geo.* III. *cap.* 81.
"An act for altering and amending the last act, by altering the time of notice ordered by the said act to be given in the service of complaints to the court of session, and for various other purposes," from p. xciii to xcvi.

1795. 35 *Geo.* III. *cap.* 65.
"An act to prevent unnecessary delay in the execution of writs, for the election of members for *Scotland*," from p. xcvii to c.

PART III.

Controverted elections determined by select committees, as well upon the *Right*, as otherwise.

ELECTION STATUTES.

ANNO 5° RICHARDI II. STAT. 2. CAP. 4.

Every one to whom it belongeth shall, upon Summons, come to the Parliament.

" ITEM, the king doth will and command, and it is assented in the parliament by the prelates, lords, and commons, That all and singular persons and commonalties, which from henceforth shall have the summons of the parliament, shall come from henceforth to the parliaments in the manner as they are bound to do and have been accustomed within the realm of *England* of old times. (2.) And if any person of the same realm, which from henceforth shall have the said summons (be he archbishop, bishop, abbot, prior, duke, earl, baron, banneret, knight of the shire, citizen of city, burgess of borough, or other singular person, or commonalty) do absent himself, and come not at the said summons, (except he

Amercement of absentees.

he may reasonably and honestly excuse him to our lord the king) he shall be amerced and otherwise punished, according as of old times hath been used to be done within the said realm in the said case. (3.) And if any sheriff of the realm be from henceforth negligent in making his returns of writs of the parliament; or that he leave out of the said returns any cities or boroughs, which be bound, and of old time were wont, to come to the parliament, he shall be amerced, or otherwise punished, in the manner as was accustomed to be done in the said case in times past." A. D. 1382.

<small>Amercement of sheriff omitting his return.</small>

ANNO 7° HENRICI IV. CAP. 15.

Manner of electing Knights of Shires.

" ITEM, our lord the king, at the grievous complaint of his commons in this present parliament, of the undue election of the knights of counties for the parliament, which be sometimes made of affection of sheriffs, and otherwise against the form of the writs directed to the sheriff, to the great slander of the counties, and hindrance of the business of the commonalty in the said county;" '(2) our sovereign lord the king willing therein to provide remedy, by the assent of the lords spiritual and temporal, and the commons in this present parliament assembled, hath ordained and established, That from henceforth the elections

elections of such knights shall be made in the form as followeth; (that is to say) at the next county to be holden after the delivery of the writ of the parliament, proclamation shall be made in the full county of the day and place of the parliament, (3) and that all they that be there present, as well suitors duly summoned for the same cause, as other, shall attend to the election of the knights for the parliament, (4) and then in the full county they shall proceed to the election freely and indifferently, notwithstanding any request or commandment to the contrary; (5) and after that they be chosen, the names of the persons so chosen (be they present or absent) shall be written in an indenture under the seals of all them that did choose them, and tacked to the same writ of the parliament, which indenture so sealed and tacked shall be holden for the sheriff's return of the said writ, touching the knights of the shires. (6) And in the writs of the parliament to be made hereafter, this clause shall be put:' " Et electionem tuam in pleno comitatu tuo factam, distincte & aperte sub sigillo tuo & sigillis eorum qui electioni illi interfuerint, nobis in cancellaria nostra ad diem & locum in brevi contentos certifices indilate."   A. D. 1405.

<small>Manner of county elections.</small>

<small>Clause to be inserted in every writ.</small>

ANNO 11° HENRICI IV. CAP. I.

Penalty on Sheriffs for making an untrue Return of the Election of the Knights of Parliament.

Enacts,

7 H. iv. c. 15.
"FIRST, Whereas in the parliament holden at Westminster, the 7th year of the reign of our said lord the king, there was ordained and established by a statute for the preservation of the liberties and franchises of the election of the knights of the shire used through the realm, a certain form and manner of the election of such knights, as in the said statute more fully is contained: (2) and forasmuch as in the same statute no penalty was ordained or limited in special upon the sheriffs of the counties, if they make any returns to the contrary of the same statute," (3) 'it is ordained and stablished, That the justices assigned to take assizes, shall have power to inquire in their sessions of assizes, of such returns made; (4) and if it be found by inquest, and due examination before the same justices, that any such sheriff hath made, or hereafter shall make, any return contrary to the tenor of the said statute, that then the said sheriff shall incur the penalty of 100l. to be paid to our lord the king; (5) and moreover, that the knights of the counties so unduly returned, shall lose their wages of the parliament, of old time accustomed.'

A. D. 1409.

ANNO

ANNO 1º HENRICI V. CAP. I.

What sort of People shall be chosen and who shall be the choosers of the Knights and Burgesses of the Parliament.

Enacts,

'FIRST, that the statutes of the election of the knights of the shires to come to the parliament be holden and kept in all points; (2) adjoining to the same, That the knights of the shires which from henceforth shall be chosen in every shire, be not chosen unless they be resident within the shire where they shall be chosen the day of the date of the writ of the summons of the parliament; (3) and that the knights and esquires, and others which shall be choosers of those knights of the shires, be also resident within the same shires, in manner and form as is aforesaid; (4) and moreover it is ordained and established, That the citizens and burgesses of the cities and boroughs be chosen men citizens and burgesses resiant, dwelling and free in the same cities and boroughs, and no other in any wise'. A. D. 1413.

<small>Residence in knights.</small>

<small>Residence in electors.</small>

ANNO 6º HENRICI VI. CAP. 4.

The Sheriff's Traverse to an Inquest found, touching returning Knights of the Shire for the Parliament.

"ITEM, Whereas it was ordained and established in the 7th year of king Henry the Fourth, grandfather of our lord the king that now is,

<small>7 H. iv. c. 15.</small>

is, that knights of shires for the parliament, should be chosen in manner and form following; that is to say, At the next county to be holden after the delivery of the writ of the parliament, proclamation shall be made in the full county of the day and place of the parliament, (2) and that all they which be present there, as well suitors duly summoned for this cause, as other, shall attend to the election of their knights for the parliament, (3) and then in full county they shall proceed to the election freely and indifferently, notwithstanding any request or commandment to the contrary; (4) and that after they be chosen, whether such persons chosen be present or absent, their names shall be written in indentures under the seals of all the choosers, and annexed to the said writ of parliament, which indenture so sealed and tacked, shall be holden for the return of the said writ, as to the knights of the said shires; (5) and also in the writs of the parliament hereafter to be made, this clause shall be put in the manner as followeth: Et electionem tuam in pleno comitatu tuo factam, distincte & aperte sub sigillo tuo & sigillis eorum qui electioni illi interfuerint, nobis in cancellaria nostra ad diem & locum in brevi contentos certifices indilate (6). And for that in the same statute no pain was ordained, nor specially set upon the sheriffs of the county, if they make their return contrary to the said statute, it

11 H. iv. c. 1. was ordained and established the 11th year of the said king Henry the Fourth, That the justices of assizes should have power to inquire in their sessions of assizes, of such returns made; (7) and if it be

found

found by inqueſt and due examination before the ſaid juſtices, that any ſuch ſheriff hath made or hereafter ſhall make any return contrary to the tenor of the ſaid ſtatute, that the ſame ſheriff ſhould incur the pain of 100 l. to be paid to our ſaid lord the king, (8) and moreover that the knights ſo unduly returned, ſhall loſe their wages of the parliament, in old times accuſtomed; (9) to the great miſchiefs of ſheriffs and knights of the ſhire, which be forebarred and put out of their anſwer againſt ſuch inqueſts or offices, taken before the ſaid judges, becauſe of the ſtatute and ordinance aforeſaid." (10) 'Our lord the king, willing in this caſe to provide remedy, hath ordained and eſtabliſhed, That all the knights of the ſhires, choſen for this preſent parliament, and the ſheriffs of the ſame counties againſt whom any inqueſts or offices of undue election be found before the juſtices of aſſizes ſhall have their anſwer and traverſe to ſuch inqueſts or offices taken; (11) and alſo all the knights from henceforth ſo to be choſen, and the ſheriffs that ſhall make ſuch elections ſhall have their anſwer and traverſe to ſuch inqueſts and offices before any juſtices of aſſizes hereafter to be taken; (12) and the ſaid knights and ſheriffs ſhall not be endamaged unto our ſaid lord the king or his ſucceſſors, for any ſuch inqueſt taken, or to be taken, until they be duly convict according to the form of the law.' A. D. 1427.

The knights choſen for the parliament, and the ſheriffs of counties may have their traverſe of an office found againſt them.

ANNO 8° HENRICI VI. CAP. 7.

What sort of Men shall be Choosers, and who shall be chosen Knights of the Parliament.

"ITEM, Whereas the elections of knights of shires to come to the parliaments of our lord the king in many counties of the realm of England, have now of late been made by very great, outrageous and excessive number of people dwelling within the same counties of the realm of England, of the which most part was of people of small substance, and of no value, whereof every of them pretended a voice equivalent, as to such elections to be made, with the most worthy knights and esquires, dwelling within the same counties, whereby manslaughter, riots, batteries, and divisions among the gentlemen and other people of the same counties, shall very likely rise and be, unless convenient and due remedy be provided in this behalf;" (2) ' our lord the king, considering the premises, hath provided, ordained and established by authority of this present parliament, That the knights of the shires to be chosen within the same realm of England, to come to the parliaments of our lord the king, hereafter to be holden, shall be chosen in every county of the realm of England, by people dwelling and resident in the same counties, whereof every one of them shall have free land or tenement to the value of forty shillings by the year,

The qualifications of the electors.

at

at the least, above all charges; (3) and that they which shall be so chosen, shall be dwelling and resident within the same counties; (4) and such as have the greatest number of them that may expend 40 s. by year, and above, as aforesaid, shall be returned by the sheriffs of every county, knights for the parliament, by indentures sealed between the said sheriffs and the said choosers so to be made. (5) And every sheriff of the realm of England, shall have power by the said authority, to examine upon the Evangelists every such chooser, how much he may expend by the year; (6) and if any sheriff return knights to come to the parliament, contrary to the said ordinance, the justices of assizes, in their sessions of assizes, shall have power by the authority aforesaid, thereof to inquire; (7) and if by inquest the same be found before the justices, and the sheriff thereof be duly attainted, that then the said sheriff shall incur the pain of 100 l. to be paid to our lord the king, and also that he have imprisonment by a year, without being let to bail or mainprize; (8) and that the knights for the parliament, returned contrary to the said ordinance, shall lose their wages.

The sheriff impowered to examine the electors upon oath, touching their estates.

Justices of assize to inquire of the returning of knights to parliament.

Penalty on the sheriff for undue returns.

Knights falsely returned shall lose their wages.

Provided always, that he which cannot expend 40 s. by year, as afore is said, shall in no wise be chooser of the knights for the parliament; and that in every writ that shall hereafter go forth to the sheriffs to choose knights for the parliament, mention be made of the said ordinances.'

A. D. 1429.

ANNO 10° HENRICI VI. CAP. 2.

Certain Things required in him who shall be a Chooser of the Knights of Parliament.

8 H. vi. c. 7.

"ITEM, whereas at the parliament holden at Westminster, the morrow of St. Matthew the apostle, the 8th year of the king that now is, it was ordained by the authority of the same parliament, that the knights of all counties within the realm of England, to be chosen to come to the Parliament hereafter to be holden, shall be chosen in every county by people dwelling and resiant in the same, whereof every one shall have freehold to the value of 40s. by year, at the least, above all charges, upon a certain pain contained in the same statute; (2) not making express mention in the same, that every man that shall be chooser of any such knights shall have freehold to the value of 40s. at the least, above all charges, within the same county, where such chooser with other like shall make such election, or elsewhere:" (3) ' and therefore our lord the king, willing to make plain declaration of the said statute, by the advice and assent aforesaid, and at the special request of the said commons, hath ordained, That the knights of all counties within the said realm, to be chosen to come to parliaments hereafter to be holden, shall be chosen in every county by people dwelling and resiant in the same, whereof every man shall have freehold to the value of
40s.

40s. by the year, at the least, above all charges within the same county where any such chooser will meddle of any such election.' A. D. 1432.

ANNO 23° HENRICI VI. CAP. 10.

The Order of levying the Wages of the Knights of the Parliament.

"ITEM, whereas before this time divers sheriffs in divers counties of England, by colour of writs to them directed, to levy the wages of the knights of the shires for the time being, of the parliament of the king that now is, and of his noble progenitors, have levied more money than hath been due to the said knights, and more than they have delivered, keeping and retaining great part of the money to their own use and profit, to their officers and servants, to the great loss of the common people of the said counties." (2) 'The king, considering the premises, hath ordained by the authority aforesaid, That the sheriff of every county for the time being, in the next county court holden in their counties after the delivery of the said writs directed to them, shall make open proclamation, that the coroners, and every chief constable of the peace of the said counties, and the baliffs of every hundred or wapentake of the same county, and all other which will be at the assessing of the wages of the knights of the shires, shall be at the next county there to be holden to assess the said wages of the

said

The penalty if the sheriff, &c. levy more money than is assessed.

said knights; (3) and that the sheriff, under-sheriff, coroners, or bailiffs for the time being, be there at the same time in their proper person, upon pain of forfeiture, to the king, of every of them that maketh default, 40s. (4) at which time the said sheriff or under sheriff, in the presence of them that shall come to the same, and of the suitors of the same counties then being there, in the full county well and duly shall assess every hundred to that assessable by itself, to pay a certain sum for the wages of the knights of the shire, so that the whole sum of all the hundreds do not exceed the sum which shall be due to the said knights. (5) And after that, in the same county, they shall assess well and lawfully every village within the said hundreds, which should be there assessable, to a certain sum for the payment of the said wages; so that the whole sum of all the towns within any of the said hundreds, do not exceed the sum assessed upon the hundred of which they be. (6) And that neither the said sheriffs, under-sheriffs, bailiffs, nor any other officers for the cause aforesaid, shall levy more money of any village than that whereunto they were assessed: (7) and if any do or will assess any hundred or village otherwise than is aforesaid, that they shall forfeit for every default to the king 20l. and to any man which will sue in this case 10l.

' And that the said sheriffs well and duly shall levy the money so assessed upon the aforesaid villages, as speedily as they well may after the said assessing, and the same shall deliver to the said knights, according to the writs thereof to be made,

made, upon the said penalties; and he that will *Who may prosecute on this act, and by what writ.* sue in this case, shall be thereunto admitted and shall have for his action in this case a *scire facias* against him that offendeth contrary to this ordinance: (3) and if the defendant, duly warned in the same, make default, or else appear, and be in the same convict, that then the plaintiffs shall recover against them which be so convict 10 l. to their own use, over the said 20 l. with their treble damages for the costs of their suits.

‘ And the justices of the king's bench and of the *The penalty on offenders.* common pleas, justices of assizes, and gaol delivery, and justices of peace in their county, shall have power to inquire, hear and determine of all the said defaults, as well by inquiry at the king's suit, as by action at the suit of the parties; and that all such expences of knights shall not be *The knight's wages shall be levied only in the accustomed places.* levied of any other villages, seigniories, or places, but of such whereof it hath been levied before this time.

‘ And that in every such writ from henceforth to be made to levy the wages of the said knights, this act shall be comprehended in the same.’

A. D. 1444.

ANNO 23°. HENRICI VI. CAP. 14.

Who shall be Knights for the Parliament. The Manner of their Election. The Remedy where one is chosen and another returned.

" ITEM, whereas by authority of a parliament holden at Westminster, the first year of the 1 H. V. c. 1.
reign

reign of king Henry, father to the king that now is, amongst other things it was ordained, that the citizens and burgesses of cities and boroughs, coming to the parliament, should be chosen men citizens and burgesses resident, abiding, and free, in the same cities and boroughs, and none other, as in the same statute more fully is contained; (2) which citizens and burgesses have always in cities and boroughs been chosen by citizens and burgesses, and no other, and to the sheriff of the counties returned, and upon their returns received and accepted by the parliaments before this holden. (3) And also, whereas by authority of a parliament holden at Westminster, the eighth year of the reign of the king that now is, it was ordained in what manner and form the knights of the shires coming to parliaments, from thenceforth to be holden, should be chosen, and how the sheriffs of the said counties thereupon should make their returns, as in the same statute more fully appeareth; (4) by force of which statute elections of knights to come to the parliaments sometimes have been duly made and lawfully returned, until now of late, that divers sheriffs of the counties of the realm of England, for their singular avail and lucre, have not made due elections of the knights, nor in convenient time, nor good men and true returned, and sometimes no return of the knights, citizens, and burgesses lawfully chosen to come to the parliaments; (5) but such knights, citizens, or burgesses have been returned, which were never duly chosen, and other citizens and burgesses than those which

8 H. vi. c. 7.

The several defaults of sheriffs in returning of knights, &c. to serve in parliament.

I   by

by the mayors and bailiffs were to the said sheriffs returned; (6) and sometimes the sheriffs have not returned the writs which they had to make election of knights to come to the parliaments, but the said writs have imbesiled, and moreover made no precept to the mayor and bailiff, or to the bailiffs or bailiff where no mayor is, of cities and boroughs, for the election of citizens and burgesses to come to the parliament by the colour of these words contained in the same writs, " Quod in pleno comitatu tuo eligi facias pro comitatu tuo duos milites, et pro qualibet civitate in comitatu tuo duo cives, et pro quolibet burgo in comitatu tuo duos burgenses;" (7) and also because sufficient penalty and convenient penalty and convenient remedy for the party in such case grieved is not ordained in the said statutes against the sheriffs, mayors, and bailiffs, which do contrary to the form of the said statutes:" ' (8) the king considering the premises hath ordained by authority aforesaid, That the said statutes shall be duly kept in all points; (9) and moreover that every sheriff, after the delivery of any such writ to him made, shall make and deliver without fraud, a sufficient precept under his seal to every mayor and bailiff, or to bailiffs or bailiff where no mayor is, of the cities and boroughs within his county, reciting the said writ, commanding them by the said precept, if it be a city, to choose by citizens of the same city, citizens, and in the same manner and form if it be a borough, by the burgesses of the same

7 H. iv. c. 15.
1 H. vi. c. 1.
6 H. vi. c. 7.

The sheriffs shall send out precepts to the mayors and bailiffs of cities and boroughs, to elect citizens and burgesses to serve in parliament.

same, to come to parliament. (10) And that the same mayor and bailiffs, or bailiffs or bailiff where no mayor is, shall return lawfully the precept to the same sheriffs, by indentures betwixt the same sheriffs and them to be made of the same elections, and of the names of the said citizens and burgesses by them so chosen, and thereupon every sheriff shall make a good and rightful return, of every such writ and of every return by the mayors and bailiffs, or bailiffs or bailiff where no mayor is, to him made.

The penalty on a sheriff making an undue return of a member of parliament.

(11) And that every sheriff at every time that he doth contrary to this statute, or any other statutes for the election of knights, citizens and burgesses to come to the parliament, before this time made, shall incur the pain contained in the said statute made the said 8th year, and moreover shall forfeit and pay to every person hereafter chosen knight, citizen, or burgess in his county, to come to any parliament and not duly returned, or to any other person, which in default of such knight, citizen, or burgess will sue, 100l. whereof every knight, citizen, and burgess so grieved, severally, or any other person which in their default will sue, shall have his action of debt against the said sheriff, or his executors or administrators, to demand and have the said 100l. with his costs spent in that case. (12) And that in such action taken by virtue of this statute the defendant shall not wage his law of the demand aforesaid in any wise, (13) and that no defendant in such action shall have any essoin. (14) And in the same manner at every time that any mayor

mayor and bailiffs, or bailiffs or bailiff where no mayor is, shall return other than those which be chosen by the citizens and burgesses of the cities or boroughs where such elections be or shall be made, shall incur and forfeit to the king 40 l. and moreover shall forfeit and pay to every person hereafter chosen citizen and burgess to come to the parliament, and not returned by the same mayor and bailiff, or bailiffs or bailiff where no mayor is, or to any other person which in default of such citizen or burgess so chosen, will sue, 40 l. whereof every of the citizens and burgesses so grieved severally, or any other person, which in default will sue, shall have his action of debt against every of the said mayor and bailiffs, or bailiffs or bailiff where no mayor is, against their executors or administrators, to demand and have of every the said mayor and bailiffs, or bailiffs or bailiff where no mayor is, 40 l. with his costs in this case expended; (15) and that in such action of debt, taken by force of this statute, no defendant in any wise shall wage his law of the said demand, nor have any essoin.

The penalty on a mayor or bailiff making an undue return.

' And that every sheriff that maketh no due election of knights to come to the parliament, in convenient time, that is to say, every sheriff in his full county, betwixt the hour of 8 and the hour of 11 before noon, without collusion in this behalf; (2) and that every sheriff that maketh not good and true return of such elections of knights to come to the parliament in time to come, as to them pertaineth, in manner and form aforesaid, shall forfeit to the king 100 l. and also shall incur

At what time of the day the knights for the shire shall be chosen.

the penalty of an 100 l. to be paid to him that will sue against him, his executors or administrators, for this cause, by way of action of debt, with his costs in this behalf expended, without waging of law of his demand, or having essoin as afore is said.

'Provided always, That every knight, citizen, and burgess, to come to any parliament, hereafter to be holden in due form, chosen and not returned as afore is said, shall begin his action of debt aforesaid, within 3 months after the same parliament commenced, to proceed in the same suit effectually without fraud; (2) and if he so do not, another that will sue shall have the said action of debt (as it is before said) and shall recover the same sum with his costs spent in this behalf, in manner and form aforesaid, so that no defendant in such action shall wage his law, nor be essoined in any wise as aforesaid; (3) and if any knight, citizen, or burgess, hereafter returned by the sheriff to come to the parliament in the manner aforesaid, after such return, be by any person put out, and another put in his place, that such person so put in the place of him which is out, if he take upon him to be knight, citizen, or burgess, at any parliament in time to come, shall forfeit to the king 100 l. and 100 l. to the knight, citizen, or burgess, so returned by the sheriff, and after as aforesaid put out; (4) and that the knight, citizen, or burgess, which is so put out, shall have an action of debt of the same 100 l. against such person put in his place, his executors or administrators; (5) provided always, That he shall begin his

Marginalia: Suits to be commenced within 3 months after the parliament begun.

Marginalia: The penalty if any chosen to be knight, citizen, or burgess, be put out and another put in his place.

his suit within three months after the parliament commenced; (6) and if he do not, then he that will sue shall have an action of debt of the same 100 l. against him, which is put in place of him that is so put out after such return, his executors, or administrators, and that no defendant in such action, shall wage his law nor be essoined; (7) and that such process shall be in the actions aforesaid, as in a writ of trespass done against the peace at the common law; (8) so that the knights of the shires for the parliament, hereafter to be chosen, shall be notable knights of the same counties for which they shall be chosen; or otherwise such notable esquires, gentlemen of the same counties, as shall be able to be knights; (9) and no man to be such knight which standeth in the degree of a yeoman and under.' A. D. 1444.

<small>What sort of persons shall be chosen knights of the shires.</small>

ANNO 6° HENRICI VIII. CAP. 16.

An Act that no Knights of Shires nor Burgesses depart before the End of Parliament.

'FORASMUCH as commonly in the end of every parliament divers and many great and weighty matters, as well touching the pleasure, weal, and surety of our sovereign lord the king, as the common weal of this his realm and subjects, are to be treated, communed of, and by authority of parliament to be concluded; (2) so it is that divers knights of shires, citizens for cities, burgesses for boroughs, and barons of the cinque ports,

ports, long time before the end of the said parliament, of their own authorities, depart and go home into their countries, whereby the said great and weighty matters are many times greatly delayed; (3) in confideration whereof, be it enacted by the king our fovereign lord, the lords fpiritual and temporal, and the commons in this prefent parliament affembled, and by authority of the fame, That from henceforth none of the faid knights, citizens, burgeffes, and barons, nor any of them that fhall hereafter be elected to come or be in any parliament, do not depart from the faid parliament, nor abfent himfelf from the fame, till the faid parliament be fully finifhed, ended, or prorogued, except he or they fo departing have licence of the fpeaker and commons, in the faid parliament affembled, and the fame licence be entered of record in the book of the clerk of the parliament, appointed or to be appointed for the commons houfe, upon pain to every of them fo departing, or abfenting themfelves in any other manner, to lofe all thofe fums of money which he or they fhould or ought to have had for his or their wages; (4) and that all the counties, cities, and boroughs, whereof any fuch perfon fhall be elected, and the inhabitants of the fame, fhall be clearly difcharged of all the faid wages againft the faid perfon and perfons, and their executors, for evermore.' A. D. 1514.

Members not to abfent themfelves without leave.

ANNO 27° HENRICI VIII. CAP. 26.

Concerning the Laws to be used in Wales.

28. AND it is further enacted by the authority aforesaid, That for this present parliament, and all other parliaments to be holden and kept for this realm, two knights shall be chosen and elected to the same parliament for the shire of Monmouth, and one burgess for the borough of Monmouth, in like manner, form, and order, as knights and burgesses of the parliament to be elected and chosen in all other shires of this realm of England; (2) and that the same knights and burgesses shall have like dignity, pre-eminence, and privilege, (3) and shall be allowed such fees as other knights and burgesses of the parliament have been allowed; (4) and the knights fees to be levied, perceived, received, gathered, and paid, in such manner, form, and order, as such fees be gathered, levied, perceived, received, and paid, in other shires of this realm of England; (5) and the burgesses fees to be levied as well within the borough of Monmouth, as within all other ancient boroughs within the said shire of Monmouth. *(Two knights for the shire of Monmouth, and one burgess for the town.)*

29. And that for this present parliament, and all other parliaments, to be holden and kept for this realm, one knight shall be chosen and elected to the same parliaments, for every of the shires of Brecknock, Radnor, Montgomery, and Denbigh, and for every other shire within the country or dominion of Wales; (2) and for every borough, being a shire town within the said country *(Knights and burgesses for the parliament in Wales, and their fees.)*

or dominion of Wales, except the shire town of the aforesaid county of Monmouth, one burgess; (3) and the election to be in like manner, form, and order, as knights and burgesses of the parliament, to be elected and chosen in other shires of this realm; (4) and that the knights and burgesses, and every of them, shall have like dignity, pre-eminence, and privilege, and shall be allowed such fees, as other knights of the parliament have and be allowed; (5) and the knights fees to be levied and gathered of the commons of the shire that they be elected in; (6) and the burgesses fees to be levied and gathered as well of the boroughs and shire towns, as they be burgesses of, as of all other boroughs within the same shires.

A. D. 1535.

ANNO 34° & 35° HENRICI VIII. CAP. 13.

An Act for making of Knights and Burgesses within the County and City of Chester.

'TO the king our sovereign lord, in most humble wise, shew unto your excellent majesty, the inhabitants of your grace's county palatine of Chester, That where the said county palatine of Chester is and hath been always hitherto exempt, excluded, and separated, out and from your high court of parliament to have any knights and burgesses within the said court; by reason whereof the said inhabitants have hitherto sustained manifold disherisons, losses, and damages,

as

as well in their lands, goods, and bodies, as in the good, civil, and politic governance and maintenance of the common-wealth of their said country: (2) and forasmuch as the said inhabitants have always hitherto been bound by the acts and statutes made and ordained by your said highness and your most noble progenitors, by authority of the said court, as far forth as other counties, cities, and boroughs have been that have had their knights and burgesses within your said court of parliament, and yet have had neither knight nor burgess there for the said county palatine, the said inhabitants, for lack thereof, have been oftentimes touched and grieved with acts and statutes made within the said court, as well derogatory unto the most ancient jurisdictions, liberties, and privileges of your said county palatine, as prejudicial unto the common-wealth, quietness, rest, and peace of your grace's most bounden subjects inhabiting within the same:' (3) for remedy whereof, may it please your said highness that it may be enacted, with the assent of the lords spiritual and temporal, and the commons in this present parliament assembled, and by the authority of the same, That from the end of this present session, the said county palatine of Chester shall have two knights for the said county palatine, and likewise two citizens to be burgesses for the city of Chester, to be elected and chosen by process to be awarded by the chancellor of England, unto the chamberlain of Chester, his lieutenant or deputy for the time being; (4) and also like process to be made by the said chamberlain, his lieutenant or deputy, to the sheriff

The county of Chester shall have two knights for the shire, and the city of Chester two burgesses for the parliament.

sheriff of the said county of Chester; (5) and the same election to be made under like manner and form to all intents, constructions, and purposes, as is used within the county palatine of Lancaster, or any other county and city within this realm of England; (6) which said knights and burgesses, and every of them so elected and chosen, shall be returned by the said sheriff into the chancery of England in due form, and upon like pains as it is ordained that the sheriff or sheriffs of any other county within this realm should make their return in like case; (7) and which said knights and burgesses, and every of them so elected and returned, shall be knights and burgesses of the court of parliament, and have like voice and authority to all intents and purposes as any other the knights and burgesses of the said court of parliament have, use, and enjoy; (8) and in like wise shall and may take all and every such like liberties, advantages, dignities, privileges, wages, fees, and commodities, concerning this said court of parliament, to all intents, constructions, and purposes, as any other the knights and burgesses of the said court shall, may, or ought to, have, take, or enjoy.

A.D. 1542.

ANNO 35° HENRICI VIII. CAP. II.

The Bill for Knights and Burgesses in Wales, concerning the Payment of their Fees and Wages.

'WHERE the knights of all and every shire of this realm of England and Wales, and the

the burgesses of all cities, towns and boroughs
of the same be named, elected, and chosen for
their assembly in the king's high court of parliament, as by ancient laudable laws and customs of this realm hath been used and accustomed, at and by the king's majesty's high
commandments, unto the which knights and
burgesses their fees and wages be assigned cer-
tainly; that is to say, to every knight by the
day 4s. and to every citizen and burgess by the
day 2s. or more, as heretofore hath been accustomed, (2) accounting for the same so many
days as the said high court of parliament en-
dureth, with addition thereunto of so many days
as every such knight and burgess may reasonably journey and resort from their habitations or
dwelling places to the said high court of parliament, and from the said high court to return
to their habitations or dwelling places, together
with their costs of writs, and other ordinary
fees and charges; (3) which wages, fees, and
charges, at all times ought to be levied and
collected by the sheriffs, and by the mayors,
bailiffs, and other head officers of and in the
cities, boroughs, and towns aforesaid, wherein
some of the said sheriffs, mayors, and bailiffs,
and other head officers, have been negligent
and laches, not endeavouring themselves in
accomplishment of their duties in collection and
payment of the same in due form, according to
justice, to the great hurt, injury, and delay of
the king's said subjects.' (4) Be it therefore
enacted by the authority of this present parliament,

The sheriff shall gather the wages of the knights in every county in Wales and in Monmouth.

ment, that the sheriffs for the time being, of every of the twelve shires in Wales, and in the county of Monmouth, from the beginning of this present parliament, shall have full power and authority by force of this act to gather and levy, or cause to be gathered and levied, the said knights fees and wages, of the inhabitants of the said twelve shires, and of the said county of Monmouth, which ought to pay the same; and the same so gathered, shall pay, or cause to be paid to every such knight or knights, or to his or their assigns, within the term of two months after that any such knight or knights shall deliver or cause to be delivered, the king's writ *de solutione feodi militis parliamenti*, to any such sheriff; (5) and every such sheriff making default of payment of the said wages or fees, in manner and form as is aforesaid, to lose and forfeit 20l. whereof the one moiety to be to the king's use, and the other to his or their use that will sue for the same in any of the king's courts of record, by information, bill, or plaint, or otherwise afore any of the king's officers, wherein no essoin, protection, or wager of law shall be admitted. (6) And if it shall happen to any sheriff, in any of the said twelve shires and county of Monmouth, to make default of payment of the said wages or fees by a longer term than two months, then every such sheriff to forfeit for every month that he or they shall make default 20l. to be forfeited and levied in manner and form as aforesaid.

And

And that every mayor and bailiff, and other head officers of cities, boroughs, and towns in every of the said twelve shires, and in the said county of Monmouth, within like term and space of two months after the receipt of the king's majesty's writ *de solutione feod' burgens' parliament'*, like as is before mentioned for gathering or levying of the knights fees, shall levy, gather and pay the wages and fees to their burgesses in like manner and form as is aforesaid, and in and under like pains and forfeitures, as be before mentioned to be levied of the goods and chattels of every such mayor, bailiff and other head officer to whom the king's said writ shall be directed for the levying of such fees, making default of payment of the said fees and wages to the burgesses in manner and form as is aforesaid.

And be it further enacted, by the authority aforesaid, forasmuch as the inhabitants of all cities and boroughs in every the said twelve shires within Wales, and in the said county of Monmouth, not finding burgesses for the parliament themselves, must bear and pay the burgesses wages within the shire towns of, and in every the said twelve shires in Wales, and in the said county of Monmouth, That from the beginning of the said parliament, the burgesses of all and every of the said cities, boroughs, and towns which be and shall be contributary to the payment of the burgesses wages of the said shire towns, shall be lawfully admonished by proclamation or otherwise, by the mayors, bailiffs, or other head officers of the said

The levying of the wages of the burgesses of parliament.

said towns, or by one of them to come and to give their votes for the electing of the said burgesses at such time and place lawful and reasonable as shall be assigned for the same intent by the said mayors, bailiffs, and other head officers of the said shire towns, or by one of them; in which elections the burgesses shall have like voice and authority to elect, name, and choose the burgesses of every the said shire towns, like and in such manner as the burgesses of the said shire towns have or use.

Who shall be choosers of the burgesses of parliament in Wales and Monmouth.

Provided always that two justices of the peace in every of the shires in Wales, and in the said county of Monmouth by force of this act, shall have full power and authority indifferently to lot and tax every city, borough, and town within the shires in Wales, wherein they do inhabit, and in the said county of Monmouth, for the portions and rates that every the said cities and boroughs shall bear and pay towards the said burgesses, within the said shire towns of every of the said shires in Wales and the county of Monmouth; (2) which rates so rated and taxed in gross by the said two justices of peace as is aforesaid, shall be again rated and taxed on the inhabitants of every the said cities and boroughs, by four or six discreet and substantial burgesses of every the said cities and boroughs in Wales, thereunto named and assigned by the mayor, bailiffs or other head officers of the said cities, towns, and boroughs, for the time being, and thereupon the mayors, bailiffs, or other head officers of every such city, borough, and town, to collect and gather the same, and thereof to make payment

Rating of boroughs and inhabitants for the burgesses wages.

payment, in manner and form as is aforesaid, to the burgesses of the parliament for the time being, within like time, and upon the like pains and forfeitures as is abovementioned. A. D. 1543.

ANNO 25° CAROLI II. CAP. 9.

An Act to enable the County Palatine of Durham to send Knights and Burgesses to serve in Parliament.

'WHEREAS the inhabitants of the county palatine of Durham, have not hitherto had the liberty and privilege of electing and sending any knights and burgesses to the high court of parliament, although the inhabitants of the said county palatine are liable to all payments, rates, and subsidies granted by parliament, equally with the inhabitants of other counties, cities, and boroughs in this kingdom who have their knights and burgesses in the parliament, and are therefore concerned equally with others the inhabitants of this kingdom, to have knights and burgesses in the said high court of parliament of their own election, to represent the condition of their county, as the inhabitants of other counties, cities, and boroughs of this kingdom have;' (2) wherefore may it please your majesty, that it may be enacted, and be it enacted by the king's most excellent majesty, by and with the advice and assent of the lords spiritual and temporal, and the commons in this present parliament assembled, and by the

The county palatine of Durham to send two knights, and the city of Durham to send two burgesses to Parliament.

the authority of the same, That from time to time, and at all times from and after the end of this present session of parliament, the said county palatine of Durham, may have two knights for the same county, and the city of Durham two citizens to be burgesses for the same city, for ever hereafter to serve in the high court of parliament; (3) to be elected and chosen by virtue of your majesty's writ, to be awarded by the lord chancellor, or lord keeper of the great seal of England for the time being, in that behalf, to the lord bishop of Durham, or his temporal chancellor of the said county of Durham, and a precept to be thereupon grounded, and made by the lord bishop of Durham, or his temporal chancellor for the time being, to the sheriff of the said county for the time being; (4) and the same election from time to time to be made in the manner and form following, that is to say, the elections of the knights to serve for the said county palatine from time to time hereafter to be made by the greater number of freeholders of the said county palatine of Durham, which from time to time shall be present at such elections, accordingly as is used in other counties in this your majesty's kingdom; (5) and that the election of the said burgesses from time to time, to serve in the high court of parliament for the city of Durham, to be made from time to time by the major part of the mayor, aldermen, and freemen of the said city of Durham, which from time to time shall be present at such elections; (6) which said knights and burgesses and every of them, so elected or returned,

How the elections are to be made.

To be returned by the sheriff.

turned, shall be returned by the said sheriff into the chancery of England, in due form, and upon the like pains as be ordained for the sheriff or sheriffs of any other county of this kingdom to make his or their returns in like cases; (7) and that the said knights and burgesses and every of them, so elected and returned, shall be by authority of this present act, knights and burgesses of the high court of parliament, to all intents and purposes, and have and use the like voice, authority, and places therein, to all intents and purposes, as any other the knights and burgesses of the said high court of parliament, have, use and enjoy, and likewise shall and may, by virtue of this present act, take, have, use, and enjoy all such and the like liberties, advantages, dignities and privileges concerning the said court of parliament to all intents, constructions and purposes as any other the knights and burgesses of the said high court of parliament have taken, had, used or enjoyed, or shall, may or ought hereafter to have, take, or enjoy. A. D. 1672.

ANNO 30° CAROLI II. STAT. 2. CAP. I.

An Act for the more effectual preserving the King's Person and Government, by disabling Papists from sitting in either House of Parliament.

'FORASMUCH as divers good laws have been made for preventing the increase and danger of popery in this kingdom, which have not had the desired effects, by reason of the free access which

which popish recusants have had to his majesty's court, and by reason of the liberty which, of late, some of the recusants have had and taken to sit and vote in parliament.'

Wherefore, and for the safety of his majesty's royal person and government, be it enacted by the king's most excellent majesty, by and with the advice and consent of the lords spiritual and temporal, and of the commons, in this present parliament assembled, and by the authority of the same, That from and after the first day of December, which shall be in the year of our Lord God 1678, no person that now is or hereafter shall be a peer of this realm, or member of the house of peers, shall vote, or make his proxy in the house of peers, or sit there during any debate in the said house of peers; (2) nor any person that now is or hereafter shall be a member of the house of commons, shall vote in the house of commons, or sit there during any debate in the said house of commons after the speaker is chosen; (3) until such peer or member shall, from time to time respectively, and in manner following, first take the several oaths of allegiance and supremacy, and make, subscribe, and audibly repeat this declaration following:

No person to be member without taking the oaths.

For these oaths see 1 W. and M. sess. 1. c. 1. § 3. &c.

The declaration.

'I, A. B. do solemnly and sincerely, in the presence of God, profess, testify, and declare, that I do believe that in the Sacrament of the Lord's Supper, there is not any transubstantiation of the elements of bread and wine into the body and blood of Christ, at or after the consecration thereof by any person whatsoever: (2) and that the invocation or adoration of the Virgin Mary, or any other saint, and the sacrifice of the Mass, as they are now used in the church of Rome, are superstitious and idolatrous. (3) And I do solemnly, in the presence of God, profess, testify, and declare, that I do make this declaration and every part thereof, in the plain and ordinary sense of the words read unto me, as they are commonly understood by English Protestants, without any evasion, equivocation or mental reservation whatsoever, and without any dispensation already granted me for this purpose by the Pope, or any other authority or person whatsoever, or without any hope of any such dispensation from any person or authority whatsoever, or without thinking, that I am or can be acquitted before God or man, or absolved, of this declaration or any part thereof, although the Pope, or any other person or persons or power whatsoever, should dispense with or annul the same, or declare that it was null or void from the beginning.'

This declaration to be subscribed by all professed Papists at their age of 18, by 1 Annæ, st. 1. c. 32. § 7.

4. Which said oaths and declarations shall be in this and every succeeding parliament, solemnly and publicly made and subscribed betwixt the hours of nine in the morning and four in the afternoon, by every such peer and member of the house of peers, at the table in the middle of the said house, before he takes his place in the said house of peers, and whilst a full house of peers is there with their speaker in his place; (2) and by every such member of the house of commons, at the table in the middle of the said house, and whilst a full house of commons is there duly sitting with their speaker in his chair; (3) and that the same

The time and place of taking the oaths and making and subscribing the declaration.

be done in either houfe, in fuch like order or me‑ thod as each houfe is called over by refpectively.

Members of parliament not fwearing and declaring as aforefaid, and recufants convict, forbidden the king's or queen's prefence.

5. And be it further enacted, That from and after the faid firft day of December, every peer of this realm and member of the houfe of peers, and every peer of the kingdom of Scotland or of the kingdom of Ireland, being of the age of one and twenty years or upwards, not having taken the faid oaths and made and fubfcribed the faid declaration; (2) and every member of the faid houfe of commons not having as aforefaid taken the faid oaths, and made and fubfcribed the faid declaration; (3) and every perfon now or hereafter convicted of Popifh recufancy, (4) who hereafter fhall at any time, after the faid firft day of December, come advifedly into or remain in the prefence of the king's majefty, or queen's majefty, or fhall come into the court or houfe where they or any of them refide, as well during the reign of his prefent majefty (whofe life God long preferve) as during the reigns of any of his royal fucceffors kings or queens of England; (5) fhall incur and fuffer all the pains, penalties, forfeitures, and difabilities, in this act mentioned or contained; (6) unlefs fuch peer, member or perfon fo convicted, do refpectively, in the next term after fuch his coming or remaining, take the faid oaths, and make and fubfcribe the faid declaration in his majefty's high court of chancery between the hours of nine and twelve in the forenoon.

6. And be it further enacted by the authority aforefaid, That if any perfon that now is, or hereafter fhall be a peer of this realm, or member of the houfe of peers, or member of the

house of commons, shall presume to do any thing contrary to this act, or shall offend in any of the cases aforesaid; That then every such peer and member so offending, shall from thenceforth be deemed and adjudged a Popish recusant convict to all intents and purposes whatsoever; (2) and shall forfeit and suffer as a Popish recusant convict; (3) and shall be disabled to hold or execute any office or place of profit or trust, civil or military, in any of his majesty's realms of England or Ireland, dominion of Wales, or town of Berwick upon Tweed, or in any of his majesty's islands, or foreign plantations to the said realms belonging; (4) and shall be disabled from thenceforth to sit or vote in either house of parliament, or make a proxy in the house of peers, (5) or to sue or use any action, bill, plaint, or information in course of law, or to prosecute any suit in any court of equity, (6) or to be guardian of any child, or executor or administrator of any person, (7) or capable of any legacy or deed of gift, (8) and shall forfeit, for every wilful offence against this act, the sum of five hundred pounds to be recovered and received by him or them that shall sue for the same, and may be prosecuted by any action of debt, suit, bill, plaint, or information in any of his majesty's courts at Westminster, wherein no essoin, protection, or wager of law shall lie.

The penalty upon members of parliament offending contrary to this act.

7. And be it further enacted by the authority aforesaid, That from the said first day of December, it shall and may be lawful, to and for the house of peers and house of commons, or either of them respectively, as often as they or either of them

Either house of parliament may cause any of their members to swear and subscribe as aforesaid.

them shall see occasion, either in this present parliament, or any other hereafter to be holden, to order and cause all or any of the members of their respective houses of parliament, openly in their respective houses of parliament, to take the said oaths, and to make and subscribe the said declaration, at such times and in such manner as they shall appoint. (2) And if any peer shall, contrary to such order made by their said house, wilfully presume to sit therein, without taking the said oaths, and subscribing the said declaration, according to the said order, every such peer or member of the house of peers, so presuming to sit, shall be adjudged, and is hereby declared, to be uncapable, and disabled in law, to all intents and purposes whatsoever, to sit in the said house of peers, and give any voice therein, either by proxy or otherwise howsoever, during that parliament; (3) and if any member or members of the house of commons shall, contrary to such order made by their house, wilfully presume to sit therein, without taking the said oaths, and making and subscribing the said declaration, every such member or members of the house of commons so presuming to sit, shall be adjudged, and is hereby declared, to be uncapable and disabled in law, to all intents and purposes whatsoever, to sit in the said house of commons, or give any voice therein during that parliament.

8. And be it enacted, That in every case where any member or members of the house of commons shall, by virtue of this act, be disabled to sit or vote in the house of commons, then and in every such case, without any further conviction

or

or other proceedings against such member or members, the place or places for which they or any of them were elected, be hereby declared void; (2) and a new writ or writs shall issue out of the high court of chancery by warrant or warrants from the speaker of the house of commons for the time being, and by order of the said house, for the election of a new member or members to serve in the house of commons, in the place or places of such member or members so disabled, to all intents and purposes, as if such member or members were naturally dead.

The places of members of the house of commons, disabled to vote, shall be void and writs issued out for new elections.

A. D. 1677.

ANNO 2° GULIELMI ET MARIÆ, SESS. I. C. 7.

An Act to declare the Right and Freedom of Election of Members to serve in Parliament for the Cinque Ports.

'WHEREAS the election of members to serve in parliament ought to be free; and whereas the late lord wardens of the cinque ports have pretended unto, and claimed as of right, a power of nominating and recommending to each of the said cinque ports, the two ancient towns, and their respective members, one person whom they ought to elect to serve as a baron or member of parliament for such respective port, ancient town, or member, contrary to the ancient usage, right and freedom of elections:'

2. Be it therefore declared and enacted by the king's and queen's most excellent majesties, by and with the advice and consent of the lords spi-

ritual

ritual and temporal and commons in this present parliament assembled, and by the authority of the same, That all such nominations or recommendations were and are contrary to the laws and constitution of this realm, and for the future shall be so deemed and construed, and hereby are declared to have been, and are, void to all intents and purposes whatsoever; any pretence to the contrary notwithstanding.   A. D. 1690.

Recommendations of members to the cinque ports.

ANNO 5° GULIELMI ET MARIÆ, CAP. 7.

An Act for granting to their Majesties certain Rates and Duties upon Salt and upon Beer, Ale, and other Liquors, for securing certain Recompences and Advantages in the said Act mentioned, to such Persons as shall voluntarily advance the sum of Ten Hundred Thousand Pounds towards carrying on the War against France.

57. PROVIDED always, and be it enacted by the authority aforesaid, That no member of the house of commons shall at any time be concerned directly or indirectly, or any other in trust for him, in the farming, collecting, or managing any of the sums of money, duties, or other aids granted to their majesties by this act, or that hereafter shall be granted by any other act of parliament; except the commissioners of the treasury, and the officers and commissioners for managing the customs and excise, not exceeding the present number in each office, and those appointed to be commissioners for putting in execution an act, intitled, an Act for granting

No members, except commissioners of treasury and land tax and T. N. &c. to be farmers.

to their majesties an aid of four shillings in the pound for one year, for carrying on a vigorous war against France, as to their executing only the authority of the said act, by which they are appointed commissioners. Provided always, That Thomas Neale, Esq. may be employed by their majesties as they shall think fit, in the ordering, or managing the several recompences and advantages hereby given to the contributors upon this act, any thing in this act contained to the contrary notwithstanding. A. D. 1694.

ANNO 5° GULIELMI ET MARIÆ, CAP. 20.

An Act for granting to their Majesties several Rates and Duties upon Tonnage of Ships and Vessels, and upon Beer, Ale, and other Liquors, for securing certain Recompences and Advantages in the said Act mentioned, to such Persons as shall voluntarily advance the Sum of Fifteen Hundred Thousand Pounds towards carrying on the War against France.

33. 'AND whereas by an act of this present session of parliament, intitled, an Act for granting to their majesties certain rates and duties upon salt, and upon beer, ale, and other liquors, for securing certain recompences and advantages, in the said act mentioned, to such persons as shall voluntarily advance the sum of ten hundred thousand pounds towards carrying on the war against France;' it is enacted, That no member of the house of commons shall at any time be concerned

To explain 5 W. & M c. 7. s. 57.

in the farming, collecting, or managing any sum or sums of money, duties, or other aids, by the said act, or any other act of parliament granted, or to be granted to their majesties, except the persons in the said act excepted; and whereas some doubts may arise, whether any member or members of parliament may be concerned in the corporation to be erected in pursuance of this act: Be it therefore declared and enacted by the authority aforesaid, That it shall and may be lawful to, and for, any member or members of the house of commons, to be a member or members of the said corporation for the purposes in this act mentioned; any thing in the said recited act contained to the contrary in any wise notwithstanding.

<small>Members of parliament may be concerned in the corporation.</small>

48. And to the end the great duties of excise, and the powers given for the collecting and levying the same, may not be employed for the influencing of elections of members to serve in parliament, which elections, by the constitution of this government, ought to be free and uncorrupt; be it enacted by the authority aforesaid, That from and after the 1st day of May, in the year of our Lord 1694, no collector, supervisor, gauger, or other officer, or person whatever concerned or employed in the charging, collecting, levying, or managing the duties of excise or any branch or part thereof, shall, by word, message, or writing, or in any other manner whatsoever endeavour to persuade any elector to give, or dissuade any elector from giving, his vote for the choice of any person to be a knight of the shire

<small>Officers in the excise not to persuade in the choice of members.</small>

shire, citizen, burgess, or baron of any county, city, borough, or cinque port, to serve in parliament, and every officer or other person offending therein shall forfeit the sum of one hundred pounds, one moiety thereof to the informer, the other moiety to the poor of the parish where such offence shall be committed, to be recovered by any person that shall sue for the same, by action of debt, bill, plaint, or information in any of their majesties courts of record at Westminster, in which no essoin, protection, privilege, or wager of law, or more than one imparlance shall be allowed; and every person convict, on any such suit, of the said offence, shall thereby become disabled and incapable of ever bearing or executing any office or place concerning or relating to the duty of excise, or any other office or place of trust whatsoever under their majesties, their heirs or successors.

Penalty.

A. D. 1694.

ANNO 6° GULIELMI ET MARIÆ, CAP. 2.

An Act for the frequent meeting and calling of Parliaments.

'WHEREAS by the ancient laws and statutes of this kingdom frequent parliaments ought to be held; and whereas frequent and new parliaments tend very much to the happy union and good agreement of the king and people;' We your majesties most loyal and obedient subjects,

jects, the lords spiritual and temporal and commons in this present parliament assembled, do most humbly beseech your most excellent majesties that it may be declared and enacted in this present parliament; and it is hereby declared and enacted by the king's and queen's most excellent majesties, by and with the advice and consent of the lords spiritual and temporal and commons in this present parliament assembled, and by the authority of the same, That from henceforth a parliament shall be holden once in three years at the least.

Parliament to be holden once in 3 years.

2. And be it further enacted by the authority aforesaid, That within three years at the farthest, from and after the dissolution of this present parliament, and so from time to time for ever hereafter, within three years at the farthest, from and after the determination of every other parliament, legal writs under the great seal shall be issued by directions of your majesties, your heirs and successors, for calling, assembling, and holding another new parliament.

Writs to be issued once in 3 years.

3. And be it further enacted by the authority aforesaid, That from henceforth no parliament whatsoever, that shall at any time hereafter be called, assembled, or held, shall have any continuance longer than for three years only at the farthest, to be accounted from the day on which, by the writs of summons, the said parliament shall be appointed to meet.

No parliament to last longer than 3 years.

4. And be it further enacted by the authority aforesaid, That this present parliament shall cease and determine on the first day of November, which shall be in the year of our Lord 1696,

Present parliament to cease 1st of November, 1696.

unless

unless their majesties shall think fit to dissolve it sooner.

A. D. 1694.

ANNO 7 GULIELMI III. CAP. 4.

An Act for preventing Charge and Expence in Elections of Members to serve in Parliament.

'WHEREAS grievous complaints are made and manifestly appear to be true in the kingdom, of undue elections of members to parliament by excessive and exorbitant expences, contrary to the laws and in violation of the freedom due to the election of representatives for the commons of England in parliament, to the great scandal of the kingdom, dishonourable, and may be destructive to the constitution of parliaments:' Wherefore, for remedy therein, and that all elections of members to parliament may be hereafter freely and indifferently made without charge or expence;' be it enacted, and declared by our sovereign lord the king's most excellent majesty, by and with the advice and consent of the lords spiritual and temporal and commons in this present parliament assembled, and by the authority of the same, That no person or persons hereafter to be elected to serve in parliament for any county, city, town, borough, port, or place within the kingdom of England, dominion of Wales, or town of Berwick upon Tweed, after the teste of the writ of summons to parliament, or after the

Candidates, after the teste of the writ or after any such place becomes vacant, giving or promising any present or reward to any person having vote, for being so elected.

the teste or the issuing out or ordering of the writ or writs of election upon the calling or summoning of any parliament hereafter, or after any such place becomes vacant hereafter in the time of this present or any other parliament, shall or do hereafter, by himself or themselves, or by any other ways or means on his or their behalf, or at his or their charge, before his or their election to serve in parliament for any county, city, town, borough, port, or place within the kingdom of England, dominion of Wales, or town of Berwick upon Tweed, directly or indirectly give, present or allow, to any person or persons having voice or vote in such election, any money, meat, drink, entertainment, or provision, or make any present gift, reward, or entertainment, or shall at any time hereafter, make any promise, agreement, obligation, or engagement to give or allow any money, meat, drink, provision, present, reward, or entertainment, to or for any such person or persons in particular, or to any such county, city, town, borough, port, or place in general, or to or for the use, advantage, benefit, employment, profit, or preferment of any such person or persons, place or places, in order to be elected, or for being elected, to serve in parliament for such county, city, borough, town, port, or place.

2. And it is hereby further enacted and declared, That every person and persons so giving, presenting, or allowing, making, promising, or engaging, doing, acting, or proceeding, shall be, and *Incapable to serve in parliament.* are hereby declared and enacted, disabled and

incapa-

incapacitated, upon such election to serve in parliament for such county, city, town, borough, port, or place; and that such person or persons shall be deemed and taken, and are hereby declared and enacted to be deemed and taken, no members in parliament, and shall not act, sit, or have any vote or place in parliament, but shall be and are hereby declared and enacted to be, to all intents, constructions, and purposes, as if they had been never returned or elected members for the parliament.

A. D. 1696.

ANNO 7° ET 8° GULIELMI III. CAP. 7.

An Act to prevent false and double Returns of Members to serve in Parliament.

'WHEREAS false and double returns of members to serve in parliament are an abuse of trust in a matter of the greatest consequence to the kingdom, and not only an injury to the persons duly chosen, by keeping them from their service in the house of commons, and putting them to great expence to make their elections appear, but also to the counties, cities, boroughs, and cinque ports, by which they are chosen, and the business of parliament disturbed and delayed thereby:' Be it therefore enacted and declared by the king's most excellent majesty, by and with the advice and consent of the lords spiritual and temporal and commons in this present parliament assembled,

Continued by 12 and 13 W. 3. c. 5.

assembled, and by the authority of the same, That all false returns, wilfully made, of any knight of the shire, citizen, burgess, baron of the cinque ports, or other member to serve in parliament, are against law, and are hereby prohibited, and in case that any person or persons shall return any member to serve in parliament for any county, city, borough, cinque port, or place, contrary to the last determination in the house of commons, of the right of election in such county, city, borough, cinque port, or place, that such return so made, shall, and is hereby adjudged to be, a false return.

False return of members prohibited.

What shall be a false return.

2. And be it further enacted, That the party grieved, to wit, every person that shall be duly elected to serve in parliament for any county, city, borough, cinque port, or place, by such false return, may sue the officers and persons making or procuring the same, and every or any of them, at his election, in any of his majesty's courts of record at Westminster, and shall recover double the damages he shall sustain by reason thereof, together with his full costs of such suit.

Party grieved may sue in any court at Westminster, and recover double damages.

3. And to the end the law may not be eluded by double returns, be it further enacted, That if any officer shall wilfully, falsely, and maliciously return more persons than are required to be chosen by the writ or precept on which any choice is made, the like remedy may be had, against him or them, and the party or parties that willingly procure the same, and every or any of them, by the party grieved, at his election.

4. And

4. And be it further enacted, That all contracts, promises, bonds, and securities whatsoever hereafter made or given, to procure any return of any member to serve in parliament, or any thing relating thereunto, be adjudged void; and that whoever makes or gives such contract, security, promise, or bond, or any gift or reward, to procure such false or double returns, shall forfeit the sum of three hundred pounds, one third part thereof to be to his majesty, his heirs and successors, another third part thereof to the poor of the county, city, borough, or place concerned, and one third part thereof to the informer, with his costs, to be recovered in any of his majesty's courts of record at Westminster, by action of debt, bill, plaint, or information, wherein no essoin, protection, or wager of law, shall be allowed, nor any more than one imparlance.

Contracts made to procure returns void.

Penalty.

5. And for the more easy and better proof of any such false or double return, be it enacted by the authority aforesaid, That the clerk of the crown for the time being shall from time to time enter, or cause to be entered, in a book for that purpose to be kept in his office, every single and double return of any member or members to serve in parliament which shall be returned or come into his office, or to his hands, and also every alteration and amendment as shall be made by him or his deputy in every such return; to which book all persons shall have free access at all seasonable times, to search and take true copies of so much thereof as shall be desired, paying a reasonable fee or reward for the same:

Clerk of the crown to enter every return and amendment.

All persons shall have access to the book, and the book or a copy may be given in evidence.

and

and that the party or parties prosecuting such suit, shall and may at any trial give in evidence such book so kept, or a true copy thereof, relating to such false or double return, and shall have the like advantage of such proof, as he or they should or might have had by producing the record itself; any law, custom, or usage to the contrary, notwithstanding; and in case the said clerk of the crown shall not, within six days after any return shall come into his office or to his hands, duly and fairly make an entry or entries as aforesaid, or shall make any alteration in any return, unless by order of the house of commons, or give any certificate of any person not returned, or shall wilfully neglect or omit to perform his duty in the premises, he shall for every such offence forfeit to the party or parties aggrieved the sum of five hundred pounds to be recovered as aforesaid, and shall forfeit and lose his said office, and be for ever incapable of having or holding the same.

Clerk not entering returns in 6 days after receipt, making any alteration, or omitting to perform his duty, to forfeit 500l. and lose his office.

6. Provided always that every information or action, grounded upon this statute, shall be brought within the space of two years after the cause of action shall arise, and not after.

Information to be within two years.

7. Provided also, and be it enacted by the authority aforesaid, that this act shall continue for the term of 7 years, and from thence to the end of the next session of parliament, and no longer.

Act to continue for 7 years. Made perpetual by 12 Annæ, stat. 1. c. 15.

A. D. 1696.

ANNO 7° ET 8° GULIELMI III. CAP. 25.

An Act for the further regulating Elections of Members to serve in Parliament, and for the preventing irregular Proceedings of Sheriffs and other Officers, in the electing and returning such Members.

'WHEREAS by the evil practices and irregular proceedings of sheriffs, under sheriffs, mayors, bailiffs, and other officers, in the execution of writs and precepts for electing of members to serve in parliament, as well the freeholders and others in their right of election, as also the persons by them elected to be their representatives, have heretofore been greatly injured and abused;' Now, for remedying the same and preventing the like for the future, be it enacted by the king's most excellent majesty, by and with the advice and consent of the lords spiritual and temporal and commons in this present parliament assembled, and by the authority of the same, That when any new parliament shall at any time hereafter be summoned or called, there shall be forty days between the teste and returns of the writs of summons; and that the lord chancellor, lord keeper, or lords commissioners of the great seal for the time being, shall issue out the writs for election of members to serve in the same parliament, with as much expedition as the same may be done; and that, as well upon the calling or summoning any new parliament, as also in case of any vacancy during this present or any future parliament, the several writs

Forty days between the teste and return of the writ.

Writ to be issued out with all expedition, and delivered to the proper officer, who is to indorse the day when received, and make out the precept.

writs shall be delivered to the proper officer to whom the execution thereof doth belong or appertain, and to no other person whatsoever; and that every such officer, upon the receipt of the same writ, shall upon the back thereof indorse the day he received the same, and shall forthwith, upon receipt of the writ, make out the precept or precepts to each borough, town corporate, port or place within his jurisdiction, where any member or members are to be elected to serve in such new parliament, or to supply any vacancy during the present or any future parliament, and within three days after the receipt of the said writ of election, shall by himself, or proper agent, deliver, or cause to be delivered, such precept or precepts to the proper officer of every such borough, town corporate, port or place within his jurisdiction, to whom the execution of such precept doth belong or appertain, and to no other person whatsoever; and every such officer upon the back of the same precept, shall indorse the day of his receipt thereof, in the presence of the party from whom he received such precept, and shall forthwith cause public notice to be given of the time and place of election, and shall proceed to election thereupon, within the space of eight days next after his receipt of the same precept, and give four days notice at least of the day appointed for the election.

Precept to be delivered in 3 days after receipt of the writ.

Officer to indorse the day of receipt, and give notice of the time of election in 8 days after.

2. And be it further enacted by the authority aforesaid, That neither the sheriff nor his under sheriff in any county or city, nor the mayor, bailiff, constable, port-reeve, or other officer or officers

Sheriff, &c. not to give or take any fee for making out receipt, &c. of any writ or precept.

officers of any borough, town corporate, port or place, to whom the execution of any writ or precept for electing members to serve in parliament doth belong or appertain, shall give, pay, receive, or take any fee, reward, or gratuity whatsoever, for the making out receipt, delivery, return or execution of any such writ or precept.

3. And be it further enacted by the authority aforesaid, That upon every election to be made of any knight or knights of the shire to serve in this present or any future parliament, the sheriff of the county where such election shall be made shall hold his county court for the same election at the most public and usual place of election within the same county, and where the same has most usually been for forty years last past, and shall there proceed to election at the next county court, unless the same fall out to be held within six days after the receipt of the writ, or upon the same day, and then shall adjourn the same court to some convenient day, giving ten days notice of the time and place of election; and in case the said election be not determined upon the view, with the consent of the freeholders there present, but that a poll shall be required for determination thereof, then the said sheriff, or in his absence his under sheriff, with such others as shall be deputed by him, shall forthwith there proceed to take the said poll in some open or public place or places, by the same sheriff, or his under sheriff as aforesaid in his absence, or others appointed for the taking thereof as aforesaid; and for the

County court to be held at the usual place, and proceed to election, unless it fall out in 6 days after receipt of the writ.

Sheriff, &c. to take the poll if required, and to appoint a number of clerks, who are to be sworn.

more

more due and orderly proceeding in the said poll, the said sheriff, or in his absence his under sheriff, or such as he shall depute, shall appoint such number of clerks as to him shall seem meet and convenient for taking thereof; which clerks shall all take the said poll, in the presence of the said sheriff or his under sheriff, or such as he shall depute; and before they begin to take the said poll, every clerk so appointed shall by the said sheriff, or his under sheriff as aforesaid, be sworn truly and indifferently to take the same poll, and to set down the names of each freeholder, and the place of his freehold, and for whom he shall poll, and to poll no freeholder who is not sworn, if so required by the candidates or any of them, (which oath of the said clerks, the said sheriff, or his under sheriff, or such as he shall depute, are hereby impowered to administer) and the sheriff, or in his absence his under sheriff, as aforesaid, shall appoint for each candidate such one person as shall be nominated to him by each candidate, to be inspectors of every clerk who shall be appointed for taking the poll; and every freeholder before he is admitted to poll at the same election, shall, if required, by the candidates or any of them, first take the oath herein-after mentioned; which oath the said sheriff, by himself or his under sheriff, or such sworn clerks by him appointed for taking of the said poll as aforesaid, are hereby authorized to administer, (viz.)

Name of each freeholder to be set down and for whom he polls, and a person for each candidate to inspect the clerks.

Freeholder to be sworn.

The oath.

" You shall swear that you are a freeholder for
" the county of   and have freehold lands
" or hereditaments of the yearly value of forty
shillings,

"shillings, lying at   within the said county
" of   and that you have not been before
" polled at this election."

4. And in case any freeholder or any other person taking the said oath, shall thereby commit wilful and corrupt perjury, and be thereof convicted, or if any person do unlawfully and corruptly procure or suborn any freeholder or other person, to take the said oath in order to be polled, whereby he shall commit such wilful and corrupt perjury, and shall be thereof convicted, he and they for every such offence, shall incur the like pains and penalties, as are in and by one act of parliament, made in the 5th year of the reign of the late queen Elizabeth, intituled, 'An act for punishment of such persons, as shall procure or commit any wilful perjury,' enacted against all such who shall commit wilful perjury, or suborn or procure any person to commit any unlawful and corrupt perjury contrary to the said act.

Persons convicted of perjury or subornation, to incur the penalty in 5 Eliz. c. 9.

5. And be it further enacted by the authority aforesaid, That the said sheriff, or in his absence his under sheriff, or such as he shall depute as aforesaid, shall at the same place of election proceed to the polling all the freeholders then and there present, and shall not adjourn the county court then and there held, to any other town or place within the same county, without the consent of the candidates, nor shall, by any unnecessary adjournment in the same place of election, protract or delay the election; but shall duly and orderly proceed in the taking of the said poll, from day to day and time to time, without any further

Sheriff not to adjourn the court, unless the candidates consent.

ther or other adjournment, without the consent of the candidates, until all the freeholders then and there present shall be polled, and no longer.

6. And be it further enacted, That every sheriff, under sheriff, mayor, bailiff, and other officer to whom the execution of any writ or precept shall belong for the electing of members to serve in parliament, shall forthwith deliver to such person or persons as shall desire the same, a copy of the poll taken at such election, paying only a reasonable charge for writing the same, and every sheriff, under sheriff, mayor, bailiff, and other officer, to whom the execution of any writ or precept for electing of members to serve in parliament doth belong, for every wilful offence contrary to this act, shall forfeit to every party so aggrieved, the sum of five hundred pounds to be recovered by him or them, his or their executors or administrators, together with full costs of suit, and for which he or they may sue by action of debt, bill, plaint, or information, in any of his majesty's courts at Westminster, wherein no essoin, protection, wager of law, privilege, or imparlance shall be admitted or allowed.

Copy of the poll to be delivered if desired; paying for writing.

Penalty on sheriff, &c. committing wilful offence.

7. And be it also enacted, That no person or persons shall be allowed to have any vote in election of members to serve in parliament, for or by reason of any trust, estate, or mortgage, unless such trustee or mortgagee be in actual possession or receipt of the rents and profits of the same estate; but that the mortgager, or *cestui que trust*, in possession, shall and may vote for the same estate, notwithstanding such mortgage

None to vote by reason of trust, &c. unless in actual possession, but mortgager may vote.

gage or truſt; and that all conveyances of any meſſuages, lands, tenements, or hereditaments, in any county, city, borough, town corporate, port or place, in order to multiply voices, or to ſplit and divide the intereſt in any houſes or lands among ſeveral perſons, to enable them to vote at elections of members to ſerve in parliament, are hereby declared to be void and of none effect, and that no more than one ſingle voice ſhall be admitted to one and the ſame houſe or tenement.

<small>Conveyance in order to multiply voices void.</small>

<small>By 10 Annæ, c. 23. § 1. All conveyances to qualify perſons for voting are made abſolute.</small>

<small>But one voice for one houſe.</small>

8. And be it further enacted, That no perſon whatſoever, being under the age of one and twenty years, ſhall at any time hereafter be admitted to give his voice for election of any member or members, to ſerve in this preſent or any future parliament; and that no perſon hereafter ſhall be capable of being elected a member to ſerve in this or any future parliament, who is not of the age of one and twenty years; and every election or return of any perſon under that age is hereby declared to be null and void, and if any ſuch minor hereafter choſen, ſhall preſume to ſit or vote in parliament, he ſhall incur ſuch penalties and forfeitures, as if he had preſumed to ſit and vote in parliament without being choſen or returned.

<small>None under twenty-one years to vote, or to be elected members.</small>

<small>Penalty.</small>

9. ‘And whereas the county court of the county of *York* is by cuſtom called and held upon *Mondays*, which hath long been complained of to be a very inconvenient day to all the ſuitors thereunto, who at the elections of knights of the ſhire and all ſervices at other times, are forced to travel upon Sundays to their attendance

dance there, to their very great diffatisfaction and grievance.'

Be it therefore enacted by the authority aforefaid, That all county courts after the 25th March, 1696, held for the county of *York*, or any other county courts which heretofore ufed to be held on a *Monday*, shall be called and held upon a *Wednefday* and not otherwife, any cuftom or ufage to the contrary notwithftanding.

County courts for York to be held on Wednefday.

10. Provided alfo, and be it enacted by the authority aforefaid, that the fheriff of the county of *Southampton*, or his deputy at the requeft of one or more of the candidates for election of a knight or knights for that county, fhall adjourn the poll from *Winchefter*, after every freeholder then and there prefent is polled, to *Newport* in the *Ifle of Wight*, for the eafe of the inhabitants of the faid Ifland; any thing in this act contained to the contrary notwithftanding.

Poll may be adjourned from Winchefter to Newport in the Ifle of Wight.

A. D. 1696.

ANNO 10° ET 11° GULIELMI III. CAP. 7.

An Act for preventing irregular Proceedings of Sheriffs, and other Officers, in making the Returns of Members chofen to ferve in Parliament.

FOR preventing abufes in the returns of writs of fummons, for the calling and affembling of any parliament for the future, or writs for the choice of any new member to ferve in parliament, and to the end fuch writs may, by the proper

per officer or his deputy, be duly returned and delivered to the clerk of the crown, to be by him filed according to the ancient and legal course; be it enacted by the king's most excellent majesty, by and with the advice and consent of the lords spiritual and temporal and commons in parliament assembled, and by authority of the same, That the sheriff, or other officer having the execution and return of any such writ which shall be issued for the future, shall, on or before the day that any future parliament shall be called to meet, and with all convenient expedition not exceeding fourteen days after any election made by virtue of any new writ, either in person or by his deputy, make return of the same to the clerk of the crown in the high court of chancery to be by him filed; and the sheriff, or other person making such return, shall pay to the said clerk of the crown the ancient and lawful fees of four shillings, and no more, for every knight of a shire, and two shillings, and no more, for every citizen, burgess, or baron of the cinque ports, returned into the said court to be by him filed; and the said sheriff or officer shall, by virtue of this act, charge the same to his majesty, his heirs or successors, and have allowance thereof in his account in the exchequer or elsewhere.

Writ when returnable.

Sheriff on return of writ to pay the ancient fees, &c. and charge the same to the king.

2. 'And whereas by an act made in the 7th and 8th years of the reign of his present majesty, intituled, An act for the further regulating election of members to serve in parliament, and for the preventing irregular proceedings of sheriffs and other officers, in the electing and returning such

7 and 8 W. 3. c. 25.

such members, it is provided and enacted, That the officer, on the receipt of any such writ, shall, within three days after such his receipt, by himself or proper agent, deliver or cause to be delivered, a precept or precepts to the proper officer of every borough, town corporate, port, or place within his jurisdiction, to whom the execution of such precept doth belong or appertain, which by experience hath been found too short a time for the performance of the same, in the cinque ports;' be it therefore enacted, by the authority aforesaid, That from henceforth the proper officer of the cinque ports, shall be allowed six days from the receipt of such writ, for the delivery of the precept, according to the purport of the said act; any thing in the said act or any other law, statute, or usage, to the contrary in any wise notwithstanding.

Officer of the cinque ports allowed six days from receipt of writ.

3. And it is further enacted by the authority aforesaid, That every sheriff or other officer, or officers aforesaid, who shall not make the returns according to the true intent and meaning of this act, shall forfeit for every such offence the sum of five hundred pounds, one moiety whereof shall be to his majesty, and the other moiety to him or them that shall sue for the same, to be recovered by action of debt, bill, plaint, or information, in any of his majesty's courts of record at Westminster, wherein no essoin, protection, privilege, or wager of law shall be allowed, nor any more than one imparlance.

Penalty on [officers...]

A. D. 1699.

ANNO

ANNO 11° & 12° GULIELMI III. CAP. 2.

An Act for granting an Aid to his Majesty by sale of the forfeited and other Estates and Interests in Ireland, and by a Land-tax in England, for the several Purposes therein mentioned.

150. AND be it further enacted by the authority aforesaid, That no member of the house of commons in this present or any future parliament, during the time of his being a member of parliament, shall, from and after the said twenty-fourth day of June, 1700, be capable of being a commissioner or farmer of the duty of excise upon beer, ale and other liquors, or of being a commissioner for determining appeals concerning the said duty, or controuling or auditing the account of the said duty, or of holding or enjoying in his own name, or in the name of any other person in trust for him, or for his use and benefit, or of executing by himself or his deputy any office, place, or employment, touching or concerning the farming, collecting, or managing the said duty of excise.

No member of parliament shall, after 24th June, 1700, be a commissioner or farmer of the excise, or a commissioner of appeals, or comptroller, or auditor of the said duty.

151. And be it further enacted, That if any member of the house of commons, in this present or any future parliament, during the time of his being a member of parliament, shall at any time after the said twenty-fourth day of June, by himself or his deputy, or any other in trust for him, or for his benefit, take, enjoy, or execute, any

any office, place or employment, touching or concerning the farming, managing, or collecting the said duty of excise, or determining appeals concerning the said duty, or controuling or auditing the accounts of the same, such person is hereby declared and enacted, to be absolutely incapable of sitting, voting, or acting as a member of the house of commons in such parliament.

Such persons incapable of sitting in the house of commons.

152. Provided always, and be it hereby declared, That nothing herein-before contained shall extend, or be construed to extend (during the continuance of this parliament) to the disabling any person, at present a member of the house of commons, from being concerned in the managing, farming, or collecting the said duties of excise, or in determining appeals concerning the same, or in controuling or auditing the accounts thereof, so as such person shall not, after the said twenty-fourth day of June, 1700, sit, vote, or act in the said house; any thing herein-before contained to the contrary notwithstanding.

But not to disable any present member, till after 24th June.

A. D. 1700.

ANNO 12° ET 13° GULIELMI III. CAP. 3.

An Act for preventing any Inconveniencies that may happen by Privilege of Parliament.

Amended by 11 Geo. 2. c. 24.

FOR the preventing all delays the king or his subjects may receive in any of his courts of law or equity, and for their ease in the recovery of of their rights and titles to any lands, tenements, or hereditaments, and their debts or other dues for which they have cause of suit or action: Be it enacted by the king's most excellent majesty, by and with the advice and consent of the lords spiritual and temporal and commons in this present parliament assembled, and by the authority of the same, That from and after the four and twentieth day of June, 1701, any person or persons shall and may commence and prosecute any action or suit in any of his majesty's courts of record at Westminster, or high court of chancery, or court of exchequer, or the dutchy court of Lancaster, or in the court of admiralty, and in all causes matrimonial and testamentary in the court of arches, the prerogative courts of Canterbury and York, and the delegates, and all courts of appeal, against any peer of this realm, or lord of parliament, or against any of the knights, citizens, and burgesses of the house of commons for the time being, or against their or any of their menial or other servants, or any other person entitled to the privilege of parliament, at any time from and immediately after the dissolution or prorogation of any parliament, until a new parliament shall meet, or the same be re-assembled, and from and immediately after any adjournment of both houses of parliament for above the space of fourteen days, until both houses shall meet or re-assemble; and that the said respective courts shall and may, after such dissolution, prorogation, or adjournment as aforesaid, proceed to give judgement, and to make final

Action may be commenced against any peer or member of parliament, &c. in the interval of parliament, &c.

And after prorogation, &c. court may give judgement.

final orders, decrees, and sentences, and award execution thereupon; any privilege of parliament to the contrary notwithstanding.

2. Provided nevertheless, That this act shall not extend to subject the person of any of the knights, citizens, and burgesses of the house of commons, or any other person entitled to the privilege of parliament, to be arrested during the time of privilege. Nevertheless, if any person, or persons, having cause of action, or complaint against any peer of this realm, or lord of parliament, such person, or persons, after any dissolution, prorogation, or adjournment as aforesaid, or before any session of parliament, or meeting of both houses as aforesaid, shall and may have such process out of his majesty's courts of king's bench, common pleas, and exchequer, against such peer, or lord of parliament as he or they might have had against him out of the time of privilege; and if any person or persons having cause of action against any of the said knights, citizens, or burgesses, or any other person entitled to privilege of parliament, after any dissolution, prorogation, or such adjournment as aforesaid, or before any sessions of parliament, or meeting of both houses as aforesaid, such person or persons shall and may prosecute such knight, citizen, or burgess, or other person entitled to the privilege of parliament, in his majesty's courts of king's bench, common pleas, or exchequer, by summons and distress infinite, or by original bill and summons, attachment and distress infinite thereupon to be issued out of any of the said

Persons may have process against any peer, &c. after dissolution of parliament.

said courts of record, which the said respective courts are hereby impowered to issue against them, or any of them, until he or they shall enter a common appearance, or file common bail to the plaintiff's action, according to the course of each respective court, and any person or persons having cause of suit or complaint, may, in the times aforesaid, exhibit any bill or complaint against any peer of this realm, or lord of parliament, or against any of the said knights, citizens, or burgesses, or other person entitled to the privilege of parliament, in the high court of chancery, court of exchequer, or dutchy court of Lancaster, and may proceed thereon by letter or *subpœna* as is usual, and upon leaving a copy of the bill with the defendant, or at his house or lodging, or last place of abode, may proceed thereon, and, for want of an appearance or answer, or for non-performance of any order or decree, or breach thereof, may sequester the real and personal estate of the party, as is used and practised where the defendant is a peer of this realm, but shall not arrest or imprison the body of any of the said knights, citizens, and burgesses, or other privileged person, during the continuance of privilege of parliament.

And may exhibit bill against any peer or member, &c.

And sequester the party's estate, but not arrest his body.

3. And be it enacted by the authority aforesaid, That where any plaintiff shall, by reason or occasion of privilege of parliament, be stayed or prevented from prosecuting any suit by him commenced, such plaintiff shall not be barred by any statute of limitation, or nonsuited, dismissed, or his suit discontinued, for want of prosecution

Plaintiff prevented from prosecuting by privilege of parliament, not to be barred by any statute of limitation, &c.

prosecution of the suit by him begun, but shall from time to time, upon the rising of the parliament, be at liberty to proceed to judgement and execution.

No action, &c. against the king's immediate debtor, &c.

4. And it is hereby enacted, That no action, suit, process, order, judgement, decree, or proceeding in law or equity against the king's original and immediate debtor, for the recovery or obtaining any debt or duty originally and immediately due or payable unto his majesty, his heirs or successors, or against any accountant, or person answerable or liable to render any account unto his majesty, his heirs or successors, for any part or branch of any of his or their revenues, or other original or immediate debt or duty, or the execution of any such process,

Shall be stayed by privilege of parliament; but person not liable to be arrested, &c.

order, judgement, decree, or proceedings, shall be impeached, stayed, or delayed, by or under the colour or pretence of any privilege of parliament; yet so, nevertheless, that the person or persons of any such debtor, or accountant, or person answerable or liable to account, being a peer of this realm or lord of parliament, shall not be liable to be arrested or imprisoned by or upon any such suit, order, judgement, decree, process, or proceedings, or being a member of the house of commons, shall not, during the continuance of the privilege of parliament, be arrested or imprisoned, by or upon any such order, judgement, decree, process, or proceedings.

Proviso.

5. Provided nevertheless, That neither this act, nor any thing herein contained, shall extend

tend to give any jurisdiction, power, or authority, to any court, to hold plea in any real or mixed actions in any other manner than such court might have done before the making this act.

A. D. 1700.

ANNO 12° ET 13° GULIELMI III. CAP. 10.

An Act for granting an Aid to his Majesty, for defraying the Expence of his Navy, Guards, and Garrisons for one Year, and for other necessary Occasions.

89. AND be it enacted by the authority aforesaid, That no member of the house of commons, from and after the dissolution of this present parliament, shall be capable of being a commissioner, or farmer of the customs, or of holding, or enjoying in his own name, or in the name of any other person in trust for him, or for his use or benefit, or of executing by himself, or his deputy, any office, place, or employment, touching or concerning the farming, collecting, or managing the customs. *After dissolution of this parliament, no member shall be a commissioner, &c. of customs.*

90. And be it further enacted, That if any member of the house of commons, from and after the dissolution of this present parliament, shall, during the time of his being a member of parliament, by himself, or his deputy, or any other in trust for him, or for his benefit, *Member executing office in customs, incapable of sitting.*

take,

take, enjoy, or execute any office, place, or employment, touching or concerning the farming, managing, or collecting the customs; such person is hereby declared and enacted to be absolutely incapable of sitting, voting, or acting as a member of the house of commons in such parliament.

<small>No officer of customs to influence any election of members.</small>

91. And be it further enacted, by the authority aforesaid, That from and after the 29th day of September 1701, no commissioner, collector, comptroller, searcher, or other officer, or person whatsoever, concerned or employed in the charging, collecting, levying, or managing the customs, or any branch or part thereof, shall by word, message, or writing, or in any other manner whatsoever, endeavour to persuade any elector to give, or dissuade any elector from giving, his vote for the choice of any person to be a knight of the shire, citizen, burgess, or baron of any county, city, borough, or cinque port, to serve in parliament; and every officer, or other person offending therein, shall forfeit the sum of 100l. one moiety thereof to the informer, the other moiety to the poor of the parish where such offence shall be committed, to be recovered by any person that shall sue for the same by action of debt, bill, plaint, or information, in any of his majesty's courts of record at Westminster, in which no essoin, protection, or wager of law, or more than one imparlance shall be allowed; and every person convict on any such suit of the said offence, shall thereby become disabled and incapable of ever bearing, or executing any office,

<small>Penalty.</small>

or

or place concerning or relating to the cuftoms, or any other office, or place of truft whatfoever under his majefty, his heirs, or fucceffors.

A. D. 1700.

ANNO 2° ET 3° ANNÆ REGINÆ, CAP. 18.

An Act for the further Explanation and Regulation of Privilege of Parliament in relation to Perfons in Public Offices.

'WHEREAS it is moft juft and reafonable that perfons employed in offices and places of public truft, fhould at all times be accountable for any mifdemeanors therein, and the public juftice of the realm requireth a vigorous profecution of fuch offenders:' To the end therefore that your majefty's good fubjects may not lie under any doubts or difcouragements whereby fuch profecution might be prevented or delayed, may it pleafe your moft excellent majefty that it may be enacted, and be it enacted by the queen's moft excellent majefty, by and with the advice and confent of the lords fpiritual and temporal, and commons in this prefent parliament affembled, and by the authority of the fame, That any action or fuit fhall and may be commenced and profecuted in any of her majefty's courts at Weftminfter, againft any officer or perfon intrufted or employed in the revenue of her majefty, her heirs or fucceffors, or any part or branch thereof, or

Action may be profecuted againft any officer of the revenue or any other place of public truft for any mifdemeanor, &c.

any other office or place of public trust, for any forfeiture, misdemeanor, or breach of trust, of, in, or relating to such office or place of trust, or any penalty imposed by law to enforce the due execution thereof, and that no such action, suit, or any other process, proceeding, judgment, or execution thereupon, although such officer or person shall be a peer of this realm, or lord of parliament, or one of the knights, citizens, or burgesses of the house of commons, or otherwise intitled to the privilege of parliaments, shall be impeached, stayed, or delayed by or under colour, or pretence of any privilege of parliament.

No such action to be stayed on pretence of privilege of parliament.

2dly. Provided nevertheless, and be it further enacted by the authority aforesaid, That nothing in this act shall extend to subject the person of such officer, being a peer of this realm, or lord of parliament, to be arrested or imprisoned, but that all process shall issue against such officer or person, being a peer of this realm, or lord of parliament, as should have issued against him out of the time of privilege. Nor shall extend to subject the person of such officer being a knight, citizen, or burgess of the house of commons, to be arrested or imprisoned, during the time of privilege of parliament, and that against such officer or other person, being a knight, citizen, or burgess of the house of commons intitled to privilege, shall be issued summons and distress infinite or original bill, summons, attachment, and distress infinite, which the said respective courts are hereby impowered to issue in such case,

Act not to subject the person of peer to imprisonment.

Nor member of the house of commons.

until

until the party shall appear upon such process according to the course of such respective court.

A. D. 1703.

ANNO 6° ANNÆ REGINÆ, CAP. 7.

An Act for the Security of her Majesty's Person and Government, and of the Succession to the Crown of Great Britain in the Protestant Line.

Sect. 4. AND be it further enacted by the authority aforesaid, That this present parliament, or any other parliament which shall hereafter be summoned and called by her Majesty Queen Anne, her heirs or successors, shall not be determined or dissolved by the death or demise of her said Majesty, her heirs or successors; but such parliament shall and is hereby enacted to continue, and is hereby empowered and required, if sitting at the time of such demise, immediately to proceed to act, notwithstanding such death or demise, for and during the term of six months, and no longer, unless the same be sooner prorogued or dissolved by such person to whom the crown of this realm of Great Britain shall come, remain, and be, according to the acts for limiting and settling the succession, and for the union above mentioned; and if the said parliament shall be prorogued, then it shall meet and sit on and upon the day unto which it shall be prorogued, and continue for the residue of the said time of

Parliament not to be dissolved by the queen's death.

But continue for six months after.

six months, unless sooner prorogued or dissolved, as aforesaid.

Sect. 5. And be it further enacted by the authority aforesaid, That if there be a parliament in being at the time of the death of her Majesty, her heirs or successors, but the same happens to be separated by adjournment or prorogation, such parliament shall, immediately after such demise, meet, convene, and sit, and shall act, notwithstanding such death or demise, for and during the time of six months, and no longer, unless the same shall be sooner prorogued and dissolved, as aforesaid.

<small>Parliament to meet immediately after the death.</small>

Sect. 6. And be it further enacted by the authority aforesaid, That in case there is no parliament in being at the time of such demise, that hath met and sat, then the last preceding parliament shall immediately convene, and sit at Westminster, and be a parliament, to continue as aforesaid, to all intents and purposes as if the same parliament had never been dissolved, but subject to be prorogued and dissolved as aforesaid.

<small>In case there be no parliament then the last preceding to meet.</small>

Sect. 7. Provided always, and it is hereby declared, That nothing in this act contained shall extend, or be construed to extend, to alter or abridge the power of the queen, her heirs or successors, to prorogue or dissolve parliaments, nor to repeal or make void one act of parliament made in England in the 6th year of the reign of their said late majesties, king William and queen Mary, intituled, An act for the frequent meeting and calling of parliaments; but that the said act shall continue in force in every thing that

<small>Not to abridge the queen's power to prorogue or dissolve parliaments.</small>

<small>6 W. and M. c. 2. confirmed.</small>

is

is not contrary to, or inconsistent with, the direction of this act, and the said act for the frequent meeting and calling of parliaments is hereby declared and enacted to extend to the parliament of Great Britain, as fully and effectually, to all intents, constructions, and purposes, as if the same were herein and hereby particularly recited and enacted.

Sect. 16. And be it further enacted by the authority aforesaid, That any nomination and appointment already made by the next successor, signified by such instruments deposited as aforesaid, pursuant to the said former act, for the better security of her majesty's person and government, and of the succession to the crown of England in the protestant line, shall be deemed and taken to be as effectual, for constituting and appointing the persons so nominated lords justices of England to be lords justices of Great Britain to all intents, constructions, and purposes, as if such nomination and appointment were made pursuant to this act.

Nomination of Lord's Justices by successor, already made, to be as effectual as if appointed by this act.

Sect. 17. And be it further enacted, That the said lords justices, constituted as aforesaid, shall not dissolve the parliament continued and ordered to assemble and sit as aforesaid, without express direction from such succeeding queen or king; and that the said lords justices shall be, and are, hereby restrained and disabled from giving the royal assent in parliament to any bill or bills for the repealing or altering the act made in England in the 13th and 14th years of the reign of King Charles the second, intituled, An act for the uniformity

Lords Justices not to dissolve the parliament without direction.

Nor alter 13 and 14 Car. 2. c. 4.

formity of public prayers and administration of sacraments, and other rites and ceremonies; and for establishing the form for making, ordaining, and consecrating bishops, priests, and deacons, in the church of England; or the act made in Scotland in the last session of parliament there, intituled, An act for securing the protestant religion and presbyterian church government; and all and every the said lords justices concurring in giving the royal assent to any bill or bills for repealing or altering the said acts, or either of them, shall be guilty of high treason, and suffer and forfeit as in cases of high treason.

Or an Act made in Scotland.

Sect. 23. And be it further declared and enacted, That if, after the death of her majesty without issue, and before the arrival of any succeeding queen or king in Great Britain, any parliament shall be called by the lords justices, by writs tested in their names; by the arrival of such succeeding queen or king in Great Britain, such parliament shall not be dissolved, but after such arrival shall proceed without any new summons.

Parliament called by Lords Justices, not to be dissolved by arrival of successor.

Sect. 25. And be it further enacted by the authority aforesaid, That no person who shall have in his own name, or in the name of any person or persons in trust for him, or for his benefit, any new office or place of profit whatsoever under the crown, which at any time since the 25th day of October, in the year of our Lord 1705, have been created, erected, or hereafter shall be erected or created, nor any person who shall be a commissioner, or sub-commissioner of prizes, secretary

Persons in office &c. made incapable of being elected members of the house of commons.

tary or receiver of the prizes, nor any comptroller of the accounts of the army, nor any commissioner of transports, nor any commissioner of the sick and wounded, nor any agent for any regiment, nor any commissioner for any wine licences, nor any governor or deputy governor of any of the plantations, nor any commissioner of the navy employed in any of the out ports, nor any person having any pension from the crown during pleasure, shall be capable of being elected, or of sitting or voting as a member of the house of commons.

Sect. 26. Provided always, that if any person being chosen a member of the house of commons, shall accept of any office of profit from the crown during such time as he shall continue a member, his election shall be, and is hereby declared to be void, and a new writ shall issue for a new election, as if such person so accepting was naturally dead. Provided nevertheless, That such person shall be capable of being again elected, as if his place had not become void as aforesaid. Accepting office of profit while a member, election void, but may be again elected.

Sect. 27. Provided also and be it enacted, That in order to prevent for the future too great a number of commissioners to be appointed or constituted for the executing of any office, that no greater number of commissioners shall be made or constituted for the execution of any office, than have been employed in the execution of such respective office at some time before the first day of this present parliament. No office to be executed by too many commissioners.

Sect. 28. Provided also, That nothing herein contained shall extend or be construed to extend Not to extend to officers in the navy or army.

to

to any member of the house of commons, being an officer in her majesty's navy or army, who shall receive any new or other commission in the navy or army respectively.

Persons disabled, if returned as members, such election and return void.

Sect. 29. And be it further enacted, That if any person hereby disabled or declared to be incapable to sit or vote in any parliament hereafter to be holden, shall nevertheless be returned as a member to serve for any county, stewartry, city, town, or cinque port, in any such parliament, such election and return are hereby enacted and declared to be void to all intents and purposes whatsoever; and if any person disabled, or declared incapable by this act to be elected, shall, after the dissolution or determination of this present parliament, presume to sit or vote as a member of the house of commons in any parliament to be hereafter summoned, such person so sitting or voting shall forfeit the sum of

Penalty on sitting.

500l. to be recovered by such person as shall sue for the same in England, by action of debt, bill, plaint, or information, wherein no essoin, protection, or wager of law shall be allowed, and only one imparlance.

Sect. 30. And be it further enacted and declared, That every person disabled to be elected, or to sit or vote in the house of commons of any parliament of England, shall be disabled to be elected, or to sit or vote in the house of commons of any parliament of Great Britain.

Sect. 31. And be it further enacted by the authority aforesaid, That no person who now is a commissioner for disposing the sum of 398,085l. 10s. and all other sums arising to Scotland by way

way of equivalent, upon the agreements and to the purposes mentioned in the articles of union of the two kingdoms, shall, for or by reason of such commission, or any other commission for disposing the said equivalent or any part thereof, or the execution of any such commission, or any thing relating thereunto, be disabled from being elected a member of parliament, or sitting or voting as such in this or any future parliament.

No commissioner for the equivalent disabled from being elected.

A. D. 1707.

ANNO 9° ANNÆ REGINÆ, CAP. 5.

An Act for securing the Freedom of Parliaments by the farther qualifying the Members to sit in the House of Commons.

FOR the better preserving the constitution and freedom of parliament, be it enacted and declared by the queen's most excellent majesty, by and with the advice and consent of the lords spiritual and temporal, and commons in this present parliament assembled, and by the authority of the same, That from and after the determination of this present parliament, no person shall be capable to sit or vote, as a member of the house of commons for any county, city, borough, or cinque port, within that part of Great Britain called England, the dominion of Wales, and town of Berwick upon Tweed, who shall not have an estate, freehold or copyhold, for his own life, or for

No person shall be a member who hath not an estate, &c.

for some greater estate, either in law or equity, to and for his own use and benefit, of or in lands, tenements, or hereditaments, over and above what will satisfy and clear all incumbrances that may affect the same, lying or being within that part of Great Britain called England, the dominion of Wales, and town of Berwick upon Tweed, of the respective annual value hereafter limited, viz. The annual value of 600 l. above reprizes for every knight of a shire, and the annual value of 300 l. above reprizes, for every citizen, burgess, or baron of the cinque ports; and that if any person who shall be elected, or returned to serve in any parliament as a knight of a shire or as a citizen, burgess or baron of the cinque ports, shall not, at the time of such election and return, be seized of or entitled to such an estate, in lands, tenements, or hereditaments, as for such knight, or for such citizen, burgess, or baron respectively, is hereinbefore required or limited, such election and return shall be void.

This act not to extend to the eldest son of a peer, or of a person qualified to serve as a knight of a shire.

2dly, Provided always, That nothing in this act contained, shall extend to make the eldest son, or heir apparent of any peer or lord of parliament, or of any person qualified by this act to serve as knight of a shire, uncapable of being elected and returned, and sitting and voting as a member of the house of commons in any parliament.

The universities may elect and return members as formerly.

3dly, Provided always, That nothing in this act contained, shall extend or be construed to extend to either of the universities, in that part of Great Britain called England, but that they,

and

and each of them may elect and return members to reprefent them in parliament as heretofore they have done; any thing herein contained to the contrary notwithftanding.

4thly, Provided always, and be it enacted by the authority aforefaid, That no perfon whatfoever, fhall be conftrued to be qualified to fit in the houfe of commons, within the meaning of this act, by virtue of any mortgage whatfoever whereof the equity of redemption is in any other perfon or perfons, unlefs the mortgagee fhall have been in poffeffion of the mortgaged premifes, for the fpace of feven years before the time of his election; any thing herein contained to the contrary notwithftanding. *None to be qualified by virtue of any mortgage, unlefs the mortgagee have been in poffeffion feven years before the election.*

5thly, Provided always, and it is hereby enacted by the authority aforefaid, That every perfon (except as aforefaid) who, from and after the determination of this prefent parliament, fhall appear as a candidate, or fhall by himfelf or any others be propofed to be elected to ferve as a member for the houfe of commons, for any county, city, borough, or cinque port in England, Wales, or Berwick upon Tweed, fhall, and he is hereby enjoined and required, upon reafonable requeft to him to be made (at the time of fuch election, or before the day to be prefixed in the writ of fummons for the meeting of the parliament) by any other perfon who fhall ftand candidate at fuch election, or by any two or more perfons having right to vote at fuch election, take a corporal oath in the form or to the effect following: *Every candidate at the requeft of another candidate, or of two of the voters, fhall take the following oath.*

' I, A. B. do fwear, that I truly and *bona fide* have fuch an eftate in law or equity, to and for *The Oath.*

for my own use and benefit, of or in lands, tenements, or hereditaments, (over and above what will satisfy and clear all incumbrances that may affect the same) of the annual value of 600l. above reprises, as doth qualify me to be elected and returned to serve as a member for the county of   according to the tenor and true meaning of the act of parliament in that behalf; and that my said lands, tenements, or hereditaments, are lying or being within the parish, township, or precincts of   or in the several parishes, townships, or precincts of   in the county of   or in the several counties of   (as the case may be).'

If the candidate be for a city &c. the oath shall relate only to 300l. per annum; mutatis mutandis.

6. And in case such candidate or person is to serve for any city, borough, or cinque port, then the said oath shall relate only to the said value of 300l. per annum, and be taken to the same effect, *mutatis mutandis,* as is hereby prescribed for the oath of a person to serve as a member for such county as aforesaid.

The oath to be administered by the sheriff, &c. who shall, within three months after the taking thereof, certify the same into the Queen's Bench or Chancery, or forfeit 100l.

7. And it is hereby enacted, That the respective oaths aforesaid shall and may be administered by the sheriff or under-sheriff for any such county as aforesaid, or by the mayor, bailiff, or other officer or officers, for any city, borough, or port, to whom it shall appertain to take the poll, or make the return, at such election for the same county, borough, or port respectively, or by any two or more justices of the peace within England, Wales, and Berwick upon Tweed; and the said sheriff, mayor, bailiff, or other officers, and the said justices of the peace respectively, who shall administer the said oaths, are hereby required,

quired to certify the taking thereof into her majesty's high court of chancery, or the queen's bench, within three months after the taking the same, under the penalty of forfeiting the sum of 100l. to wit, one moiety thereof to the queen, and the other moiety thereof to such person or persons as will sue for the same, to be recovered, with full costs of suit, by action of debt, bill, plaint, or information, in any of her majesty's courts of record at Westminster; and if any of the said candidates, or persons proposed to be elected as aforesaid, shall wilfully refuse, upon reasonable request to be made at the time of the election, or at any time before the day upon which such parliament, by the writ of summons, is to meet, to take the oath hereby required, then the election or return of such candidate or person shall be void. *One moiety to the queen, the other to him who will sue, &c. with costs.* *Candidate refusing to take the oath, his election to be void.*

8. And it is hereby enacted, That no fee or reward shall be taken for administering any such oath, or making, receiving, or filing the certificate thereof, except one shilling for administering the oath, and two shillings for making the certificate, and two shillings for receiving and filing the same, under the penalty of 20l. to be forfeited by the offender, and to be recovered and divided as aforesaid. *One shilling only for administering the oath, two shillings for certificate, and two shillings for filing.* *Penalty 20l.*

A. D. 1710.

ANNO 9° ANNÆ REGINÆ, CAP. 10.

An Act for establishing a General Post Office for all her Majesty's Dominions, and for settling a weekly Sum out of the Revenues thereof, for the Service of the War and other her Majesty's Occasions.

No officer of the post-office to intermeddle in elections.

Sect. 44. AND be it further enacted by the authority aforesaid, That no postmaster or postmasters general, or his or their deputy, or deputies, or any person employed by, or under him or them, in the receiving, collecting, or managing the revenue of the post office, or any part thereof, shall by word, message, or writing, or in any manner whatsoever, endeavour to persuade any elector to give, or dissuade any elector from giving, his vote for the choice of any person to be a knight of the shire, citizen, or burgess, or baron of any county, city, borough, or cinque port, to serve in parliament; and every officer, or other person offending therein, shall forfeit the sum of

Penalty.

100l. one moiety thereof to the informer, the other moiety to the poor of the parish, where such offence shall be committed, to be recovered by action of debt, bill, plaint, or information in any of her majesty's courts of record, at Westminster, or in the court of exchequer in Scotland, for the said offences committed in England and Scotland respectively, wherein no essoin, protection, or wager of law, or any more than one imparlance shall be allowed; and every person convict on any such suit of the said offence, shall thereby become disabled and incapable

pable of ever bearing or executing any office or place of truft whatfoever under her majefty, her heirs or fucceffors. A. D. 1710.

ANNO 9° ANNÆ, CAP. II.

An Act for levying certain Duties upon Hides and Skins tanned, tawed, or dreſſed, and upon Vellum and Parchment, for the Term of Thirty-two Years, for profecuting the War and other her Majefty's moſt preſſing Occaſions.

49. 'AND be it further enacted by the authority aforefaid, That no commiffioner, officer, or other perfon, concerned or employed in the charging, collecting, receiving, or managing any of the duties granted by this act, fhall by word, meffage, or writing, or in any other manner, endeavour to perfuade any elector to give, or diffuade any elector from giving, his vote for his choice of any perfon to be a knight of the fhire, commiffioner, citizen, burgefs, or baron, for any county, city, borough, or cinque port; and every officer or other perfon offending therein fhall forfeit the fum of one hundred pounds, one moiety thereof to the informer, the other moiety thereof to the ufe of the poor of the parifh or place where fuch offence fhall be committed, to be recovered by any perfon that fhall fue for the fame by action of debt, bill, plaint, or information, in any of her majefty's courts of record at Weftminfter, or in the court of exchequer in that part of Great Britain called Scotland, in which no effoin, protection,

Commiffioners, officers, &c. not to intermeddle with elections.

Penalty.

tection, privilege, or wager of law, or more than one imparlance shall be allowed; and every person convict on any such suit shall thereby become disabled and incapable of ever bearing or executing any office or place of trust whatsoever under her majesty, her heirs or successors.

Made perpetual 3 Geo. 1. c. 7.

A. D. 1710.

ANNO 9° ANNÆ REGINÆ, CAP. 20.

An Act for rendering the Proceedings upon Writs of Mandamus *and Informations, in the Nature of a* Quo Warranto *more speedy and effectual; and for the more easy trying and determining the Rights of Offices and Franchises in Corporations and Boroughs.*

8. 'AND whereas in divers counties, boroughs, towns corporate, and cinque ports where the mayor, bailiffs, or other officer or officers to whom it belongs to preside at the election, and make return of any member to serve in parliament, ought to be annually elected, the same person hath been re-elected into such office for several years successively, which hath been found inconvenient:' Be it enacted and declared by the authority aforesaid, That no person or persons, who hath been, or shall be in such annual office for one whole year, shall be capable to be chosen into the same office for the year immediately ensuing; and where any such annual officer or officers is or are to continue for a year, and until some person or persons shall be chosen and sworn into such office, if any such officer or officers shall voluntarily

No annual officer shall be re-elected.

voluntarily and unlawfully obstruct and prevent the choosing another person or persons to succeed into such office at the time appointed for making another choice, shall forfeit one hundred pounds for every such offence, to be recovered with costs of suit by such person as will sue for the same in any of her majesty's courts of record before mentioned, by action of debt, bill, plaint, or information, wherein no essoin, protection, or wager of law, shall be allowed, nor any more than one imparlance; one moiety thereof to her majesty, her heirs and successors, and the other moiety to him or them that will sue for the same.   A. D. 1710.

Such annual officer obstructing the election of his successor to forfeit 100l.

One moiety to the queen, the other to the prosecutor.

ANNO 10° ANNÆ REGINÆ, CAP. 19.

An Act for laying several Duties upon all Soap and Paper made in Great Britain, or imported into the same, and upon chequered and striped Linens imported, and upon certain Silks, Callicoes, Linens, and Stuffs, printed, painted, or stained, and upon several Kinds of stamped Vellum, Parchment, and Paper, and upon certain printed Papers, Pamphlets, and Advertisements, for raising the Sum of Eighteen Hundred Thousand Pounds, by Way of Lottery, towards her Majesty's Supply; and for licensing an additional Number of Hackney Chairs, and for charging certain stocks of Cards and Dice, and for better securing her Majesty's Duties to arise in the Office for the stamped Duties by Licenses for Marriages and otherwise, and for Relief of Persons who have not claimed their

Lottery

Lottery Tickets in due Time, or have lost Exchequer Bills or Lottery Tickets, and for borrowing Money upon Stock (Part of the Capital of the South-Sea Company) for the Use of the Public.

The commissioners and officers appointed by this act not to intermeddle with elections.

182. AND be it further enacted by the authority aforesaid, That no commissioner, officer, or other person, concerned or employed in the charging, collecting, receiving, or managing, any of the duties granted by this act, shall, by word, message, or writing, or in any other manner, endeavour to persuade any elector to give, or dissuade any elector from giving, his vote for his choice of any person to be knight of the shire, commissioner, citizen, burgess, or baron, for any county, city, borough, or cinque port, and every officer or other person offending therein,

Penalty.

shall forfeit the sum of one hundred pounds one moiety thereof to the informer, the other moiety thereof to the use of the poor of the parish or place where such offence shall be committed, to be recovered by any person that shall sue for the same, by action of debt, bill, plaint, or information, in any of her majesty's courts of record at Westminster, or in the court of exchequer in that part of Great Britain called Scotland, in which no essoin, protection, privilege, or wager of law, or more than one imparlance, shall be allowed, and every person convict on any such suit shall thereby become disabled, and incapable of ever bearing or executing any office or place of trust whatsoever, under her majesty, her heirs and successors.

ANNO 10° ANNÆ REGINÆ, CAP. 23.

An Act for the more effectual preventing fraudulent Conveyances, in order to multiply Votes for electing Knights of Shires to serve in Parliament.

'WHEREAS by an act of parliament made in the 7th year of the reign of his late majesty king William the third, intituled, An act for the further regulating elections of members to serve in parliament, and for the preventing irregular proceedings of sheriffs, and other officers, in the electing and returning such members, it is amongst other things enacted, That all conveyances of any messuages, lands, tenements, or hereditaments, in any county, city, borough, town-corporate, port or place, in order to multiply voices, or to split and divide the interest in any houses or lands amongst several persons, to enable them to vote at elections of members to serve in parliament, shall be void, and of none effect; and that no more than one single voice shall be admitted for one and the same house and tenement: And whereas (notwithstanding this provision to the contrary) many fraudulent and scandalous practices have been used of late, to create and multiply votes at the election of knights of the shire to serve in parliament, to the great abuse of the ancient law and custom of that part of Great Britain called England, to the great injury of those persons who have just right to elect, and in prejudice of the freedom of such elections:' Therefore, for the more effec-

7 and 8 W. 3. c. 25.

tual preventing of such undue practices, be it enacted by the queen's most excellent majesty, by and with the advice and consent of the lords spiritual and temporal, and commons in this present parliament assembled, and by the authority of the same, That all estates and conveyances whatsoever, made to any person, or persons, in any fraudulent or collusive manner, on purpose to qualify him or them to give his or their vote or votes at such elections of knights of the shire (subject nevertheless to conditions or agreements to defeat or determine such estate, or to reconvey the same) shall be deemed and taken against those persons who executed the same, as free and absolute, and be holden and enjoyed by all and every such person or persons to whom such conveyance shall be made, as aforesaid, freely and absolutely acquitted, exonerated, and discharged of and from all manner of trusts, conditions, clauses of re-entry, powers of revocation, provisoes of redemption, or other defeazances whatsoever, between or with the said parties, or any other person or persons in trust for them; and that all bonds, covenants, collateral or other securities, contracts, or agreements, between or with the said parties, or any other person or persons in trust for them, or any of them, for the redeeming, revoking, or defeating such estate or estates, or for the restoring or re-conveying thereof, or any part thereof, to any person or persons who made or executed such conveyance, or to any other person or persons in trust for them, or any of them, shall be null and void to all intents and purposes whatsoever; and that every person who shall make and

All conveyances fraudulently made to qualify any person to vote (subject to conditions to defeat the same) shall be discharged of such conditions, &c.

And all bonds, &c. for defeating such estate shall be void.

and execute such conveyance or conveyances as aforesaid, or being privy to such purpose, shall devise or prepare the same; and every person who, by colour thereof, shall give any vote at any election of any knight or knights of a shire, to serve in parliament, shall, for every such conveyance so made, or vote so created or given, forfeit the sum of forty pounds, to any person who shall sue for the same, to be recovered, together with full costs of suit, by action of debt, bill, plaint, or information, in any of her majesty's courts of record at Westminster, wherein no essoin, privilege, protection, wager of law, or more than one imparlance shall be admitted or allowed.

Persons making, &c. such conveyances, or voting by colour thereof, shall, for every such offence, forfeit 40l.

2. And be it further enacted by the authority aforesaid, That from and after the first day of May, which shall be in the year of our Lord 1712, no person shall vote for the electing of any knight of a shire, within that part of Great Britain called England, in respect or in right of any lands or tenements which have not been charged or assessed to the public taxes, church rates, and parish duties, in such proportion as other lands or tenements of forty shillings per annum, within the same parish or township where the same shall lie or be, are usually charged, and for which such person shall not have received the rents or profits, or be entitled to have received the same to the full value of forty shillings or more, to his own use, for one year before such election, unless such lands or tenements came to such person within the time aforesaid, by descent, marriage, marriage settlement, devise, or presentation to some benefice in the church, or by promotion to some office, unto

After 1st May, 1712, no persons shall vote for a knight of a shire, in right of lands which have not been charged to public taxes, &c. and for which such person has not received the rents for one year before, unless such lands came to him by descent, &c. on penalty of 40l.

This clause explained by 12 Ann. stat. 1. c. 5. repealed by 18 Geo. 2. c. 18.

which

which such freehold is affixed; and if any person shall vote in any such election, contrary to the true intent and meaning hereof, he shall, for every such offence, forfeit the sum of forty pounds, one moiety thereof to the poor of the parish or parishes where the lands or tenements lie, for which such person shall vote, and the other moiety to the person or persons who shall sue for the same, to be recovered by action of debt, bill, plaint, or information, in any of her majesty's courts of record at Westminster, wherein no essoin, privilege, protection, or wager of law, shall be allowed, or more than one imparlance.

The oath required by the act 7 W. 3. c. 25. repealed.

3. And whereas, by the above recited act it is also further enacted, That upon every election to be made of any knight or knights of the shire to serve in parliament, every freeholder, before he is admitted to poll at the same election, shall (if required by the candidates, or any of them) first take the oath therein-after mentioned; be it enacted by the authority aforesaid, That the said act, as to so much only as concerns the said oath, shall be and is hereby repealed.

4. And be it further enacted by the authority aforesaid, That upon every election to be made of any knight or knights of a shire within that part of Great Britain called England, to serve in parliament, every freeholder, before he is admitted to poll at the same election, shall (if required by the candidates, or any of them, or any other person having a right to vote at such election) first take the oath following, viz.

Their oath.
Another oath is appointed by 18 Geo. 2. c. 18.

'You shall swear that you are a freeholder in the county of   and have freehold lands, or hereditaments,

ditaments, lying or being at   in the same county of   of the yearly value of forty shillings above all charges payable out of the same; and that such freehold estate hath not been made or granted to you fraudulently on purpose to qualify you to give your vote; and that the place of your abode is at   in   and that you have not been polled before at this election.'

Which oath, the sheriff by himself, his under sheriff, or such sworn clerk or clerks (as shall be by him appointed for taking the poll, pursuant to the said recited act) is hereby required to administer; and in case any freeholder, or other person, taking the said oath hereby appointed, shall thereby commit wilful and corrupt perjury, and be thereof convicted, or if any person do unlawfully and corruptly procure or suborn any freeholder, or other person, to take the said oath, in order to be polled, whereby he shall commit such wilful and corrupt perjury, and shall be thereof convicted, he and they, for every such offence, shall incur the like pains and penalties as are in and by one act of parliament, made in the fifth year of the reign of the late queen Elizabeth, intituled, an act for punishment of such persons as shall procure or commit any wilful perjury, enacted against all such who shall commit wilful perjury, or suborn or procure any person to commit any unlawful or corrupt perjury, contrary to the said act.

To be administered by the sheriff, &c.

Freeholder committing wilful perjury, or any person suborning him to to do, shall incur the penalties of 5 Eliz. c. 9.

5. And the better to detect and punish any offenders against this act, be it enacted by the authority aforesaid, That in taking the poll, the sheriff, or his under sheriff, and clerks, shall enter not only the place of the elector's freehold, but also the

The elector's name, &c. to be entered.

the place of his abode, as he shall declare the same at the time of the giving his vote, and shall also make or enter *jurat* against the name of every such voter who shall be tendered and take the oath hereby required; and that the said sheriff, or returning officer, shall, within the space of twenty days next after such election, faithfully deliver over upon oath (which oath the two next justices of the peace, one of whom to be of the quorum, are hereby enabled and required to administer) unto the clerk of the peace of the same county, all the poll-books of such respective election without any embezzlement or alteration, and in such counties where there are more than one clerk of the peace of the same county, then the original poll-books to one of such clerks of the peace, and attested copies thereof to the rest, to be carefully kept and preserved amongst the records of the sessions of the peace of and for the said county.

<small>Poll-books to be delivered upon oath to the clerk of the peace, to be kept among the records of the sessions.</small>

6. And be it further enacted by the authority aforesaid, That the sheriff of the county of York, for the time being, shall be and is hereby required to appoint seven convenient tables, or places for taking the poll of the said county, upon any new election of a knight or knights of the shire for the said county, at the proper costs and charges of the candidates for the same, to continue 'till the poll be concluded.

<small>Sheriff of York to appoint 7 tables for taking the poll, at the costs of the candidates.</small>

7. And be it further enacted by the authority aforesaid, That the sheriff of the county palatine of Chester for the time being, against every election of a knight or knights of the shire to serve in parliament for the said county, shall and is hereby required to cause seven convenient tables

<small>Sheriff of Cheshire to do the like.</small>

bles or places, and no more, to be made at the costs and charges of the candidates, within the shire hall of the said county, for taking the poll at such elections; that is to say, two at the upper end, two at each side, and one at the lower end of the said hall; and shall at such place take the poll at such elections 'till the same be concluded.

8. Provided always, and be it enacted by the authority aforesaid, That if any person being a *Quaker*, during the continuance of an act, passed the seventh year of his late majesty's reign, intituled, an Act that the solemn affirmation and declaration of the people called *Quakers*, shall be accepted instead of an oath in the usual form, shall, upon such election as aforesaid, if required by the candidates, or any of them, declare the effect of the said oath upon his solemn affirmation, in such manner and form as is directed by the said act of parliament, made in the seventh year of the reign of his late majesty king William the third, intituled, An act that the solemn affirmation and declaration of the people called *Quakers*, shall be accepted instead of an oath in the usual form; every such *Quaker* shall be capable and admitted to give his vote for the election of any such member as aforesaid, to serve in the house of commons, within that part of Great Britain called England; and every sheriff by himself, or such his proper officer as aforesaid, is hereby authorized and required to accept such affirmation instead of the said oath, and shall also make or enter *affirmat* against the name of every such *Quaker*; and in case any such *Quaker* shall be convicted wilfully, falsely, and corruptly to have affirmed or declared any matter or thing, which,

Quakers declaring the effect of the oath on their affirmation, as directed by 7 & 8 W. 3. c. 34, shall be admitted to vote.

which, if the same had been in the usual form, would have amounted to wilful and corrupt perjury, every such *Quaker* so offending, shall incur the same penalties and forfeitures as are herein-before enacted against persons convicted of wilful and corrupt perjury.   A. D. 1711.

And affirming any thing false, shall incur the penalties before enacted against perjury.

ANNO 12° ANNÆ REGINÆ, CAP. 5.

An Act to explain a Clause in an Act of the last Session of Parliament, intituled, An Act for the more effectual preventing fraudulent Conveyances, in order to multiply Votes for the electing Knights of Shires to serve in Parliament, as far as the same relates to the ascertaining the Value of Freeholds of 40s. per Annum.

'WHEREAS by an act made in the last session of parliament, intituled, An act for the more effectual preventing fraudulent conveyances, in order to multiply votes for electing knights for shires to serve in parliament, it is amongst other things enacted, That from and after the first day of May, which should be in the year of our Lord 1712, no person shall vote for the electing of any knight of a shire, within that part of Great Britain called England, in respect or in right of any lands or tenements which have not been charged or assessed to the public taxes, church rates, and parish duties, in such proportions as other lands or tenements of 40s. per annum, within the same parish and township where the same shall lie or be, are usually charged, under a penalty therein expressed; and whereas some

10 Ann. c. 23.

doubts

doubts have arisen whether parsons, vicars, and other persons, having messuages, lands, rents, tithes, or other hereditaments, are not thereby restrained from voting at such elections, in regard that such messuages, lands, rents, tithes, or hereditaments, have not been usually charged or assessed to the public taxes, church rates, and parish duties, and to every of them.' Now, for as much as it was only intended thereby to ascertain the value of lands or tenements, by making the proportion paid to the public taxes, church rates, and parish duties, or such of them to which the same were usually charged or assessed, the measure of the value thereof; and for the removing such doubts, be it enacted and declared by the queen's most excellent majesty, by and with the advice and consent of the lords spiritual and temporal, and commons in this present parliament assembled, and by the authority of the same, That the said act, or any thing therein contained shall not extend, or be construed to restrain any person from voting in such election of any knight of a shire within that part of Great Britain called England, in respect or in right of any rents, tithes, or other incorporeal inheritances, or any messuages or lands in extra-parochial places, or any chambers in the inns of court, or inns of chancery, or any messuages or seats belonging to any offices, in regard or by reason that the same have not usually been, or shall not be charged or assessed to all or any the public taxes, church rates, and parish duties, as mentioned in the above recited act, or in respect or in right of any other messuages or lands not herein before

The act 10 Ann. c. 23. not to restrain any person from voting in respect of any rents, &c. or chambers in inns of court, in regard of their not being charged to public taxes, &c.

before specified, in regard or by reason that the same have not been usually charged or assessed to all and every the public taxes, church rates, and parish duties aforesaid. Provided, That such messuages or lands have usually been charged or assessed to some one or more of the said public taxes, rates, or duties, in such proportion as other messuages or lands of forty shillings per annum within the same parish or township where the same shall lie or be, are usually charged to the same; any thing contained in the said recited act to the contrary thereof in any wise notwithstanding. A. D. 1713.

Provided that they have been assessed as other messuages of 40s. per ann. in the same parish, &c.

ANNO 12° ANNÆ REGINÆ, STAT. I. CAP. 15.

An Act for making perpetual an Act made in the seventh Year of the Reign of the late King William, intituled, An Act to prevent false and double Returns of Members to serve in Parliament.

'WHEREAS in the 7th year of the reign of the late king William the Third, an act was made, intituled, An act to prevent false and double returns of members to serve in parliament, and was thereby enacted to continue for the term of seven years, and from thence to the end of the next session of parliament, and no longer; which act, by another act made in the 12th year of the reign of the late king, intituled, An act for continuing a former act to prevent false and double returns of members to serve in parliament, was enacted, should therefore be in force for, and during the term of eleven years, and from thence to

7 & 8 W. 3. c. 7.

12 & 13 W. 3. c. 5.

to the end of the first session of the next parliament, and no longer; which said act has been found by experience to be very useful for the preservation of the rights of the several counties, cities, and boroughs of this kingdom, in the election of members to serve in parliament, and being near expiring:' Be it therefore enacted by the queen's most excellent majesty, by and with the advice and consent of the lords spiritual and temporal, and commons in this present parliament assembled, and by the authority of the same, That the said act made in the 7th year of the reign of the late king William the Third, intituled, An act to prevent false and double returns of members to serve in parliament, and every clause, matter, and thing therein contained, shall be, and is hereby declared to be in full force, and is hereby made perpetual. A. D. 1713.

<small>The act 7 & 8 W. 3. c. 7. made perpetual.</small>

ANNO 1° GEORGII REGIS, CAP. 38.

An Act for enlarging the Time of Continuance of Parliaments appointed by an Act made in the sixth Year of the Reign of King William and Queen Mary, intituled, An Act for the frequent meeting and calling of Parliaments.

'WHEREAS in and by an act of parliament made in the sixth year of the reign of their late majesties king William and queen Mary (of ever blessed memory) intituled, An act for the frequent meeting and calling of parliaments, it was amongst other things enacted, That from thenceforth no parliament whatsoever, that should at any

<small>6 W. & M. c. 2.</small>

any time then after be called, assembled, or held, should have any continuance longer than for three years only at the farthest, to be accounted from the day on which, by the writ of summons, the said parliament should be appointed to meet; and whereas it hath been found by experience, that the said clause hath proved very grievous and burthensome, by occasioning much greater and more continued expences, in order to elections of members to serve in parliament, and more violent and lasting heats and animosities among the subjects of this realm, than were ever known before the said clause was enacted, and the said provision, if it should continue, may probably, at this juncture, when a restless and popish faction are designing and endeavouring to renew the rebellion within this kingdom, and an invasion from abroad be destructive to the peace and security of the government:' Be it enacted by the king's most excellent majesty, by and with the advice and consent of the lords spiritual and temporal and commons in parliament assembled, and by the authority of the same, That this present parliament, and all parliaments that shall at any time hereafter be called, assembled, or held, shall and may respectively have continuance for seven years, and no longer, to be accounted from the day on which, by the writ or summons, this present parliament hath been, or any future parliament shall be, appointed to meet, unless this present or any such parliament hereafter to be summoned, shall be sooner dissolved by his majesty, his heirs or successors.

Parliament shall have continuance for seven years, unless sooner dissolved by the king.

A. D. 1715.

ANNO 1° GEORGII I. STAT. 2. CAP. 56.

An Act to disable any Person from being chosen a Member of, or from sitting and voting in, the House of Commons, who has any Pension for any Number of Years from the Crown.

'WHEREAS by an act, intituled, An act for the security of her majesty's person and government, and of the succession to the crown of Great Britain in the Protestant line, and made in the sixth year of the late queen Anne, it was provided, that no person, having any pension from the crown during pleasure, should be capable of being elected, or of sitting or voting as member of the house of commons in any parliament, which should be then after summoned and holden;' to the end therefore, that the provision intended by that law, for securing the honour of the house of commons, may not in future times be defeated or eluded by any person, who shall be a member of the house of commons, accepting any pension for any term or number of years; be it enacted by the king's most excellent majesty, by and with the advice and consent of the lords spiritual and temporal and commons in this present parliament assembled, and by the authority of the same, That no person, having any pension from the crown for any term or number of years, either in his own name, or in the name or names of any other person or persons in trust for him, or for his benefit, shall be capable of being elected or chosen member of, or sitting

6 Annæ, c. 7.

No person having a pension from the crown shall be capable of being elected, &c. a member of the house of commons.

or voting as a member of, this present or any future house of commons, which shall be hereafter summoned.

Any person having such pension, and who, being elected, shall sit in the house, shall forfeit 20l. per diem to the prosecutor.

2. And be it further enacted by the authority aforesaid, That if any person who shall have such pension as aforesaid, at the time of his being so elected, or at any time after, during such time as he shall continue or be a member of the house of commons, shall presume to sit or vote in that house, then and in such case, he shall forfeit twenty pounds for every day in which he shall so sit or vote in the said house of commons, to such person or persons who shall sue for the same, in any of his majesty's courts in Westminster hall; and the monies so forfeited shall be recovered by the person so suing, with full costs of suit, in any of the said courts by action of debt, bill, plaint or information, in which no essoin, privilege, protection, or wager of law, shall be allowed, and only one imparlance. A. D. 1715.

ANNO 11° GEORGII I. CAP. 18.

An Act for regulating Elections within the City of London, and for preserving the Peace, good Order, and Government of the said City.

'WHEREAS of late years great controversies and dissentions have arisen in the city of London, at the elections of citizens to serve in parliament and of mayors, aldermen, sheriffs, and other officers of the said city; and many evil minded persons having no right of voting, have unlawfully intruded themselves into the assemblies

semblies of the citizens and presumed to give their votes at such elections, in manifest violation of the rights and privileges of the citizens, and of the freedom of their election, and to the disturbance of the public peace; and whereas great numbers of wealthy persons not free of the said city, do inhabit and carry on the trade of merchandize and other employments within the said city, and refuse or decline to become freemen of the same, by reason of an ancient custom within the said city restraining the freemen of the same from disposing of their personal estates by their last wills and testaments; and whereas great dissentions have arisen between the aldermen and commons, of the common-council of London, in or concerning the making or passing of acts, orders or ordinances in common council, which, if not timely settled and determined, may occasion great obstructions of the public business and concerns of the said city, and create many expensive controversies and suits at law, and be attended with other dangerous consequences:' Now, to the intent that suitable remedies may be provided, for preserving the privileges of the city of London and the freedom of election therein, and for settling the right of such elections, and putting a stop to the aforesaid controversies and dissentions and the ill consequences of the same, and that a constant supply may be had of able officers, capable of supporting the dignity of, and maintaining good order and government within, that ancient, populous and loyal city, which is of the greatest consequence to the whole kingdom: Be it enacted, by the king's moſt excellent majeſty, by and with the advice and conſent of the lords ſpiritual and temporal and commons in this preſent parliament aſſembled, and by the authority of the ſame, That at all times from and after the firſt day of June, 1725, upon every election of a citizen or citizens to ſerve for the ſaid city of London in parliament, and upon all elections of mayors, ſheriffs, chamberlains, bridge maſters, auditors of chamberlains and bridge maſters accounts, and all and every other officer and officers to be choſen in and for the ſaid city, by the liverymen thereof, and upon all elections of aldermen and common-councilmen, choſen at the reſpective wardmotes of the ſaid city, the preſiding officer or officers at ſuch elections ſhall, in caſe a poll be demanded by any of the candidates, or any two or more of the electors, appoint a convenient number of clerks to take the ſame, which clerks ſhall take the ſaid poll in the preſence of the preſiding officer or officers, and be ſworn by ſuch officer or officers, truly and indifferently to take the ſame, and to ſet down the name of each voter and his place of reſidence or abode and for whom he ſhall poll, and to poll no perſon who ſhall not be ſworn, or being a *Quaker*, ſhall not affirm according to the direction of this act; and every perſon before he is admitted to poll, at any election of any citizen or citizens to ſerve in parliament, or of any officer or officers uſually choſen by the liverymen of the ſaid city as aforeſaid, ſhall take the oath herein-after mentioned, or being one of the people

On all elections by the liverymen, and at the wardmotes, preſiding officer to appoint a convenient number of clerks to take the poll, &c.

None to be polled who is not ſworn.

people called *Quakers*, shall solemnly affirm the effect thereof, that is to say,

"You do swear, That you are a freeman of London, and a liveryman of the company of   and have so been for the space of twelve kalendar months; and that the place of your abode is at   in   and that you have not polled at this election. So help you God."

Liveryman's oath at elections.

And in case of any election of any alderman, or common-councilman, every person before he is admitted to poll, shall take the oath hereinafter mentioned, or being one of the people called *Quakers*, shall solemnly affirm the effect thereof, that is to say,

"You do swear, That you are a freeman of London and an housholder in the ward of   and have not polled at this election.   So help you God."

Oath at wardmotes.

And if any person or persons shall refuse or neglect to take the oaths hereby respectively appointed to be taken, or being a *Quaker*, shall refuse or neglect to make such solemn affirmation as aforesaid, then and in every such case the poll or vote of such person or persons so neglecting or refusing shall be, and the same is hereby declared to be, null and void, and as such shall be rejected and disallowed.

On refusal to swear, poll to be rejected.

2dly. And be it further enacted by the authority aforesaid, That at all times from and after the said first day of June, 1725, upon every election of such citizen or citizens, officer or officers, by the liverymen of the said city, and upon every election of such officer or officers, at any wardmote of the said city as aforesaid, all and every person and persons having a right to vote or poll at such election or elections, shall, before he be admitted to vote or poll thereat, (if required by any of the candidates, or any two or more of the electors) first take the oaths in and by an act made in the first year of his majesty's reign, intituled, ' An act for the further security of his majesty's person and government, and the succession of the crown in the heirs of the late princess Sophia, being Protestants, and for extinguishing the hopes of the pretended prince of Wales, and his open and secret abettors,' appointed to be taken, or being one of the people called *Quakers*, shall, if required as aforesaid, solemnly affirm the effect thereof; and if any person or persons shall, being required thereunto as aforesaid, refuse or neglect to take the said oaths by the said act appointed to be taken, or to affirm the effect thereof as aforesaid, that then the poll or vote of such person or persons so neglecting or refusing shall be, and the same is hereby declared to be, null and void, and as such shall be rejected and disallowed; and the presiding officers at all and every the respective elections aforesaid, and such sworn clerks as shall be by them appointed, are hereby respectively authorized and impowered to administer the above mentioned oaths and affirmations; and if any such presiding officer or officers, sworn clerk or clerks, shall neglect or refuse so to do, or shall otherwise offend in the premises, contrary to the true intent and meaning of this act, every such officer and sworn clerk, shall for every such offence forfeit the sum of sixty pounds, of

The oaths to be taken, if required, as appointed by 1 Geo. 1. stat. 2. c. 13.

Presiding officer and sworn clerk to administer the oaths, on penalty of 60l.

lawful

lawful money of Great Britain, besides costs of suit.

3. And it is hereby further enacted, That if any person or persons shall wilfully, falsely, and corruptly take the said oaths or affirmations set forth and appointed in and by this act, or either of them, and be thereof lawfully convicted by indictment or information, or if any person or persons shall corruptly procure or suborn any other person to take the said oaths or affirmations, or either, whereby he shall wilfully and falsely take the said oaths or affirmations, or either of them, and the person so procuring or suborning shall be thereof convicted by indictment or information; every person so offending shall for every such offence incur and suffer such penalties, forfeitures, and disabilities as persons convicted of wilful and corrupt perjury, at the common law, are liable unto. *Penalty on falsely taking the oaths, or suborning.*

4. "And to the intent that the poll at every such election may be expeditiously and duly taken;" Be it further enacted by the authority aforesaid, That if a poll shall be demanded at any of the elections before-mentioned, after the said first day of June, 1725, the presiding officer or officers at such elections shall begin such poll the day the same shall be demanded, or the next day following at the farthest, unless the same shall happen on a *Sunday*, and then on the next day after, and shall duly and orderly proceed thereon from day to day (Sundays excepted) until such poll be finished, and shall finish the poll at elections by the liverymen within seven days, exclusive of Sundays, and the poll at the wardmotes *Presiding officer how to act, if a poll be demanded.* *When the poll to be finished, &c.*

within

within three days, exclusive of Sunday, after the commencing the same respectively, and shall upon adjourning the poll on each day at all and every the elections aforesaid, seal up the poll books with the seals and in the presence of such of the respective candidates or persons deputed by them as shall desire the same, and the said poll book shall not be opened again, but at the time and place of meeting, in pursuance of such adjournment, and after the said poll is finished, the said poll books being sealed as aforesaid, shall within two days after be publicly opened at the place of election and be duly and truly cast up, and within two days after such casting up, the numbers of the votes or polls for each candidate shall be truly, fairly, and publicly declared to the electors at the place of election, by the officer or officers presiding at such election; and if a scrutiny shall, upon such declaration made, be lawfully demanded, the same shall be granted and proceeded upon, and the respective candidates shall immediately nominate to the presiding officer, or

If a scrutiny be demanded, scrutineers not to exceed 6 on each side.

officers at such elections, any number of persons qualified to vote at such elections not exceeding six, to be scrutineers for and on behalf of the candidate or candidates on each side, to whom the presiding officer or officers at such election shall, within six days next after such scrutiny shall be demanded, upon request and at the charge of the candidate or candidates or any of the scrutineers on his or their behalfs, deliver or cause to be delivered to him or them a true copy, signed by such officer or officers, of the poll taken at such election; and all and every the scrutinies, to be be had or taken upon any election to be made by the liverymen of the said city, shall begin within ten days after the delivery of the copies of the said polls, and be proceeded on day by day, (Sundays excepted) and shall be finished within fifteen days after the commencement of such scrutiny; and thereupon the presiding officer or officers, shall, within four days after the finishing such scrutiny, publicly declare at the place of such election, which of the candidates is or are duly elected and the number of legal votes, for each candidate, appearing to him or them upon such scrutiny; and on the election of any officer or officers at the respective wardmotes of the said city if a scrutiny be demanded, the candidates or scrutineers nominated on their behalf respectively, shall within ten days next after the receipt of the copy or copies of the polls taken at such election, deliver or cause to be delivered to the presiding officer or officers, the names in writing, of the several persons who have polled in the said election, against whose votes they shall object, with the particular objections against each respective name; and the presiding officer or officers, shall thereupon within three days then next following, at the request and charges of any candidate or candidates, or the scrutineers named on his or their behalfs, deliver or cause to be delivered to him or them, one or more true copy or copies (signed as aforesaid) of the paper containing such names and objections as aforesaid; and the said presiding officer or officers, within ten days then next following (exclusive of Sundays) after having fully heard such of the said

Scrutiny when to begin, and when to finish, on election by liverymen.

Scrutinies on elections at Wardmotes.

True copies of the objections against the polls.

can-

candidates as shall desire the same, or some person appointed by him or them touching such objections, shall at or in the place of election, openly and publicly declare which of the said candidates is or are duly elected, and the number of legal votes for each candidate appearing to him or them upon such scrutiny; and if the said presiding officer or officers, or any other person or persons shall offend in the premises, every such offender shall forfeit for every such offence the sum of two hundred pounds of lawful money of Great Britain, with full costs of suit, over and above all other penalties and forfeitures inflicted by any other act or acts of parliament.

Penalty 200l. &c. with costs, besides all other penalties.

5. And be it further enacted by the authority aforesaid, That after any election made and scrutiny taken, as is herein-before provided and directed, the presiding officer or officers at such election and scrutiny shall deliver, under his or their hand or hands, a true list of the voters by him or them disallowed upon such scrutiny, to any of the candidates who shall, upon the final declaration of the election as aforesaid, demand the same within six days after such demand made, such candidate paying for the same: Provided always, That no such list as is hereby directed to be given, nor any thing therein contained, shall be admitted to be given in evidence on any action or occasion whatsoever.

A true list to be given of the voters disallowed.

6. And be it further enacted by the authority aforesaid, That the mayor of the city of London for the time being, upon request to him made by any candidate or candidates, his or their agent

Mayor to issue precepts to the companies to bring in lists.

or

or agents, at any election of a citizen or citizens to serve in parliament for the said city, or of a mayor or any other officer or officers to be chosen by the liverymen thereof, where a scrutiny is demanded and granted, shall issue his precepts as has been usual, requiring the masters and wardens of the livery companies of the said city respectively, to cause their clerks forthwith to return to him two true lists of all the liverymen of their respective companies; and the said clerks shall return such their respective lists upon oath within three days after the receipt of any such precepts, one of which lists so returned, the said mayor shall, and he is hereby required forthwith to deliver, or cause to be delivered to the candidate or candidates on each side at such election, or to his or their agent or agents respectively.

14. And it is hereby further enacted, That no person or persons whatsoever shall, from and after the said first day of June, 1725, have any right or title to vote at any election of a citizen or citizens to serve in parliament for the said city, or of any mayor or other officer or officers to be chosen by the liverymen thereof, who have not been upon the livery by the space of twelve kalendar months before such election, and who shall not have paid their respective livery fines, or who having paid the same, shall have received such fines back again in part or in all, or shall have had any allowance in respect thereof; and no person or persons whatsoever shall have any right to vote at any election of a citizen or citizens to serve in parliament, or of any mayor, alderman,

Persons excluded from voting.

or

or other officer or officers of or for the said city, or any the wards or precincts thereof, who have, at any time within the space of two years next before such election or elections, requested to be, and accordingly have been, discharged from paying to the rates and taxes to which the citizens of London inhabiting therein are or shall be liable as aforesaid, or any of them, or who have within the time aforesaid had or received an alms whatsoever; and the vote of every such person shall be void.

Forfeitures how to be distributed.

20. And be it further enacted by the authority aforesaid, That all and every the forfeitures hereby enacted or inflicted, shall be distributed in the manner following, that is to say, one third part thereof to the king's most excellent majesty; one third part thereof to the chamberlain of the said city, to the use of the mayor, commonalty, and citizens of the said city; and the remaining third part thereof to him or them that will sue for the same within six kalendar months next after the same shall be incurred, to be recovered by action of debt, bill, plaint, or information, in any of his majesty's courts of record at Westminster, wherein no essoin, privilege, protection, or wager of law, shall be allowed, nor any more than one imparlance.   A. D. 1724.

ANNO 2° GEORGII II. CAP. 24.

An Act for the more effectual preventing Bribery and Corruption in the Elections of Members to serve in Parliament.

'WHEREAS it is found by experience that the laws already in being have not been sufficient

ficient to prevent corrupt and illegal practices in the election of members to serve in parliament:' For remedy therefore of so great an evil, and to the end that all elections of members to serve in parliament may hereafter be freely and indifferently made, without charge or expence, be it enacted by the king's most excellent majesty, by and with the advice and consent of the lords spiritual and temporal and commons in this present parliament assembled, and by the authority of the same, That from and after the twenty-fourth day of June, 1729, upon every election of any member or members to serve for the commons in parliament, every freeholder, citizen, freeman, burgess, or person having or claiming to have a right to vote or be polled at such election, shall, before he is admitted to poll at the same election, take the following oath (or being one of the people called *Quakers*, shall make the solemn affirmation appointed for *Quakers*) in case the same shall be demanded by either of the candidates, or any two of the electors; that is to say,

Extended to elections of delegates in Scotland, by 16 Geo. 2. c. 11.

Electors of Parliament men to take the following oath if demanded.

" I, A. B. do swear (or being one of the people called *Quakers*, I, A. B. do solemnly affirm) I have not received, or had, by myself or any person whatsoever in trust for me, or for my use and benefit, directly or indirectly, any sum or sum of money, office, place, or employment, gift, or reward, or any promise or security for any money, office, employment, or gift, in order to give my vote at this election, and that I have not been before polled at this election."

Electors oath.

Which oath or affirmation the officer or officers presiding or taking the poll at such election,

Presiding officers to administer it, on forfeiture of 50l.

is and are hereby impowered and required to administer *gratis*, if demanded as aforesaid, upon pain to forfeit the sum of fifty pounds of lawful money of Great Britain, to any person that shall sue for the same, to be recovered together with full costs of suit, by action of debt, bill, plaint, or information, in any of his majesty's courts of record at Westminster, wherein no essoin, protection, wager of law, or more than one imparlance shall be admitted or allowed; and if the said offence shall be committed in that part of Great Britain called Scotland, then to be recovered, together with full costs of suit, by summary action or complaint before the court of session, or by prosecution before the court of justiciary there, for every neglect or refusal so to do; and no person shall be admitted to poll, till he has taken and repeated the said oath in a public manner, in case the same shall be demanded as aforesaid, before the returning officer, or such others as shall be legally deputed by him.

Sheriff or other returning officer admitting any to be polled before sworn, to forfeit 100l.

2. And be it further enacted, That if any sheriff, mayor, bailiff, or other returning officer, shall admit any person to be polled without taking such oath or affirmation, if demanded as aforesaid, such returning officer shall forfeit the sum of one hundred pounds, to be recovered in manner aforesaid, together with full costs of suit; and that if any person shall vote or poll at such election, without having first taken the oath, or if a *Quaker*, having made his affirmation as aforesaid, if demanded,

Voters to incur the like penalty.

such person shall incur the same penalty which the officer is subject to for the offence above-mentioned.

3. And

3. And be it further enacted by the authority aforesaid, that every sheriff, mayor, bailiff, headborough, or other person being the returning officer of any member to serve in parliament, shall immediately after the reading the writ, or precept for the election of such member, take and subscribe the following oath, *viz.*

Returning officers after reading the writ, to take the following oath.

" I, A. B. do solemnly swear, That I have not, directly or indirectly, received any sum or sums of money, office, place or employment, gratuity or reward, or any bond, bill, or note, or any promise or gratuity whatsoever, either by myself or any other person to my use, or benefit, or advantage, for making any return at the present election of members to serve in parliament; and that I will return such person or persons as shall, to the best of my judgment, appear to me to have the majority of legal votes."

Repealed so far as it relates to the returning officers in Scotland, by 16 Geo. 2, c. 11. s. 38.

Which oath any justice or justices of the peace of the said county, city, corporation, or borough, where such election shall be made, or, in his or their absence, any three of the electors are hereby required and authorized to administer; and such oath, so taken, shall be entered among the records of the sessions of such county, city, corporation, and borough as aforesaid.

4. And be it enacted by the authority aforesaid, That such votes shall be deemed to be legal, which have been so declared by the last determination in the house of commons; which last determination concerning any county, city, shire, borough, cinque port, or place, shall be final to all intents

What votes shall be deemed legal.

intents and purposes whatsoever, any usage to the contrary notwithstanding.

5. And be it further enacted by the authority aforesaid, That if any returning officer, elector, or person taking the oath or affirmation hereinbefore mentioned, shall be guilty of wilful and corrupt perjury, or of false affirming, and be thereof convicted by due course of law, he shall incur and suffer the pains and penalties which by law are enacted or inflicted in cases of wilful and corrupt perjury.

Persons convicted of wilful perjury, never capable to vote.

6. And be it further enacted by the authority aforesaid, That no person convicted of wilful and corrupt perjury, or subornation of perjury, shall, after such conviction, be capable of voting in any election of any member or members to serve in parliament.

Persons taking money or reward for their vote, &c. forfeit 500l. and are disabled to vote, &c.

7. And be it further enacted by the authority aforesaid, That if any person, who hath or claimeth to have, or hereafter shall have or claim to have, any right to vote in any such election, shall, from and after the said twenty-fourth day of June, which shall be in the year of our Lord, 1729, ask, receive, or take any money, or other reward, by way of gift, loan, or other device, or agree or contract for any money, gift, office, employment, or other reward whatever, to give his vote, or to refuse or forbear to give his vote in any such election, or if any person, by himself or any person employed by him, doth or shall, by any gift or reward, or by any promise, agreement, or security for any gift or reward, corrupt or procure any person or persons to give his or their

vote

vote or votes, or to forbear to give his or their vote or votes in any such election, such person so offending in any of the cases aforesaid shall, for every such offence, forfeit the sum of five hundred pounds of lawful money of Great Britain, to be recovered as before directed, together with full costs of suit; and every person offending in any of the cases aforesaid, from and after judgement obtained against him in any such action of debt, bill, plaint, or information, or summary action or prosecution, or being any otherwise lawfully convicted thereof, shall for ever be disabled to vote in any election of any member or members to parliament, and also shall for ever be disabled to hold, exercise, or enjoy any office or franchise, to which he and they then shall or at any time afterwards may be entitled, as a member of any city, borough, town corporate, or cinque port, as if such person was naturally dead.

8. And be it further enacted by the authority aforesaid, That if any person offending against this act, shall within the space of twelve months next after such election as aforesaid, discover any other person or persons offending against this act, so that such person or persons so discovered be thereupon convicted, such person so discovering, and not having been before that time convicted of any offence against this act, shall be indemnified and discharged from all penalties and disabilities, which he shall then have incurred by any offence against this act.

Offenders, in twelve months after the election discovering others, indemnified.

9. And for the more effectual observance of this act, be it enacted, That all and every the sheriffs,

riffs, mayors, bailiffs, and other officers, to whom the execution of any writ or precept, for electing any member or members to serve in parliament, shall belong or appertain, shall and are hereby required, at the time of such election, immediately after the reading such writ or precept, to read or cause to be read openly before the electors there assembled, this present act, and every clause therein contained, and the same shall also openly be read once in every year at the general quarter sessions of the peace, to be holden next after Easter, for any county or city, and at every election of the chief magistrate in any borough, town corporate, or cinque port, and at the annual election of the magistrates and town counsellors for every borough, within that part of Great Britain called Scotland.

<small>The act to be read by the sheriff, &c. after reading the writ, and at the quarter sessions after Easter.</small>

10. And be it further enacted by the authority aforesaid, That every sheriff, under sheriff, mayor, bailiff, and other officer, to whom the execution of any writ or precept, for the electing of members to serve in parliament doth belong, for every wilful offence, contrary to this act, shall forfeit the sum of fifty pounds to be recovered, together with full costs of suit, in the manner before directed.

<small>Wilful offence, forfeits 50l.</small>

11. Provided always, and it is hereby declared and enacted by the authority aforesaid, That no person shall be made liable to any incapacity, disability, forfeiture, or penalty by this act laid or imposed, unless prosecution be commenced within two years after such incapacity, disability, forfeiture, or penalty shall be incurred, or in case of a prosecution, the same be carried on without

<small>Prosecution to commence within two years.</small>

wilful delay; any thing herein contained to the contrary notwithstanding.

A. D. 1729.

ANNO 3° GEORGII II. CAP. 8.

An Act for the better regulating Elections in the City of Norwich, *and for preserving the Peace, good Order, and Government, in the said City.*

"WHEREAS many unhappy controversies and diffentions have of late years arisen in the city of *Norwich*, at the elections of citizens to serve in parliament, and also of mayors, sheriffs, aldermen, and common-councilmen of and for the said city, touching the legality and validity of the votes of many persons who in such elections have offered to vote; and whereas the time appointed by the charters of the said city is not sufficient to elect so great a number of common-councilmen for each great ward, as are thereby yearly directed to be chosen when such elections happen to be controverted; and whereas great differences and diffentions have arisen between the mayor, sheriffs, and aldermen, and the commons of the common-council of the said city, in or concerning the making or passing of acts, orders, or ordinances, in common-council, or assembly of the representative body of the said city, which have often obstructed the public business and concerns thereof:" Now to the intent that a stop may be put to all such controversies and diffentions as aforesaid, touching the legality of voters, that the number of common-councilmen may be yearly elected, and that the public business of the said city may not be obstructed: Be it enacted, &c.

" Oaths to be tendered at elections in *Norwich*. Refusing to swear, the vote or poll disallowed. One of the checks, &c. may go into the prisons to take the votes there. The oaths, 1 Geo. I. st. 2. c. 13. to be taken by electors, if required. Three common-councilmen for each great ward, to elect the remaining number of common-councilmen. Vacancies to be filled up in forty-eight hours after notice. None but Inhabitants to be chosen sheriffs. No act valid, without assent of the major part, &c. Mayors to nominate officers as customary. Penalty on absence from the quarterly assemblies."

A. D. 1730.

ANNO 6° GEORGII II. CAP. 23.

An Act to explain and amend an Act made in the 7th and 8th Years of the Reign of King William the Third, intituled, " An Act for the further regulating Elections of Members to serve in Parliament, and for the preventing irregular proceedings of Sheriffs and other Officers in the electing and returning such Members, so far as the same relates to the holding of County Courts.

7 & 8 W. 3. c. 25.

' WHEREAS by an act passed in the 7th and 8th years of the reign of king William the

the Third, intituled, An act for the further regulating elections of members to serve in parliament, and for the preventing irregular proceedings of sheriffs and other officers in the electing and returning such members, it was, amongst other things, enacted, That the sheriff of any county, upon the election to be made of any knight or knights of the shire, should proceed to election at the next county court, unless the same should fall out to be held within six days after the receipt of the writ, or upon the same day, and then should adjourn the said court to some convenient day, giving ten days notice of the time and place of election; and whereas by the same act it was also enacted, That all county courts held for the county of York, or any other county courts which were used to be held on a Monday, should from henceforth be called and begun on Wednesdays; and whereas there was no express provision to prevent the adjournment of any county court to a Monday, whereby doubts have arisen whether the same might not be adjourned to a Monday, which is declared by the said act to be a very inconvenient day to all the suitors thereunto, which hath given occasion to county courts being frequently adjourned over to a Monday, to the great inconvenience of such suitors, who, at elections for knights of the shire, and their services at other times, are thereby obliged to travel on Sundays; and whereas there is no provision made by the said act with relation to not adjourning county courts to a Friday or Saturday, which is as inconvenient to all suitors as if the same were adjourned to a Monday:' For remedy whereof be it therefore enacted by the king's most excellent majesty, by and with the advice and consent of the lords spiritual and temporal and commons in this present parliament assembled, and by the authority of the same, That from and after the twenty-fourth day of June, 1733, no county court whatsoever held within that part of Great Britain called England, shall be adjourned to a Monday, a Friday, or Saturday, and that all and every such adjournment and adjournments, and all and every act and deed done or performed at such courts so adjourned, shall be deemed, adjudged, and taken to be utterly null and void to all intents and purposes whatsoever, any law, custom, or usage to the contrary thereof in any wise notwithstanding.

After 24 June, 1733, no county court in Great Britain to be adjourned to a Monday, Friday, or Saturday.

Repealed by 18 Geo. 2. c. 18. sect. 11.

2. Provided nevertheless, That any county court begun, holden on, or adjourned to a day not prohibited by this act, or the said other recited act, for electing any knight or knights of the shire for any county, or for hearing and determining causes, or such other matters and business as are usually transacted at county courts within the limits aforesaid, may be adjourned over from day to day, though the same may happen on a Monday, Friday, or Saturday, until such election, or such other matters as aforesaid, be fully finished and determined, any thing in this present act contained to the contrary in any wise notwithstanding.

But county courts begun on any other days, may be adjourned to those.

A. D. 1733.

ANNO 8° GEORGII II. CAP. 30.

An Act for regulating the quartering of Soldiers during the Time of the Elections of Members to serve in Parliament.

'WHEREAS by the ancient common law of this land, all elections ought to be free; and whereas by an act passed in the 3d year of the reign of king Edward the First, of famous memory, it is commanded upon great forfeiture, that no man by force of arms, nor by malice, or menacing shall disturb any to make free election; and forasmuch as the freedom of elections of members to serve in parliament is of the utmost consequence to the preservation of the rights and liberties of this kingdom; and whereas it hath been the usage and practice to cause any regiment, troop, or company, or any number of soldiers which hath been quartered in any city, borough, town, or place, where any election of members to serve in parliament hath been appointed to be made, to remove and continue out of the same during the time of such election, except in such particular cases as are herein-after specified:' To the end therefore that the said usage and practice may be settled and established for the future; be it enacted by the king's most excellent majesty, by and with the advice and consent of the lords spiritual and temporal and commons in parliament assembled, and by the authority of the same, That when and as often as any election

Ed. 1. c. 5.

On notice of election of a member, the secretary at war, or person acting as such, to send proper orders in writing for removing soldiers 2 miles from the place of election.

election of any peer or peers to represent the peers of Scotland in parliament, or of any member or members to serve in parliament, shall be appointed to be made the secretary at war for the time being, or in case there shall be no secretary at war, then such person who shall officiate in the place of the secretary at war, shall, and is hereby required, at some convenient time before the day appointed for such election, to issue and send forth proper orders in writing for the removal of every such regiment, troop, or company, or other number of soldiers as shall be quartered or billetted in any such city, borough, town, or place, where such election shall be appointed to be made, out of every such city, borough, town, or place, one day at the least before the day appointed for such election, to the distance of two or more miles from such city, borough, town, or place, and not to make any nearer approach to such city, borough, town, or place as aforesaid, until one day at the least after the poll to be taken at such election shall be ended, and the poll-books closed.

2. And be it further enacted by the authority aforesaid, That in case the secretary at war shall neglect or omit to issue or send forth such orders as aforesaid; or if any person who shall officiate in the place of the secretary at war, shall neglect or omit to issue or send forth such orders as aforesaid, according to the true intent and meaning of this act, and shall be thereof lawfully convicted upon any indictment to be preferred at the next assizes, or sessions of oyer and terminer to be

held

held for the county where such offence shall be committed, or on an information to be exhibited in the court of king's bench within six months after such offence committed, such secretary at war, or person who shall officiate in the place of the secretary at war, shall for such offence be discharged from their said respective offices, and shall from thenceforth be utterly disabled, and made incapable to hold any office or employment, civil or military, in his majesty's service.

On penalty of forfeiting his office, &c.

3. Provided always, That nothing in this act contained, shall extend or be construed to extend to the city and liberty of Westminster, or the borough of Southwark, for and in respect of the guards of his majesty, his heirs, or successors, nor to any city, borough, town, or place, where his majesty, his heirs or successors, or any of his royal family shall happen to be, or reside at the time of any such election as aforesaid, for or in respect of such number of troops or soldiers only as shall be attendant as guards to his majesty, his heirs or successors, or to such other person of the royal family as is aforesaid, nor to any castle, fort, or fortified place, where any garrison is usually kept, for or in respect of such number of troops or soldiers only whereof such garrison is composed.

Not to extend to Westminster, or other place of residence of the royal family, &c.

Or to fortified places,

4. Provided likewise, That nothing in this act contained, shall extend, or be construed to extend, to any officer or soldier who shall have a right to vote at any such election as aforesaid, but that every such officer and soldier may freely and without interruption attend and give his vote at such election;

Or to any officer, &c. having a right to vote at such election.

election; any thing herein-before contained to the contrary thereof notwithstanding.

<small>The secretary at war, &c. not liable in case of vacancy, unless notice of the writ be given by the clerk of the crown.</small>

5. Provided always, That the secretary at war, or in case there shall be no secretary at war, then such person who shall officiate in the place of the secretary at war, shall not be liable to any forfeiture or incapacity for not sending such order as aforesaid upon any election to be made of a member to serve in parliament on a vacancy of any seat there, unless notice of the making out any new writ for such election shall be given to him by the clerk of the crown in chancery, or other officer making out any new writ for such election, which writ he is hereby directed and required to give with all convenient speed after making out the said writ.

A. D. 1735.

ANNO 9° GEORGII II. CAP. 38.

An Act to explain and amend so much of an Act made in the 2d Year of his present Majesty's Reign, intituled, An Act for the more effectual preventing Bribery and Corruption in the Elections of Members to serve in Parliament, as relates to the commencing and carrying on of Prosecutions grounded upon the said Act.

<small>2 Geo. 2. c. 24.</small>

'WHEREAS by an act of parliament made in the 2d year of the reign of his present majesty, intituled, An act for the more effectual preventing bribery and corruption in the election of of members to serve in parliament, it is enacted, That no person shall be made liable to any incapacity, disability, forfeiture, or penalty, by the said act laid or imposed, unless prosecution be commenced within two years after such incapacity, disability, forfeiture, or penalty, shall be incurred, or in case of a prosecution, the same be carried on without wilful delay; and whereas prosecutions may have been, or may be commenced against persons offending against the said act, by suing out original or other writs or processes against such persons so offending within two years after the incurring any incapacity, disability, forfeiture, or penalty, laid or imposed by the said act, and persons so suing out such original or other writs or processes, may have delayed, or may delay to serve the same, without giving the persons against whom such original or other writs or processes may have been or may be sued out, any notice thereof, by reason of which practice the said provision for limiting the time for the prosecution of persons offending against the said act is or may be evaded: Now, for explaining and amending the said provision, be it enacted by the king's most excellent majesty, by and with the advice and consent of the lords spiritual and temporal and commons in this present parliament assembled, and by the authority of the same, That no person shall be made liable to any incapacity, disability, forfeiture, or penalty, by the said act laid or imposed, unless such person has been, or shall be, actually and legally arrested, summoned, or otherwise served with

any

any such original or other writ or process, within the space of two years after any offence against the said act has been, or shall be committed, so as the service of any such original or other writ or process hath not been, or shall not be prevented by such person absconding or withdrawing out of this kingdom.

<small>No person liable to any penalty by the said act, unless personally served with the process in two years after the fact.</small>

A. D. 1736.

ANNO 11° GEORGII II. CAP. 24.

An Act to Amend an Act passed in the 12th and 13th Years of the Reign of King William the Third, intituled, " An Act for preventing any Inconveniences that may happen by Privilege of Parliament."

'WHEREAS for the preventing all delays the king or his subjects may receive in any of his courts of law or equity, and for their ease in the recovery of their rights and titles to any lands, tenements, or hereditaments, and their debts or other dues, for which they have cause of suit or action, an act was made in the 12th and 13th years of the reign of king William the Third, intituled, "An act for preventing any inconveniences that may happen by privilege of parliament," whereby, nevertheless, the privilege of parliament is restrained only in actions or suits commenced or prosecuted in the courts, and for the causes therein particularly mentioned; and whereas great inconveniences may happen to his

<small>12 & 13 W. 3. c. 3.</small>

his majesty, and his subjects, with respect to their rights and titles of lands, tenements, or hereditaments, and their debts or other dues for which they have cause of suit or action, if the privilege of parliament be not restrained upon actions or suits commenced or prosecuted in other courts within Great Britain and Ireland: For remedy thereof be it enacted, by the king's most excellent majesty, by and with the advice and consent of the lords spiritual and temporal and commons in this present parliament assembled, and by the authority of the same, That from and after the first day of June, 1738, any person and persons shall and may commence and prosecute in Great Britain or Ireland any action or suit in any court of record, or court of equity, or of admiralty, and in all causes matrimonial and testamentary, in any court having cognizance of causes matrimonial and testamentary, against any peer, or lord of parliament of Great Britain, or against any of the knights, citizens, and burgesses of the house of commons of Great Britain for the time being, or against their or any of their menial or other servants, or any other person entitled to the privilege of the parliament of Great Britain, at any time from and immediately after the dissolution or prorogation of any parliament, until a new parliament shall meet, or the same be re-assembled, and from and immediately after any adjournment of both houses of parliament for above the space of fourteen days, until both houses shall meet or re-assemble, and that the said respective courts, shall and may after such dissolution, prorogation,

Persons may prosecute actions against members of parliament in the intervals of sessions.

rogation, or adjournment as aforesaid, proceed to give judgement, and to make final orders, decrees, and sentences, and award execution thereupon, any privilege of parliament to the contrary notwithstanding.

Members not liable to be arrested during privilege.

2. Provided nevertheless, That this act shall not extend to subject the person of any of the knights, citizens, and burgesses of the house of commons of Great Britain, or any other person entitled to the privilege of parliament, to be arrested during the time of privilege, ne-

The courts of Great Sessions in Wales, and sessions in counties palatine to proceed against members, as the courts at Westminster.

vertheless, it shall and may be lawful to and for any of the courts of great sessions in Wales, courts of session, in the counties palatine of Chester, Lancaster, and Durham, courts of king's bench, common pleas, and exchequer in Ireland, after any dissolution, prorogation, or such adjournment as aforesaid, or before any session of parliament, or meeting of both houses as aforesaid, to have and use such and the like methods of proceeding, and to issue such and the like process against any such peer, or lord of parliament, or against any of the said knights, citizens, and burgesses, or other persons entitled to the privilege of the parliament of Great Britain, as the courts of king's bench, common pleas, and exchequer in England, are by the said recited act impowered and directed to use and issue respectively; and that it shall and may be lawful to and for the court of chancery of Ireland, and the court of equity of the exchequer there, to have and use such and the like methods of proceeding, and to issue such and the like process

within

within the times and against the persons aforesaid, as the high court of chancery of Great Britain, and the court of exchequer in England, are by the said recited act respectively directed and impowered to use and issue; and that it shall and may be lawful to and for any of the other courts herein-before described, the process whereof is not particularly directed by the said recited act, or by this act, after any dissolution, prorogation, or such ajournment as aforesaid, or before any session of parliament, or meeting of both houses as aforesaid, to issue such and the like process against any such peer, or lord of parliament, or against any of the said knights, citizens, or burgesses, or other person entitled to the privilege of parliament, as such courts may now lawfully issue against persons not liable to be arrested or imprisoned.

3. And be it enacted by the authority aforesaid, That where any plaintiff shall, by reason or occasion of privilege of parliament, be stayed or prevented from prosecuting any suit by him commenced, such plaintiff shall not be bound by any statute of limitation, or nonsuited, dismissed, nor his suit discontinued for want of prosecution of the suit by him begun, but shall, from time to time, upon the rising of the parliament, be at liberty to proceed to judgement and execution. *Plaintiff's not barred or nonsuited,*

4. And it is hereby enacted, That no action, suit, process, order, judgement, decree, or proceeding in law or equity, against the king's original and immediate debtor, for the recovery or obtaining *Nor process against the king's debtor to be stayed by privilege of parliament,*

obtaining of any debt or duty originally and immediately due or payable unto his majesty, his heirs or successors, or against any accountant, or person answerable, or liable to render any account unto his majesty, his heirs or successors, for any part or branch of any of his or their revenues, or other original and immediate debt, or duty, or the execution of any such process, order, judgement, decree, or proceedings, shall be impeached, stayed, or delayed in any court in Great Britain or Ireland, by and under the colour or pretence of any privilege of the parliament of Great Britain; yet so nevertheless, that the person of any such debtor, or accountant, or person answerable or liable to account, being a peer, or lord of parliament of Great Britain, shall not be liable to be arrested or imprisoned, by or upon any such suit, order, judgement, decree, process, or proceedings; or being a member of the house of commons of Great Britain, shall not, during the continuance of the privilege of parliament, be arrested or imprisoned by or upon any such order, judgement, decree, process, or proceedings.

But the persons not to be arrested.

Proviso.

5. Provided nevertheless, That neither this act, nor any thing therein contained, shall extend to give any jurisdiction, power, or authority to any court, to hold plea in any real or mixt action, in any other manner than such court might have done before the making this act.

A. D. 1738.

ANNO 13° GEORGII II. CAP. 20.

An Act for the more effectually preventing fraudulent Qualifications of Persons to vote as Freeholders, in the Election of Members to serve in Parliament, for such Cities and Towns as are Counties of themselves, in that Part of Great Britain called England.

"WHEREAS by an act made in the 10th year of the reign of queen Anne, intituled, 'An act for the more effectual preventing fraudulent conveyances, in order to multiply votes for electing knights of shires to serve in parliament,' it is enacted, That all estates and conveyances whatsoever, made to any person or persons in any fraudulent or collusive manner, on purpose to qualify him or them, to give his or their vote or votes at such elections of knights of the shire, subject nevertheless to conditions or agreements to defeat or determine such estate, or to re-convey the same, shall be deemed and taken against those persons who executed the same as free and absolute, and be holden and enjoyed by all and every such person or persons, to whom such conveyance shall be made as aforesaid, freely and absolutely acquitted, exonerated, and discharged, of and from all manner of trusts, conditions, clauses of re-entry, powers of revocation, provisoes of redemption, or other defeazances whatsoever, between or with the said parties, or any other person or persons in trust for them, and that all bonds, covenants, collateral or other securi-

10 Annæ, c. 23.

ties,

ties, contracts, or agreements, between or with the said parties, or any other person or persons in trust for them, or any of them for the redeeming, revoking, or defeating, such estate or estates, or for the restoring or re-conveying thereof, or any part thereof, to any person or persons who made or executed such conveyance, or to any other person or persons in trust for them, or any of them, shall be null and void to all intents and purposes whatsoever; and that every person who shall make and execute such conveyance or conveyances as aforesaid, or, being privy to such purpose, shall devise or prepare the same, and every person who, by colour thereof, shall give any vote at any election of any knight or knights of the shire to serve in parliament, shall, for every such conveyance so made, or vote so created or given, forfeit the sum of forty pounds to any person who shall sue for the same, to be recovered together with full costs of suit, by action of debt, bill, plaint, or information, in any of the courts of record at Westminster, wherein no essoin, privilege, protection, wager of law, or more than one imparlance shall be admitted or allowed; and it is thereby further enacted, That no person shall vote for the electing of any knight of a shire within that part of Great Britain called England in respect or in right of any lands or tenements, which have not been charged or assessed to the public taxes, church rates, and parish

Voters to be possessed of lands &c. to the value of 40s. per annum a full year before the election.

duties, in such proportion as other lands or tenements of forty shillings *per annum*, within the same parish or township where the same shall lie, or be usually charged, and for which such person

son shall not have received the rents or profits, or be entitled to have received the same, to the full value of forty shillings or more, to his own use for one year before such election, unless such lands or tenements came to such person within the time aforesaid by descent, marriage, marriage settlement, devise, or presentation to some benefice in the church, or by promotion to some office, unto which such freehold is affixed, and that, if any person shall vote in any such election contrary to the true intent and meaning of the said act, he shall, for every such offence, forfeit the sum of forty pounds, one moiety thereof to the poor of the parish or parishes, where the lands or tenements lie, for which such person shall vote, and the other moiety to the person or persons who shall sue for the same to be recovered by action of debt, bill, plaint, or information, in any of the courts of record at Westminster, wherein no essoin, privilege, protection, or wager of law shall be allowed, or more than one imparlance; and whereas by an act, made in the next session of parliament, to explain a clause in the said last recited act, made in the 10th year of the reign of queen Anne, it is enacted, That the said act made in the 10th year of the reign of queen Anne, or any thing therein contained, shall not extend or be construed to restrain any person from voting in such election of any knight of a shire, within that part of Great Britain called England, in respect or in right of any rents, tythes, or other incorporeal inheritances, or any messuages or lands in any extra-parochial places, or any chambers in the inns

Unless such lands came by descent, &c. within the time,

On penalty of 40l.

12 Annæ, st. 1, c. 5.

inns of courts or inns of chancery, or any messuages or seats belonging to any offices, in regard or by reason that the same have not usually been, or shall not be charged or assessed to all or any of the public taxes, church rates, and parish duties, as mentioned in the said act made in the 10th year of the reign of queen Anne, or in respect or right of any other messuages or lands not therein-before specified in regard or by reason that the same have not been usually charged or assessed to all and every the public taxes, church rates, and parish duties aforesaid, provided that such messuages or lands, have usually been charged or assessed to some one or more of the said public taxes, rates, or duties, in such proportion as other messuages or lands of forty shillings *per annum* within the same parish or township, where the same shall lie or be, are usually charged to the same, any thing contained in the said act made the the 10th year of the reign of queen Anne, to the contrary thereof in any wise notwithstanding; and whereas it is reasonable, that provision should likewise be made to prevent any fraudulent conveyances of lands and tenements, in order to multiply votes for electing members to serve in parliament, for such cities and town as are counties of themselves, wherein persons have a right to vote for electing such members, for or in respect of lands, tenements, or hereditaments of the yearly value of forty shillings:" Be it enacted by the king's most excellent majesty, by and with the advice and consent of the lords spiritual and temporal and commons in this present parliament assembled, and by the authority of the same, that from

and

and after the twenty-fifth day of March, 1740, the said provisions contained in the said in part recited act, made in the 10th year of the reign of queen Anne, for preventing fraudulent conveyances in order to multiply votes for electing knights for shires, and in the said act made in the next sessions of parliament, shall be extended and construed to extend, to such lands or tenements, for or in respect of which any person shall vote for the election of any member to serve in parliament for any such city or town as aforesaid, being a county of itself in that part of Great Britain called England, and that if any person shall vote for the election of any such member as a freeholder, not having such an estate for one year before the same election, and so charged or assessed as in the said acts or one of them is described, except in cases therein excepted, every such person shall be subject to the like penalties and forfeitures, as are by the said act, made in the 10th year of the reign of queen Anne, imposed on persons voting for knights of shires, not having the qualifications thereby required. A. D. 1740.

Persons voting as freeholders not having an estate one year before election, subject to the penalties and forfeitures ordained by 10 Annæ.

Exception.

In part repealed by 19 Geo. 2. c. 28.

ANNO 15° GEORGII II. CAP. 13. S. 8.

An Act for establishing an Agreement with the Governor and Company of the Bank of England, for advancing the Sum of One Million Six Hundred Thousand Pounds, towards the Supply for the Service of the Year 1742.

8. AND it is hereby further enacted by the authority aforesaid, That no person in respect of

The being governor, &c. of the bank to create no disability.

of his being governor, deputy governor, director, manager, or member of the said company, or for having any stock or share therein, or for any matter or thing to be by him done or performed in the affairs of the said corporation, shall be now or at any time hereafter disabled from being or continuing, or from being elected or serving as a member of parliament, or be liable or subject to any penalty, forfeiture, or disability prescribed by any other act or acts of parliament, for not qualifying himself to execute his trust with respect to the affairs of the said corporation, as persons who shall take or execute any office or place of profit or trust, are subject and liable unto by any law now in force, or be adjudged liable to be a bankrupt, within the intent or meaning of all or any the statutes made against or concerning bankrupts; any law, statute, or provision to the contrary thereof in any wise notwithstanding.

A. D. 1742.

ANNO 15° GEORGII II. CAP. 22.

An Act to exclude certain Officers from being Members of the House of Commons.

FOR further limiting or reducing the number of officers capable of sitting in the house of commons, be it enacted by the king's most excellent majesty, by and with the advice and consent of the lords spiritual and temporal and commons in this present parliament assembled,

and

and by the authority of the fame, That from and after the diffolution, or other determination of this prefent parliament, no perfon who fhall be commiffioners of the revenue in Ireland, or commiffioner of the navy or victualling offices, nor any deputies or clerks in any of the faid offices, or in any of the feveral offices following; that is to fay, the office of lord high treafurer, or the commiffioners of the treafury, or of the auditor of the receipt of his majefty's exchequer, or of the tellers of the exchequer, or of the chancellor of the exchequer, or of the lord high admiral, or the commiffioners of the admiralty, or of the paymafters of the army or of the navy, or of his majefty's principal fecretaries of ftate, or of the commiffioners of the falt, or of the commiffioners of the ftamps, or of the commiffioners of appeals, or of the commiffioners of wine licences, or of the commiffioners of hackney coaches, or of the commiffioners of hawkers and pedlars, nor any perfons having any office, civil or military, within the ifland of Minorca or in Gibraltar, other than officers having commiffions in any regiment there only, fhall be capable of being elected, or of fitting or voting as a member of the houfe of commons in any parliament which fhall be hereafter fummoned and holden.

Defcription of officers not admitted to fit in parliament.

2. And be it further enacted, by the authority aforefaid, That if any perfon hereby difabled or declared to be incapable to fit or vote in any parliament hereafter to be holden, fhall neverthelefs be returned as a member to ferve for any county, ftewartry, city, borough, town, cinque port,

port, or place, in parliament, such election and return are hereby enacted and declared to be void to all intents and purposes whatsoever; and if any person disabled and declared incapable by this act to be elected, shall after the dissolution, or other determination of this present parliament, presume to sit or vote as a member of the house of commons in any parliament to be hereafter summoned, such person so sitting or voting, shall forfeit the sum of twenty pounds for every day in which he shall sit or vote in the said house of commons, to such person or persons who shall sue for the same in any of his majesty's courts at Westminster, and the money so forfeited shall be recovered by the persons so suing, with full costs of suit, in any of the said courts, by action of debt, bill, plaint, or information, in which no essoin, privilege, protection, or wager of law, shall be allowed, and only one imparlance, and shall from thenceforth be incapable of taking, holding, or enjoying any office of honour or profit under his majesty, his heirs or successors.

Returns of such members declared void.

Penalty on persons sitting or voting, after disabled by this act.

Proviso.

3. Provided always, and it is hereby enacted and declared by the authority aforesaid, That nothing in this act shall extend or be construed to extend or relate to, or exclude the treasurer or comptroller of the navy, the secretaries of the treasury, the secretary to the chancellor of the exchequer, or secretaries of the admiralty, the under secretary to any of his majesty's principal secretaries of state, or the deputy paymaster of the army, or to exclude any person having or holding any office or employment for life, or for

so

so long as he shall behave himself well in his office; any thing herein contained to the contrary notwithstanding.

A. D. 1742.

ANNO 18° GEORGII II. CAP. 18.

An Act to explain and amend the Laws touching the Elections of Knights of the Shire to serve in Parliament for that Part of Great Britain called England.

'WHEREAS several delays and inconveniencies have arisen in elections of knights of shires to serve in parliament, to the great trouble and expence of the candidates and electors:' For remedy thereof, be it enacted, by the king's most excellent majesty, by and with the advice and consent of the lords spiritual and temporal and commons in this present parliament assembled, and by the authority of the same, That from and after the twenty-fourth day of June, 1745, upon every election to be made within that part of Great Britain called England, or dominion of Wales, of any knight or knights of the shire to serve in parliament, every freeholder instead of the oath or affirmation prescribed to be taken, by An act of parliament made in the 10th year of the reign of her late majesty queen Anne, intituled, an act for the more effectual preventing fraudulent conveyances in order to multiply votes for electing knights

Instead of the oath by 10 Annæ, c. 23, another is appointed for freeholders.

knights of shires to serve in parliament, before he is admitted to poll at the said election, shall (if required by the candidates or any of them, or any other person having a right to vote at the said election) first take the oath (or being one of the people called *Quakers*, the solemn affirmation) following, *videlicet*,

The oath.

' You shall swear (or being one of the people called *Quakers*, you shall solemnly affirm) that you are a freeholder in the county of   and have a freehold estate, consisting of   (specifying the nature of such freehold estate, whether messuage, land, rent, tythe, or what else; and if such freehold estate consists in messuages, lands, or tythes, then specifying in whose occupation the same are; and if in rent, then specifying the names of the owners or possessors of the lands or tenements, out of which such rent is issuing, or of some or one of them) lying or being at   in the county of   of the clear yearly value of forty shillings over and above all rents and charges payable out of, or in respect of the same; and that you have been in the actual possession or receipt of the rents and profits thereof, for your own use, above twelve kalendar months, or that the same came to you within the time aforesaid, by descent, marriage, marriage settlement, devise, or promotion to a benefice in a church, or by promotion to an office; and that such a freehold estate has not been granted or made to you fraudulently on purpose to qualify you to give your vote; and that the place of your abode is at   in   and

and that you are twenty-one years of age as you believe, and that you have not been polled before at this election.'

Which oath (or solemn affirmation) the sheriff by himself, his under-sheriff, or such sworn clerk or clerks, as shall be by him appointed for the taking of the poll, is hereby required to administer; and in case any freeholder or other person taking the said oath or affirmation hereby appointed, shall thereby commit wilful perjury and be thereof convicted; and if any person do unlawfully or corruptly procure, or suborn any freeholder or other person, to take the said oath or affirmation in order to be polled, whereby he shall commit such wilful perjury, and shall be thereof convicted; he and they for every such offence, shall incur such pains and penalties, as are in and by two acts of parliament, the one made in the 5th year of the reign of the late queen Elizabeth, intituled, an act for punishing such persons as shall procure or commit wilful perjury, or suborn or procure any person to commit any wilful or corrupt perjury, the other made in the 2d year of his present majesty, intituled, an act for the more effectual preventing and further punishment of forgery, perjury, and subornation of perjury, and to make it felony to steal bonds, notes, or other securities for payment of money, contrary to the said acts.

By whom to be administered.

Penalty of perjury or subornation, the same as by 5 Eliz. c. 9. & 2 Geo. 2. c. 25.

2. 'And whereas by the said act made in the 10th year of the reign of her late majesty queen Anne, It is enacted as follows: *videlicet,* That from and after the first day of May, which was in the year 1712, no person shall vote

for the election of any knight of a shire within that part of Great Britain called England, in respect or in right of any lands or tenements which have not been charged or assessed to the public taxes, church rates, and parish duties in such proportion as other lands or tenements of forty shillings *per annum* within the same parish or township wherein the same shall lie or be, are usually charged; and whereas by an act of parliament made in the 12th year of the reign of her said late majesty queen Anne, for explaining the said recited clause, it is enacted, That the said act, or any thing therein contained, shall not extend or be construed to restrain any person from voting in such election of any knight of a shire within that part of Great Britain called England, in respect or in right of any rents, tythes, or other incorporeal inheritances, or any messuages or lands in any extra-parochial places, or any chambers in the inns of court or inns of chancery, or any messuages or seats belonging to any offices, in regard or by reason that the same have not been usually charged or assessed to all or any the public taxes, church rates, and parish duties as mentioned in the above recited act, or in respect or right of any other messuages or lands not herein-before specified in regard or by reason that the same have not been usually charged or assessed to all and every the public taxes, church rates, and parish duties aforesaid; provided that such messuages or lands have usually been charged or assessed to some one or more of the said public taxes, rates, or duties, in such proportion as other messuages or lands of forty

Marginalia:
Clauses repealed of 10 Annæ, c. 23. § 2.

And 12 Annæ, st. 1. c. 5.

forty shillings *per annum* in the same township or parish where the same shall lie or be, are usually charged to the same:' Be it enacted by the authority aforesaid, That so much of the said recited act as disables any person to vote for knights of shires in respect or in right of any lands or tenements which have not been charged or assessed as therein mentioned, shall from and after the said twenty-fourth day of June, be and is hereby repealed. {*In part repealed.*}

3. Provided always, that from and after the said twenty-fourth day of June, no person shall vote for the electing of a knight or knights of the shire to serve in parliament, within that part of Great Britain called England, or the principality of Wales, in respect or in right of any messuages, lands, or tenements, which have not been charged or assessed towards some aid granted, or hereafter to be granted to his majesty, his heirs or successors, by a land tax in Great Britain, twelve kalendar months next before such election. {*Qualification of electors.*}

4. Provided also, That this act, or any thing therein contained, shall not extend, or be construed to extend to restrain any person from voting in any such election of any knight or knights of a shire within that part of Great Britain called England, or the principality of Wales, in respect or in right of any rents or any chambers in the inns of court or inns of chancery, or any messuages or seats belonging to any offices, in regard or by reason that the same have not been usually charged or assessed to the aid commonly called the land tax; and that the acting commissioners of the land tax for the time being, or any {*Exception for voting in right of chambers or offices.*}

any three or more of them, at their meetings for the respective divisions, shall sign and seal one other duplicate of the copies of the respective assessments, to be delivered to them by the several assessors after all appeals determined, and the same to deliver, or cause to be delivered, to the clerks of the peace for their respective counties, to be by them kept amongst the records of the sessions, to which all persons may resort at all seasonable times and inspect the same, paying sixpence for such inspection; and the said clerks of the peace or their deputies, are hereby required forthwith to give copies of the said duplicates or any part thereof, to any such person or persons who shall require the same, paying after the rate of six-pence for every three hundred words, and so in proportion for any greater or lesser number.

Duplicates of the land tax assessments to be kept among the records of the sessions;

To be inspected, or copies taken.

5. And be it further enacted by the authority aforesaid, That from and after the said twenty-fourth day of June, 1745, no person shall vote in any such election without having a freehold estate in the county for which he votes, of the clear yearly value of forty shillings over and above all rents and charges payable out of or in respect of the same, or without having been in the actual possession, or in the receipt of the rents and profits thereof for his own use above twelve kalendar months, unless the same came to him within the time aforesaid, by descent, marriage, marriage settlement, devise, or promotion to any benefice in a church, or by promotion to an office, or shall vote in respect or in right of any freehold estate which was made or granted to him fraudulently,

Further qualifications of electors.

lently, on purpose to qualify him to give his vote, or shall vote more than once at the same election, and if any person shall vote in any such election contrary to the true intent and meaning hereof, he shall forfeit to any candidate to whom such vote shall not have been given, and who shall first sue for the same, the sum of forty pounds to be recovered by him or them, his or their executors or administrators together with full costs of suit, by action of debt in any of his majesty's courts of record at Westminster, wherein no essoin, protection, wager of law, privilege, or imparlance shall be admitted or allowed; and in every such action the proof shall lie on such person against whom the same was brought, unless the fact on which such action is grounded, be the having polled more than once at the same election. *Penalty of 40l.*

6. And be it declared by the authority aforesaid, That no public or parliamentary tax, county, church, or parish rate, or duty, or any other tax, rate, or assessment whatsoever, to be assessed or levied upon any county, division, rape, lathe, wapentake, ward, or hundred, is or shall be deemed or construed to be any charge payable out of or in respect of any freehold estate within the meaning and intention of this act, or of the oath or solemn affirmation herein-before directed to be administered to, and taken by, every freeholder if required as aforesaid. *No public tax to be deemed a charge on a freehold.*

7. And be it further enacted by the authority aforesaid, That from and after the said twenty-fourth day of June, 1745, at every such election within that part of Great Britain called England,

and

and dominion of Wales, the sheriff, or in his absence, the under sheriff, or such as he shall depute, shall appoint, make or erect, or cause to be appointed, made, or erected, at the expence of the candidates, such number of convenient booths or places for taking the poll as the candidates or any of them shall three days at least before the commencement of the poll desire, so as the same do not exceed the number of rapes, lathes, wapentakes, wards, or hundreds within the said county, and not exceeding in the whole the number of fifteen; and shall affix, or cause to be affixed on the most public part of each of the said booths or polling places the name or names of the rape, wapentake, lathe, ward, or hundred, or rapes, wapentakes, lathes, wards, or hundreds, for which such booth or polling place is allotted or designed; and the said sheriff, under sheriff, or such person as he shall depute, shall appoint a proper clerk or clerks at each of the said booths or polling places to take the poll (which said clerk or clerks shall be at the expence of the candidates, and be paid not exceeding one guinea *per* day each clerk), and the said sheriff or under sheriff shall also make out a list for each of the said booths or polling places respectively, of all the several towns, villages, parishes, and hamlets, lying or being wholly or in part in the rape, wapentake, lathe, ward, or hundred, or in the several rapes, wapentakes, lathes, wards, or hundred, for which such booth or polling place is allotted or designed; and shall, upon request made, deliver a true copy thereof to any of the candidates,

Marginalia:
- Booths to be erected at the expence of the candidates;
- Proportioned to the hundreds, &c. and not exceeding 15.
- The sheriff to appoint a clerk at each booth for polling at the candidates' expence.
- List of towns, &c. for each booth, of which copies to be given at 2s. each.

dates, or their agents, who shall desire the same, taking for each of the said copies the sum of two shillings and no more.

8. And be it further enacted by the authority aforesaid, That no sheriff, under-sheriff, or clerk, appointed to take the poll at any of the said booths or polling places, shall admit any person to vote for any lands, tenements, or other freehold estate, sworn by the said oath to be lying and being at some parish, town, or place, or parishes, towns, or places, which parish, town, or place, or parishes, towns, or places, or any of them, or any part of them, is not or are not mentioned in the list so made out for such booths or polling places as aforesaid, unless such lands, tenements, or estate lie or be in some town, liberty, or place not mentioned in any of the lists so made out for all the said booths or polling places as aforesaid. *Voting at each booth to be regulated by the list.*

Exception.

9. And be it further enacted by the authority aforesaid, That the sheriff, or in his absence the under-sheriff, or such as he shall depute, shall at every such election allow a cheque book for every poll book for each candidate, to be kept by their respective inspectors at every place where the poll for such election shall be taken or carried on. *A cheque book for every poll book allowed each candidate.*

10. 'And whereas by an act made in the 7th and 8th years of the reign of king William the Third, intituled, An act for further regulating elections of members to serve in parliament, and for the preventing irregular proceedings of sheriffs and other officers in the electing and re- *7 & 8 W. 3.*

turning such members, it is enacted, That upon every election to be made of any knight or knights of the shire, the sheriff of the county where such election shall be made, shall proceed to election at the next county court, unless the same fall out to be held within six days after the receipt of the writ, or upon the same day, and then shall adjourn the same court to some convenient day, giving ten days notice of the time and place of election; And whereas sheriffs have frequently in such cases, where the county court fell out to be held within six days after the receipt of the writ, or upon the same day, made long adjournments of the same in order to delay proceeding to election:' For remedy thereof for the future, be it enacted by the authority aforesaid, That from and after the said twenty-fourth day of June, no sheriff shall in such case take upon himself to adjourn such court for longer than sixteen days, any law, usage, or custom, to the contrary notwithstanding.

No sheriff to adjourn a county court for longer than 16 days.

11. 'And whereas by an act made in the 6th year of the reign of his present majesty, intituled, An act to explain and amend an act made in the 7th and 8th years of the reign of king William the third, intituled, An act for the further regulating elections of members to serve in parliament, and for the preventing irregular proceedings of sheriffs, and other officers, in the electing and returning such members, so far as the same relates to holding of county courts, it is, among other things, enacted, That no county court whatsoever held within that part of Great Britain

Clause of 6 Geo. 2, c. 23. repealed.

Britain called England, shall be adjourned to a Monday, a Friday, or Saturday; and that all and every such adjournment and adjournments, and all and every act and deed done or performed at such courts so adjourned, shall be deemed, adjudged, and taken to be utterly null and void to all intents and purposes whatsoever; and whereas the same hath been found inconvenient:' Be it therefore enacted by the authority aforesaid, That from and after the said twenty-fourth day of June, so much of the said act, as is herein-before recited, shall be, and is hereby repealed.

12. And be it further enacted by the authority aforesaid, That in case any such sheriff or under-sheriff, who shall preside at any election of any such knight or knights of the shire within that part of Great Britain called England, or the dominion of Wales, shall wilfully offend against or act contrary to the true intent and meaning of this act, every such sheriff or under-sheriff shall be liable to be prosecuted by information or indictment in his majesty's court of king's bench at Westminster, or in the courts of great sessions in the principality of Wales, or at the sessions held for the counties palatine of Chester, Lancaster, and Durham, or at the assizes for the county, city, town, or place where such offence shall be committed, in which no *Noli prosequi*, or *Cesset processus*, shall be granted; any law, custom, or usage to the contrary thereof, in any wise notwithstanding.

Sheriff, &c. offending to be prosecuted.

No Noli prosequi, or Cesset processus to be granted.

13. And be it further enacted by the authority aforesaid, That it shall and may be sufficient for the plaintiff in any action of debt given by

The manner o proceeding in case of offence against this act.

by this act, to set forth in the declaration or bill that the defendant is indebted to him in the sum of   and to alledge the particular offence for which the action or suit is brought, and that the defendant hath acted contrary to this act, without mentioning the writ of summons to parliament, or the return thereof; and it shall be sufficient in any indictment or information for any offence committed contrary to this act, to alledge the particular offence charged upon the defendant; and that the defendant is guilty thereof, without mentioning the writ of summons to parliament, or the return thereof; and upon trial of any issue in such action, suit, indictment, or information, the plaintiff, prosecutor, or informer, shall not be obliged to prove the writ of summons to parliament, or the return thereof, or any warrant or authority to the sheriff, grounded upon any such writ of summons.

Limitations of actions.

14. Provided always, That every action, suit, indictment, or information given by this act, shall be commenced within the space of nine kalendar months, after the fact upon which the same is grounded shall have been committed.

Statutes of jeofails, &c. extended to proceedings on this act.

15. And be it further enacted by the authority aforesaid, That all the statutes of jeofails and amendments of law whatsoever, shall and may be construed to extend to all proceedings in any action, suit, indictment, or information given or allowed by this act, or which shall be brought in pursuance thereof.

16. Provided always, and be it further enacted by the authority aforesaid, That in case the plaintiff

tiff or informer in any action, suit, indictment, or information given by this act, shall discontinue the same or be nonsuited, or judgement be otherwise given against him; then, and in any of the said cases the defendant against whom such action, suit, or information shall have been brought, shall recover his treble costs.

Treble costs.

A. D. 1745.

ANNO 19° GEORGII II. CAP. 28.

An Act for the better regulating of Elections of Members to serve in Parliament for such Cities and Towns, in that Part of Great Britain called England, as are Counties of themselves.

'WHEREAS by an act made and passed in the last session of parliament, intituled, An act to explain and amend the laws touching the elections of knights of the shire to serve in parliament for that part of Great Britain called England, several good provisions were enacted for the better regulating the said elections; and whereas it is reasonable, that like provisions should be made for the due election of members to serve in parliament for such cities and towns in that part of Great Britain called England as are counties of themselves, and in which persons have a right to vote for electing such members for and in respect of freehold lands, tenements, or hereditaments, of the yearly value of forty shillings:' Therefore, be it enacted by the king's

18 Geo. 2. c. 18.

king's most excellent majesty, by and with the advice and consent of the lords spiritual and temporal and commons in this present parliament assembled, and by the authority of the same, That from and after the twenty-fourth day of June, 1746, every person, demanding to vote for the election of any member to serve in parliament for such city or town being a county of itself, in that part of Great Britain called England, for and in respect of any freehold estate of forty shillings a year, shall, before he is admitted to poll at the said election (if required by the candidates or any of them, or any person having a right to vote at the said election), first take the oath (or being a *Quaker*, the solemn affirmation) following, viz.

Persons demanding to vote for election of members, if required, to take the oath following, &c.

The oath.

' You shall swear (or being a *Quaker*, you shall solemnly affirm), That you have a freehold estate, consisting of (specifying the nature of such freehold estate, whether messuage, land, rent, tythe, or what else; and if such freehold estate consists in messuages, lands, or tythes, then specifying in whose occupation the same are; and if rent, then specifying the names of the owners, or possessors of the lands or tenements, out of which such rent is issuing, or some or one of them), lying or being in the city and county, or town and county (as the case may be) of   of the clear yearly value of forty shillings over and above all rents and charges payable out of, or in respect of the same; and that you have been in the actual possession or receipt of the rents and profits thereof for your own use, above twelve kalendar months; or that the same came to you within the time aforesaid by descent, marriage,

marriage, marriage, settlement, devise or promotion to a benefice in a church, or by promotion to an office; and that such freehold estate has not been granted or made to you fraudulently on purpose to qualify you to give your vote; and that the place of your abode is at
in   and that you are twenty-one years of age, as you believe, and that you have not been polled before at this election.'

Which oath (or solemn affirmation) the sheriff or sheriffs, by him or themselves, or his or their under-sheriff or under-sheriffs, or such sworn clerk or clerks as shall be by him or them appointed for the taking of the poll is and are hereby required to administer; and in case any freeholder or other person, taking the said oath or affirmation hereby appointed, shall thereby commit wilful perjury, and be thereof convicted; and if any person do unlawfully and corruptly procure or suborn any freeholder or other person to take the said oath or affirmation in order to be polled, whereby he shall commit such wilful perjury and shall be thereof convicted, he and they for every such offence shall incur such pains and penalties as are in and by two acts of parliament, (the one made in the 5th year of the reign of the late queen Elizabeth, intituled, An act for punishment of such persons as shall procure or commit wilful perjury; the other made in the 2d year of the reign of his present Majesty, intituled, An act for the more effectual preventing and further punishment of forgery, perjury, subornation of perjury, and to make it felony to steal

The oath, &c. by whom to be administered.

Wilful perjury, and subornation to be punished as by,

5 Eliz. c. 9.

And 2 Geo. 2. c. 25.

bonds,

bonds, notes, and other securities for payment of money;) directed to be inflicted for offences committed contrary to the said acts.

10 Annæ, c. 23.

2. "And whereas by an act made in the 10th year of the reign of Queen Anne, intituled, An act for the more effectual preventing fraudulent conveyances in order to multiply votes for electing knights of shires to serve in parliament, it was enacted, That no person should vote for the electing a knight of the shire within that part of Great Britain called England, in respect or in right of any lands or tenements which had not been charged or assessed to the public taxes, church rates, and parish duties in such proportion as other lands or tenements of forty shillings *per annum* within the same parish or township where the same should lie or had been usually charged; And whereas by an

12 Ann. st. 1. c. 5.

act of parliament made in the 12th year of the reign of her said late majesty queen Anne for explaining the said recited clause, it is enacted, that the said act, or any thing therein contained shall not extend, or be construed to restrain any person from voting in such election of any knight of a shire within that part of Great Britain called England, in respect or in right of any rents, tithes, or other incorporeal inheritances, or any messuages or lands in extra-parochial places, or any chambers in the inns of court, or inns of chancery, or any messuages or seats belonging to any offices, in regard or by reason that the same have not been usually charged or assessed to all or any the public taxes, church rates, and parish duties aforesaid, or in respect or right of

any

any other messuages or lands not therein before specified in regard or by reason that the same have not been usually charged or assessed to all and every the public taxes, church rates, and parish duties aforesaid, provided that such messuages or lands have usually been charged or assessed to some one or more of the said public taxes, rates, or duties, in such proportion as other messuages or lands of forty shillings *per annum*, in the same parish or township where the same shall lie or be, are usually charged to the same; which said provisions are recited in an act of parliament made in the 13th year of the reign of his present majesty, intituled, An act for the more effectually preventing fraudulent qualifications of persons to vote as freeholders in the election of members to serve in parliament for such cities and towns as are counties of themselves, in that part of Great Britain called England; and are therein enacted to extend and to be construed to extend to such lands or tenements for or in respect of which any person shall vote for the election of any member to serve in parliament for any such city or town as aforesaid, being a county of itself in that part of Great Britain called England; And whereas by an act passed in the last session of this present parliament, it is enacted, That so much of the said recited acts of the 10th and 12th years of the reign of the late queen Anne, as disables any person to vote for knights of shires in respect or in right of any lands or tenements which have not been charged or assessed as therein mentioned, shall be and is repealed:" Be it enacted by the authority

13 Geo. 2. c. 20.

18 Geo. 2. c. 18.

authority aforesaid, That so much of the said recited act of the 13th year of the reign of his present majesty as extends the said provisions to such cities and towns that are counties of themselves as aforesaid, shall also from and after the said twenty-fourth day of June, 1746, be and it is hereby repealed.

<small>Part of the act of 13 Geo. 2. repealed.</small>

3. Provided always that from and after the said twenty-fourth day of June, 1746, no person shall vote for the electing a member or members to serve in parliament for such city or town, being a county of itself as aforesaid, within that part of Great Britain called England, in respect or in right of any freehold, messuages, lands, or tenements, of the yearly value of forty shillings as aforesaid, which have not been charged or assessed towards some aid granted or hereafter to be granted to his majesty, his heirs or successors by a land tax in Great Britain, twelve kalendar months next before such election. Provided, that nothing herein contained shall extend, or be construed to restrain any person from voting in any such election for cities and towns as are counties of themselves as aforesaid, in respect or in right of any rents, or any messuages or seats belonging to any offices in regard or by reason that the same have not been usually charged or assessed to the aid commonly called the land tax; and the acting commissioners of the land tax for the time being, or any three or more of them at their meetings, shall sign and seal one other duplicate of the copies of the assessment or assessments, to be delivered to them by the assessors after all appeals determined, and the same shall deliver, or cause to be delivered

<small>Qualification of persons who shall vote for members for cities or towns being counties.</small>

<small>Exception.</small>

<small>Commissioners of the land tax to sign duplicates of the assessments to be delivered to the clerks of the peace, &c. and filed.</small>

delivered to the persons officiating as clerks of the peace within the districts of the said cities and towns, being counties of themselves as aforesaid respectively, to be by them kept amongst the records of the sessions, to which all persons may resort at all seasonable times, and inspect the same, paying six-pence for such inspection; and the said persons officiating as clerks of the peace or their deputies, are hereby required forthwith to give copies of the said duplicates, or any part thereof, to any person or persons who shall require the same, paying after the rate of six-pence for every three hundred words, and so in proportion for any greater or less number. *Copies to be given to persons paying for them.*

4. And be it further enacted by the authority aforesaid, That from and after the said twenty-fourth day of June, 1746, no person shall vote in such election of a member or members to serve in parliament for any city or town, being a county of itself, and in which persons have a right to vote for such members, for and in respect of lands, tenements, or hereditaments of the yearly value of forty shillings, unless such persons shall have a freehold estate in the city and county, or town and county, for which he votes, of the clear yearly value of forty shillings, over and above all rents and charges payable out of or in respect of the same, and shall have been in the actual possession or in receipt of the rents and profits thereof for his own use above twelve kalendar months, except the same came to him within the time aforesaid, by descent, marriage, marriage settlement, devise, or promotion to any *Persons voting, to have a freehold estate of 40s. &c.* *And to be in possession above 12 months.* *Exception.*

benefice

benefice in a church, or by promotion to an office; and no person shall vote in respect or in right of any freehold estate which was made or granted to him fraudulently, on purpose to qualify him to give his vote, or shall vote more than once at the same election; and if any person shall vote in any such election contrary to the true intent and meaning hereof, he shall forfeit to any candidate for whom such vote shall not have been given, and who shall first sue for the same, the sum of forty pounds, to be recovered by him or them, his or their executors or administrators, together with full costs of suit, by action of debt in any of his majesty's courts of record at Westminster, wherein no essoin, protection, wager of law, privilege, or imparlance shall be admitted or allowed; and in every such action the proof shall lie on such person against whom the same was brought, unless the fact, on which such action is grounded, be the having polled more than once at the same election.

Penalty of fraudulent qualifications, &c.

The proof where to lie, &c.

5. And be it declared by the authority aforesaid, That no public or parliamentary tax, church or parish rate or duty, or any other tax, rate, or assessment whatsoever, to be assessed or levied within such cities or towns, being counties of themselves as aforesaid, is or shall be deemed or construed to be any charge payable out of or in respect of any freehold estate, within the meaning and intention of this act, or of the oath or solemn affirmation herein-before directed to be administered to, and taken by, every freeholder, if required, as aforesaid.

Taxes not within this act.

6. And

6. And be it further enacted by the authority aforesaid, That the sheriff or sheriffs of any city or town, being a county of itself in that part of Great Britain called England, or in his or their absence, his or their under-sheriff or under-sheriffs, or such other person as he or they shall depute, shall, at every election of any member or members to serve in parliament for such city or town, allow a cheque book for every poll book for each candidate, to be kept by their respective inspectors, at the place where the poll for such election shall be taken or carried on. *Sheriff to allow a cheque book for every poll book.*

7. And be it further enacted by the authority aforesaid, That from and after the said twenty-fourth day of June, 1746, the sheriff or sheriffs of every city or town being a county of itself, and having a right to elect a member or members of parliament by virtue of the writ issuing out of chancery, without any precept thereupon, within that part of Great Britain called England, shall forthwith, upon the receipt of the writ for election of a member or members to serve in parliament for such city or town, cause public notice to be given of the time and place of election, and shall proceed to election thereupon within the space of eight days next after that of his receipt of the said writ, and give three days notice thereof at least, exclusive of the day of the receipt of the writ, and of the day of election. *Sheriffs to give public notice, &c.* *And to proceed to election within 8 days after receipt of the writ.*

8. And be it further enacted by the authority aforesaid, That in case any sheriff or under-sheriff presiding at any election of a member or members to serve in parliament for any such city or

or town, being a county of itself as aforesaid, within that part of Great Britain called England, shall wilfully offend against or act contrary to the true intent and meaning of this act, every such sheriff or under-sheriff shall be liable to be prosecuted by information or indictment in his majesty's court of king's bench at Westminster, or at the assizes for the city or town where such offence shall be committed, in which no *Noli prosequi* or *Cesset processus* shall be granted; any law, custom, or usage to the contrary thereof in any wise notwithstanding.

May be prosecuted in the king's bench, &c.

9. And be it further enacted by the authority aforesaid, That it shall and may be sufficient for the plaintiff in any action of debt given by this act, to set forth in the declaration or bill, that the defendant is indebted to him in the sum of and to alledge the particular offence for which the action or suit is brought, and that the defendant hath acted contrary to this act, without mentioning the writ of summons to parliament, or the return thereof; and it shall be sufficient in any indictment or information for any offence committed contrary to this act to alledge the particular offence charged upon the defendant, and that the defendant is guilty thereof, without mentioning the writ of summons to parliament, or the return thereof; and upon trial of any issue in any such action, suit, indictment, or information, the plaintiff, prosecutor, or informer, shall not be obliged to prove the writ of summons to parliament or the return thereof, or

Plaintiffs how to proceed.

any warrant or authority to the sheriff or sheriffs grounded upon any such writ of summons.

10. Provided always, That every action, suit, indictment, or information, given by this act, shall be commenced within the space of nine kalendar months after the fact upon which the same is grounded shall have been committed. *Suits to be commenced within nine months.*

11. And be it further enacted by the authority aforesaid, That all the statutes of jeofails and amendments of the law whatsoever, shall and may be construed to extend to all proceedings in any action, suit, indictment, or information given or allowed by this act, or which shall be brought in pursuance thereof. *Statutes of jeofails extended to such proceedings.*

12. Provided always, and be it further enacted by the authority aforesaid, That in case the plaintiff or informer in any action, suit, indictment, or information given by this act, shall discontinue the same or be nonsuited, or judgement be otherwise given against him, then and in any of the said cases, the defendant against whom such action, suit, or information shall have been brought, shall recover his treble costs. *Plaintiff discontinuing, &c. shall pay treble costs.*

13. Provided always, and be it enacted by the authority aforesaid, That this act, or any thing therein contained (other than, and except such clauses and provisions as are by this act made for or concerning allowing cheque books, or for or concerning notice to be given of the time and place of election, and proceeding to election thereupon) shall not extend, or be construed to extend, to any city or town, being a county of itself or to any person or persons, where the right of voting *Limitation of this act.*

for

for any member or members of any such city or town is, for or in respect of burgage tenure, or where the right of voting for such member or members for or in respect of a freehold, does not require the same to be of the yearly value of forty shillings.

A. D. 1746.

ANNO 31° GEORGII II. CAP. 14.

An Act for further explaining the Laws touching the Electors of Knights of the Shire to serve in Parliament for that Part of Great Britain called England.

WHEREAS by an act made, in the 18th year of the reign of his present majesty, intituled, 'An act to explain and amend the laws touching the elections of knights of the shire, to serve in parliament for that part of Great Britain called England,' it is enacted, That no person shall vote at the election of any knight or knights of a shire, within that part of Great Britain called England, or principality of Wales, without having a freehold estate in the county for which he votes, of the clear yearly value of forty shillings, over and above all rents and charges payable out of or in respect of the same; and whereas, notwithstanding the said act, certain persons who hold their estates by copy of court roll pretend to have a right to vote and have, at certain times, taken upon them to vote at such elections;

elections: Be it therefore enacted by the king's most excellent majesty, by and with the advice and consent of the lords spiritual and temporal and commons in this present parliament assembled, and by the authority of the same, That from and after the twenty-fourth day of June, 1758, no person who holds his estate by copy of court roll shall be entitled thereby to vote at the election of any knight or knights of a shire, within that part of Great Britain called England, or principality of Wales; and if any person shall vote in any such election, contrary to the true intent and meaning hereof, every such vote shall be void to all intents and purposes whatsoever; and every person so voting shall forfeit to any candidate for whom such vote shall not have been given, and who shall first sue for the same, the sum of fifty pounds; to be recovered by him or them, his, her, or their executors and administrators, together with full costs of suit, by action of debt in any of his majesty's courts of record at Westminster, wherein no essoin, protection, wager of law, privilege, or imparlance, shall be admitted or allowed; and in every such action the proof shall lie on the person against whom such action shall be brought.

Copyholders disabled from voting for knights of the shire;

their vote void, and they to forfeit 50 l.

with full costs of suit.

Onus probandi.

2. And be it further enacted by the authority aforesaid, That it shall and may be sufficient for the plaintiff in any such action of debt to set forth in the declaration or bill, that the defendant is indebted to him in the sum of fifty pounds and to alledge the offence for which the action or suit is brought, and that the defendant hath acted contrary

Plaintiff's plea the action upon the case.

trary to this act, without mentioning the writ of summons to parliament, or the return thereof; and upon trial of any issue in any such action or suit, the plaintiff shall not be obliged to prove the writ of summons to parliament or the return thereof, or any warrant or authority to the sheriff grounded upon any such writ of summons.

Limitation of actions.

3. Provided always, That every such action or suit shall be commenced within the space of nine kalendar months next after the fact, upon which the same is grounded, shall have been committed.

Statutes of jeofails, &c. extended to suits.

4. And be it further enacted by the authority aforesaid, That all the statutes of jeofails, and amendments of the law whatsoever, shall and may be construed to extend to all proceedings in in any such action or suit.

Plaintiff nonsuited, &c. to pay treble costs.

5. Provided always, and be it further enacted by the authority aforesaid, That in case the plaintiff in any such action or suit shall discontinue the same, or be nonsuited, or judgement be otherwise given against him; then, and in any of the said cases, the defendant, against whom such action or suit shall have been brought, shall recover his treble costs.

A. D. 1757.

ANNO 33° GEORGII II., CAP. 20.

An Act to enforce and render more effectual the Laws relating to the Qualification of Members to sit in the House of Commons.

WHEREAS by an act passed in the 9th year of the reign of her late majesty queen Anne, intituled,

intituled, 'An act for securing the freedom of parliaments, by the farther qualifying the members to sit in the house of commons,' it was enacted, That no person should be capable to sit or vote, as a member of the house of commons, for any county, city, borough, or cinque port, within that part of Great Britain, called England, the dominion of Wales, and town of Berwick upon Tweed, who should not have an estate, freehold or copyhold, for his own life, or for some greater estate, either in law or equity, to and for his own use and benefit, of or in lands, tenements, or hereditaments, over and above what would satisfy and clear all incumbrances that might affect the same, lying or being within that part of Great Britain called England, the dominion of Wales, and town of Berwick upon Tweed, of the respective annual value therein limited; *viz.* the annual value of six hundred pounds, above reprizes, for every knight of a shire; and the annual value of three hundred pounds, above reprizes, for every citizen, burgess, or baron of the cinque ports: Now, in order to enforce and render the said act more effectual, be it enacted by the king's most excellent majesty, by and with the advice and consent of the lords spiritual and temporal and commons in this present parliament assembled, and by the authority of the same, that from and after the determination of this present parliament, every person, except as is herein-after excepted, who shall be elected a member of the house of commons, shall, before he presumes to vote in the house of commons, or sit there during any debate

All members in future parliaments (not particularly excepted), before they act, are to deliver in at the table, while the house is sitting, a signed schedule of their respective qualifications.

debate in the said house of commons after their speaker is chosen, produce and deliver in to the clerk of the said house, at the table in the middle of the said house, and whilst the house of commons is there duly sitting, with their speaker in the chair of the said house, a paper or account, signed by every such member, containing the name or names of the parish, township, or precinct, or of the several parishes, townships, or precincts, and also of the county, or of the several counties, in which the lands, tenements, or hereditaments, do lie, whereby he makes out his qualification, declaring the same to be of the annual value of six hundred pounds above reprizes, if a knight of the shire; and of the annual value of three hundred pounds, above reprizes, if a citizen, burgess, or baron of the cinque ports; and shall also, at the same time, take and subscribe the following oath; *viz.*

and take and subscribe the following oath;

' I, A. B. do swear, That I truly and *bona fide* have such an estate in law or equity, and of such value, to and for my own use and benefit, of or in lands, tenements, or hereditaments, over and above what will satisfy and clear all incumbrances that may affect the same, as doth qualify me to be elected and returned to serve as a member for the place I am returned for, according to the tenor and true meaning of the acts of parliament in that behalf; and that such lands, tenements, or hereditaments, do lie as described in the paper or account signed by me, and now delivered to the clerk of the house of commons.

So help me God.'

And

And the said house of commons is hereby impowered and required to administer the said oath and subscription, according to the directions of this act, as occasion shall be, from time to time, to every person duly demanding the same, immediately after such person shall have taken the oaths of allegiance, supremacy, and abjuration, at the said table: and the said oath and subscription herein-before directed to be taken and made, shall be entered in a parchment roll, to be provided for that purpose by the clerk of the house of commons; and the said papers or accounts, so signed and delivered in to the said clerk as aforesaid, shall be filed and carefully kept by him.

which is to be administered by the house, and inrolled, after the usual oaths of qualification have been taken;

and the schedules to be filed.

2. And be it further enacted by the authority aforesaid, That if any person, who shall be elected to serve in any future parliament as a knight of a shire, or as a citizen, burgess, or baron of the cinque ports, shall presume to sit or vote as aforesaid as a member of the house of commons, before he has delivered in such paper or account, and taken and subscribed such oath as aforesaid, or shall not be qualified according to the true intent and meaning of the said recited act, and of this act; his election shall be and is hereby declared to be void, and a new writ shall be issued to elect another member in the said person's room.

Any member presuming to act contrary thereto,

or without being duly qualified, his election is void, and a new writ to be issued.

3. Provided always, That nothing in this act contained, shall extend to the eldest son or heir-apparent of any peer or lord of parliament, or of any person qualified to serve as a knight of a shire

Persons excepted out of the general qualifications.

shire, or to the members for either of the universities in that part of Great Britain called England, or to the members for that part of Great Britain called Scotland.

A. D. 1759.

ANNO 3° GEORGII III. CAP. 15.

An Act to prevent occasional Freemen from voting at Elections of Members to serve in Parliament for Cities and Boroughs.

WHEREAS great abuses have been committed in making freemen of corporations, in order to influence elections of members to serve in parliament, to the great infringement of the rights of freemen of such corporations, and of the freedom of elections; to prevent such practices for the future, be it enacted by the king's most excellent majesty, by and with the advice and consent of the lords spiritual and temporal and commons in parliament assembled, and by authority of the same, That from and after the first day of May, 1763, no person whatsoever claiming as a freeman to vote at any election of members to serve in parliament for any city, town, port, or borough in England, Wales, and the town of Berwick upon Tweed, where such voter's right of voting is as a freeman only, shall be admitted to give his vote at such election, unless such person shall have been admitted to the freedom of such city, town, port, or borough,

None to vote as freemen, at elections of members, but such as have been admitted to their freedom twelve months before such election.

twelve

twelve kalendar months before the first day of such election; and if any person shall presume to give his vote as a freeman at any election of members to serve in parliament, contrary to the true intent and meaning of this act, he shall, for every such offence, forfeit and pay the sum of one hundred pounds to him, her, or them, who shall inform and sue for the same; and the vote given by such person shall be void and of no effect.

On penalty of 100l.

2. Provided always, That nothing herein contained shall extend, or be construed to extend, to any person entitled to his freedom by birth, marriage, or servitude, according to the custom or usage of such city, town, port, or borough.

Persons entitled to their freedom, by birth, marriage, or servitude, excepted.

3. And be it further enacted by the authority aforesaid, That if any mayor, bailiff, sheriff, town clerk, or other officer of any corporation, or other person whatsoever, shall wilfully and fraudulently antedate, or cause to be antedated, any admission of any freeman, such mayor, bailiff, sheriff, town clerk, officer, or other person, shall, for every such offence, forfeit and pay the sum of five hundred pounds to him, her, or them, who shall inform and sue for the same.

Penalty of antedating the admission of any freeman, 500l.

4. And be it further enacted by the authority aforesaid, That the mayor, bailiff, sheriff, town clerk, or other officer of any corporation, having the custody of, or power over, the records of the same, shall, upon the demand of any candidate, or his agent, or any two freemen, on the payment of one shilling, permit such candidate, agent, or freemen, between the hours of nine in the morning and three in the afternoon, at any time

The books and papers of admission of freemen to be open to inspection, upon demand of a candidate, his agent, or two freemen, upon payment of 1s.

before,

before, and within one month after, any such election as aforesaid, to inspect the books and papers wherein the admission of freemen shall be entered; and to have copies or minutes of the admission of so many freemen as such candidate, agent, or freemen, shall think fit, upon paying to such mayor, bailiff, sheriff, town clerk, or other officer, a reasonable charge for writing the same; and such books and papers shall, if demanded by such candidate, agent, or freemen, be produced by such mayor, bailiff, sheriff, town clerk, or other officer, at every election, and be referred to, in case any dispute shall arise touching the right of any person to give his vote thereat; and if such mayor, bailiff, sheriff, town clerk, or other officer, shall refuse or deny such candidate, agent, or freemen, the inspection of such books and papers, or to have copies or minutes thereof, or shall refuse or neglect to produce such books and papers at any election, if demanded and paid for in the manner herein-before set forth, such mayor, bailiff, sheriff, town clerk, or other officer, shall, for every such offence, forfeit and pay the sum of one hundred pounds to him, her, or them, who shall inform and sue for the same.

And copies and minutes of the admission to be given, paying reasonably for writing the same;

And the books, &c. to be produced, if demanded, at every election,

On penalty of 100l.

5. And be it further enacted by the authority aforesaid, That all forfeitures or penalties laid or imposed by this act, shall be recovered, with full costs of suit, by action of debt, bill, plaint, or information, in any of his majesty's courts of record at Westminster; wherein no essoin, protection,

The penalties may be recovered with full costs of suit;

tection, wager of law, or more than one imparlance shall be allowed.

6. Provided always, and it is hereby further enacted and declared, by the authority aforesaid, That no person shall be liable to any forfeiture or penalty by this act laid or imposed, unless prosecution be commenced within one year after such forfeiture or penalty shall be incurred. *Provided the prosecution be commenced within a year.*

7. And be it further enacted by the authority aforesaid, That the returning officer shall read, or cause to be read, openly, this act, at the time of election of members to serve in parliament for cities, towns, ports, or boroughs, where the right of election is in the whole, or in part, in freemen as aforesaid, immediately after the reading of the act passed in the 2d year of his late majesty's reign, intituled, An act for the more effectual preventing bribery and corruption in the elections of members to serve in parliament. *This act to be openly read by the returning officer, at all elections by freemen, immediately after act 2 Geo. 2.*

8. And be it further enacted by the authority aforesaid, That nothing in this act shall extend, or be construed to extend, to the cities of *London* or *Norwich*. *This act not to extend to London or Norwich.*

A. D. 1762.

ANNO 3° GEORGII III. CAP. 24.

An Act to prevent fraudulent and occasional Votes in the Elections of Knights of the Shire, and of Members for Cities and Towns which are Counties of themselves, so far as relates to the Right of Voting by virtue of Annuity or Rent Charge.

WHEREAS annuities or rent charges granted for a life or lives, or a greater estate, issuing out of freehold lands or tenements, are of a private nature, and therefore liable to fraudulent practices in the elections of knights of shires, to the prejudice of the candidates, and of those who have just right to vote at such elections; and whereas the right of election of members to serve in parliament for several cities and towns which are counties of themselves, in that part of Great Britain called England, is vested partly, or in the whole, in freeholders, in respect of freeholds of the yearly value of forty shillings, lying within such cities and towns; and whereas annuities and rent charges for a life or lives, or a greater estate, issuing out of such freehold lands or tenements, are liable to the like fraudulent practices: For remedy whereof, be it enacted by the king's most excellent majesty, by and with the advice and consent of the lords spiritual and temporal and commons in this present parliament assembled, and by the authority of the same, That

That from and after the first day of August, 1764, no person shall vote for electing any knight or knights of a shire, citizen or citizens, burgess or burgesses, of any such city or town for that part of Great Britain called England, for or in respect of any annuity or rent charge issuing out of freehold lands or tenements, and granted before the first day of June, 1763, unless a certificate, upon oath, shall have been entered twelve kalendar months, at least, before the first day of such election, with the clerk of the peace for the county, riding, or division, or with the clerk of the peace, town clerk, or other public officer, having the custody of the records within such city or town where such lands or tenements do lie, as follows, (that is to say),

"I, A. B. of   am really and *bona fide* seized of an annuity or rent charge, for my own use and benefit, of the clear yearly value of forty shillings, above all rents and charges payable out of the same, wholly issuing out of freehold lands, tenements, or hereditaments, belonging to C. D. of   situate, lying, and being, in the parish, township, or place, or in the parishes, townships, or places of E. in the county of   without any trust, agreement, matter, or thing to the contrary notwithstanding; and I, or the person or persons under whom I claim, was or were seized of the said annuity or rent charge before the first day of June, 1763."

2. And be it further enacted by the authority aforesaid, That no person shall vote for the electing

No person may vote in elections of knights of the shire, or of members for cities and towns which are counties of themselves, in right of any annuity or rent charge granted before 1 June, 1763, unless a certificate be entered with the clerk of the peace, or other proper officer 12 months before any such elections begin;

and in like manner with respect to such qualifications as shall come by descent, marriage, devise, presentation, or promotion:

ing any knight or knights of a shire, or for a citizen or citizens, burgess or burgesses, of any such city or town, for that part of Great Britain called England, in respect of any annuity or rent charge issuing out of freehold lands, tenements, or hereditaments, which shall come to such person by descent, marriage, marriage settlement, devise, or presentation to a benefice in a church, or promotion to an office, within twelve kalendar months next before such election respectively, unless a certificate upon oath, or affirmation if a *Quaker*, shall have been entered with the clerk of the peace, town clerk, or other officer as aforesaid, before the first day of such election, as follows; that is to say,

"I, A. B. of   am really and *bona fide* seized of an annuity or rent charge, to my own use and benefit, of the clear yearly value of forty shillings a year, above all rents and charges payable out of the same, wholly issuing out of freehold lands, tenements, or hereditaments, belonging to C. D. of   situate, lying, and being in the parish, township, or place, or in the parishes, townships, or places of   in the county of   without any trust, agreement, matter, or thing to the contrary notwithstanding; and I became seized of the said annuity or rent charge, on the   day of   last past, by descent or otherwise" *(as the case may happen.)*

Nor may any person vote in any election as aforesaid, after 1 Aug. 1764,

3. And be it further enacted by the authority aforesaid, That from and after the said first day of August, 1764, no person shall vote at any election

election of a knight or knights of the shire, or of any citizen or citizens, burgess or burgesses, of any such city or town, within that part of Great Britain called England, for or in respect of any annuity or rent charge to be granted after the said first day of June, 1763, unless a memorial of the grant of such annuity or rent charge shall have been registered with the clerk of the peace of the county, riding, or division, or with the clerk of the peace, town clerk, or other public officer, having the custody of the records, within such city or town where the lands or tenements out of which such annuity or rent charge issues shall lie, twelve kalendar months at least before the first day of such election; which memorial shall be wrote on parchment, and directed to such clerk of the peace, town clerk, or other public officer, and shall be under the hand and seal of the grantor or grantors, and attested by two witnesses, one whereof to be one of the witnesses to the execution of such grant; which witness shall, upon oath, before such clerk of the peace, town clerk, or other officer as aforesaid, or their deputies, prove the sealing and delivering of such grant, and the signing and sealing of such memorial; and which memorial shall contain the day and year of the date, and the names, additions, and abodes, of the parties and witnesses, and all the lands and tenements out of which the annuity or rent charge issues, and the parish, township, or place, or the parishes, townships, or places, where such lands and tenements lie; and that every such grant, of which such memorial is so to

in respect of any annuity or rent charge granted after the said 1 June, 1763, unless a memorial of the grant duly attested, be registered as aforesaid.

Such grant to be produced at the time of registering, and the day and year of en-

<small>tering the memorial to be indorfed thereon by the proper officer:</small>

to be regiſtered, ſhall, at the time of entering ſuch memorial, be produced to ſuch clerk of the peace, town clerk, or other officer, as aforeſaid, or their deputies, who ſhall thereon indorſe a certificate, in which ſhall be mentioned the day and year on which ſuch memorial ſhall be ſo entered.

<small>Nor may any one vote in right of any aſſignment of any annuity or rent charge made before 1763,</small>

4. And be it further enacted, by the authority aforeſaid, That from and after the ſaid firſt day of Auguſt, 1764, no perſon ſhall vote at any election of a knight or knights of the ſhire, or of any citizen or citizens, burgeſs or burgeſſes of any ſuch city or town, in that part of Great Britain called England, by reaſon of an aſſignment of any annuity or rent charge, or any part or parts thereof,

<small>unleſs a certificate of the original annuity be entered as aforeſaid;</small>

made before the ſaid firſt day of June, 1763, unleſs a certificate of ſuch aſſignment upon oath, to the purport herein-before mentioned, with reſpect to an original annuity or rent charge, ſhall have been entered with ſuch clerk of the peace, town clerk, or other officer as aforeſaid, twelve kalendar months at leaſt before the firſt day of ſuch

<small>and if the aſſignment be made after the ſaid 1 June, then a memorial thereof, and of the grant, to be atteſted and regiſtered as is directed in caſes of original grants.</small>

election; and that no perſon ſhall vote at any ſuch election as aforeſaid, by reaſon of an aſſignment of any annuity or rent charge, or any part or parts thereof, made after the firſt day of June, 1763, unleſs a memorial of ſuch aſſignment, and alſo a memorial of the grant of ſuch annuity or rent charge of which ſuch aſſignment ſhall be made, ſhall have been atteſted and regiſtered twelve kalendar months at leaſt before the firſt day of ſuch election, in the ſame manner as is herein-before directed with reſpect

to

to the memorial of an original grant of an annuity or rent charge.

5. And be it further enacted by the authority aforesaid, That the clerk of the peace for every county, riding, or division, and the clerk of the peace, town clerk, or other officer as aforesaid, of every such city or town, shall keep a book or books for the entering of every such certificate and memorial, and shall be allowed for the entry of every such certificate the sum of one shilling, and of every such memorial, two shillings, and no more; and for every search for any certificate or memorial, one shilling, and no more: and that any person or persons may, at all seasonable times, resort to, and inspect the certificates, memorials, and books of entries thereof; and such clerk of the peace, town clerk, or other officer as aforesaid, or their deputies, is hereby directed and required forthwith to give a copy of any certificate or memorial to any person or persons who shall desire the same, paying for such copy, if it contains not more than two hundred words, the sum of six-pence; and so in proportion for any greater number of words; and such clerk of the peace, town clerk, or other officer as aforesaid, or their deputies, is hereby impowered to administer an oath in all cases where an oath is required by this act; and true copies of the aforesaid certificates and memorials attested by such respective clerks of the peace, town clerk, or other officer as aforesaid, or their deputies, shall, at all times, be allowed and admitted

admitted as legal evidence in all cafes whatfoever.

Memorials of grants or affignments made and executed above 40 miles from the office of clerk of the peace, &c. to be regiftered, upon producing an affidavit made by one of the witneffes before one of the judges at Weftminfter, or a mafter in chancery.

6. Provided always, and be it further enacted by the authority aforefaid, That a memorial of fuch grant or affignment as fhall be made and executed in any place not within forty miles of the office of the clerk of the peace for the refpective county, riding, or divifion, or of the town clerk, or other officer as aforefaid, fhall be entered and regiftered by fuch clerk of the peace, town clerk, or other officer as aforefaid, or their deputies, in cafe an affidavit fworn, or affirmation of a *Quaker*, before one of the judges at Weftminfter, or a mafter in chancery ordinary or extraordinary, be brought with the faid memorial to the faid clerk of the peace, town clerk, or other officer, as aforefaid, wherein one of the witneffes to the execution of fuch grant or affignment fhall fwear that he or fhe faw the fame executed; and the fame fhall be a fufficient authority to the clerk of the peace, town clerk, or other officer, or their deputies, to give the party that brings fuch memorial a certificate of the regiftering fuch memorial; which certificate, figned by the faid clerk of the peace, town clerk, or other officer, as aforefaid, or their deputies, fhall be taken and allowed as evidence of the regiftry of the fame memorial in all courts of record whatfoever; any thing herein contained to the contrary notwithftanding.

Officer, or deputy, to attend, upon reafonable notice and fatisfaction, with the

7. And be it further enacted by the authority aforefaid, That the clerk of the peace of every county, riding, or divifion, and the clerk of the peace,

peace, town clerk, or other officer, as aforesaid, of every such city or town, or their deputies, shall, upon reasonable notice, attend at any such election with the book or books of entries of every such certificate and memorial, at the request of any candidate or candidates; he or they making him reasonable satisfaction for such attendance.

books of entries at any such election.

8. And be it further enacted, by the authority aforesaid, That if any clerk of the peace, town clerk, or other officer, as aforesaid, shall be guilty of any wilful neglect, misdemeanor, or fraudulent practice, contrary to the true intent and meaning of this act, every such clerk of the peace, town clerk, or other officer, as aforesaid, shall for every such offence, forfeit one hundred pounds to the person who shall sue for the same, by action of debt, bill, plaint, or information, in any of his majesty's courts of record at Westminster; wherein no essoin, protection, wager of law, or more than one imparlance, shall be allowed.

Officer guilty of any neglect &c misdemeanor, forfeits 100l.

9. Provided always, and it is hereby further enacted and declared by the authority aforesaid, That no person shall be liable to any forfeiture or penalty by this act laid or imposed, unless prosecution be commenced within twelve months after such forfeiture or penalty shall be incurred.

Limitation of prosecutions.

A. D. 1762.

ANNO 10° GEORGII III. CAP. 16.

An Act to regulate the Trials of controverted Elections or Returns of Members to serve in Parliament.

'WHEREAS the present mode of decision upon petitions, complaining of undue elections or returns of members to serve in parliament, frequently obstructs public business; occasions much expence, trouble, and delay to the parties; is defective, for want of those sanctions and solemnities which are established by law in other trials; and is attended with many other inconveniencies: For remedy thereof, be it enacted by the king's most excellent majesty, by and with the advice and consent of the lords spiritual and temporal and commons in this present parliament assembled, and by the authority of the same, That after the end of the present session of parliament, whenever a petition, complaining of an undue election or return of a member or members to serve in parliament, shall be presented to the house of commons, a day and hour shall by the said house be appointed for taking the same into consideration; and notice thereof in writing shall be forthwith given, by the speaker, to the petitioners and the sitting members, or their respective agents, accompanied with an order to them to attend the house, at the time appointed, by themselves, their counsel, or agent.

After the present session, on complaint of undue election, &c. a precise time to be fixed for considering thereof.

Speaker to give notice thereof, and order attendance.

2. Provided

2. Provided always, That no such petition shall be taken into consideration within fourteen days after the appointment of the committee of privileges. *But not within 14 days after appointment of committee of privileges.*

3. Provided also, That the house may alter the day and hour so appointed for taking such petition into consideration, and appoint some subsequent day and hour for the same as occasion shall require; giving to the respective parties the like notice of such alteration, and order to attend on the said subsequent day and hour, as aforesaid. *House may alter the time on like notice and order.*

4. And be it further enacted, That at the time appointed for taking such petition into consideration, and previous to the reading of the order of the day for that purpose, the serjeant at arms shall be directed to go with the mace to the places adjacent, and require the immediate attendance of the members on the business of the house; and that after his return the house shall be counted, and if there be less than one hundred members present, the order for taking such petition into consideration shall be immediately adjourned to a particular hour on the following day, *Sunday* and *Christmas-day* always excepted; and the house shall then adjourn to the said day; and the proceedings of all committees, subsequent to such notice from the said serjeant, shall be void; and, on the said following day, the house shall proceed in the same manner; and so, from day to day, till there be an attendance of one hundred members at the reading of the order of the day, to take such petition into consideration. *Serjeant at arms, before the reading of the order of the day, to require the attendance of the members: At his return, house to be counted. For want of 100 members, to adjourn, Till 100 be present.*

5. And

5. And be it further enacted, That if after summoning the members, and counting the house as aforesaid, one hundred members shall be found to be present, the petitioners, by themselves, their counsel, or agents, and the counsel or agents of the sitting members, shall be ordered to attend at the bar, and then the door of the house shall be locked, and no member shall be suffered to enter into or depart from the house until the petitioners, their counsel, or agents, and the counsel or agents for the sitting members, shall be directed to withdraw, as herein-after is mentioned; and when the door shall be locked, as aforesaid, the order of the day shall be read, and the names of all the members of the house, written or printed on distinct pieces of parchment or paper, being all as near as may be of equal size, and rolled up in the same manner, shall be put in equal numbers into six boxes or glasses, to be placed on the table for that purpose, and shall there be shaken together; and then the clerk or clerk assistant attending the house shall publicly draw out of the said six boxes or glasses, alternately, the said pieces of parchment or paper, and deliver the same to the speaker, to be by him read to the house; and so shall continue to do, until forty-nine names of the members then present be drawn.

In presence of 100, The petitioners, &c. to be ordered to the bar.

Names of the members to be put into six boxes or glasses; to be drawn alternately, and read by the Speaker, till 49 be drawn.

6. Provided always, That if the name of any member who shall have given his vote at the election so complained of as aforesaid, or shall be a petitioner complaining of an undue election or return, or against whose return a petition shall be then

Voting members at the election,

or complainants,

then depending, or whose return shall not have been brought in fourteen days, shall be drawn; his name shall be set aside, with the names of those who are absent from the house.

To be set aside.

7. Provided also, That if the name of any member of sixty years of age or upwards be drawn, he shall be excused from serving on the select committee, to be appointed as herein-after is mentioned, if he require it, and verify the cause of such requisition upon oath.

All above 60 years old excused,

8. Provided also, That if the name of any member who has served in such select committee during the same session be drawn, he shall, if he require it, be excused from serving again in any such select committee, unless the house shall, before the day appointed for taking the said petition into consideration, have resolved, that the number of members who have not served on such select committee, in the same session, is insufficient to fulfil the purposes of this act, respecting the choice of such select committee.

Or those who have served on select committees in the same session,

Unless the number who have not served be insufficient.

9. Provided always, That no member, who after having been appointed to serve in any such select committee shall, on account of inability or accident, have been excused from attending the same throughout, shall be deemed to have served on any such select committee.

Members excused shall not be deemed to have served.

10. And be it further enacted, That if any other member shall offer and verify upon oath any other excuse, the substance of the allegations so verified upon oath shall be taken down by the said clerk, in order that the same may be afterwards entered on the journals, and the opinion of the

Members verifying other excuses, allegation to be entered.

the house shall be taken thereon; and if the house shall resolve, that the said member is unable to serve, or cannot without great and manifest detriment serve, in such select committee, he also shall be excused from such service.

And if the house resolve that they are unable, &c.
Are to be excused.

11. And be it further enacted, That instead of the members so set aside and excused, the names of other members shall be drawn; who may, in like manner, be set aside or excused, and others drawn to supply their places, until the whole number of forty-nine members, not liable to be so set aside or excused, shall be compleat; and the petitioners, or their agents, shall then name one, and the sitting members, or their agents, another, from among the members then present, whose names shall not have been drawn, to be added to those who shall have been so chosen by lot.

Instead of whom, others to be drawn to compleat the number 49, &c.
Petitioners may name one, and sitting members another,

12. Provided always, That either of the members so nominated shall or may be set aside, for any of the same causes as those chosen by lot; or shall, if he require it, be excused from serving on the said select committee; and the party who nominated the member so set aside or excused, shall nominate another in his stead, and so continue to do as often as the case shall happen, until his nominee is admitted.

Who may for like causes be set aside,
Or excused,
And others named.

13. And be it further enacted, That as soon as the said forty-nine members shall have been so chosen by lot, and the two members to be added thereunto shall have been so nominated as aforesaid, the door of the house shall be opened, and the house may proceed upon any other business; and

Door to be opened, and the house may proceed on other business.

lists

lists of the forty-nine members, so chosen by lot shall then be given to the petitioners, their counsel, or agents, and the counsel or agents for the sitting members, who shall immediately withdraw, together with the clerk appointed to attend the said select committee; and the said petitioners and sitting members, their counsel or agents, beginning on the part of the petitioners, shall alternately strike off one of the said forty-nine members, until the said number shall be reduced to thirteen; and the said clerk, within one hour at farthest from the time of the parties withdrawing from the house, shall deliver in to the house the names of the thirteen members then remaining; and the said thirteen members, together with the two members nominated as aforesaid, shall be sworn at the table, well and truly to try the matter of the petition referred to them, and a true judgement to give according to the evidence; and shall be a select committee to try and determine the merits of the return or election appointed by the house to be that day taken into consideration; and the house shall order the said select committee to meet at a certain time to be fixed by the house, which time shall be within twenty-four hours of the appointment of the said select committee, unless a *Sunday* or *Christmas-day* shall intervene; and the place of their meeting and sitting shall be some convenient room or place adjacent to the house of commons, or court of requests, properly prepared for that purpose.

14. Provided always, That on the parties withdrawing as aforesaid, the house shall continue sitting;

Lists of the 49 to be then given to the petitioners, &c.

Who with the clerk are to withdraw,

And to strike off one alternately, till the number be reduced to 13;

Clerk within one hour to deliver a list of them;

And they, with the nominees shall be sworn a select committee.

House to order them to meet in 24 hours.

On withdrawing the members not to do ought till the meeting of committee be fixed.

fitting; and the said fifty-one members, so chosen and nominated, shall not depart the house till the time for the meeting of the said select committee shall be fixed.

Petitioners, &c. declaring that any member drawn is intended for a nominee,

15. Provided always, and be it further enacted, That if upon the drawing out the name of any member by lot, as aforesaid, the said petitioners or sitting members, or their agents, shall declare, that such member is intended to be one of the two nominees to be nominated by them respectively,

And member consenting thereto,

and if such member shall consent to such nomination, the name of such member so drawn by lot shall be set aside, and, unless objected to

He is to serve as such,
And another to be drawn to supply his place;

as aforesaid, he shall serve as such nominee, and the name of another member shall be drawn to supply his place, to complete the number of forty-nine members to be drawn by lot; and if the said petitioners or sitting members, or their agents, shall not respectively nominate a member then present, who shall be admitted according to the directions of this act, then the want of such nomination shall be supplied, by drawing out, instead thereof, the name of one or two members, as the case shall require; who shall be drawn by lot in the like manner, and subject to the like objections and excuses as the other forty-nine members already drawn by lot, and shall be added to the lists of the said forty-nine members, and shall be liable to be struck off in the same manner;

But on neglect of nomination,

Deficiencies to be supplied by lot;

Leaving always 15 as a select committee.

leaving always the number of fifteen members in the whole, and no more, as a select committee for the purposes aforesaid.

16. And,

16. And, for the greater dispatch and certainty in the proceeding herein-before described, be it further enacted, That the names of all the members so written and rolled up as herein-before directed, shall, previous to the day appointed for taking any such petition into consideration, be prepared by the said clerk, or clerk assistant, and by him put into a box or parcel, in the presence of the Speaker, together with an attestation, signed by the said clerk, or clerk assistant, purporting, that the names of all the members were by him put therein the   day of   in the year   which said box or parcel the Speaker shall seal with his own seal; and to the outside thereof shall annex an attestation, signed by himself, purporting, that the said box or parcel was on the   day of   in the year   made up in his presence, in the manner directed by this act; and that as soon as the parties shall be withdrawn as aforesaid, and before the house shall enter on any other business, any member may require, that the names of all the members, which remain undrawn, shall be drawn, and read aloud by the said clerk or clerk assistant.

Previous to taking Petition into consideration,

Clerk to put the names of the members drawn into a box or parcel, and attest the same;

Speaker to seal the same, and attest the making up thereof in his presence.

Names of Members undrawn may be read by the clerk.

17. And be it further enacted, That the said select committee shall, on their meeting, elect a chairman from among such of the members thereof as shall have been chosen by lot; and if in the election of a chairman there be an equal number of voices, the member whose name was first drawn in the house shall have a casting voice; so likewise, in case there should ever be occasion for electing

Chairman to be elected out of members chosen by lot;

And in case of equality in election,

Member first drawn to have a casting voice.

electing a new chairman, on the death, or necessary absence of the chairman first elected.

Select committee impowered to send for persons, &c.

Examine witnesses,

And determine finally.

House thereupon to confirm, or alter the return;

Or issue writ for new election.

18. And be it further enacted, That the said select committee shall have power to send for persons, papers, and records; and shall examine all the witnesses who come before them upon oath; and shall try the merits of the return, or election, or both; and shall determine, by a majority of voices of the said select committee, whether the petitioners or the sitting members, or either of them, be duly returned or elected, or whether the election be void; which determination shall be final between the parties to all intents and purposes; and the house, on being informed thereof by the chairman of the said select committee, shall order the same to be entered in their journals, and give the necessary directions for confirming or altering the return, or for the issuing a new writ for a new election, or for carrying the said determination into execution, as the case may require.

Select committee not to adjourn for more than 24 hours without leave.

If House then sitting, business to be stayed,

And motion made for further adjournment.

19. And be it further enacted, That the said select committe shall sit every day (*Sunday* and *Christmas-day* only excepted) and shall never adjourn for a longer time than twenty-four hours, unless a *Sunday* or a *Christmas-day* intervene, without leave first obtained from the house, upon motion, and special cause assigned for a longer adjournment; and in case the house shall be sitting at the time to which the said select committee is adjourned, then the business of the house shall be stayed, and a motion shall be made for a further adjournment, for any time to be fixed by the house, not exceeding twenty-four hours,

hours, unless a *Sunday* or *Christmas-day* intervene.

20. And be it further enacted, That where the time prescribed by this act for the meeting, sitting, or adjournment of the said select committee, shall, by the intervention of a *Sunday* or *Christmas-day*, exceed twenty-four hours, such meeting, sitting, or adjournment, shall be within twenty-four hours from the time of appointing or fixing the same, exclusive of such *Sunday* or *Christmas-day*.

Sunday or Christmas day intervening not to be deemed included.

21. And be it further enacted, That no member of the said select committee shall be allowed to absent himself from the same, without leave obtained from the house, or an excuse allowed by the house at the next sitting thereof, on special cause shewn and verified upon oath; and the said select committee shall never sit, until all the members to whom such leave has not been granted, nor excuse allowed, are met; and in case they shall not all meet within one hour after the time to which the said select committee shall have been adjourned, a further adjournment shall be made in the manner as before directed, and reported, with the cause thereof, to the house.

Select committee-man not to absent without leave,

nor committee to sit, till all, who have not leave, be met.

On failure of meeting within one hour, a further adjournment to be made, and reported, with the cause thereof.

22. And be it further enacted, That the chairman of the said select committee shall, at the next meeting of the house, always report the name of every member thereof who shall have been absent therefrom without such leave or excuse as aforesaid; and such member shall be directed to attend the house at the next sitting thereof, and shall then be ordered to be taken into the custody

Chairman, at next meeting to report absentees,

who are to be directed to attend next sitting;

tody of the serjeant at arms attending the house, for such neglect of his duty, and otherwise punished or censured at the discretion of the house; unless it shall appear to the house, by facts specially stated and verified upon oath, that such member was, by a sudden accident, or by necessity, prevented from attending the said select committee.

and be censured or punished at discretion,

unless absence proved unavoidable.

23. And be it further enacted, That if more than two members of the said select committee shall on any account be absent therefrom, the said select committee shall adjourn in the manner herein-before directed; and so, from time to time, until thirteen members are assembled.

If 13 do not attend, committee to adjourn;

24. And be it further enacted, That in case the number of members able to attend the said select committee shall, by death or otherwise, be unavoidably reduced to less than thirteen, and shall so continue for the space of three sitting days, the said select committee shall be dissolved, and another chosen to try and determine the matter of such petition in manner aforesaid; and all the proceedings of the said former select committee shall be void, and of no effect.

if less for 3 days, then to be dissolved and another chosen;

and past proceedings to be void.

25. And be it further enacted, That if the said select committee shall come to any resolution other than the determination above mentioned, they shall, if they think proper, report the same to the house for their opinion, at the same time that the chairman of the said select committee shall inform the house of such determination; and the house may confirm or disagree with such reso-

Resolutions of committee, other than determination of complaint,

may be reported,

and the house may make order thereon.

resolution, and make such orders thereon, as to them shall seem proper.

26. Provided always, That if any person summoned by the said select committee, shall disobey such summons; or if any witness before such select committee shall prevaricate, or shall otherwise misbehave in giving, or refusing to give evidence; the chairman of the said select committee, by their direction, may at any time, during the course of their proceedings, report the same to the house, for the interposition of their authority or censure, as the case shall require.

Persons disobeying summons, or prevaricating,

to be reported by the chairman.

27. And be it further enacted, That whenever the said select committee shall think it necessary to deliberate amongst themselves, upon any question which shall arise in the course of the trial, or upon the determination thereof, or upon any resolution concerning the matter of the petition referred to them as aforesaid; as soon as the said select committee shall have heard the evidence and counsel on both sides relative thereunto, the room or place wherein they shall sit shall be cleared, if they shall think proper, while the members of the said select committee consider thereof; and all such questions, as well as such determination, and all other resolutions, shall be by a majority of voices; and if the voices shall be equal, the chairman shall have a casting voice.

When committee shall deliberate, room to be cleared.

Questions to be determined by a majority.

Chairman to have a casting voice.

28. Provided always, That no such determination as aforesaid shall be made, nor any question be proposed, unless thirteen members shall be present;

No determination, unless 13 be present;

fent; and no member shall have a vote on such determination, or any other question or resolution, who has not attended during every sitting of the said select committee.

nor any member to vote who has not attended every sitting.

29. And be it further enacted, That the oaths by this act directed to be taken in the house, shall be administered by the said clerk or clerk assistant, in the same manner as the oaths of allegiance and supremacy are administered in the house of commons; and that the oaths by this act directed to be taken before the said select committee, shall be administered by the clerk attending the said select committee; and that all persons who shall be guilty of wilful and corrupt perjury in any evidence which they shall give before the house, or the said select committee, in consequence of the oath which they shall have taken by the direction of this act, shall, on conviction thereof, incur and suffer the like pains and penalties to which any other person, convicted of wilful and corrupt perjury, is liable by the laws and statutes of this realm.

Oaths taken in the house to be administered by the clerk;

and those before the select committee, by the clerk.

Penalties on perjury extended thereto.

30. And be it further enacted, That this act shall continue in force seven years, and till the end of the session of parliament next after the expiration of the said seven years, and no longer.

Act to continue for seven years.

A. D. 1770.

ANNO

ANNO 10º GEORGII III. CAP. 41.

An Act to enable the Speaker of the House of Commons to issue his Warrants to make out new Writs for the Choice of Members to serve in Parliament, in the Room of such Members as shall die during the Recess of Parliament.

WHEREAS many inconveniencies have happened, and many disorders have been occasioned, for want of more speedy elections of members of the house of commons, in the room of such who have died during the recess of parliament: For remedy whereof, be it enacted by the king's most excellent majesty, by and with the advice and consent of the lords spiritual and temporal and commons in this present parliament assembled, and by the authority of the same, That, from and after the end of the present session of parliament, it shall and may be lawful for the speaker of the house of commons for the time being, during the recess of parliament for more than twenty days, whether by prorogation or adjournment, and he is hereby required to issue his warrants to the clerk of the crown to make out new writs for electing members of the house of commons, in the room of such members who shall happen to die during such recess of parliament, so soon as such speaker shall have had due notice of the decease of such members.

After the end of the present session, the speaker of the house of commons, during recess, may issue warrants for making out writs for new elections.

2. Provided always, That no such warrant shall be issued by the speaker of the house of commons,

Proofs to be certified by two members;

mons, unless the death of such member shall be certified to him by two members of the house of commons, by writing under their hands.

3. Provided always, and be it further enacted, That the speaker of the house of commons shall forthwith, after the receipt of the certificate of the death of such member, cause notice thereof to be inserted in the London Gazette, and shall not issue his warrant till fourteen days after the insertion of such notice in the Gazette; any thing herein contained to the contrary notwithstanding.

and notified by the speaker in the London Gazette.

4. Provided also, and be it further enacted, That nothing herein contained shall extend to authorize the speaker of the house of commons for the time being, to issue his warrant to the clerk of the crown to make out a new writ for the electing a member of the house of commons in the room of any member deceased, unless the return of the writ, by virtue of which such member deceased was elected, shall have been brought into the office of the clerk of the crown, fifteen days at the least before the end of the session of parliament immediately preceding the death of such member.

Speaker not to issue his warrant, unless the return of the writ for election of deceased member be brought to the crown office,

15 days before the end of the preceding session.

A. D. 1770.

ANNO 10º GEORGII III. CAP. 50.

An Act for the further preventing Delays of Justice by reason of Privilege of Parliament.

WHEREAS the several laws heretofore made for restraining the privilege of parliament, with respect to actions or suits commenced and prose-

prosecuted at any time from and immediately after the dissolution or prorogation of any parliament, until a new parliament should meet, or the same be re-assembled, and from and immediately after an adjournment of both houses of parliament for above the space of fourteen days, until both houses should meet or assemble, are insufficient to obviate the inconveniencies arising from the delay of suits by reason of privilege of parliament; whereby the parties often lose the benefit of several terms: For the preventing of all delays the king or his subjects may receive in prosecuting their several rights, titles, debts, dues, demands, or suits, for which they have cause, be it enacted by the king's most excellent majesty, by and with the advice and consent of the lords spiritual and temporal and commons in this present parliament assembled, and by the authority of the same, That from and after the twenty-fourth day of June, 1770, any person or persons shall and may, at any time, commence and prosecute any action or suit in any court of record, or court of equity, or of admiralty, and in all causes matrimonial and testamentary, in any court having cognizance of causes matrimonial and testamentary, against any peer or lord of parliament of Great Britain, or against any of the knights, citizens, and burgesses, and the commissioners for shires and burghs of the house of commons of Great Britain for the time being, or against their or any of their menial or any other servants, or any other person entitled to the privilege of parliament of Great Britain; and no such action,

After 24 June, 1770, suits may be prosecuted in courts of record, equity, or admiralty, and courts having cognizance of causes matrimonial and testamentary, against peers, and members of the house of commons, and their servants, &c.

suit,

suit, or any other process or proceeding thereupon, shall at any time be impeached, stayed, or delayed, by or under colour or pretence of any privilege of parliament.

But the persons of members of the house of commons, not to be arrested or imprisoned.

2. Provided nevertheless, and be it further enacted by the authority aforesaid, That nothing in this act shall extend to subject the person of any of the knights, citizens, and burgesses, or the commissioners of shires and burghs of the house of commons of Great Britain for the time being, to be arrested or imprisoned upon any such suit or proceedings.

Court out of which writ proceeds, may order the issues to be sold, and money arising thereby to be applied to pay costs to plaintiff.

3. And whereas the process by *distringas* is dilatory and expensive: for remedy thereof, be it enacted by the authority aforesaid, That the court, out of which the writ proceeds, may order the issues levied from time to time to be sold, and the money arising thereby to be applied to pay such costs to the plaintiff, as the said court shall think just, under all the circumstances, to order; and

Surplus to be retained till appearance of defendant, &c.

the surplus to be retained until the defendant shall have appeared, or other purpose of the writ be answered.

When purpose is answered, issues to be returned; or, if sold, money remaining to be repaid.

4. Provided always, when the purpose of the writ is answered, That then the said issues shall be returned; or, if sold, what shall remain of the money arising by such sale, shall be repaid to the party distrained upon.

Obedience to rule of the court of king's bench, common pleas, or exchequer, may be enforced by distress infinite.

5. And be it further declared and enacted by the authority aforesaid, That obedience may be enforced to any rule of his majesty's courts of king's bench, common pleas, or exchequer, against any person entitled to privilege of parliament, by

distress

distress infinite, in case any person or persons entitled to the benefit of such rule shall chuse to proceed in that way.

6. And whereas an act was made in the 12th and 13th years of the reign of king William the Third, intituled, 'An act for preventing any inconveniencies that may happen by privilege of parliament;' be it enacted by the authority aforesaid, That from and after the said twenty-fourth day of June, the said act, and also this act, shall extend to that part of Great Britain called *Scotland*. A. D. 1770.

Act 12 and 13 Will. 3.

and this act

extended to Scotland.

ANNO 11° GEORGII III. CAP. 42.

An Act to explain and amend an Act, made in the last Session of Parliament, intituled, 'An Act to regulate the Trials of controverted Elections, or Returns of Members to serve in Parliament.'

WHEREAS an act was passed in the last session of parliament, intituled, 'An act to regulate the trials of controverted elections, or returns of members to serve in parliament;' And whereas further provisions may be necessary to prevent all obstructions and difficulties, which in certain cases may arise in the execution of the said act: Be it therefore enacted by the king's most excellent majesty, by and with the advice and consent of the lords spiritual and temporal and commons in this present parliament assembled, and by the authority of the same, That from and after

10 Geo. 3.

After passing thereof, on complaint of an undue election, &c. notice and orders to be given to parties and their agents.

after the passing of this act, if several parties, on distinct interests or grounds of complaint, shall present separate petitions, complaining of an undue election, or return of a member or members to serve in parliament, the same notices and orders shall be given to all such parties, or their respective agents, as by the said act are directed to be given to the sitting members, or the petitioners therein mentioned, or their respective agents.

Clause in act 10 Geo. 3. repealed.

2. And be it further enacted, That the clause in the said act, which provides that no petition shall be taken into consideration within fourteen days after the appointment of the committee of privileges, be repealed; and that from henceforth no petition, complaining of an undue election, or return of a member or members to serve in parliament, shall be taken into consideration within fourteen days after the commencement of the session of parliament in which it is presented, nor within fourteen days after the return to which it relates, shall be brought into the office of the clerk of the crown.

If at the time of drawing, 49 members cannot be compleated,

3. And be it further enacted, That if at the time of drawing by lot the names of the members, in manner prescribed by the said act, the number of forty-nine members, not set aside nor excused, cannot be compleated, the house shall proceed in

the house to proceed in manner directed by act 10 Geo. 3.

the manner they are directed by the said act to proceed, in case there be less than one hundred members present at the time therein prescribed for counting the house; and so, from day to day, as often as the case shall happen.

4. And

4. And be it further enacted, That on the day appointed for taking any petition, complaining of an undue election, or return of a member or members to serve in parliament, into consideration, the house shall not proceed to any other business whatsoever, except the swearing of members, previous to the reading of the order of the day for that purpose.

On the day appointed for hearing complaints of undue elections, the house shall not proceed to other business previous to the reading the order.

5. And be it further enacted, That if the select committee shall have occasion to apply or report to the house, in relation to adjournment of the said select committee, the absence of the members thereof, or the non-attendance or misbehaviour of witnesses summoned to appear, or appearing before them, and the house shall be then adjourned for more than three days, the said select committee may also adjourn to the day appointed for the meeting of the house.

Manner of adjourning the select committee.

6. And be it further enacted, That if on a complaint by petition of an undue election or return, there shall be more than two parties before the house, on distinct interest, or complaining or complained of upon different grounds, whose right to be elected or returned may be affected by the determination of the said select committee, each of the said parties shall successively strike off a member from the forty-nine members to be chosen by lot, until the same number be reduced to thirteen, in the same manner as by the said act is directed for the striking off a member alternately by the parties therein mentioned; and the lists of the forty-nine members chosen by lot shall, for this purpose, be given to all the said parties,

If on complaint of undue election, there shall be more than two parties on distinct interest,

each party shall strike off a member of the 49, successively, until reduced to 13.

N 3 and

and the order in which the said parties shall so strike off the said members shall be determined by lot after they are withdrawn from the bar, and in such case, neither of the said parties (there being more than two) shall be permitted to name a member to be added to the members so drawn by lot as aforesaid; but that as soon as the list of thirteen members shall be returned by the parties to the house, such thirteen members shall immediately withdraw, and shall by themselves chuse two members then present in the house, whose names shall not have been drawn, to be added to the said thirteen members; and shall, within one hour from the time of their withdrawing, report the names of such two members to the house; which two members shall be liable to be set aside, on the like objections for which nominees may be set aside by virtue of the said act; and in case such two members, or either of them, shall be set aside for any of the causes aforesaid, then the said thirteen members shall chuse one or two other members, as the case shall require, until two members are chosen, against whom none of the objections to nominees mentioned in the said act shall be taken and allowed; and that the names of such two members shall be then added to the said list of thirteen members; and all the said fifteen members shall be sworn at the table, and they shall be the select committee appointed for the purposes expressed in this and the said former act.

When the list is returned to the house, the 15 members to withdraw;

and, within one hour, report the names of such two members.

In case such two members shall be set aside, they sha'l chuse others, until two are not objected against.

7. And be it further enacted, That where the said nominees are by this act directed to be named

Where the nominees are directed to be

named by the said thirteen members, no member present at the time of the ballot shall depart from the house until the time for the meeting of the said select committee shall be fixed.

A. D. 1771

ANNO 11° GEORGII III. CAP. 55.

An Act to incapacitate John Burnett, *&c. and others from voting at Elections of Members to serve in Parliament, and for the preventing Bribery and Corruption in the Election of Members to serve in Parliament for the Borough of* New Shoreham, *in the County of Sussex.*

'WHEREAS a wicked and corrupt society calling itself the Christian society, hath for several years subsisted in the borough of *New Shoreham* in the county of Sussex, and consisted of a great majority of persons having a right to vote at elections of members to serve in parliament for the said borough; and whereas it appears that the chief end of the institution of the said society, was for the purpose of selling, from time to time, the seat or seats in parliament for the said borough; and whereas *John Burnett*, &c. and others were members of the said society:' In order therefore to prevent such unlawful practices for the future, and that the said borough from henceforth be duly represented in parliament; be it enacted by the king's most excellent majesty, by and with the advice and consent of the lords spiritual and temporal and commons in this present

sent parliament assembled, and by the authority of the same, That the said *John Burnett,* &c. and others shall be, and by virtue of this act are, from henceforth incapacitated and disabled from giving any vote at any election for the chusing a member or members to serve in parliament.

2. And be it further enacted by the authority aforesaid, That from henceforth it shall and may be lawful to and for every freeholder, being above the age of twenty-one years, who shall have within the rape of *Bramber,* in the said county of Sussex, a freehold of the clear yearly value of forty shillings, to give his vote at every election of a burgess or burgesses to serve in parliament, for the said borough of *New Shoreham.*

Freeholders above 21 years of age, of 40s. annually, entitled to vote.

3. And be it further enacted by the authority aforesaid, That the right of election of a member or members to serve in parliament, for the said borough of *New Shoreham,* shall be and is hereby declared to be in such freeholders as aforesaid, and in the persons who by the custom and usage of the said borough have, or shall hereafter have, a right to vote at such election, those whose names are mentioned herein and incapacitated and disabled by this act only excepted; and the constable or other proper officer for the time being, to whom the return of such precept or writ does belong, is hereby required to return the person or persons, to serve in parliament for the said borough, who shall have the major number of votes of such freeholders, and other persons having a right to vote at such election, (except such persons as are herein-

Right of election, in whom vested.

herein-before excepted) any law or usage to the contrary notwithstanding.

4. And be it further enacted by the authority aforesaid, that every such freeholder before he is admitted to poll at any election for the said borough, shall, if required by the candidates, or any of them, or any other person having a right to vote at the said election, first take the oath, (or being one of the people called *Quakers*, the solemn affirmation) following, *viz.* Freeholder, before admitted to poll, to take the following

" You shall swear, or being a *Quaker* solemnly affirm, That you are a freeholder in the rape of *Bramber*, in the county of Sussex, and have a freehold estate, consisting of Oath.

(specifying the nature thereof, and if it consists in messuages, lands or tithes, in whose occupation the same are; and if in rent, the names of the owners or possessors of the tenements, out of which such rent is issuing, or some of them) lying or being at   within the rape of *Bramber*, in the county of Sussex, of the clear yearly value of forty shillings, over and above all rents and charges payable out of or in respect of the same; and that you have been in the actual possession or receipt of the rents and profits thereof, for your own use above twelve kalendar months; (or that the same came to you within the time aforesaid by descent, marriage, marriage settlement, devise, or promotion to a benefice in a church, or by promotion to an office) and that such freehold estate has not been granted or made to you fraudulently, on purpose to qualify you to give your vote; and
that

"that the place of your abode is at   in   and that you are twenty-one years of age as you believe; and that you have not been polled before at this election."

Which oath or solemn affirmation, the constable, or other proper officer to whom the return of any writ or precept for such election shall belong, is hereby required to administer; and in case any freeholder or other person, taking the said oath or affirmation hereby appointed, shall thereby commit wilful perjury, and be thereof convicted; or if any person shall unlawfully and corruptly procure or suborn any freeholder or other person to take the said oath or affirmation, in order to be polled, whereby he shall commit such wilful perjury, and shall be thereof convicted, he and they, for every such offence respectively, shall incur such penalties as are inflicted on persons guilty of perjury or subornation of perjury, in and by two acts of parliament, one made in the 5th year of the reign of Queen Elizabeth, (intituled, An act for punishing such persons as shall procure or commit wilful perjury, or suborn or procure any person to commit any wilful or corrupt perjury); and the other made in the 2d year of his late majesty's reign, (intituled, An act for the more effectual preventing and further punishment of forgery, perjury, and subornation of perjury, and to make it felony to steal bonds, notes, or other securities for payment of money), contrary to the said acts.

Persons guilty of perjury, &c. liable to the penalties as directed by

Act 5 Eliz. and

Act 2 Geo. 2.

5. And be it further enacted by the authority aforesaid, that such constable, or other proper officer

Constable to back a precept the day of the receipt thereof.

officer to whom any writ or precept shall be directed for making any election for the said borough, shall, upon the reception of such writ or precept, indorse, upon the back thereof the day of his receipt thereof, in the presence of the party from whom he received such precept; and shall forthwith cause public notice to be given within the said borough of *New Shoreham*, and at the towns of *Bramber* and *Steyning*, in the said county of Sussex, by fixing up a notice thereof in writing on the market houses or on the doors of the churches of the said towns, of the day of election; and shall proceed to election thereupon within the space of twelve days, and not less than eight days, next after his receipt of the same precept.

6. And be it further enacted, by the authority aforesaid, That this act shall be publicly read at every election for the said borough of *New Shoreham*, immediately after the acts directed by any act of parliament to be read thereat, and before the persons present shall proceed to make such election.

The act to be read publicly.

A. D. 1771.

ANNO 12° GEORGII III. CAP. 21.

An Act for giving relief in Proceedings upon Writs of Mandamus *for the Admission of Freemen into Corporations; and for other Purposes therein mentioned.*

WHEREAS divers persons, who have a right to be admitted citizens, burgesses, or freemen, of divers cities, towns corporate, boroughs, cinque ports, and places, within that part of Great Britain called England and Wales, being refused to be admitted thereto, have, in many cases, no other ordinary remedy to procure themselves to be admitted to the franchises of being citizens, burgesses, or freemen, than by writs of *mandamus*, the proceedings on which are very dilatory and expensive; and, although any such writ of *mandamus* is obeyed, the person applying is nevertheless put to great and unnecessary trouble, delay, and expence; and whereas by the laws now in being, in many cases, no provision is made for giving costs to the party suing out any such writ where the same is obeyed: For remedy whereof, be it enacted, by the king's most excellent majesty, by and with the advice and consent of the lords spiritual and temporal and commons in this present parliament assembled, and by the authority of the same, That from and after the first day of August, 1772,

After August 1, 1772, any per-

where any person shall be entitled to be admitted a citizen, burgess, or freemen, of any such city, town corporate, borough, cinque port, or place, and shall apply to the mayor, or other person, officer, or officers, in such city, town corporate, borough, cinque port, or place, who hath or have authority to admit citizens, burgesses, and freemen therein, to be admitted a citizen, burgess, or freemen thereof; and shall give notice, specifying the nature of his claim, to such mayor, or other officer or officers, that if he or they shall not so admit such person a citizen, burgess, or freeman, within one month from the time of such notice, the court of king's bench will be applied to for a writ of *mandamus*, to compel such admission; and if such mayor, or other officer or officers, shall, after such notice, refuse or neglect to admit such person, and a writ of *mandamus* shall afterwards issue to compel such mayor, or other officer or officers, to make such admission, and, in obedience to such writ, such persons shall be admitted by the said mayor, or other officer or officers, a citizen, burgess, or freeman of such city, town corporate, borough, cinque port, or place, then such person shall (unless the court shall see just cause to the contrary) obtain and receive from the said mayor, or other officer or officers, so neglecting or refusing as aforesaid, all the costs to which he shall have been put in applying for obtaining and serving such writ of *mandamus*, and enforcing the same, by a rule to be made by the court out of which such writ shall issue, for the

pay-

[marginal notes: son entitled to be admitted a citizen, &c. of any city, and applying to the mayor, &c. for that purpose, giving him notice, specifying the nature of his claim, &c. If such mayor, &c. shall refuse to admit such person, and a mandamus shall issue, for compelling his admission, the mayor to pay all costs.]

payment thereof, together with the costs of applying for, obtaining, serving, and enforcing the said rule; and if the rule so to be made shall not be obeyed, then the same shall be enforced in such manner as other rules made by the said court are or may be enforced by law.

<small>Freemen to be admitted to inspect the entries of admission, &c. and to take copies thereof.</small>

2. And, in order that it may be known what persons are, from time to time, admitted freemen or burgesses of any city, corporation, borough, or cinque port, be it further enacted by the authority aforesaid, That the mayor, bailiff, town clerk, or other officer of any city, corporation, borough, or cinque port, having the custody of, or power over, the records of the same, shall, upon the demand of any two freemen or burgesses, permit such freemen or burgesses, and their agent or agents, at any time whatsoever, between the hours of nine in the morning and three in the afternoon, to inspect the entries of admission of freemen, burgesses, or other inferior corporaters, and to take copies or extracts therefrom, paying for every such inspection two shillings and six-pence; and for every such copy or extract, not exceeding seventy-two words, the sum of four-pence; and so in proportion for all such copies or extracts: and if any mayor, bailiff, town clerk, or other officer, shall refuse or deny the inspection of any such entries, or to give copies or extracts thereof, as before directed; he or they shall, for every such denial or refusal, forfeit and pay the sum of one hundred pounds to any person who shall sue for the same; to be recovered, with full costs of suit, by action

<small>Mayor, bailiff, &c. denying inspection of such entries, or to give copies thereof, shall, for every refusal, forfeit 100l.</small>

of debt, in any of his majesty's courts of record at Westminster; in which action, it shall be sufficient for the plaintiff to alledge in his declaration, that the defendant or the defendants is or are indebted to the said plaintiff in the sum of one hundred pounds for money had and received to his use; provided that such action shall be commenced within the space of one year after the cause of it shall have arisen, and not afterwards.

to be recovered by action of debt.

to be commenced within one year after the cause shall have arisen.

A. D. 1772.

ANNO 14° GEORGII III. CAP. 15.

An Act for making perpetual Two Acts, passed in the 10th and 11th Years of the Reign of His present Majesty for regulating the Trials of controverted Elections, or Returns of Members to serve in Parliament.

WHEREAS an act, passed in the 10th year of the reign of his present majesty, intituled, 'An act to regulate the trials of controverted elections, or returns of members to serve in parliament,' which act was made to continue for a limited time only; and whereas another act, passed in the 11th year of the reign of his said majesty, intituled, 'An act to explain and amend an act, made in the last session of parliament, intituled, An act to regulate the trials of controverted elections, or returns of members to serve in parliament;' and whereas the provisions of the said

Act 10 Geo. 3.

and

Act 11 Geo. 3.

said recited acts are well adapted to procure to the commons of this realm a free and impartial trial of controverted elections of members to serve in parliament, and have been found, by experience, to be practicable and beneficial: May it therefore please your majesty that it may be enacted, and be it enacted by the king's most excellent majesty, by and with the advice and consent of the lords spiritual and temporal and commons in this present parliament assembled, and by the authority of the same, that the said recited acts, passed in the 10th and 11th years of his present majesty, shall be, and are hereby made, perpetual.   A. D. 1774.

made perpetual by this act.

ANNO 14° GEORGII III. CAP. 58.

An Act for repealing an Act made in the First Year of the Reign of King Henry the Fifth, and so much of several Acts of the 8th, 10th, and 23d Years of King Henry the Sixth, as relates to the Residence of Persons to be elected Members to serve in Parliament, or of the Persons by whom they are to be chosen.

WHEREAS an act of parliament was made in the first year of the reign of king Henry the fifth, ordaining and establishing what sort of people shall be chosen, and who shall be the chusers of the knights and burgesses of the parliament; and also an act in the 8th year of the reign of king Henry the sixth, ordaining what sort

Act 1 Hen. 5.

Act 8 Hen. 6.

sort of men shall be chusers, and who shall be chosen knights of the parliament: and also an act in the 10th year of the reign of his said majesty, requiring certain things in him who shall be a chuser of the knights of parliament; and also an act in the 23d year of the reign of his said majesty, directing who shall be knights for the parliament, the manner of their election, and the remedy where one is chosen and another returned: and whereas several provisions contained in the said acts have been found, by long usage, to be unnecessary, and are become obsolete; in order therefore to obviate all doubts that may arise upon the same, may it please your majesty that it may be enacted, and be it enacted by the king's most excellent majesty, by and with the advice and consent of the lords spiritual and temporal and commons in this present parliament assembled, and by the authority of the same, That the said act, made in the 1st year of the reign of his majesty king Henry the Fifth, and every part thereof; and so much of the said several acts, made in the 8th, the 10th, and the 23d years of the reign of his majesty king Henry the 6th, as relates to the residence of persons to be elected members to serve in parliament, or of the persons by whom they are to be chosen, shall be, and the same are hereby repealed.

Act 10 Hen. 6.

and

Act 23 Hen. 6.

So far as relates to the residence of persons to be elected members of parliament, &c.

repealed.

A. D. 1774.

ANNO 15° GEORGII III. CAP. 36.

An Act to explain and amend an Act made in the 10th Year of the Reign of his present Majesty, intituled, An Act to enable the Speaker of the House of Commons to issue his Warrants to make out New Writs for the Choice of Members to serve in Parliament, in the room of such Members as shall die during the Recess of Parliament; and for enabling the Speaker of the House of Commons to make out New Writs for the Choice of Members to serve in Parliament, in the room of such Members as shall, during the recess of Parliament, become Peers of Great Britain, and be summoned to Parliament; and for suspending the Execution of the said Act with respect to the Borough of Shaftesbury, *in the County of* Dorset, *during the next Recess of Parliament.*

10 Geo. 3.

Whereas by an act, passed in the 10th year of his present majesty's reign, (intituled, An act to enable the speaker of the house of commons to issue his warrants to make out new writs for the choice of members to serve in parliament, in the room of such members as shall die during the recess of parliament,) the speaker of the house of commons is required to issue his warrants to the clerk of the crown to make out new writs in the room of members who die during a recess of parliament for more than twenty days, whether by prorogation or adjournment, the deaths

deaths of such members having been certified in writing to him under the hands of two members of the house of commons, and fourteen days notice being first given by the speaker of the house of commons thereof, and of his intentions to issue such warrants, by inserting such notice in the London Gazette; and whereas inconveniencies might arise if such notice should be inserted in the London Gazette, and such warrant should be issued by the speaker of the house of commons, in the case of the death of a member, which shall not be certified to the speaker of the house of commons so long before the actual meeting of the house of commons for the dispatch of business as that the said notice may be inserted, and the fourteen days expire, before the said meeting of the house of commons; or in the case of the death of a member against whose election or return a petition had been presented to the house of commons, and was depending at the time of such prorogation or adjournment: For preventing the same, be it declared and enacted by the king's most excellent majesty, by and with the advice and consent of the lords spiritual and temporal and commons in this present parliament assembled, and by the authority of the same, That nothing in the said act contained extends, or shall be construed to extend, to require the speaker of the house of commons to insert notice in the London Gazette, or issue his warrant to make out a new writ in the room of any member deceased, whose death shall not be duly certified to the speaker of the house of commons so long before the actual meeting of the house of commons

Explanation of said act with respect to the issuing of writs for members to serve in parliament.

for the dispatch of business as that the speaker of the house of commons may be able to insert notice thereof, and of his intention to issue such warrant, fourteen days at the least before such meeting of the house of commons; or for the election of a member to serve in parliament for any county, shire, city, borough, cinque port, or place, in the room of any member deceased, against whose election or return for such county, shire, city, borough, cinque port, or place, a petition had been presented to the house of commons, and was actually depending at the time of such prorogation or adjournment.

2. And whereas it would tend still further to promote the purposes of the said act of the 10th year of his present majesty, and to prevent those inconveniences and disorders which may be occasioned for want of more speedy elections of members of the house of commons, if the provisions of the said act were extended to the cases of members who shall become peers of Great Britain, be it enacted by the authority aforesaid, That from and after the end of this present session of parliament, it shall and may be lawful for the speaker of the house of commons for the time being, during the recess of parliament for more than twenty days, whether by prorogation or adjournment, and he is hereby required to issue his warrants to the clerk of the crown, to make out new writs for electing members of the house of commons in the room of such members as shall, during such recess, become peers of Great Britain, as soon as he shall receive notice, by a certificate under the hands of two members of the house of commons,

Speaker to issue his warrants, during a recess, for electing members in the room of those become peers of Great Britain.

that a writ of summons hath been issued under the great seal of Great Britain to summon the said members to parliament.

3. Provided also, That after the receipt of such certificate, the like notice in the London Gazette shall be given by the speaker, as is required in the case of members deceased; and such notice and warrant shall be subject and liable to the same exceptions and regulations as are required by the said act and by this present act, in the case of notices to be given, and warrants to be issued in the room of members dying during a recess.

The like notice to be given as of members deceased.

4. And whereas it has appeared to the house of commons, that there was the most notorious bribery and corruption at the last election of members to serve in this present parliament for the borough of *Shafton* otherwise *Shaftesbury*, in the county of *Dorset*; and whereas in consequence thereof, and until the house of commons shall have an opportunity of making a further enquiry into the persons concerned in the said bribery and corruption, the house of commons have provided, that no writ do issue for the electing of a burgess to serve in parliament for the said borough during the present session of parliament; but as it may happen that, during the next recess of parliament, the speaker of the house of commons may, by virtue of the said recited act of the 10th year of his present majesty, be required to issue his warrant to the clerk of the crown to make out a new writ for the electing of a burgess to serve in parliament for the said borough of *Shaftesbury*; and whereas the issuing such writ, during the next re-

cess of parliament, might tend to defeat those measures which it may be proper to take in consequence of the said notorious bribery and corruption: Be it enacted by the authority aforesaid, That the speaker of the house of commons shall not be enabled, by virtue of the said recited act, to issue his warrant to the clerk of the crown to make out a new writ for the said borough of *Shafton* otherwise *Shaftesbury*, in the county of *Dorset*, during the said next recess of Parliament.

Speaker not to issue any warrant, &c. for the borough of Shafton.

A. D. 1775.

ANNO 20° GEORGII III. CAP. I.

An act for holding the ensuing Election of a Knight of the Shire for the County of Southampton, *at the Town of* New Alresford *in the said County.*

WHEREAS by an act, made in the 8th year of the reign of his late majesty king George the Second, intituled, 'An act for regulating the quartering of soldiers during the time of the elections of members to serve in parliament,' it is enacted, That when and as often as any election of any member or members to serve in parliament shall be appointed to be made, the secretary at war, or the person who shall officiate in the place of the secretary at war, shall, at some convenient time before the day appointed for such election, issue and send forth proper orders for the removal of all soldiers, who shall be quartered

8 Geo. 2.

or billetted in any city, borough, town, or place, where such election shall be appointed to be made, out of every such city, borough, town, or place, one day at least before the day appointed for such election, to the distance of two or more miles from such city, borough, town, or place, and not to make any nearer approach thereto, until one day at the least after the poll to be taken at such election shall be ended, and the poll books closed, under certain penalties and disabilities in the said act mentioned; and whereas by an act, made in the 7th and 8th years of king William the Third, for the further regulating elections of members to serve in parliament, and for the preventing irregular proceedings of sheriffs, and other officers, in electing and returning such members, it is enacted, That upon every election of any knigt of the shire, the sheriff shall hold his county court at the most public and usual place of election, and where the same has been usually held for forty years; and whereas an election is soon to be held for a knight of the shire for the county of *Southampton*, and if not otherwise provided for, will be held at the city of *Winchester* (being the usual place for holding elections for the said county) at which place many French and Spanish prisoners are now confined, for the safe keeping of which a number of troops or soldiers are absolutely necessary, and cannot be removed from thence without manifest danger, as well to the inhabitants of the said city and all persons resorting thereto, as to the public in general: Be it therefore enacted by the king's most excellent majesty, by

Enfuing election for Hampshire to be held at New Alresford, instead of Winchester.

by and with the advice and consent of the lords spiritual and temporal and commons in this present parliament assembled, and by the authority of the same, that the said election shall be begun and held at the town of *New Alresford*, in the said county of *Southampton*; and that the county court for the said county at which the said election shall be made (whether the same county court be holden by adjournment, or otherwise) shall be holden at the said town of *New Alresford*, and not at *Winchester* aforesaid; and the adjournment of the said county court, if any such has been made, and is now depending, to the said city of *Winchester*, or any other place, shall be deemed and taken to be legally made to the said town of *New Alresford*; any law, usage, or custom to the contrary notwithstanding; and the sheriff of the said county, or his deputy, are hereby authorised and required to adjourn the poll, from the said town of *New Alresford*, to *Newport* in the *Isle of Wight*, in the manner directed in and by an act made in the 7th and 8th years of the reign of king William the Third, (intituled, An Act for the further regulating elections of members to serve in parliament, and for the preventing irregular proceedings of sheriffs, and other officers in the electing and returning such members,) in relation to adjourning the poll from the said city of *Winchester*.

A. D. 1780.

ANNO 20° GEORGII III. CAP. 17.

An Act to remove certain Difficulties relative to Voters at County Elections.

WHEREAS the several laws now in being for ascertaining the rights of persons claiming to vote in the elections of knights of the shire to serve in parliament, for that part of Great Britain called England, are difficult to be carried into execution, and great delays and inconveniencies have been occasioned by the numberless disputes which have arisen at county elections concerning such rights: for remedy whereof, be in enacted by the king's most excellent majesty, by and with the advice and consent of the lords spiritual and temporal and commons in this present parliament assembled, and by the authority of the same, That, from and after the first day of January, 1781, no person shall vote for the electing of any knight or knights of the shire to serve in parliament, within that part of Great Britain called England, or the principality of Wales, in respect of any messuages, lands, or tenements, which have not, for six kalendar months next before such election, being charged or assessed towards some aid granted or to be granted to his majesty, his heirs or successors, by a land tax, (in case any such aid be then granted and assessable,) in the name of the person or persons who shall claim to vote at such election for or in respect

After Jan. 1, 1781, no person to vote at any county election in England, or Wales, who has not been assessed to the land tax for his qualification, 6 months previous to the time of election.

of

of any such messuages, lands, or tenements, or in the name of his or their tenant or tenants, actually occupying the same as tenant or tenants of the owner or landlord thereof.

Certain cases to which this act shall not extend.

2. Provided always, That this act, with respect to such rating and assessing as aforesaid, shall not extend, or be construed to extend, to annuities or fee-farm rents (duly registered) issuing out of any messuages, lands, or tenements, rated or assessed as aforesaid: nor shall the same extend, or be construed to extend, to any person who became entitled to such messuages, lands, or tenements, for which he shall vote, or claim to vote as aforesaid, by descent, marriage, marriage settlement, devise, or promotion to any benefice in a church, or by promotion to an office, within twelve kalendar months next before such election; *Provided the claimant's qualification has been assessed to the land tax, in the name of his predecessor, within two years before the election.* but such person shall be entitled to vote at such election, if the messuages, lands, or tenements, for which he shall vote, or claim to vote, as aforesaid, have been, within two years next before such election, rated or assessed to the land tax, in the name of the person or persons by or through whom such person voting, or claiming to vote, as aforesaid, shall derive his title to the messuages, lands, or tenements, for which he shall vote, or claim to vote, as aforesaid, or in the name of some predecessor, within two years next before such election, of such person claiming to vote in respect of any promotion to any benefice in a church, or promotion to an office, or in the name of the tenant or tenants of such person or persons, such tenant

or

or tenants actually occupying such messuages, lands, or tenements.

3. And be it further enacted, That the commissioners of the land tax for that part of Great Britain called England, or the principality of Wales, at their respective meetings held for appointing assessors of the land tax for the several parishes and places lying within the division for which such commissioners shall act, shall cause to be delivered to each of the said assessors, a printed form of assessment, as set forth in the schedule hereunto annexed; and the said assessors are hereby required to make their assessments according to the said form; and shall make three duplicates of such assessments; and shall (at least fourteen days before such assessment shall be delivered to the commissioners of the land tax for the county, riding, or division, within which the parish or place for which such assessment shall be made shall lie) cause one of the said duplicates, or a fair copy thereof, to be stuck up upon one of the doors of the church or chapel of the parish or place for which such assessment shall be made; but in case such assessment shall be made for an extra-parochial or any other place, where there is not any church or chapel, then such assessment shall be stuck up upon one of the doors of the church or chapel in a parish next adjoining; and if any person or persons (renting, holding, or occupying, any messuages, lands, or tenements, in any such parish or place) shall rent, hold, or occupy messuages, lands, or tenements, belonging to different owners or proprietors, the same shall be separately and distinctly rated

Commissioners of the land tax to deliver to assessors a printed form of an assessment, who are to make their assessments according thereto.

A duplicate of assessments to be stuck up on the door of the parish church, &c.

rated and assessed in such assessments, that the proportion of the land tax to be paid by each separate owner or proprietor respectively may be known and ascertained; and the said duplicates shall be delivered to the land tax commissioners, at their meeting for the receipt of assessments; and if the name of any owner or owners of any messuages, lands, or tenements, in such parish or place, entitled to vote as aforesaid, shall not appear or be included in such assessment, it shall and may be lawful for such person or persons, by himself or themselves, or by his or their agent or agents, to appeal to the commissioners of the land tax, to whom such assessments shall be returned; and every person so intending to appeal shall, and is hereby required to give notice thereof in writing to one or more of the assessors of the parish or place wherein he is rated; and the said commissioners, on sufficient cause to be shewn, shall amend the duplicates of such assessments, by inserting therein the name or names of the actual occupier or occupiers, and of the owner or owners of such messuages, lands, or tenements, or the person or persons entitled to, or in the actual receipt of the rents, issues, and profits thereof, or by erasing the name of any person who shall appear to them to have been improperly inserted therein; and the said commissioners are hereby required to cause one of the said duplicates so amended (after the same shall be duly signed and sealed by the said commissioners, or any three of them) to be returned to the said assessors, or one of them; and such assessors are hereby required to deliver such duplicate, so amended, within ten days after the receipt

Qualified persons, whose names are omitted in assessments, may appeal to the commissioners;

who are to amend the assessments where defective.

An amended duplicate to be returned to the assessors, and delivered to the clerk of the peace at the next quarter sessions.

receipt thereof, to one of the chief conſtables of the hundred, lathe, or wapentake, within which the pariſh or place for which ſuch aſſeſſment was made ſhall lie, taking the receipt of ſuch chief conſtable for the ſame, and which receipt ſuch chief conſtable is hereby required to give; and ſuch chief conſtable is hereby alſo required to deliver ſuch duplicate upon oath (which oath the ſaid magiſtrates are hereby impowered to adminiſter) without any alteration, at the next general quarter ſeſſions of the peace for the county, riding, or diviſion, within which ſuch aſſeſſment ſhall be made, in open court, the firſt day of ſuch ſeſſions, to the clerk of the peace attending ſuch ſeſſions, to be by him filed and kept amongſt the records of the ſeſſions.

4. And be it further enacted, That if any aſſeſſor ſhall neglect to deliver ſuch duplicate ſo amended, to ſuch chief conſtable as aforeſaid, or if ſuch chief conſtable, to whom the ſame ſhall be delivered, ſhall neglect to deliver the ſame to ſuch clerk of the peace, at the next general quarter ſeſſions of the peace as aforeſaid, or ſhall wilfully alter or deface any ſuch duplicate; every ſuch aſſeſſor and chief conſtable ſo offending ſhall, for every ſuch offence, and for every ſuch duplicate ſo neglected to be delivered as aforeſaid, forfeit the ſum of five pounds, to be levied and recovered in the manner herein-after mentioned.

Penalty on aſſeſſor, &c. who ſhall alter or neglect to deliver any duplicate as above directed.

5. And be it further enacted, That at the Michaelmas ſeſſions in every year, the clerk of the peace, or his deputy, attending ſuch ſeſſions, in every county, riding, or diviſion, as aforeſaid, ſhall, before

If clerk of the peace ſhall not receive all the duplicates before the end of Michaelmas ſeſſions yearly, the court ſhall immediate-

ly fine the chief constables making default.

before the conclusion of such sessions, examine whether the duplicates of all the assessments within such county, riding, or division, shall have been delivered for that year; and if it shall appear that any such duplicates have not been received by or delivered to such clerk of the peace, or his deputy, by the proper chief constables, then and in such case such clerk of the peace, or his deputy, shall report the same to the court, and the court shall immediately set and impose the said fine or fines of five pounds upon such chief constables, for the hundred, lathe, or wapentake, within which the parish or place for which such duplicate or duplicates, of the assessment or assessments not returned shall lie; and the said clerk of the peace, or his deputy, shall give to such chief constables immediate notice of such fine or fines; and if the same is or are not immediately paid, the justices assembled in the said quarter sessions shall, by order of court, issue a warrant

On failure of payment, fines may be levied by distress.

of distress for the recovery thereof, directed to the constable or constables of the respective parishes or places where such chief constables shall live; and such warrant shall be delivered or transmitted by the clerk of the peace, or his deputy, to such constables, or one of them, who is and are hereby required to levy such fine or fines, by distress and sale of the goods and chattels of such chief constables, rendering the overplus (if any) to the owners of such goods and chattels, after deducting the reasonable charges of such distress.

In case chief constables make oath that asses-

6. Provided always, That if such chief constables shall voluntarily make oath at such sessions, that such

such duplicate or duplicates was or were not delivered to them, or either of them, by such assessor or assessors, then, and in such case, the said fine or fines, herein-before directed, shall be set and imposed upon such assessor or assessors, of the parish or place, parishes or places, for which such duplicate or duplicates shall not be returned; and the justices assembled in such quarter sessions shall, by order of court, issue a warrant of distress for the recovery thereof, directed to the constable or constables of such parish or place, or respective parishes or places, or to such other person or persons as such justices shall think proper; and also shall, by order of court, require the chief constables, or one of them, to give notice to such assessor or assessors, that such fines have been set and imposed; and such chief constables are hereby required to serve such notices upon such assessors within fourteen days next after such sessions; and if such assessors, or one of them, shall not deliver such duplicate, or the chief constables' receipt for the same, to the clerk of the peace, or his deputy, for such county, riding, or division, within ten days after being served with such notice, then and in such case the said clerk of the peace, or his deputy, shall deliver or transmit such warrant of distress against the assessor, to the person or persons to whom the same shall be directed, who is hereby required to levy the said fine set upon such assessor by distress and sale of the goods and chattels of such assessor or assessors, rendering the overplus

sors neglected to deliver said duplicates to them,

then the fines shall be levied on the said assessors, except they deliver the duplicates, &c. within 10 days after notice:

(if

(if any) to the owner or owners, after deducting the reasonable charges of such distress.

<small>But if assessors, within the said time, shall produce to the clerk of the peace the chief constables' receipt, then the fine shall be levied on said constables.</small>

7. Provided always, That if such assessors, or either of them, shall, within the said ten days after such notice, produce to the said clerk of the peace, or his deputy, the receipt of such chief constables, or one of them, for such duplicate, then and in such case such clerk of the peace, or his deputy, shall deliver or transmit the warrants against such chief constables, or such of them who shall have signed such receipt, to the proper constable or constables to whom the same shall be directed, that the same may be executed as aforesaid, and the warrant or warrants for levying the fine or fines upon such assessor or assessors shall not be executed.

8. And be it further enacted by the authority aforesaid, That the fines to be set and imposed upon such chief constables and assessors as aforesaid, shall, after the same shall be so levied and recovered, be, by the person or persons who shall <small>Fines to be paid to the treasurer of the county, &c.</small> levy and recover the same, paid to the treasurer of the county, riding, or division, wherein the same shall be levied or recovered, or the lawful deputy of such treasurer, to be applied and disposed of as part of the county stock, under the direction of the sessions of such county, riding, or division.

<small>When assessments are no made, and returned to the clerk of the peace, justices may order them to be made and returned forthwith.</small>

9. And be it further enacted, That whenever any assessment shall not have been made by the assessor or assessors of any parish or place, and returned to the chief constable, and by the chief constable to the clerk of the peace, by the neglect

or

or default of any person concerned therein, it shall and may be lawful for the said justices at the said quarter sessions, or any two justices for such county, riding, or division, out of sessions, to order and direct such assessment or assessments forthwith to be made and returned in manner aforesaid; and such assessments, so made and returned, shall have the same and the like effect as if made and returned at the time and in the manner herein-before directed.

10. And be it further enacted, That if any person or persons shall be dissatisfied, or shall think himself or themselves aggrieved by any determination of the said commissioners of the land tax, it shall and may be lawful for such person or persons to appeal against such determination to the general quarter sessions of the peace for the county, riding, or division, within which such commissioners shall act, which shall happen next after the cause of complaint shall have arisen, giving ten days notice of such appeal to one of the commissioners signing the duplicate of the said assessment, and also to one of the assessors of the parish or place where the estate, belonging to the person or persons who shall think himself or themselves aggrieved, shall lie; and the justices assembled in such sessions are hereby authorized and required, by examination upon oath (which oath the said justices are hereby authorized to administer), to hear and determine the matter of such appeal, and to amend such assessments where they shall think necessary; and also to award such costs as to them in their discretion shall seem reasonable;

Persons aggrieved may appeal to the quarter sessions;

giving ten days notice.

Justices may award costs.

fonable; and by their order or warrant to levy the cofts which fhall be fo awarded, by diftrefs and fale of the goods and chattels of the perfon or perfons againft whom the fame fhall be fo awarded, rendering the overplus (if any) to the owner or owners, after deducting the reafonable charges of fuch diftrefs.

Any perfon, whofe name, on appeal, fhall appear to have been improperly left out of any affeffment, fhall be deemed to have been rated therein.

11. And be it further enacted, That if the faid commiffioners, upon any appeal before them, and alfo the faid juftices in feffions upon any appeal before them, fhall find it requifite to infert in fuch affeffments, or the duplicates thereof, the names of any perfon or perfons, which fhall appear to fuch commiffioners, or to fuch juftices, to have been improperly omitted, fuch perfon or perfons fhall be taken and deemed to be rated in fuch affeffment or affeffments, as effectually, to all intents and purpofes, as if the name or names of fuch perfon or perfons had been originally inferted in fuch affeffment by the affeffors.

Hufbands of women entitled to dower out of the eftates of their former hufbands, may vote in refpect thereof, although the faid dower has not been fet out by metes or bounds.

12. And whereas difputes have arifen, whether the hufbands of women entitled to the dower or thirds, at common law, out of the eftates of their former hufbands, fhall be entitled to vote in the election of members of parliament, unlefs dower has been affigned and fet out, by metes and bounds, for fuch women; be it therefore further enacted, That where any woman, the widow of any perfon tenant in fee or in tail, fhall be entitled to dower or thirds, by the common law, out of the freehold eftate which her hufband died feifed or poffeffed of, and fhall intermarry with a fecond hufband,

husband, such second husband shall be entitled to vote in respect of such dower or thirds, if such dower or thirds shall be of the clear yearly value of forty shillings, or upwards, although the same has not been assigned or set out by metes or bounds, if such second husband shall be in the actual receipt of the profits of such dower, and the estate from whence the same issues is rated to, and contributes to the land tax in the name of the actual owner of the lands or tenements, from whence such dower or thirds arises or issues.

13. And be it further enacted by the authority aforesaid, That it shall and may be lawful for all and every person or persons, at all seasonable times, to resort to and inspect the said duplicates, or any part thereof, in the hands of such clerk of the peace, or his deputy, paying for every search into, or inspection of, such duplicates, or any part thereof, one shilling, and no more; and the said clerk of the peace, or his deputy, is hereby required and directed, upon demand, to deliver a true copy or copies of all such duplicates, or of such part or parts of them, or any of them, of which a copy shall be demanded, to any person or persons who shall demand or desire the same, (such copy or copies to be signed by such clerk of the peace, or his deputy, purporting the same to be a true copy or true copies,) and for which copy or copies such clerk of the peace, or his deputy, shall be paid at and after the rate of sixpence, and no more, for every three hundred words or figures, and so in proportion for any lesser

Duplicates may be inspected.

Clerk of the peace to deliver signed copies of duplicates, on demand,

and being paid 6d. for every 300 words.

lesser number of words or figures; which said duplicates, and also a true copy of them, or any of them, or any part of them, signed as aforesaid, and also the duplicate of any assessment in the possession of the commissioners of the land tax, or in the possession of the receiver-general of the county, or a copy of the said duplicates, signed by such commissioners, and purporting the same to be a true copy, shall, at all times and in all places, be allowed and admitted as legal evidence of such assessments, certificates, memorials, and books of entries, in all cases whatsoever; and such copy shall be delivered in a reasonable time after the same shall be demanded.

Duplicates, &c. to be deemed legal evidence.

14. And be it further enacted by the authority aforesaid, That such clerk of the peace of every county, riding, or division, in whose office such duplicates shall be filed as aforesaid, or his deputy, shall, upon reasonable notice, attend at every election of a knight or knights of the shire for such county, with the said original duplicates, at the request of any candidate, or the agent or agents of any candidates; the person or persons requesting the same making such clerk of the peace, or his deputy, a satisfaction for such attendance, at and after the rate of two guineas for each day of his attendance at such election, together with an allowance of one shilling and sixpence a mile for the costs and charges he may be at, or put unto, in his journey from the place of his abode to and from the place of such election.

Clerk of the peace, or his deputy, to attend at every election of a knight of the shire, with original duplicates, at the request of any candidate:

Such candidate to pay him 2l. 2s. for each day's attendance, and 1s. 6d. per mile for travelling charges.

15. And

15. And be it further enacted, That after issuing any writ or precept for the election of a knight or knights of the shire for any county within that part of Great Britain called England, or the dominion of Wales, the clerk of the peace, or his deputy, shall, and he is hereby required to attend, *gratis*, from day to day, from the hour of nine in the forenoon to three in the afternoon, in each day, at the place where the records of such county, riding, or division, are usually kept, from the time of the delivery of such notice to the day immediately preceding the day of election of such knight or knights, for the purpose of receiving applications for the inspection of such duplicates, and for making copies of them, or any of them, or of so much of them, or any of them, which he shall be requested to copy as aforesaid.

After issuing any writ for election of a county member, the clerk of the peace shall attend gratis, from 9 to 3 each day, where the records of the county are usually kept, to make copies of duplicates, &c.

16. And be it further enacted, That if any clerk of the peace, or his deputy, shall neglect or refuse to permit such duplicates, or any of them, or any part of them, or any of them, to be inspected by any person or persons who shall request the same as aforesaid, or shall neglect or refuse to deliver any copy or copies of the same, or any part thereof, within the time before mentioned, or shall neglect to attend as aforesaid at the place where the records of such county, riding, or division, are usually kept, or at any county election, with such duplicates, in pursuance of the directions of this act; every such clerk of the peace, or his deputy, shall, for every such offence, forfeit the sum of five hundred pounds to the party aggrieved,

Penalty on clerk of the peace, or his deputy, making default.

Action to be brought within two months, &c.

grieved, provided such action is brought within two months after the offence shall have been committed; and if no such action shall be brought within the said time, then to any person who shall sue for the same in the manner herein-after mentioned; and shall also forfeit his office of clerk of the peace, or deputy, the same to be absolutely void on such clerk of the peace, or his deputy, being convicted of such offence; and such clerk of the peace, or deputy clerk of the peace, shall be rendered incapable of being again appointed a clerk of the peace, or deputy clerk of the peace, or of acting as such, in or for any county, riding, or division, whatsoever.

Final judgement upon any verdict against a clerk of the peace, shall be deemed sufficient conviction.

17. And be it further enacted by the authority aforesaid, That final judgement upon any verdict to be obtained against such clerk of the peace, or deputy clerk of the peace, for the recovery of such forfeiture, shall be deemed and taken to be a sufficient conviction of such offence, without any other prosecution or conviction whatsoever; and immediately after such judgement, the said office of clerk of the peace, or deputy clerk of the peace, shall be absolutely void, to all intents and purposes whatsoever.

Penalties how to be recovered.

18. And be it further enacted by the authority aforesaid, That the forfeitures or penalties laid or imposed against such clerk of the peace, or deputy clerk of the peace, by this act, shall and may be recovered, with full costs of suit, by action of debt, bill, plaint, or information, in any of his majesty's court of record at Westminster, wherein no essoin, protection, or wager of law,

law, or more than one imparlance, shall be allowed.

19. Provided always, and be it further enacted and declared, That no person shall be liable to any forfeiture or penalty by this act laid or imposed, unless prosecution be commenced within twelve kalendar months next after such forfeiture or penalty shall be incurred. A. D. 1780.

Prosecutions to be commenced within twelve months.

FORM OF ASSESSMENT.

County of N to wit:
For the parish of
in the said county.
} An assessment made in pursuance of an act of parliament, passed in the
year of his majesty's reign, for granting an aid to his majesty by a land tax, to be raised in Great Britain, for the service of the year 17

Form of assessment.

Names of Proprietors.	Names of Occupiers.	Sums assessed.
A. B. —	Himself. —	— —
A. B. —	C. D. —	— —
E. F. —	C. D. —	— —
C. D. —	G. H. —	— —
I. K. and } — L. M.	N. O. —	— —
P. Q. —	{ R. S. and } — T. U. }	— —

Signed this   day of
    17   by us
        A. B. }
        C. D. } Assessors.

ANNO 21° GEORGII III. CAP. 43.

An Act for continuing an Act, made in the 20th Year of the Reign of his present Majesty, intituled, an Act for exempting the City of Winchester, *the County of* Southampton, *the Town of* Shrewsbury, *and the County of* Salop, *out of the Provisions of an Act, made in the 8th Year of the Reign of his late Majesty King George the Second, intituled,* 'An Act for regulating the Quartering of Soldiers during the Time of the Elections of Members to serve in Parliament,' *so far as the same relates to the Removal of Troops during the Elections of Members to serve in Parliament, for a limited Time.*

20 Geo. 3. c. 50.

WHEREAS an act was made in the last session of parliament, (intituled, An Act for exempting the city of *Winchester*, the county of *Southampton*, the town of *Shrewsbury*, and the county of *Salop*, out of the provisions of an act, made in the 8th year of the reign of his late majesty king George the Second, intituled, ' An act for regulating the quartering of soldiers during the time of the elections of members to serve in parliament,' so far as it relates to the removal of troops during the elections of members to serve in parliament, for a limited time,) which was to continue in force until the end of this present session of parliament; and whereas it is expedient that the said act should be continued or a further term: be it therefore enacted by the king's most excellent majesty, by and with the advice and consent of the lords spiritual and temporal and commons in this present parliament assembled, and by the authority of the same, That the said act shall be further continued until the end of the next session of parliament.

and further continued until the end of the next session of parliament.

A. D. 1780.

ANNO 21° GEORGII III. CAP. 54.

An Act for the better regulating Elections of Citizens to serve in Parliament for the City of Coventry.

WHEREAS the right of election of citizens to serve in parliament for the city of *Coventry*, is, by the last determination of the house of commons, of the twentieth day of November, 1722, declared to be in such freemen as have served seven years apprenticeship to one and the same trade in the said city, or the suburbs thereof, and do not receive alms or weekly charity, such freemen being duly sworn and inrolled; and whereas great frauds and abuses were committed, in clandestinely admitting persons, having no such right to the freedom of the city of *Coventry*, during the last election of members to serve in parliament for the said city, in order to influence the said election, to the great infringement of the rights of the true electors of the said city, and in violation of the freedom of elections: to prevent such practices for the future, be it enacted by

An open council to be held at St. Mary's Hall, on the first and last Tuesday in every month.

by the king's most excellent majesty, by and with the advice and consent of the lords spiritual and temporal and commons in this present parliament assembled, and by the authority of the same, That, from and after the passing of this act, an open council shall be held at *Saint Mary's Hall* in the said city, on the first and last *Tuesday* in every kalendar month, for the purpose, on the first *Tuesday* in each month, of receiving and proclaiming aloud the names of every person or persons who shall then present, or cause to be presented, an account in writing of the particulars of his or their claim to the freedom of the said city, and for the purpose, on the last *Tuesday* in each month, of admitting to the freedom of the said city such person or persons as shall then appear and claim to be so admitted, he or they first verifying upon oath the particulars of his or their claim delivered in at the preceding council; and that the council which shall be holden on the first *Tuesday* in each month shall assemble at ten in the morning, and continue open a convenient time, for receiving such claims as shall then be preferred; and the council which shall be holden on the last *Tuesday* in each month shall continue open from the hour of ten in the morning till three o'clock in the afternoon of the same day, or for such shorter time as shall be found sufficient for hearing and determining any claims which shall then have been preferred; and if any such claims shall then remain unheard or undetermined, the said council shall be adjourned from day to day, and continue

tinue open on each day in manner aforesaid, for hearing and determining such claims.

2. And be it further enacted by the authority aforesaid, That, from and after the passing of this act, no greater fee than three shillings, over and above the expence of the necessary stamps, shall be demanded or taken of any person or persons who shall be so admitted to his or their freedom at any such council. *Limitation of the expence of taking up the freedom.*

3. And be it further enacted, by the authority aforesaid, That no person shall be admitted to the freedom of the said city, at any council to be held for that purpose, who shall not produce evidence of regular indentures or deeds of apprenticeship for seven years, as required by the resolution aforesaid, and who shall not also declare upon oath the name or names of his master or masters, the trade to which he served under him or them, the place of his or their residence during the time he served, and of his own residence at the time of his claiming to be admitted to the freedom of the said city; and that it shall be lawful for such persons so claiming their freedom as aforesaid, to come to such council attended with their agents, who shall be present at their admission, if they so require it; and such council are hereby authorized and required to administer such oath as aforesaid. *Particulars to be observed by those who take it up.*

4. And be it further enacted by the authority aforesaid, That the town clerk shall enter all the above particulars in the admission book under the name of each person who is admitted to the freedom of the said city; and that the said town clerk *Town clerk to enter the above particulars in a book.*

and the mayor, and each of the members composing the council at which such freemen shall be admitted, shall openly subscribe their names to the said entries.

Lists of the names of all the freemen, &c. admitted, to be pasted on the church doors.

5. And be it further enacted by the authority aforesaid, That lists of the names of all persons claiming to be admitted freemen, and of all the freemen admitted at any council to be held in the manner aforesaid, shall be made out in writing, and signed by the town clerk, and be pasted or fixed upon the doors of all the churches in *Coventry*, within twenty-four hours after the holding of such council.

Councils not to be held during a certain time specified.

6. And be it further enacted by the authority aforesaid, That no council shall be held for receiving claims of persons claiming to be admitted to the freedom of the said city after the day on which notice shall be given by the sheriff or sheriffs, according to the statute, of any election for a member or members to serve in parliament for the said city, till after the final close of every such election.

7. And be it further enacted by the authority aforesaid, That, at every election of members to serve in parliament for the said city, every person who shall come to poll at such election, shall, if required by any candidate at such election, or by any two or more persons having a right to vote at such elections, previous to his

Electors to be sworn.

being permitted to poll, take the following oath, or, being one of the persons called *Quakers*, shall solemnly affirm the effect thereof (that is to say)

" You

" You do swear, That your name is A. B. and that you have been admitted to the freedom of the city of *Coventry* under indentures, or deeds of apprenticeship, and that you have served seven years apprenticeship to one and the same trade in the said city, or the suburbs thereof; and that you are of the age of twenty-one years, or upwards; and have not been polled before at this election.   So help you God." The oath.

Which oath the returning officer or officers, or his deputy, is hereby impowered to administer.

8. And be it further enacted by the authority aforesaid, That all persons who shall be guilty of wilful and corrupt perjury, in consequence of any oath which they shall have taken by the direction of this act, shall, on conviction thereof, incur and suffer the like pains and penalties to which any other person convicted of wilful and corrupt perjury is liable by the laws and statutes of this realm. Penalty on persons guilty of perjury.

9. And be it further enacted by the authority aforesaid, That if the returning officer or officers, at any election of a member or members to serve in parliament for the said city, shall wilfully admit any person to poll at such election without his having first taken the above-mentioned oath, if required so to do, in manner aforesaid, the said returning officer or officers shall, for every such offence, forfeit and pay the sum of one hundred pounds to him, her, or them, who shall sue for the same. Penalty on returning officer for admitting persons to poll without being sworn;

10. And be it further enacted by the authority aforesaid, That if the mayor, and the other members And on members of the council for refusing to admit electors, &c.

members composing any council to be held for the purpose of proclaiming the persons presenting accounts of their claim to the freedom of the said city, or for the purpose of admitting such persons to the freedom of the said city, shall refuse to proclaim, or to admit such person or persons as shall come and prove their titles according to the provisions of this act, they shall, for every such offence, forfeit and pay the sum of one hundred pounds.

Proviso.

11. Provided always, That if any doubts shall arise as to the legality of the titles so sworn to, it shall and may be lawful for the said council to hear witnesses, and admit evidences to disprove the same.

12. And be it further enacted by the authority aforesaid, That if the town clerk shall neglect to make the proper entries, or shall make any false and fraudulent entries in the admission book; or if he shall neglect to make out and sign the lists of the freemen admitted, and cause them to be pasted or fixed on the doors of the churches in manner herein-before directed; or if he shall make out, sign, or cause to be pasted or fixed on the doors of the churches as aforesaid, any false or fraudulent list, he shall, for every such offence, forfeit the sum of ten pounds.

Penalty on town clerk for making fraudulent entries, &c.

13. Provided also, and it is hereby enacted and declared, That this act shall not extend, nor be construed to extend, to any freemen of the said city but such as have a right to vote in the election of members to serve in parliament for the said city.

To what freemen this act shall extend.

14. And

14. And be it further enacted, That the returning officer or officers shall, at all future elections of citizens to serve in parliament for the said city, cause the booth for holding such election to be erected in the widest and most convenient part of the open market-place called Cross-cheaping, not contiguous to any other building. *Election booth where to be erected.*

15. And be it further enacted by the authority aforesaid, That all penalties laid or imposed by this shall be recovered, with full costs of suit, by action of debt, bill, plaint, or information, in any of his majesty's courts of record at Westminster, wherein no essoin, protection, wager of law, or more than one imparlance, shall be allowed. *Penalties how to be recovered.*

16. Provided always, and it is hereby further enacted and declared by the authority aforesaid, That no person shall be liable to any penalty by this act laid or imposed, unless prosecution be commenced within one year after such penalty shall be incurred. *Limitation of actions.*

17. And it is further enacted by the authority aforesaid, That this act shall be deemed, adjudged, and taken to be a public act; and be judicially taken notice of as such, by all judges, justices, and other persons whomsoever, without specially pleading the same. *Public act.*

18. And be it further enacted by the authority aforesaid, that the dates of all deeds or indentures of apprenticeship, together with the names of the parties, and their places of abode, which, from and after the passing of this act, shall be made and executed between any person or *Deeds or indentures of apprenticeship, &c. shall be registered by the town clerk.*

persons residing in the said city of *Coventry*, or the suburbs thereof, and his, her, or their apprentice or apprentices, under which such apprentice or apprentices may hereafter have a right to be admitted to the freedom of the said city, shall be registered in a book to be kept for that purpose by the town clerk of the same city for the time being, within the space of six kalendar months next after the execution thereof; which the said town clerk is hereby required to register, and on such deeds or indenture to indorse a certificate of such register; and in default thereof, such deeds or indentures shall, to all intents and purposes, be null and void.

A. D. 1780.

ANNO 22° GEORGII III. CAP. 29.

An Act for further continuing an Act, made in the 20th Year of the Reign of His present Majesty, intituled, An Act for exempting the City of Winchester, the County of Southampton, the Town of Shrewsbury, and the County of Salop, out of the Provisions of an Act, made in the 8th Year of the Reign of His late Majesty King George the Second, intituled, " An Act for regulating the quartering of Soldiers during the Time of the Elections of Members to serve in Parliament;" so far as the same relates to the Removal of Troops during the Elections of Members to serve in Parliament, for a limited Time.

WHEREAS

WHEREAS an act was made in the 20th year of the reign of his present majesty, intituled, 'An act for exempting the city of Winchester, the county of Southampton, the town of Shrewsbury, and the county of Salop, out of the provisions of an act, made in the 8th year of the reign of his late majesty king George the Second, intituled, An act for regulating the quartering of soldiers during the time of the election of members to serve in parliament; so far as the same relates to the removal of troops during the elections of members to serve in parliament, for a limited time;' which was to continue in force until the end of the last session of parliament; which said act was, by another act, made in the last session of parliament, continued until the end of this present session of parliament; and whereas it is expedient that the said act should be continued for a further term: Be it therefore enacted by the king's most excellent majesty, by and with the advice and consent of the lords spiritual and temporal and commons in this present parliament assembled, and by the authority of the same, That the said act shall continue in force during the present hostilities with France, Spain, and Holland, or either of them.

20 Geo. 3. c. 50.

Further continued during the present hostilities.

A. D. 1781.

ANNO 22° GEORGII III. CAP. 31.

An Act for the preventing of Bribery and Corruption in the Election of Members to serve in Parliament for the Borough of Cricklade, *in the County of* Wilts.

WHEREAS there was the most notorious bribery and corruption at the last election of burgesses to serve in parliament for the borough of *Cricklade* in the county of *Wilts*; and whereas such bribery and corruption is likely to continue and be practised in the said borough in future, unless some means are taken to prevent the same: in order, therefore, to prevent such unlawful practices for the future, and that the said borough may from henceforth be duly represented in parliament: Be it enacted by the king's most excellent majesty, by and with the advice and consent of the lords spiritual and temporal, and commons, in this present parliament assembled, and by the authority of the same, That from henceforth it shall and may be lawful to and for every freeholder, being above the age of twenty-one years, who shall have, within the hundreds or divisions of Highworth, Cricklade, Staple, Kingsbridge, and Malmsbury, or one or more of them, in the county of Wilts, a freehold of the clear yearly value of forty shillings, to give his vote at every election of a burgess or burgesses to serve in parliament for the said borough of Cricklade.

Certain freeholders intitled to vote for the borough of Cricklade:

2dly.

2dly. And be it further enacted by the authority aforesaid, That the right of election of a member or members to serve in parliament for the said borough of Cricklade, shall be, and is hereby declared to be, in such freeholders as aforesaid, and in the persons who, by the custom and usage of the said borough, have, or shall hereafter have, a right to vote at such election; and the proper officer for the time being, to whom the return of every writ or process does belong, is hereby required to return the person or persons to serve in parliament for the said borough who shall have the major number of votes of such freeholders and other persons having a right to vote at such election; any law or usage to the contrary notwithstanding.

Customary voters also intitled.

3dly. Provided always, That such freeholders only shall be entitled to vote as shall be duly qualified to vote at elections for knights of the shire for the said county of Wilts, according to the laws now in being for regulating county elections.

No freeholders to vote but such as are qualified to be county voters.

4thly. And be it further enacted by the authority aforesaid, That every such freeholder, before he is admitted to poll at any election for the said borough, shall, if required by the candidates, or any of them, or any other person having a right to vote at the said election, first take the oath, or, being one of the people called *Quakers*, the solemn affirmation following, viz.

Freeholders to be sworn.

" I do swear, [or, being a *Quaker*, solemnly affirm] That I am a freeholder in the hundreds or divisions of Highworth, Cricklade, Staple,

The oath.

Malm-

Malmſbury, and Kingſbridge, or any one or more of them, in the county of Wilts, and have a freehold eſtate, confiſting of

[ſpecifying the nature thereof; and if it conſiſts in meſſuages, lands, tenements, or tithes, in whoſe occupation the ſame are; and if in rents, the names of the owners or poſſeſſors of the tenements out of which ſuch rent is iſſuing, or ſome of them], ſituate, lying, or being at

in the aforeſaid hundreds or diviſions, or in one or more of them, of the clear yearly value of forty ſhillings, over and above all rents and charges payable out of, or in reſpect of the ſame; and that I have been in the actual poſſeſſion or receipt of the rents and profits thereof, for my own uſe, above twelve kalendar months, [or, that the ſame came to me within the time aforeſaid by deſcent, marriage, marriage ſettlement, deviſe, or promotion to a benefice in a church, or by promotion to an office]; and that ſuch freehold eſtate has not been granted or made to me fraudulently, on purpoſe to qualify me to give my vote; and that the place of my abode is at

in   , and that I am twenty-one years of age, as I believe, and that I have not been polled before at this election."

Which oath, or ſolemn affirmation, the proper officer, to whom the return of any writ or precept for ſuch election ſhall belong, is hereby required to adminiſter: And in caſe any freeholder, or other perſon taking the ſaid oath or affirmation hereby appointed, ſhall thereby commit wilful perjury, and be thereof convicted; or if any perſon
ſhall

shall unlawfully and corruptly procure or suborn any freeholder or other person to take the said oath or affirmation, in order to be polled, whereby he shall commit such wilful perjury, and shall be thereof convicted, he and they, for every such offence respectively, shall incur such penalties as are inflicted on persons guilty of perjury, or subornation of perjury, in and by two acts of parliament one made in the 5th year of the reign of queen Elizabeth, intituled, An act for punishing such persons as shall procure or commit wilful perjury, or suborn or procure any person to commit any wilful or corrupt perjury; and the other, made in the 2d year of the reign of his late majesty king George the Second, intituled, An act for the more effectual preventing and further punishment of forgery, perjury, and subornation of perjury, and to make it felony to steal bonds, notes, or other securities for payment of money, contrary to the said acts. *Penalty on committing perjury, or subornation thereof. As by 5 Eliz. And 2 Geo. 2.*

5thly. And be it further enacted by the authority aforesaid, That such proper officer, to whom any writ or precept shall be directed for making any election for the said borough, shall, upon the receipt of such writ or precept, indorse upon the back thereof the day of his receipt thereof, in the presence of the party from whom he received such precept, and shall forthwith cause public notice to be given within the said borough of Cricklade, and the several towns of Highworth, Malmsbury, Swindon, and Wotton Basset, by affixing up a notice thereof in writing on the market- *How officer to proceed on receiving any writ for election.*

market-houses, or on the doors of the churches of the said towns, of the day of election; and shall proceed to election thereupon within the space of twelve days, and not less than eight days, next after his receipt of the same precept.

This act to be read previous to any election.

6thly. And be it further enacted by the authority aforesaid, That this act shall be publicly read at every election for the said borough of Cricklade, immediately after the acts directed by any act of parliament to be read thereat, and before the persons present shall proceed to make such election.

A. D. 1781.

ANNO 22° GEORGII III. CAP. 41.

An Act for better securing the Freedom of Elections of Members to serve in Parliament, by disabling certain Officers, employed in the Collection or Management of His Majesty's Revenues, from giving their Votes at such Elections.

From Aug. 1, 1782, no commissioner or officer employed in collecting or managing the duties of excise, customs, &c. shall have any vote in the election of members of parliament.

FOR the better securing the freedom of elections of members to serve in parliament, be it enacted by the king's most excellent majesty, by and with the advice and consent of the lords spiritual and temporal and commons in this present parliament assembled, and by the authority of the same, That from and after the first day of of August, 1782, no commissioner, collector, supervisor, gauger, or other officer or person whatsoever, concerned or employed in the charging, collecting, levying, or managing the duties

of

of excise, or any branch or part thereof; nor any commissioner, collector, comptroller, searcher, or other officer or person whatsoever, concerned or employed in the charging, collecting, levying, or managing the customs, or any branch or part thereof; nor any commissioner, officer, or other person concerned or employed in collecting, receiving, or managing, any of the duties on stamped vellum, parchment, and paper, nor any person appointed by the commissioners for distributing of stamps; nor any commissioner, officer, or other person employed in collecting, levying, or managing any of the duties on salt; nor any surveyor, collector, comptroller, inspector, officer, or other person employed in collecting, managing, or receiving the duties on windows or houses; nor any postmaster, postmasters general, or his or their deputy or deputies, or any person employed by or under him or them in receiving, collecting, or managing the revenue of the post-office, or any part thereof; nor any captain, master, or mate of any ship, packet, or other vessel employed by or under the postmaster or postmasters general in conveying the mail to and from foreign ports, shall be capable of giving his vote for the election of any knight of the shire, commissioner, citizen, burgess, or baron to serve in parliament for any county, stewartry, city, borough, or cinque port, or for chusing any delegate in whom the right of electing members to serve in parliament, for that part of Great Britain called Scotland, is vested: And if any person,

hereby

hereby made incapable of voting as aforesaid, shall nevertheless presume to give his vote, during the time he shall hold, or within twelve kalendar months after he shall cease to hold, or execute any of the offices aforesaid, contrary to the true intent and meaning of this act, such votes so given shall be held null and void to all intents and purposes whatsoever; and every person so offending shall forfeit the sum of one hundred pounds; one moiety thereof to the informer, and the other moiety thereof to be immediately paid into the hands of the treasurer of the county, riding, or division, within which such offence shall have been committed, in that part of Great Britain called England; and into the hands of the clerk of the justices of the peace of the counties or stewartries, in that part of Great Britain called Scotland, to be applied and disposed of to such purposes as the justices at the next general quarter session of the peace to be held for such county, stewartry, riding, or division, shall think fit; to be recovered by any person that shall sue for the same, by action of debt, bill, plaint, or information, in any of his majesty's courts of record at Westminster, in which no essoin, protection, privilege, or wager of law, or more than one imparlance, shall be allowed, or by summary complaint before the court of session in Scotland; and the person convicted on any such suit shall thereby become disabled and incapable of ever bearing or executing any office or place of trust whatsoever under his majesty, his heirs and successors.

Penalty on persons voting who are disqualified by this act.

2dly.

2dly. Provided always, and be it enacted, That nothing in this act contained shall extend, or be construed to extend, to any person or persons for or by reason of his or their being a commissioner or commissioners of the land tax, or for or by reason of his or their acting by or under the appointment of such commissioners of the land tax, for the purpose of assessing, levying, collecting, receiving, or managing the land tax, or any other rates or duties already granted or imposed, or which shall hereafter be granted or imposed by authority of parliament. *Not to extend to commissioners of the land tax, or persons acting under them;*

3dly. Provided also, and be it further enacted, That nothing in this act contained shall extend, or be construed to extend, to any office now held, or usually granted to be held, by letters patent for any estate of inheritance or freehold. *Nor to offices held by letters patent for any estate of inheritance;*

4thly. Provided always, and be it enacted by the authority aforesaid, That nothing herein contained shall extend to any person who shall resign his office or employment on or before the said first day of August, 1782. *Nor to persons who shall resign their offices before Aug. 1, 1782.*

5thly. Provided also, and be it enacted, That no person shall be liable to any forfeiture or penalty by this act laid or imposed, unless prosecution be commenced within twelve months after such penalty or forfeiture shall be incurred. *Limitation of actions.*

A. D. 1781.

ANNO 22° GEORGII III. CAP. 45.

An Act for restraining any Person concerned in any Contract, Commission, or Agreement, made for the Public Service, from being elected, or sitting and voting as a Member of the House of Commons.

FOR further securing the freedom and independence of parliament, be it enacted by the king's most excellent majesty, by and with the advice and consent of the lords spiritual and temporal and commons in this present parliament assembled, and by the authority of the same, That, from and after the end of this present session of Parliament, any person who shall, directly or indirectly, himself, or by any person whatsoever in trust for him, or for his use or benefit, or on his account, undertake, execute, hold, or enjoy, in the whole or in part, any contract, agreement, or commission, made or entered into with, under, or from the commissioners of his majesty's treasury, or of the navy or victualling-office, or with the master general or board of ordnance, or with any one or more of such commissioners, or with any other person or persons whatsoever, for or on account of the public service; or shall knowingly and willingly furnish or provide, in pursuance of any such agreement, contract, or commission, which he or they shall have made or entered into as aforesaid, any money to be remitted abroad, or any wares

[margin: After the end of this session, all persons holding contracts for the public service, shall be incapable of being elected, or sitting in the house of commons.]

wares or merchandize to be used or employed in the service of the public, shall be incapable of being elected, or of sitting or voting as a member of the house of commons, during the time that he shall execute, hold, or enjoy, any such contract, agreement, or commission, or any part or share thereof, or any benefit or emolument arising from the same.

2dly. And be it further enacted by the authority aforesaid, That if any person, being a member of the house of commons, shall directly or indirectly, himself, or by any other person whatsoever in trust for him, or for his use or benefit, or on his account, enter into, accept of, agree for, undertake, or execute, in the whole or in part, any such contract, agreement, or commission, as aforesaid; or if any person, being a member of the house of commons, and having already entered into any such contract, agreement, or commission, or part or share of any such contract, agreement, or commission, by himself, or by any other person whatsoever in trust for him, or for his use or benefit, or upon his account, shall, after the commencement of the next session of parliament, continue to hold, execute, or enjoy the same, or any part thereof, the seat of every such person in the house of commons shall be, and is hereby declared to be void.

Any member accepting a contract, or continuing to hold any contract after the commencement of the next session, his seat shall be void.

3dly. Provided always, and be it enacted, That nothing herein contained shall extend, or be construed to extend, to any contract, agreement, or commission made, entered into, or accepted, by any incorporated trading company in its corporate

Not to extend to incorporated trading Companies.

porate capacity, nor to any company now existing or established and consisting of more than ten persons, where such contract, agreement, or commission, shall be made, entered into, or accepted, for the general benefit of such incorporation or company.

Not to extend to contracts already made for one year.

4thly. Provided also, and be it enacted, That nothing in this act contained shall extend, or be construed to extend, to any contract, agreement, or commission, made, entered into, or accepted, before the passing of this act, the term whereof will expire in the space of one year from the time of making thereof.

Clause relative to contracts which are not to expire until a year's notice be given.

5thly. Provided also, and be it enacted, That where any contract, agreement, or commission, has been made, entered into, or accepted, with a provision that the same shall continue until a year's notice be given of the intended dissolution thereof, the same shall not disable any person from sitting and voting in parliament until one year after the said notice shall be actually given for the determination of the said contract, agreement, or commission, or till after twelve kalendar months, to be computed from the time of passing this act.

Not to extend to contracts, by descent, &c. until after 12 months possession.

6thly. Provided also, and be it enacted, That nothing herein contained shall extend, or be construed to extend, to any person on whom, after the passing of this act, the completion of any contract, agreement, or commission, shall devolve by descent or limitation, or by marriage, or as devisee, legatee, executor, or administrator,

tor, until twelve kalendar months after he shall have been in possession of the same.

7thly. Provided also, and be it enacted, That any person who is now a member of the house of commons, and holds and enjoys any such contract, agreement, or commission, as aforesaid, may be discharged from the execution thereof on giving twelve months notice to the person or persons with or from whom such contract, agreement, or commission, is made, entered into, or accepted, of his desire that the same shall cease and determine; and such contract, agreement, or commission, after the expiration of the term aforesaid, shall be null and void.

Members holding contracts may be discharged therefrom on giving 12 months notice.

8thly. Provided also, That if any person actually possessed of a patent for a new invention, or a prolongation thereof by act of parliament, and having contracted with government concerning the object of the said patent before the passing of this act, shall give notice of his intention to dissolve the said contract, the same shall be null and void from the time of giving such notice.

Clause relative to patentees for new inventions.

9thly. And be it further enacted by the authority aforesaid, That if any person hereby disabled, or declared to be incapable to sit or vote in parliament, shall nevertheless be returned as a member to serve for any county, stewartry, city, borough, town, cinque port, or place, in parliament, such election and return are hereby enacted and declared to be void; and if any person, disabled and declared incapable by this act to be elected, shall, after the end of this present session of

If any person hereby disqualified, shall be elected, such election shall be void.

Disabled persons who shall sit in the house of commons after this session, shall forfeit £500 for each day.

of parliament, presume to sit or vote as member of the house of commons, such person so sitting or voting shall forfeit the sum of five hundred pounds for every day in which he shall sit or vote in the said house, to any person or persons who shall sue for the same, in any of his majesty's courts at Westminster; and the money so forfeited shall be recovered by the person or persons so suing, with full costs of suit, in any of the said courts, by any action of debt, bill, plaint, or information, in which no essoin, privilege, protection, or wager of law, or more than one imparlance, shall be allowed; or by summary complaint before the court of session in Scotland; and every person, against whom any such penalty or forfeiture shall be recovered by virtue of this act, shall be from thenceforth incapable of taking or holding any contract, agreement, or commission, for the public service, or any share thereof, or any benefit or emolument from the same, in any manner whatsoever.

A condition to be inserted in all public contracts, that no member of the house of commons shall have any share thereof.

10thly. And be it enacted, That in every such contract, agreement, or commission, to be made, entered into, or accepted, as aforesaid, there shall be inserted an express condition, that no member of the house of commons be admitted to any share or part of such contract, agreement, or commission, or to any benefit to arise therefrom; and

Penalty on contractors who shall admit any member of the house of commons to any share of their contracts.

that in case any person or persons who hath or have entered into or accepted, or who shall enter into or accept, any such contract, agreement, or commission, shall admit any member or members of the house of commons to any part or share

share thereof, or to receive any benefit thereby, all and every such person and persons shall, for every such offence, forfeit and pay the sum of five hundred pounds, to be recovered, with full costs of suit, in any of his majesty's courts of record at Westminster, by any person or persons who shall sue for the same, by any action of debt, bill, plaint, or information, in which no essoin, privilege, protection, or wager of law, or more than one imparlance, shall be allowed; or by summary complaint before the court of session in Scotland.

11thly. Provided also, and be it enacted, That *Limitation of actions.* person shall be liable to any forfeiture or penalty inflicted by this act, unless a prosecution shall be commenced within twelve kalendar months after such penalty or forfeiture shall be incurred.

A. D. 1781.

ANNO 24° GEORGII III. CAP. 26.

An Act to repeal so much of two Acts, made in the 10th and 15th Years of the reign of his present Majesty, as authorizes the Speaker of the House of Commons to issue his Warrant to the Clerk of the Crown for making out Writs for the Election of Members to serve in Parliament, in the Manner therein mentioned; and for substituting other Provisions for the like Purposes.

WHEREAS by an Act, made in the 10th year of the reign of his present majesty, intituled, "An act to enable the speaker of the 10 Geo. 3. c. 41. the house of commons to issue his warrants to

make

make out new writs for the choice of members to ferve in parliament, in the room of fuch members as fhall die during the recefs of parliament;" and alfo by another act paffed in the 15th year of the reign of his prefent majefty, "for explaining and amending the faid act, and for enabling the fpeaker of the houfe of commons to make out new writs for the choice of members to ferve in parliament, in the room of fuch members as fhall, during the recefs of parliament, become peers of Great Britain, and be fummoned to parliament," and for other the purpofes therein mentioned; feveral provifions were made for enabling the fpeaker of the houfe of commons to iffue his warrants to the clerk of the crown to make out new writs for electing members of the houfe of commons in the room of fuch members as fhould happen to die, or become peers of Great Britain, at the times, in the manner, and under the reftrictions in the faid feveral acts mentioned; and whereas the faid acts have been found highly advantageous to the public, by caufing fpeedy elections of members of the houfe of commons, and it is therefore expedient, that the provifions therein contained fhould be further extended, and freed from certain of the reftrictions in the faid acts particularly fpecified, and alfo that fome further provifions fhould be made for carrying the faid powers into execution, in the cafes of the death of the fpeaker of the houfe of commons for the time being, or of his feat in parliament becoming vacant, or of his abfence out of the realm; and it would be alfo convenient that the provifions contained

and 15 Geo. 3. c. 56.

tained in the said two several acts of parliament, and of this act, should be reduced into one act of parliament, and that, for that purpose, those provisions contained in the said two several acts should be repealed: Be it therefore enacted by the king's most excellent majesty, by and with the advice and consent of the lords spiritual and temporal and commons in this present parliament assembled, and by the authority of the same, That, from and after the passing of this act, the said act, passed in the 10th year of the reign of his present majesty, and also so much of the said act, passed in the 15th year of the reign of his present majesty, as enables the speaker of the house of commons to issue his warrants to make out new writs for the election of members to serve in parliament, shall be, and the same are hereby repealed.

The recited act of 10 Geo. 3 repealed; and part of 15 Geo. 3, c. 36.

2dly. And be it enacted, That, from and after the passing of this act, it shall and may be lawful for the speaker of the house of commons for the time being, during any recess of the said house, whether by prorogation or adjournment, and he is hereby required to issue his warrant to the clerk of the crown, to make out a new writ for electing a member of the house of commons in the room of any member of the said house who shall happen to die, or who shall become a peer of Great Britain, either during the said recess, or previous thereto, as soon as he shall receive notice, by a certificate, under the hands of two members of the house of commons, of the death of such member, in the first case; and in the

Speaker to issue his warrant, during a recess, for making out writs for electing members in the room of those who shall die or become peers of Great Britain.

R   second

second case, that a writ of summons hath been issued, under the great seal of Great Britain, to summon such peer to parliament; which certificate may be in the form, or to the effect, comprized in the schedule hereunto annexed.

<small>Certificates of vacancies to be notified in the Gazette.</small>

3dly. Provided always, and be it enacted, That the speaker of the house of commons shall forthwith, after his receiving such certificate, cause notice thereof to be inserted in the London Gazette, and shall not issue his warrant until fourteen days after the insertion of such notice in the Gazette.

<small>Certain restrictions on the speaker relative to issuing his warrant.</small>

4thly. Provided also, That nothing herein contained shall extend to enable the speaker of the house of commons to issue his warrant for the purposes aforesaid, unless the return of the writ (by virtue of which such member deceased, or become a peer of Great Britain, was elected) shall have been brought into the office of the clerk of the crown, fifteen days at the least before the end of the last sitting of the house of commons immediately preceding the time when such application shall be made to the speaker of the house of commons to issue such warrant as aforesaid, nor unless such application shall be made so long before the then next meeeting of the house of commons for the dispatch of business, as that the writ for the election may be issued before the day of such next meeting of the house of commons; nor in case such application shall be made with respect to any seat in the house of commons which shall have been vacated in either of the methods before-mentioned, by any member

ber of that house against whose election or return to serve in parliament a petition was depending, at the time of the then last prorogation of parliament, or adjournment of the house of commons.

5thly. And whereas the due execution of this act may be prevented or impeded by the death of the speaker of the house of commons for the time being, or by his seat in parliament becoming vacant, or by his absence out of the realm, for which inconveniencies it is expedient to provide a remedy; be it therefore enacted by the authority aforesaid, That it shall and may be lawful for the present speaker of the house of commons, and he is hereby required, within a convenient time after the passing of this act, and for every future speaker of the house of commons, and he is hereby required within a convenient time after he shall be in that office, at the beginning of any parliament, by any instrument in writing under his hand and seal, to nominate and appoint a certain number of persons, not more than seven, nor less than three, members of the house of commons at the time being, thereby authorizing them, or any one of them, to execute all and singular the powers given to the speaker of the house of commons for the time being, for issuing such warrants as aforesaid, by virtue of this act, subject nevertheless to such regulations and exceptions as are herein also contained; which instrument of appointment and authority shall, notwithstanding the death of the speaker of the house of commons making and executing the same, or

Speaker to authorize a certain number of members of the house of commons to execute the powers given to him by this act.

the vacating his seat in parliament, continue and remain in full force until the dissolution of the parliament in which it shall be made.

When such number shall be reduced to less than 3, a new appointment to be made.

6thly. Provided always, and be it enacted, That whenever and as often as the said number of persons, so to be appointed as aforesaid, shall, by death, or by their seats in parliament being vacated, happen to be reduced to less than three, it shall and may be lawful for the speaker of the house of commons for the time being to make a new appointment in the manner herein-before directed.

Appointments to be entered in the journals of the house, and published in the Gazette.

7thly. Provided also, That every such appointment shall be entered in the journals of the house of commons, and be also published once in the London Gazette; and the instrument of such appointment shall be preserved by the clerk of the house of commons, and a duplicate thereof shall be filed in the office of the clerk of the crown in chancery.

In what cases only such persons are impowered to act.

8thly. Provided also, That nothing in this act contained shall extend, or be construed to extend, to give any power or authority whatsoever to any person so to be nominated and appointed as aforesaid, except in the case of there being no speaker of the house of commons, or of his being absent out of the realm, nor for any longer time than such person, so to be appointed as aforesaid, shall continue a member of the house of commons; any thing herein contained to the contrary notwithstanding.

Publisher of the Gazette to give receipts for notices.

9thly. And be it enacted, That the publisher of the Gazette for the time being, when any such notice as aforesaid of the issuing of any such warrant

rant shall be brought to him, signed by any person so appointed as aforesaid, shall give a receipt for the same, specifying the day and hour when the same was received; and in case more than one such notice shall be brought to him, relative to the same election, such publisher shall insert in the Gazette only the notice first received.

SCHEDULE.

WE whose names are underwritten, being two members of the house of commons, do hereby certify, That *M. P.* late a member of the said house, serving as one of the knights of the shire for the county of   [*or as the case may be*] died upon the   day of
[*or* is become a peer of Great Britain], and that a writ of summons hath been issued, under the great seal of Great Britain, to summon him to parliament [*or as the case may be*]; and we give you this notice, to the intent that you may issue your warrant to the clerk of the crown, to make out a new writ for the election of a knight to serve in parliament for the said county of
[*or as the case may be*] in the room of the said *M. P.* Given under our hands, this   day of

To the Speaker of
the House of Commons.

Note, That in case there shall be no speaker of the house of commons, or of his absence out of the realm, such certificate may be addressed to any one of the persons appointed according to the directions of this act.

ANNO 25° GEORGII III. CAP. 17.

An Act to enable the House of Commons to authorize the Select Committee, appointed to try the Merits of the Petition of the Honourable Saint Andrew Saint John, *complaining of an undue Election for the County of Bedford, to proceed in case the said Select Committee shall be reduced to a less Number than is prescribed by an Act, made in the* 10*th Year of the Reign of His present Majesty, intituled,* An Act *to regulate the Trials of Controverted Elections, or Returns of Members to serve in Parliament.*

WHEREAS the select committee appointed to try and determine the merits of the petition of the honourable *Saint Andrew Saint John*, complaining of an undue election and return for the county of Bedford, have made a considerable progress in the matters to them referred, but are now, by the indisposition of two of the members of the said select committee, reduced to thirteen; and if the said committee should be further reduced, by the indisposition or death of any of the members remaining on the said select committee, the same would be dissolved, which would be attended with manifest injury and inconvenience to the parties concerned: Be it therefore enacted by the king's most excellent majesty, by and with the advice and consent of the lords spiritual and temporal and commons in this present parliament assembled, and by the authority of the same, That if the said select committee shall, by the indisposition or death of any of the said members of the said select committee, be further reduced to eleven, it shall be lawful for the house of commons, upon application made to them for that purpose, to authorize and direct the said select committee to proceed in the matters referred to them, and report upon the same; which report shall be deemed to be as valid as if the number of the said select committee had not been reduced to eleven; any thing in an act made in the 10th year of the reign of his present majesty, intituled, An act to regulate the trials of controverted elections, or returns of members to serve in parliament, to the contrary thereof in any wise notwithstanding.

If the committee shall be reduced to 11, the house of commons may direct them to proceed, and to make report.

A. D. 1785.

ANNO 25° GEORGII III. CAP. 84.

An Act to limit the Duration of Polls and Scrutinies, and for making other Regulations touching the Election of Members to serve in Parliament for Places within England and Wales, and for Berwick upon Tweed; and also for removing Difficulties which may arise for want of Returns being made of Members to serve in Parliament.

FOR the better regulation of polls and scrutinies, be it enacted by the king's most excellent majesty,

majesty, by and with the advice and consent of the lords spiritual and temporal and commons in this present parliament assembled, and by the authority of the same, That, from and after the first day of August 1785, every poll which shall be demanded at any election for a member or members to serve in parliament for any county, city, borough, or other place, within England, Wales, or for the town of Berwick upon Tweed, shall commence on the day upon which the same shall be demanded, or upon the next day at farthest, (unless it shall happen to be a Sunday, and then on the day after;) and shall be duly and regularly proceeded in from day to day (Sundays excepted) until the same be finished, but so as that no poll for the election of any member or members to serve in parliament, shall continue more than fifteen days at most (Sundays excepted); and if such poll shall continue until the fifteenth day, then the same shall be finally closed at or before the hour of three in the afternoon of the same day; and the returning officer or officers at every such election shall, immediately, or on the day next after the final close of the poll, truly, fairly, and publicly declare the name or names of the person or persons who have the majority of votes on such poll, and shall forthwith make a return of such person or persons, unless the returning officer or officers, upon a scrutiny being demanded by any candidate, or any two or more electors, shall deem it necessary to grant the same; in which case, it shall and may be lawful for him so to do, and to proceed there-

From Aug. 1, 1785, every poll must commence, at the latest, the day after it is demanded, unless it be Sunday, and must not continue more than 15 days.

Return to be made at the close of the poll, or the day after, unless a scrutiny is demanded.

thereupon, but so as that in all cases of a general election, every returning officer or officers having the return of a writ, shall cause a return of a member or members to be filed in the crown office on or before the day on which such writ is returnable; and every other returning officer or officers, acting under a precept or mandate, shall make a return of a member or members, in obedience to such precept or mandate, at least six days before the day of the return of the writ by virtue of which such election has been made; and so that in case of any election, upon a writ issued during a session or prorogation of parliament, and a scrutiny being granted as aforesaid, then that a return of a member or members shall be made within thirty days after the close of the poll, (or sooner, if the same can conveniently be done).

Regulations for making returns in case of a scrutiny.

2dly. And be it enacted, That whenever a scrutiny shall be granted as aforesaid, and there shall be more parties than one objecting to votes on such scrutiny, the returning officer or returning officers, shall decide alternately, or by turns, on the votes given for the different candidates who shall be parties to such scrutiny, or against whom the same shall be carried on.

Objections to voters to be decided alternatively.

3dly. And, in order that electors may have full time and opportunity to poll, be it enacted, That all and every returning officer and officers, unless prevented by any unavoidable accident, shall, during the continuance of the poll, on every day subsequent to the commencement of the same,

cause

Poll to be kept open seven hours daily.

cause the said poll to be kept open for seven hours at the least in each day, between the hours of eight in the morning and eight at night.

4thly. And whereas inconveniencies may arise from the time allowed by the laws now in being for proceeding to an election of a knight or knights to serve in parliament, for any county or shire in England or Wales; be it enacted, That, immediately after the receipt of the writ for making any such election, and indorsing on the back thereof the day of receiving the same, as by law required, it shall and may be lawful for the sheriff of such county or shire, and he is *Within two days after receipt of the writ, proclamation to be made of the election, which must begin between the 10th and 16th days after proclamation.* hereby required, within two days after the receipt thereof, to cause proclamation to be made at the place where the ensuing election ought by law to be holden, of a special county court to be there holden for the purpose of such election only, on any day, Sunday excepted, not later from the day of making such proclamation than the sixteenth day, nor sooner than the tenth day; and that he shall proceed in such election, at such special county court, in the same manner as if the said election was to be held at a county court, or at an adjourned county court, according to the laws now in being: provided always, That the usual county court for all other purposes, or any adjournment made thereof, shall take place, be held, and proceeded in, by the sheriff, or his deputy, and may from time to time be further adjourned and proceeded in, in such and the same manner, and at the same times and places, as if

the

the writ for the election of a knight or knights of the shire had not been received.

5thly. And whereas, although from the various and disputed rights of voting in several cities, boroughs and other places, a positive oath of qualification cannot be required from the electors, yet it is apprehended that unqualified persons may be deterred from polling at such elections, under fictitious names or otherwise, by requiring from electors previously to their polling, the oath or affirmation herein-after mentioned; be it therefore further enacted, That, from and after the said first day of August, 1785, upon every election to be made, within that part of Great Britain called England, or Wales, or town of Berwick upon Tweed, of any member or members to serve in parliament, in all cases where no oath or affirmation of qualification, other than the oaths or affirmations against bribery, or of allegiance, supremacy, and abjuration, can now by law be required, every person claiming to give his vote at the said election, shall (if required by any candidate, or any person having a right to vote at such election), before he is admitted to poll, take the oath (or, being one of the people called *Quakers*, make the solemn affirmation) following; (that is to say), An oath to be taken previous to polling.

" I do swear, *(or being a Quaker*, do affirm,) That my name is *A. B.* and that I am [*specifying the addition, profession, or trade of such person*], and that the place of my abode is at   in the county of

[*and*

[*and if it is a town consisting of more streets than one, specifying what street*]; and that I have not before polled at this election; and that I verily believe myself to be of the full age of twenty-one years."

Which oath, or solemn affirmation, the returning officer or officers at such election, and his or their deputies and poll clerks, is or are hereby authorized and required to administer.

6thly. And be it further enacted, That, from and after the first day of August, 1785, upon every election of any member or members to serve in parliament for any county, city, borough, or place, within England or Wales, or for Berwick upon Tweed, it shall and may be lawful for the returning officer or officers, if he or they see cause, and he and they are in such case authorized, during the continuance of any scrutiny which shall have been granted as aforesaid, to administer an oath to any person whatsoever consenting to take the same, touching the right of any person having voted at such election, or touching any other matter or thing material or necessary towards carrying on such scrutiny.

<small>Returning officers authorized to administer oaths during a scrutiny.</small>

7thly. And whereas it is expedient that all persons employed as poll clerks at elections, should take an oath for the faithful discharge of their office, but the same is not at present required or authorized by law, except in counties and other places for which there are express provisions made by statute; be it therefore further enacted, That, from and after the said first day of August, 1785, at every

every election of any member or members of parliament for any city, borough or other place, within England or Wales, or town of Berwick upon Tweed, every person whom the returning officer or officers shall retain to act as a clerk in taking the poll shall, before beginning to take such poll, be sworn by such returning officer or officers truly and indifferently to take the said poll, and to set down the name of each voter, and his addition, profession, or trade, and the place of his abode, and for whom he shall poll; and to poll no person who is not sworn or put to his affirmation, where, by this or any other statute, any oath or affirmation now is or hereafter shall be required, which oath of every such poll clerk the said returning officer or officers is or are hereby authorized and required to administer.

Poll clerks to take an oath for the faithful discharge of their duty.

8thly. And be it further enacted, That if any person, in taking any oath or affirmation hereinbefore appointed or authorized to be taken before any returning officer or officers, shall thereby commit wilful perjury, and be thereof convicted; or if any person shall unlawfully and corruptly procure or suborn any other person to take any such oath or affirmation, whereby he or she shall commit such wilful perjury, and shall be thereof convicted, he or she so offending shall incur such pains and penalties as are inflicted in and by two acts of parliament, the one made in the 5th year of the reign of the late Queen Elizabeth (intituled, An act for punishment of such person as shall procure or commit any wilful perjury); the other made in the

Persons taking, or suborning others to take, a false oath, liable to the pains inflicted by 5 Eliz. c. 9; and 2 Geo. 2, c. 25.

the 2d year of his late majesty king George the Second (intituled, An act for the more effectual preventing and further punishment of forgery perjury, and subornation of perjury; and to make it felony to steal bonds, notes, or other securities for payment of money), for any perjury or subornation of perjury, contrary to the said acts.

<small>Not to extend to places where particular regulations have been enacted by statute.</small>

9thly. Provided always, and be it enacted, That nothing in this act before contained shall extend to, or in any wise affect, alter, or regulate the mode or time of proceeding at any election of any member or members for any place where particular regulations, touching the duration of polls and scrutinies, are specially enacted by statute, but that every such election shall be begun and carried on in the same manner as if this act had not been made.

10thly. And whereas an act was passed in the 10th year of his present majesty's reign (intituled, An act to regulate the trials of controverted elections, or returns of members to serve in Parliament); and another act was passed in the 11th year of his said majesty's reign, for explaining and amending the said former act; and whereas no provision is made therein for the hearing and determining any petition, unless the same shall complain of an undue election or return of members to serve in parliament; be it therefore

<small>Where returns have not been duly made, a select committee may be appointed, conformable to 10 Geo. 3, c. 16, and 11 Geo. 3, c. 42.</small>

enacted, That, from and after the first day of August, 1785, if upon any writ or writs to be issued for the election of any member or members to serve in parliament, no return shall be made to the same on or before the day on which such writ

writ is made returnable; or if a writ shall have been issued during any session or prorogation of parliament, and no return shall be made to the same within fifty-two days after the day on which such writ bears date; or if the return made in either of such cases shall not be a return of a member or members, according to the requisition thereof, but contain special matters only concerning such election; it shall and may be lawful for any person or persons, having had, or claiming to have had, a right to vote at such election, or claiming to have had a right to be returned as duly elected thereat, who shall think himself or themselves aggrieved, to petition the house of commons concerning the same; and upon such petition being presented, a day and hour shall be appointed for taking the same into consideration, and notice thereof in writing shall be forthwith given by the speaker to the petitioners, and to the returning officer or officers by whom such return ought to have been made, or shall have been made, accompanied with an order to him or them to attend the house at the time appointed, by himself or themselves, his or their council or agents; and a select committee shall be appointed according to the directions of the said two recited acts, for regulating the trial of controverted elections; which committee shall try and determine whether any, and which of the person or persons named in such petition ought to have been returned, or whether a new writ ought to issue; which determination shall be final to all intents and purposes; and the house being informed thereof

Notice of the meeting of committees to be given to the petitioners and returning officers.

thereof by the chairman of the said select committee, shall order the same to be entered in their journals, and give the necessary directions for ordering a return to be made, or for altering the return if made, or for the issuing a new writ for a new election, or for carrying the said determination into execution, as the case may require.

Regulations of 10 Geo. 3. c. 16; and 11 Geo. 3. c. 42, extended to this act.

11thly. And be it further enacted, That all and every the rules, regulations, authorities, and powers, given or prescribed by either of the said recited acts for regulating the trial of controverted elections, with respect to select committees to be appointed by virtue of the said acts, or either of them, shall be in full force and effect with respect to select committees to be appointed by virtue of this present act, in as full and ample manner as if the same were herein repeated and particularly and specially enacted concerning the same.

When returning officers cannot be found, or do not appear at committees, other persons may be appointed to appear in their stead, and where more than one petition is presented, the house to determine turning officer is to strike off from the list of members drawn by lot.

12thly. Provided always, That if the returning officer or officers, by whom such return ought to have been made, or has been made, cannot be found so as to be served with the notice or order herein-before mentioned, or being served shall not appear by himself or themselves, his or their council or agents, at the day or time appointed for taking such petition into consideration, it shall and may be lawful for the house to permit or authorize any person to appear in the stead of him or them; and in case there shall be more petitions than one presented, complaining of such return, or omission of a return, on distinct interests, or complaining upon different grounds, the

the house shall determine, from the nature of the case, whether the returning officer or officers, or person appearing in the stead of him or them, shall, together with such petitioners, be entitled to strike off from the list of members drawn by lot, in the manner directed by the said act, passed in the 11th year of the reign of his present Majesty, in the case where there shall be more than two parties before the house, or whether such list shall be reduced by the parties severally presenting the said petitions only.

13thly. And be it enacted, That if any sheriff, or other returning officer or officers, who shall preside at any election of a member or members to serve in parliament for any county, city, borough, or place, shall wilfully offend against, or act contrary to the true intent and meaning of this act, every such person shall be liable to be prosecuted, by information or indictment, in his majesty's court of king's bench, or at any court of oyer and terminer, great sessions, or gaol delivery, for the county, city, town, or place, where such offence shall be committed, in which no *noli prosequi* or *cesset processus* shall be granted; any law, custom, or usage to the contrary notwithstanding.

Returning officers liable to prosecution for offences against this act.

14thly. And be it further enacted, That if any sheriff or returning officer shall wilfully delay, neglect, or refuse duly to return any person who ought to be returned to serve in parliament for any county, city, borough, or place within Great Britain, every such person may, in case it shall have been determined by a select committee,

Returning officers may be sued for neglecting to return persons duly elected.

committee, appointed in the manner hereinbefore directed, that such person was entitled to have been returned, sue the sheriff, or other officer or officers, having so wilfully delayed, neglected, or refused, duly to make such return, and every or any of them, at his election, in any of his majesty's courts of record at Westminster, or of the court of session in Scotland; and shall recover double the damages he shall sustain by reason thereof, together with full costs of suit.

Actions to be commenced within one year after the offence, or six months after conclusion of proceedings in the house.

15thly. Provided always, and be it further enacted, That every indictment, information, or action, for any offence against this act, shall be found, filed, or commenced within one year after commission of the fact on which such indictment, information, or action shall be grounded, or within six months after the conclusion of any proceedings in the house of commons relating to such election.

Poll may be adjourned from Winchester to Newport in the Isle of Wight, &c.

16thly. Provided always, That, notwithstanding any thing in this act contained, it shall and may be lawful for the sheriff of the county of Southampton, and he is hereby required, after any poll for the said county shall have closed at Winchester, and which shall always be closed within the space of fifteen days at the most, in the manner above required, to adjourn the poll to Newport in the Isle of Wight, in case the same shall be required by one or more of the candidates, so that every such adjourned poll shall commence within four days from the close of the poll at Winchester, and shall not continue longer than three days at the most.

A. D. 1785.

ANNO

ANNO 26° GEORGII III. CAP. 100.

An Act to prevent occasional Inhabitants from voting in the Election of Members to serve in Parliament, for Cities and Boroughs, in that Part of Great Britain called England, and the Dominion of Wales.

WHEREAS it frequently happens, in cities and boroughs where the right of election of members to serve in parliament is in the inhabitants paying scot and lot, or in the inhabitants householders, housekeepers, and pot-wallers, legally settled, or in the inhabitants householders, housekeepers, and pot-wallers, or in the inhabitants householders resiants, or in the inhabitants within such cities or boroughs, that much trouble, expence, and litigation, is created by occasional voters, to the great prejudice of the real inhabitants, who bear the burthens of such cities and boroughs, and to whom the right of sending members to parliament belongs: For remedy thereof, be it enacted by the king's most excellent majesty, by and with the advice and consent of the lords spiritual and temporal and commons in this present parliament assembled, and by the authority of the same, That from and after the first day of August 1786, no person shall be admitted to vote at any election of a member or members to serve in parliament for any city or borough of that part of Great Britain called England,

From Aug. 1, 1786, any person voting as an inhabitant, paying scot and lot, &c. who shall not have been so 6 months previous to the election, to forfeit 20l.;

land, or the dominion of Wales, as an inhabitant paying scot and lot, or as an inhabitant householder, housekeeper, and pot-waller, legally settled, or as an inhabitant householder, housekeeper, and pot-waller, or as an inhabitant householder resiant, or as an inhabitant of such city or borough, unless he shall have been actually and *bona fide* an inhabitant paying scot and lot, or an inhabitant householder, housekeeper, and pot-waller, legally settled, or an inhabitant householder, housekeeper, and pot-waller, or an inhabitant householder resiant, or an inhabitant within such city or borough, six kalendar months previous to the day of the election at which he shall tender his vote; and if any person shall vote at any such election, contrary to the true intent and meaning of this act, his vote shall be deemed null and void, and he shall forfeit, to any person who shall sue for the same, the sum of twenty pounds to be recovered by him or her, by action of debt, in any of his majesty's courts of record at Westminster, wherein no essoin, protection, wager of law, privilege, or imparlance, shall be admitted or allowed; and in every such action the proof of inhabitancy, as aforesaid, shall lie upon the person against whom the same shall be brought: Provided nevertheless, That such action be commenced within six kalendar months after the cause of action accrued: Provided also,

<small>but not to extend to persons acquiring possession by descent, &c.</small> that nothing in this act contained shall extend, or be construed to extend, to any person acquiring the possession of any house, in any city or borough, by descent, devise, marriage, or marriage settlement, or promotion to any office or benefice.

2dly.

2dly. Provided alfo, and be it further enacted, That this act fhall relate only to thofe perfons who claim to exercife the franchife of voting as inhabitants paying fcot and lot, or as inhabitants houfeholders, houfekeepers, and potwallers, legally fettled, or as inhabitants houfeholders, houfekeepers, and potwallers, or as inhabitants houfeholders refiants, or as inhabitants within fuch cities or boroughs, and fhall not extend to any other defcription of perfons who may claim to vote at any election for members to ferve in parliament for fuch cities or boroughs, by any other title, or by any other fuperadded qualification.

nor to perfons claiming a right to vote under any other defcription than inhabitants paying fcot and lot, &c.

A. D. 1786.

ANNO 28° GEORGII III. CAP. 52.

An Act for the further Regulation of the Trials of controverted Elections, or Returns of Members to ferve in Parliament.

WHEREAS, by an act of parliament paffed in the 10th year of the reign of his prefent majefty, intituled, ' An act to regulate the trials of controverted elections, or returns of members to ferve in parliament,' certain regulations were eftablifhed, for a time therein limited, for the trials of controverted elections, or returns of members to ferve in parliament; and whereas, by an act paffed in the 11th year of the reign of his prefent majefty, intituled, ' An act to explain and amend an act made in the laft feffion of parliament, intituled, An act to regulate the trials of controverted elections, or returns of members to

10 Geo. 3. c. 16.

11 Geo. 3. c. 42.

serve in parliament,' further regulations were made therein; and whereas the provisions of the the said acts were, by an act passed in the 14th year of the reign of his present majesty, continued and made perpetual; and whereas, by an act passed in the 25th year of the reign of his present majesty, intituled, ' An act to limit the duration of polls and scrutinies, and for making other regulations touching the election of members to serve in parliament for places within England and Wales, and for Berwick upon Tweed, and also for removing difficulties which may arise for want of returns being made of members to serve in parliament,' the provisions of the said acts were extended, in the manner therein mentioned, to petitions complaining that no return has been made to a writ, issued for the election of a member or members to serve in parliament, within the times limited in the said act, or that such return is not a return of a member or members according to the requisition of the writ; and whereas it is expedient that further regulations should be made for the execution of the said several acts, and that provision should be made for discouraging persons from presenting frivolous or vexatious petitions, or setting up frivolous or vexatious defences, in any of the cases to which the above-recited acts relate, and that provision should also be made for the final decision of questions respecting the rights of voting at such elections, or of nominating or appointing the returning officer or returning officers who are to preside thereat: Be it therefore enacted by the king's most excellent majesty,

and 25 Geo. 3. c. 84. recited.

majesty, by and with the advice and consent of the lords spiritual and temporal and commons in this present parliament assembled, and by the authority of the same, That no petition complaining of an undue election or return, or of the omission of a return, or of the insufficiency of a return, shall be proceeded upon, in the manner prescribed in the said above recited acts, unless the same shall be subscribed by some person or persons claiming therein to have had a right to vote at the election to which the same shall relate, or to have had a right to be returned as duly elected thereat, or alledging himself or themselves to have been a candidate or candidates at such election: Provided always, That in any case where a writ has been issued for the election of a member to serve in parliament for any district of burghs in that part of Great Britain called Scotland, any such petition as aforesaid shall and may be so proceeded upon, if the same shall be subscribed by any person or persons claiming therein to have had a right to vote at the election of any delegate or delegates, commissioner or commissioners, for chusing a burgess for such district.

No petition complaining of an undue election or return, to be proceeded upon, unless subscribed as herein mentioned.

2dly. And be it further enacted, That if, at any time, before the day appointed for taking any such petition into consideration, the speaker of the house of commons shall be informed, by a certificate in writing, subscribed by two of the members of the said house, of the death of the sitting member or sitting members, or either of them, whose election or return is complained of in such petition, or of the death of any member or members

In the cases herein specified, notice to be sent by the speaker to the returning officer of the place to which any such petition relates.

bers returned upon a double return, whofe election or return is complained of in fuch petition, or that a writ of fummons has been iffued, under the great feal of Great Britain, to fummon any fuch member or members to parliament as a peer of Great Britain; or if the houfe of commons fhall have refolved that the feat of any fuch member is by law become vacant; or if the faid houfe fhall he informed, by a declaration in writing, fubfcribed by fuch member or members, or either of them, as the cafe fhall be, and delivered in at the table of the houfe, that it is not the intention of fuch member or members to defend his or their election or return; in every fuch cafe notice thereof fhall immediately be fent by the fpeaker to the fheriff, or other returning officer for the county, borough, or place to which fuch petition fhall relate, and fuch fheriff or other returning officer fhall caufe a true copy of the fame to be affixed on the doors of the county hall or town hall, or of the parifh church neareft to the place where fuch election has ufually been held, and fuch notice fhall alfo be inferted, by order of the fpeaker, in the next London Gazette; and the order for taking fuch petition into confideration fhall, if neceffary, be adjourned, fo that at the leaft thirty days may intervene between the day on which fuch notice fhall be inferted in the faid Gazette, and the day on which fuch petition fhall be taken into confideration.

A copy thereof to be affixed on the doors of the county or town hall, or neareft church, and faid notice to be inferted in the Gazette.

Order for taking fuch petitions into confideration may be adjourned,

3dly. And be it enacted, That it fhall and may be lawful, at any time within thirty days after the day on which fuch notice fhall have been inferted in

Within 30 days after notice is fo inferted in the

in the said Gazette, for any person or persons claiming to have had a right to vote at such election, or at the election of delegates or commissioners for making such election, to petition the house, praying to be admitted as a party or parties, in the room of such member or members, or either of them; and such person or persons shall thereupon be so admitted as a party or parties, and shall be considered as such, to all intents and purposes whatever.

Gazette, any voter may petition to be admitted a party in the complaint.

4thly. And be it enacted, That whenever the member or members, whose election or return is so complained of in such petition, shall have given such notice as aforesaid of his or their intention not to defend the same, he or they shall not be admitted to appear or act as a party or parties against such petition, in any subsequent proceedings thereupon, any thing in the above recited acts to the contrary notwithstanding; and he or they shall also be restrained from sitting in the house, or voting in any question, until such petition shall have been decided upon in the manner prescribed by the above recited acts and by this act.

Members giving notice of their intention not to defend their election, not to be admitted as parties against any such petition, &c.

5thly. And be it further enacted, That no proceeding shall be had upon any petition, by virtue of the above recited acts or of this act, unless the person or persons subscribing the same, or some one or more of them, shall, within fourteen days after the same shall have been presented to the house, or within such further time as shall be limited by the house, personally enter into a recognizance to our sovereign lord the king, according

No proceedings to be had upon any petition, unless one of the subscribers enter into a recognizance to appear before the house at the time fixed for taking it into consideration,

cording to the form hereunto annexed, in the sum of two hundred pounds, with two sufficient sureties, in the sum of one hundred pounds each, to appear before the house at such time or times as shall be fixed by the house for taking such petition into consideration, and also to appear before any select committee which shall be appointed by the house for the trial of the same, and to renew the same in every subsequent session of parliament, until a select committee shall have been appointed by the house for the trial of the same, or until the same shall have been withdrawn by the permission of the house; and if, at the expiration of the said fourteen days, such recognizance shall not have been so entered into, or shall not have been received by the speaker of the house of commons, the speaker shall report the same to the house, and the order for taking such petition into consideration shall thereupon be discharged, unless, upon matter specially stated, and verified to the satisfaction of the house, the house shall see cause to enlarge the time for entering into such recognizance; and whenever such time shall be so enlarged, the order for taking such petition into consideration shall, if necessary, be postponed, so that no such petition shall be so taken into consideration till after such recognizance shall have been entered into and received by the speaker: Provided always, That the time for entering into such recognizance shall not be enlarged more than once, nor for any number of days exceeding thirty.

and if no recognizance be duly entered into, the order for taking the petition into consideration to be discharged, unless cause shall be seen for enlarging the time, &c.

6thly.

6thly. And be it enacted, That the said recognizance shall be entered into before the speaker of the house of commons, who is hereby authorized and empowered to take the same; and the sufficiency of the sureties named therein shall be judged of and allowed by the said speaker, on the report of two persons appointed by him to examine the same, of which two persons the clerk, or clerk assistant of the house, shall always be one, and one of the following officers, not being a member of the said house, shall be the other; (that is to say) masters of the high court of chancery, clerks in the court of king's bench, prothonotaries in the court of common pleas, and clerks in the court of exchequer; and the said persons so appointed are hereby authorized and required to examine the same, and to report their judgement thereupon; and are also hereby authorized to demand and receive such fees, for such examination and report, as shall be, from time to time, fixed by any resolution of the house of commons.

Recognizances to be entered into before the speaker, and the sufficiency of the sureties to be allowed of by him, on the report of the persons herein mentioned.

7thly. Provided always, and be it further enacted, That in case where the party or parties, who are to enter into such recognizance, or his or their sureties, or either of them, shall reside at a greater distance from London than forty miles, it shall and may be lawful for such party or parties, surety or sureties, respectively, to enter into such recognizance before any of his majesty's justices of the peace; and his majesty's justices of the peace, or any of them, is and are hereby authorized and empowered to take the same;

Sureties living more than 40 miles from London may enter recognizance before a justice.

fame; and such recognizance, being duly certified under the hand of such justice, and being transmitted to the speaker of the house of commons, shall have the same force and effect as if the same had been entered into before the said speaker: provided nevertheless, that it shall and may be lawful for the persons to whom it is referred by the speaker to examine the sufficiency of such surety or sureties, to receive as evidence, in their said examination, any affidavits relating

Affidavits made before a master in chancery, or a justice, to be received as evidence of the sufficiency of sureties.

thereto, which shall be sworn before any master of the high court of chancery, or before any of his majesty's justices of the peace; and such master of the high court of chancery, or justice of the peace, respectively, is hereby authorized to administer such oath, and is authorized and required to certify such affidavit under his hand.

No petition to be withdrawn unless the member's seat shall have been vacated.

8thly. And be it enacted, That the house shall not permit any such petition to be withdrawn, except so far as the same may relate to the election or return of any member or members who shall, since the same shall have been presented, have vacated his or their seat by death, or in any other manner.

Recognizances of petitioners not appearing before the house at the time fixed for proceeding to the appointment of a select committee, &c. to be certified into the exchequer.

9thly. And be it enacted, That if the petitioner or petitioners, who shall have entered into such recognizance as aforesaid, shall not appear before the house by himself or themselves, or by his or their counsel or agents, within one hour after the time fixed, in pursuance of the above recited acts, and of this act, for calling in the respective parties, their counsel or agents, for the purpose of proceeding to the appointment of a select

committee;

committee; or if the select committee, appointed in pursuance of the said acts, and of this act, for the trial of such petition, shall inform the house that such person or persons did not appear before the said committee, by himself or themselves, or by his or their counsel or agents, to prosecute their said petition; or if such person or persons shall neglect to renew their said petition within four sitting days after the day of the commencement of every session of the same parliament, subsequent to that in which such petition was first presented, and until a select committee shall have been appointed for trial of the same, or until the same shall have been withdrawn by the permission of the house, in every such case such person or persons shall be held to have made default in his or their said recognizance; and the speaker of the house of commons shall thereupon certify such recognizance into the court of exchequer, and shall also certify that such person or persons have made default therein, and such certificate shall be conclusive evidence of such default, and the recognizance being so certified shall have the same effect as if the same were estreated from a court of law: Provided always, That such recognizance and certificate shall in every such case be delivered, by the clerk or clerk assistant of the house of commons, into the hands of the lord chief baron of the exchequer, or of one of the barons of the exchequer, or of such officer of the court of exchequer as shall be appointed by the said court to receive the same.

Recognizance and certificate to be delivered, by the clerk or clerk assistant, into the exchequer.

10thly.

10thly. And whereas, by several provisions contained in the above recited acts, made in the 10th and 11th years of the reign of his present majesty, *Sunday* and *Christmas day* are excepted from the general regulations of the said acts; be it hereby enacted, That in every such case, *Good Friday* shall also be excepted therefrom, in the same manner as if the same had been specially excepted in the said acts.

<small>*Good Friday* to be excepted from the regulations of the recited acts.</small>

11thly. And be it also enacted, That if, on the day immediately preceding any of the three following days, that is to say, *Christmas day*, *Whit-Sunday*, or *Good Friday*, after reading the order of the day for taking any such petition as aforesaid into consideration, it shall be found that there are not one hundred members present, or that the number of forty-nine members, not set aside or excused, cannot be completed, it shall and may be lawful for the house, if they shall think fit, any thing in the above-recited acts to the contrary notwithstanding, to direct that the said order shall be adjourned for any number of days, and the house shall then immediately be adjourned to the hour and day to which such order shall be so adjourned.

<small>If on the day preceeding *Christmas day*, &c. there shall not be 100 members present, or 49 not excused cannot be completed, the order for taking any such petition into consideration, and the house may be adjourned for any number of days.</small>

12thly. And whereas it is enacted, by the said act passed in the 11th year of the reign of his present majesty, that on the day appointed for taking such petition into consideration, the house shall not proceed to any other business whatsoever, except the swearing of members, previous to the reading of the order of the day for that purpose; be it hereby enacted, That it shall and may

may be lawful for the house, previous to reading such order, to receive any report from any select committee appointed in pursuance of the above-recited acts, or of this act, and to enter the same upon their journals, and to give the necessary orders and directions thereupon; and that previous to reading the said order, the clerk of the crown may be admitted to alter or amend any return, in pursuance of an order made on a preceding day, or on that day; and also, that it shall and may be lawful for the house, previous to reading the said order, to postpone the same, for the purpose of attending his majesty, or his majesty's commissioners, in the house of lords, in consequence of any message from his majesty, or from his majesty's commissioners, signified to the house in the usual manner.

On days appointed for taking petitions into consideration, reports from select committees, &c. may be received previous to reading the order of the day.

13thly. And be it also enacted, That if, within one hour after the time fixed in pursuance of above-recited acts, and of this act, for calling in the respective parties, their counsel or agents, for the purpose of proceeding to the appointment of a select committee, the petitioner or petitioners, or some one or more of them, who shall have signed any such petition, shall not appear by himself or themselves, or by his or their counsel or agents, the order for taking such petition into consideration shall thereupon be discharged, and such petition shall not be any further proceeded upon in the manner directed in the above-recited acts, and in this act.

If petitioners do not appear within an hour after the time fixed for appointing select committees, the order for taking such petitions into consideration to be discharged.

14thly. And be it enacted, That if, within one hour after the time so appointed as aforesaid, the sitting

Regulations for trial of the merits of petitions, where no party appears to oppose them.

fitting member or fitting members, or other party or parties opposing the petition, shall not appear by himself or themselves, or by his or their counsel or agents, or if, at the time so appointed as aforesaid, there shall be no party before the house opposing the petition, the house shall proceed to appoint a select committee, to try the merits of such petition, in the following manner; (that is to say,) That the names of forty-nine members shall be drawn, in the manner prescribed in the above-recited acts, but in reducing the list of such names to thirteen, the place of a party opposing the petition shall be supplied by the clerk appointed to attend the said committee, who shall, as often as it shall come to his turn as supplying the place of the party opposing the petition to strike out a name, strike out that name which then shall be first in the said list; and in every case where the party opposing the petition would be impowered, by the above-recited acts, to nominate one member to be added to the said thirteen, the said thirteen shall, from among the persons present in the house at the time of drawing the names of the members, chuse one person to supply the place of the member to have been so nominated, in the same manner as is directed by the above-recited act made in the 11th year of his majesty's reign, in the case where there are more than two parties on distinct interests.

The aforegoing method of reducing the list to 13 members, &c. to be follow-

15thly. And be it further enacted, That the same method of reducing the list of members drawn to thirteen, and of nominating a member to be added

added to the thirteen remaining on the said list, shall be respectively followed, whenever any party shall wave his right of striking off names from the said list, or of nominating a member to be added to the said thirteen.

ed when any party shall wave his right to do it.

16. And be it further enacted, That if any person summoned to attend the said select committee, by the warrant of the speaker of the said house or by order of the said committee, shall disobey such summons, or shall give false evidence, or prevaricate, or otherwise misbehave in giving, or in refusing to give, evidence before the said committee, the said committee shall have power, by a warrant to be signed by the chairman, and directed to the serjeant at arms attending the house of commons, or to his deputy or deputies, to commit such person (not being a peer of the realm or a lord of parliament) to the custody of the said serjeant, without bail or mainprize, for any time not exceeding twenty-four hours if the house shall then be sitting, or if not, then for a time not exceeding twenty-four hours after the hour to which the house shall then be adjourned.

Witnesses not attending the select committee, or giving false evidence, &c. to be committed.

17. And whereas it is enacted by the said act made in the 10th year of his majesty's reign, That if more than two members of the said select committee shall, on any account, be absent therefrom, the said select committee shall adjourn in the manner in the said act directed, and so from time to time, until thirteen members are assembled; and that no such determination as in the said act is mentioned shall be made, nor any question be proposed, unless thirteen members shall

shall be present; and that no member shall have a vote on such determination, or any other question or resolution, who has not attended during every sitting of the said select committee; and that, in case the number of members able to attend the said committee shall, by death or otherwise, be unavoidably reduced to less than thirteen, and shall so continue for the space of three sitting days, the said committee shall be dissolved, and another chosen to try and determine the matter of such petition, in the manner in the said act before provided. Be it hereby enacted, That whenever any committee shall have sat for business fourteen days, not including those days on which they shall have adjourned on account of the absence of any member, nor including *Sunday*, *Christmas day*, or *Good Friday* it shall and may be lawful for them to proceed to business, if a number of members not less than twelve be present; and in such case, the committee shall not be dissolved by reason of the absence of the members, unless the number of members able to attend the same shall, by death or otherwise, be unavoidably reduced to less than twelve, and shall so continue for the space of three sitting days; and whenever any committee shall in like manner have sat for business twenty-five days, it shall and may be lawful for them to proceed to business, if a number of members not less than eleven be present; and in such case, the committee shall not be dissolved by reason of the absence of the members, unless the number of members able to attend the same shall, by death or otherwise, be unavoidably reduced to less than eleven,

marginalia: If a committee shall have sat for business 14 days, 12 members may proceed therein;

and if 25 days, 11 members may proceed

eleven, and shall so continue for the space of three sitting days.

18. And be it further enacted, That every such committee, at the same time that they report to the house their final determination on the merits of the petition which they were sworn to try, shall also report to the house whether such petition did, or did not, appear to them to be frivolous or vexatious; and that they shall in like manner report, with respect to every party or parties who shall have appeared before them in opposition to such petition, whether the opposition of such party or parties respectively did, or did not, appear to them to be frivolous or vexatious; and that if no party shall have appeared before them in opposition to such petition, they shall then report to the house whether such election or return, or such alledged omission of a return, or such alledged insufficiency of a return, as shall be complained of in such petition, according as the case shall be, did, or did not appear to them to be vexatious or corrupt.

Committees in their reports to mention whether petitions, &c. appear to be frivolous or vexatious.

19. And be it enacted, That whenever any such committee shall report to the house, with respect to any such petition, that the same appeared to them to be frivolous or vexatious, the party or parties, if any, who shall have appeared before the committee in opposition to such petition, shall be entitled to recover, from the person or persons, or any of them, who shall have signed such petition, the full costs and expences which such party or parties shall have incurred in opposing the same; such costs and expences to be ascertained in the manner herein-after directed.

Parties opposing petitions reported vexatious, or frivolous,

20. And

and petitioners reported to have been vexatiously or frivolously opposed, to be entitled to costs and expences.

20. And be it also enacted, That whenever any such committee shall report to the house, with respect to the opposition made to such petition by any party or parties who shall have appeared before them, that such opposition appeared to them to be frivolous or vexatious, the person or persons who shall have signed such petition shall be entitled to recover from such party or parties, or any of them, with respect to whom such report shall be made, the full costs and expences which such petitioner or petitioners shall respectively have incurred in prosecuting their said petition; such costs and expences to be ascertained in the manner herein-after directed.

Where no party appears in opposition to any such petition, the costs and expences to be paid by the sitting members, &c.

21. And be it also enacted, That whenever, in any case where no party shall have appeared before such committee in opposition to such petition, such committee shall report to the house, with respect to the election or return, or to the alledged omission of a return, or to the alledged insufficiency of a return, complained of in any such petition, that the same appeared to them to be vexatious or corrupt, the person or persons who shall have signed such petition shall be entitled to recover from the sitting member or sitting members (if any) whose election or return shall be complained of in such petition, such sitting member or sitting members not having given notice as aforesaid of his or their intention not to defend the same, or from any other person or persons whom the house shall have admitted or directed to be made a party or parties to oppose such petition, the full costs and expences which such

such petitioner or petitioners shall have incurred in prosecuting their said petition; such costs and expences to be ascertained in the manner hereinafter directed.

22. And be it enacted, That in the several cases herein-before mentioned, the costs and expences of prosecuting or opposing any such petition shall be ascertained in manner following; (that is to say), That on application made to the speaker of the house of commons, by any such petitioner or petitioners, or party or parties, as before-mentioned, for ascertaining such costs and expences, he shall direct the same to be taxed by two persons, of whom the clerk or clerk assistant of the house shall always be one, and one of the following officers, not being a member of the house shall be the other; (that is to say), masters in the high court of chancery, clerks in the court of king's bench, prothonotaries in the court of common pleas, and clerks in the court of exchequer; and the persons so authorized and directed to tax such costs and expences shall, and they are hereby required to examine the same, and to report the amount thereof to the speaker of the said house, who shall, on application made to him, deliver to the party or parties a certificate, signed by himself, expressing the amount of the costs and expences allowed in such report; and the persons so appointed to tax such costs, and report the amount thereof, are hereby authorized to demand and receive, for such taxation and report, such fees as shall be, from time to time, fixed by any resolution of the house.

How such costs and expences are to be ascertained.

23. And

If costs, &c. be not paid on demand, they may be recovered by action of debt, &c.

23. And be it enacted, That it shall and may be lawful for the party or parties entitled to such costs and expences, or for his, her, or their executors or administrators, to demand the whole amount thereof, so certified as above, from any one or more of the persons respectively, who are herein-before made liable to the payment thereof, in the several cases herein-before mentioned: and in case of nonpayment thereof, to recover the same by action of debt, in any of his majesty's courts of record at Westminster; in which action it shall be sufficient for the plaintiff or plaintiffs to declare that the defendant or defendants is or are indebted to him or them (in the sum to which the costs and expences, ascertained in manner aforesaid, shall amount) by virtue of this act; and the certificate of the speaker of the house of commons, under his signature, of the amount of such costs and expences, together with an examined copy of the entries in the journals of the house of commons, of the resolution or resolutions of the said select committee or committees, shall be deemed full and sufficient evidence in support of such action of debt. Provided always, That in every such action of debt, no wager of law, or more than one imparlance shall be allowed; and the party or parties in whose favour judgement shall be given in any such action, shall recover his or their costs.

Judgement in such actions to entitle the party to costs.

Persons paying costs may recover a proportion thereof from any other persons liable thereto.

24. And be it further enacted, That in every case where the amount of such costs and expences shall have been so recovered from any person or persons, it shall and may be lawful for such person or persons to recover in like manner from

from the other persons, or any of them, if such there shall be, who shall be liable to the payment of the said costs and expences, a proportionable share thereof, according to the number of persons so liable.

25. And be it further enacted, That whenever any such select committee, appointed to try the merits of any such petition as aforesaid, shall be of opinion that the merits of such petition do wholly or in part depend on any question or questions which shall be before them respecting the right of election for the county, city, borough, district of burghs, or other place to which such petition shall relate, or respecting the right of chusing, nominating, or appointing the returning officer or returning officers, who is or are to make return of such election, the said committee, in such case, shall require the counsel or agents for the several parties, or if there shall be none such before them, shall then require the parties themselves to deliver to the clerk of the said committee, statements in writing of the right of election, or of chusing, nominating, or appointing returning officers, for which they respectively contend; and the committee shall come to distinct resolutions on such statements, and shall, at the same time that they report to the house their final determination on the merits of such petition, also report to the house such statement or statements, together with their judgement with respect thereto; and such report shall thereupon be entered in the journals of the house, and notice thereof shall be sent by the speaker to the sheriff or other returning officer of the place to which the same shall relate;

When the merits of petitions depend on questions respecting the right of election, &c. Statements of such right to be delivered in writing; and the committee to report, with their determination on the merits of the petition, their judgement on such statements.

Report to be entered in the journals, and notice thereof sent to the returning officer, &c.

relate; and a true copy of such notice shall, by such sheriff or other returning officer, be forthwith affixed to the doors of the county hall or town hall, or of the parish church nearest to the place where such election has usually been held; and such notice shall also be inserted, by order of the speaker, in the next London Gazette.

Persons may, within twelve months after such report, petition to be admitted to oppose the right of election, &c. thereby established.

26. And be it enacted, That it shall and may be lawful for any person or persons, at any time within twelve kalendar months after the day on which such report shall have been made to the house, or within fourteen days after the day of the commencement of the next session of parliament after that in which such report shall have been made to the house, to petition the house to be admitted as a party or parties to oppose that right of election, or of chusing, nominating, or appointing the returning officer or returning officers, who is or are to make return of such election, which shall have been deemed valid in the judgement of such committee.

But if no such petition shall be so presented, the judgement of the committee to be conclusive.

27. And be it enacted, That if no such petition shall be so presented within the time above limited for presenting the same, the said judgement of such committee, on such question or questions, shall be held and taken to be final and conclusive in all subsequent elections of members of parliament for that place to which the same shall relate, and to all intents and purposes whatsoever; any usage to the contrary notwithstanding.

Forty days to intervene between the presenting and hearing such petitions, &c.

28. And be it enacted, That whenever any such petition shall be so presented, a day and hour shall be appointed by the house for taking the same into consideration; so that the space of forty

forty days at the least shall always intervene between the day of presenting such petition and the day appointed by the house for taking the same into consideration; and notice of such day and hour shall be inserted, by order of the speaker, in the next London Gazette, and shall also be sent by him to the sheriff or other returning officer for the place to which such petition shall relate; and a true copy of such notice shall, by the said sheriff or other returning officer, be forthwith affixed to the doors of the county hall, or town hall, or of the parish church nearest to the place where such election has usually been held.

29. And be it enacted, That it shall and may be lawful for any person or persons, at any time before the day so appointed for taking such petition into consideration, to petition the house to be admitted as a party or parties to defend such right of election, or of chusing, nominating, or appointing the returning officer or returning officers; and such person or persons shall thereupon be so admitted, and shall be considered as such to all intents and purposes whatever.

Before the hearing such petition, any person may petition to be admitted to defend such right of election, &c.

30. And be it enacted, That at the hour appointed by the house for taking such petition into consideration, the house shall proceed to appoint a select committee to try the merits thereof, according to the directions of the above-recited acts, and of this act; and such select committee shall be sworn to try and determine the merits of such petition, so far as the same relate to any question or questions respecting the right of election for the place to which the petition shall relate;

Committee to be appointed to try the merits of such petition, who shall be sworn, &c.

late, or respecting the right of appointing, nominating, or chusing, the returning officer or returning officers who are to make return of such election; and the determination of such committee on such question or questions, shall be be entered in the journals of the house, and shall be held and taken to be final and conclusive in all subsequent elections of members of parliament for that place to which the same shall relate, and to all intents and purposes whatever, any usage to the contrary notwithstanding.

<small>2 Geo. 2. c. 24, in part recited;</small>

31. And whereas it is amongst other things enacted, by an act passed in the 2d year of the reign of his late majesty, king George the Second, intituled, An act for the more effectual preventing bribery and corruption in the elections of members to serve in parliament, that such votes shall be deemed to be legal which have been so declared by the last determination in the house of commons; which last determination concerning any county, shire, city, borough, cinque port, or place, shall be final to all intents and purposes whatever, any usage to the contrary notwithstanding: Be it enacted, That so much of the said act as is above recited shall be, and the same is hereby repealed, in so far only as the same relates, or might be construed to relate, to any such determination to be made in the house of commons subsequent to the passing of this act.

<small>And the same repealed in as far as it may relate to any determination subsequent to passing this act.</small>

<small>Rules, &c. of recited acts to be in force with ref. &c. to committees appointed under this act.</small>

32. And be it enacted, That all and every the rules, regulations, authorities, or powers, prescribed and given by the above-recited acts, or by this act, to select committees for the trial of controverted elections or returns shall be in full

full force and effect with respect to select committees appointed by virtue of this act for the trial of such question or questions of right as aforesaid, in as full and ample a manner as if the same were herein repeated, and particularly and specially enacted, concerning such select committees: Provided always, That the several rules and regulations herein-before enacted, by which certain persons are directed to enter recognizances, and by which certain persons are made liable to the payment of costs, in the particular manner, and in the several cases herein-before specified, shall not be construed to apply to the case of any petition presented in pursuance of this act, and relating solely to any question or questions respecting the right of election, or of chusing, nominating, or appointing a returning officer or returning officers.

Regulations touching recognizances and payment of costs not to apply to petitions relating solely to questions respecting right of election.

33. And be it further enacted, That whenever it shall happen that parliament shall be prorogued while any select committee shall be sitting for the trial of any such petition as aforesaid, and before they shall have reported to the house their determination thereon, such committee shall not be dissolved by such prorogation; but shall be thereby adjourned to twelve of the clock on the day immediately following that on which parliament shall meet again for the dispatch of business, (*Sundays*, *Good Friday*, and *Christmas Day*, always excepted,) and all former proceedings of the said committee shall remain and continue to be of the same force and effect as if parliament had not been so prorogued; and such committee shall meet on the day and hour to which

Committees not to be dissolved by the prorogation of parliament.

which it shall be so adjourned, and shall thenceforward continue to sit from day to day, in the manner provided in the above recited acts, and in this act, until they shall have reported to the house their determination on the merits of such petition.

FORM OF THE RECOGNIZANCE REFERRED TO IN THIS ACT.

"Be it remembered, That on the   day of   in the year of our Lord   before me A. B. [speaker of the house of commons] or [one of his majesty's justices of the peace for the county of   ] came C. D. E. F. and J. G. and severally acknowledged themselves to owe to our sovereign lord the king the following sums; that is to say, the said C. D. the sum of two hundred pounds, and the said E. F. and the said J. G. the sum of one hundred pounds each, to be levied on their respective goods and chattels, lands, and tenements, to the use of our said sovereign lord the king, his heirs and successors, in case the said C. D. shall fail in performing the condition hereunto annexed.

The condition of this recognizance is, that if the said C. D. shall duly appear before the house of commons, at such time or times as shall be fixed by the said house for taking into consideration the petition signed by the said C. D. complaining of an undue election or return for the
   of   [*Here specify the county, city, borough, or district of burghs*]
or

or, complaining that no return has been made for the said [   ] of [   ] within the time limited by act of parliament, or, that the return made for the said [   ] of [   ] is not a return of a member or members according to the requisition of the writ, and shall appear before any select committee which shall be appointed by the house of commons for the trial of the same, and shall renew his said petition in every subsequent session of this present parliament, until a select committee shall have been appointed by the said house for the trial of the same, or until the same shall have been withdrawn by the permission of the said house; then this recognizance to be void, otherwise to be of full force and effect.   A. D. 1787.

ANNO 30° GEORGII III. CAP. *.

An Act to explain and amend an Act passed in the 20th Year of the Reign of his present Majesty, touching the Election for Knights of the Shire to serve in Parliament for that Part of Great Britain called England.

WHEREAS an act was passed in the 20th year of the reign of his present majesty, intituled, ' An act to remove certain difficulties

20 Geo. 3. c. 17.

* This was printed before it could be ascertained, what would be the number of the chapter.

relative

relative to voters at county elections,' whereby it is, among other things, enacted, That from and after the first day of January, 1781, no person shall vote for electing of any knight or knights of the shire to serve in parliament, within that part of Great Britain called England, or the principality of Wales, in respect of any messuages, lands, or tenements, which have not, for six kalendar months next before such election, been charged or assessed towards some aid granted, or to be granted to his majesty, his heirs or successors, by a land tax, (in case any such aid be then granted and assessable), in the name of the person or persons who shall claim to vote at such election for or in respect of any such messuages, lands, or tenements, or in the name of his or their tenant or tenants actually occupying the same as tenant or tenants of the owner or landlord thereof:

And whereas the form of assessment prescribed by the said Act, and thereunto annexed, denotes that the names, both of the proprietor and of the occupier, ought to be specified; and doubts have arisen, whether, if such form be not strictly pursued, the suffrage of the person claiming to vote be admissible:

22 Geo. 3. c. 31. And whereas an act was passed in the 22d year of his present Majesty's reign, intituled, 'An act for the preventing of bribery and corruption in the election of members to serve in parliament for the borough of *Cricklade*, in the county of *Wilts*,' whereby it is enacted, That such freeholders only shall be entitled to vote

vote in the election of members to serve in parliament for the said borough of *Cricklade*, as shall be duly qualified to vote at elections for knights of the shire for the county of *Wilts*, according to the laws in force for regulating county elections at the time of passing the same act.

Be it therefore enacted by the king's most excellent majesty, by and with the advice and consent of the lords spiritual and temporal and commons in this present parliament assembled, and by the authority of the same, That nothing in the said acts contained shall extend, or be construed to extend, to prevent any person from voting at any election of a knight or knights of a shire to serve in parliament within that part of Great Britain called England, or the principality of Wales, or at any election of a burgess or burgesses to serve in parliament for the borough of *Cricklade*, in the county of *Wilts*, for or in respect of any messuages, lands, or tenements, which have been charged or assessed for six kalendar months next before such election, towards some aid granted, or to be granted to his majesty, his heirs or successors, by a land tax, in the name of the person claiming to vote, or for or in respect of any messuages, lands, or tenements, to which the person so claiming to vote shall have become entitled by descent, marriage, marriage settlement, devise, promotion to any benefice in a church, or promotion to any office, within twelve kalendar months next before such election, and which messuages, lands, or tenements, shall have been within two years next before such election charged

Person may vote a though tenant's name is not in the assessment.

or

or assessed to the land-tax, in the name of the person or persons by or through whom such person so claiming to vote shall derive his title to such messuages, lands, or tenements, or of some predecessor of such person so claiming to vote, although the name of the tenant or tenants actually occupying such messuages, lands, or tenements, shall not be inserted in such assessment, according to the form of assessment to the said first recited act annexed.

and although his own name is not in the assessment.

2. And be it further enacted by the authority aforesaid, That nothing in the said acts contained shall extend, or be construed to extend, to prevent any person from voting at any such election of a knight or knights of any shire, or of a burgess or burgesses for the said borough of *Cricklade*, for or in respect of any messuages, lands, or tenements, which have been charged or assessed, for six kalendar months next before such election, towards some aid granted, or to be granted to his majesty, his heirs or successors, by a land tax, in the name of a tenant or tenants actually occupying the same at the time of such assessment being made, although the name of the person so claiming to vote, or the person or persons by or through whom such person so claiming to vote derives his title, or of the predecessor of the person so claiming to vote, shall not be inserted in the assessment, according to the form of the assessment to the said first recited act annexed.

ANNO 31º GEORGII III. CAP. 3.

An Act to give further Time to John Macbride, *Esquire, and his Sureties, for entering into their Recognizances, in respect of his Petition presented to the House of Commons, complaining of an undue Election and Return for the Borough of* Plymouth, *in the County of* Devon.

WHEREAS by an act, made in the twenty-eighth year of the reign of his present majesty, intituled, ' An act for the further regulation of the trials of controverted elections, or returns of members to serve in parliament,' it is enacted, that no proceeding shall be had in the house of commons upon any petition presented to the said house, complaining of an undue election, or return of a member or members to serve in parliament, by virtue of the said act, or of any of the acts therein mentioned, unless the person or persons subscribing such petition, or some one or more of them, shall, within fourteen days after the same shall have been presented to the said house, or within such further time as shall be limited by the house, under such restrictions as are therein also mentioned, personally enter into a recognizance to our sovereign lord the king in the sum of two hundred pounds, with two sufficient sureties in the

28 Geo. III. cap. 52, recited.

sum of one hundred pounds each, in the form, and upon the condition particularly mentioned in the said act: And whereas *John Macbride*, Esquire, a captain in his majesty's royal navy, and now commander of his majesty's ship *Cumberland*, who was a candidate at the last election for the borough of *Plymouth* in the county of *Devon*, to be one of the representatives for the said borough in parliament, sailed from this country on his majesty's service on or about the twenty-third day of October one thousand seven hundred and ninety, having left behind him a petition signed by him, complaining of an undue election and return for the said borough; which petition was presented to the house of commons on the third day of December, one thousand seven hundred and ninety, and which is ordered by the house of commons to be taken into consideration on the nineteenth day of April one thousand seven hundred and ninety one: And whereas the said *John Macbride* being still absent on his majesty's service, the house of commons have enlarged the time for his entering into such recognizance for thirty days, being the full extent of the time allowed by the said act for that purpose; but it being yet uncertain when he will return to this country, it is expedient that the time given to the said *John Macbride* and his sureties to enter into the recognizance aforesaid should be further enlarged; be it therefore enacted by the king's most excellent

lent majesty, by and with the advice and consent of the lords spiritual and temporal, and commons, in this present parliament assembled, and by the authority of the same, that in case the said *John Macbride* shall, within thirty days next after his return to this country, enter into the recognizances required by the said act, with sufficient sureties, in the manner and form therein mentioned, the same shall be as valid and effectual to all intents and purposes whatsoever, as if the same had been entered into within the time limited by the said act, any thing in the said act to the contrary notwithstanding.

If captain Macbride within 30 days after his return to this country, enters into the recognizances required by the recited acts, the same shall be valid.

A. D. 1791.

ANNO 32° GEORGII III. CAP. I.

An Act to extend the Provisions of certain Acts of Parliament made to regulate the Trials of Controverted Elections, or Returns of Members to serve in Parliament.

WHEREAS by an act, passed in the eleventh year of the reign of his present majesty, intituled, ' An act to explain and amend an act, made in the last session of parliament, intituled, An act to regulate the trials of controverted elections, or returns of members to serve in parliament;' it is enacted, that, on the day appointed by the house of commons for taking

11 Geo. III. cap. 42. recited.

U 2 into

into confideration any petition complaining of an undue election, or return of any member to ferve in parliament, the houfe fhall not proceed to any other bufinefs whatfoever, except the fwearing of members, previous to the reading the order of the day for that purpofe: and whereas by an act, paffed in the twenty-eighth year of the reign of his prefent majefty, intituled, 'An act for the further regulation of the trials of controverted elections, or returns of members to ferve in parliament,' it is enacted, that it fhall and may be lawful for the houfe, previous to the reading fuch order, to proceed to fuch other bufinefs as in the faid act is particularly fpecified: And whereas it is of importance, that the like power fhould be extended to the feveral cafes herein-after mentioned, be it enacted by the king's moft excellent majefty, by and with the advice and confent of the lords fpiritual and temporal, and commons, in this prefent parliament affembled, and by the authority of the fame, that on the day appointed by the houfe for taking into confideration any petition complaining of an undue election, or return of any member to ferve in parliament, or the petition of any perfon or perfons defiring to oppofe any right of election, or the right of chufing, nominating, or appointing any returning officer or returning officers, which fhall have been deemed valid by the determination of any felect committee, it

and 28 Geo. III, cap. 52, recited.

On days appointed by the commons for taking petitions into confideration, meffages from the lords may be received previous to reading the order of the day; and on days appointed for trial of articles of impeachment, bufinefs neceffary for carrying on the profecution may in like manner be proceeded on.

fhall

shall and may be lawful for the house, previous to the reading the order or orders for taking any such petition or petitions into consideration, to receive any message or messages from the lords; and also that it shall and may be lawful for the house, on the days appointed for the trial of any articles of impeachment exhibited or to be exhibited by the commons before the lords in parliament, previous to the reading any such order or orders as aforesaid, to proceed to any business that may be necessary for the purpose of carrying on the prosecution of such impeachment.

A. D. 1792.

ANNO 33° GEORGII III. CAP. 64.

An Act to explain and amend an Act, passed in the Seventh and Eighth Years of King William the Third, intituled, 'An Act for the further regulating Elections of Members to serve in Parliament, and for the preventing irregular Proceedings of Sheriffs and other Officers in the electing and returning such Members,' so far as relates to the Publication of Notices of the Time and Place of Election.

WHEREAS by an act, made and passed in the seventh and eighth years of the late king William the third, intituled, 'An act for

7 & 8 Gul. III. cap. 25. recited.

the further regulating elections of members to serve in parliament, and for the preventing irregular proceedings of sheriffs and other officers in the electing and returning such members,' it is enacted, that the proper officers therein mentioned shall, upon the receipt of precepts for the election of members to serve in parliament, forthwith cause public notice to be given of the time and place of election, and shall proceed to election thereupon within the time by the said act limited, and give four days notice at least of the day appointed for the election; but it is not in the said act specified at what time or within *what hours of the day* it shall be incumbent on the proper officer to give such public notice as aforesaid: And whereas, by reason of such uncertainty, great inconveniences may arise from the undue practices of returning officers and others: May it please your majesty that it may be enacted; and be it enacted by the king's most excellent majesty, by and with the advice and consent of the lords spiritual and temporal, and commons, in this present parliament assembled, and by the authority of the same, that, from and after the passing of this act, all notices to be given of the time and place of any election for members to serve in parliament, shall be publicly given at the usual place or places within the hours of *eight* of the clock in the forenoon and *four* of the clock in the afternoon, from the *twenty-fifth* day

Notices of the time and place of elections for members of parliament to be given within certain hours.

day of *October* to the *twenty fifth* day of *March* inclusive, and within the hours of *eight* of the clock in the forenoon and *six* of the clock in the afternoon from the *twenty-fifth* day of *March* to the *twenty-fifth* day of *October* inclusive, and not otherwise; and that no notice to be given of the time and place of elections of members to serve in parliament shall be deemed or taken to be a good or valid notice for any purposes, or to any effect whatsoever, which shall not be made and published in the manner and within the time of day aforesaid; any law, statute, usage, or custom to the contrary notwithstanding.

A. D. 1793.

ANNO 34° GEORGII III. CAP. 73.

An Act for directing the Appointment of Commissioners, to administer certain Oaths and Declarations required by Law to be taken and made by Persons offering to vote at the Election of Members to serve in Parliament.

WHEREAS great delays have arisen in the election of members to serve in parliament for places in *England*, *Wales*, and the town of *Berwick upon Tweed*, by the time and place in which the oaths of allegiance, supremacy, the declaration of fidelity, the oath of abjuration, and the declaration or affirmation of the effect thereof, are usually administered to electors; and in many places it might thereby be rendered impracticable to receive the votes of all persons claiming and having a right to vote within the time limited by law for the duration of the polls at such elections: Be it enacted by the king's most excellent majesty, by and with the advice and consent of the lords spiritual and temporal, and commons, in this present parliament assembled, and by the authority of the same, that from and after the passing of this act, when a poll shall be demanded at any election of a member or members to serve in parliament for any county, city, borough, or other place in *England* or *Wales*, or for the town of *Berwick upon Tweed*, the returning officer or officers at every such election, after such poll shall be demanded, shall, at the instance and request in writing of any of the candidates, under his or their hand or hands, immediately after such request, and before he or they shall proceed further in taking the poll, retain, nominate, and appoint, two or more persons to administer the oaths of allegiance, supremacy, the declaration of fidelity, the oath of abjuration, and the declaration or affirmation of the effect thereof, now required by law to be taken, made, or subscribed by voters at elections of members to serve in parliament, and to certify the names of the respective electors who shall take such oaths,

Returning officers, on request of candidates, to appoint persons to administer the oaths of allegiance, &c.

oaths, or subscribe and make such declarations or affirmations respectively, in manner hereinafter mentioned; and the persons to be appointed as aforesaid, or in manner herein-after mentioned, shall respectively have full power, and each of them is hereby authorized and required to administer all and every such respective oaths, declarations, and affirmations to every such elector who shall desire or be required to take the same oaths, or any of them, or to subscribe or make the said declarations and affirmations respectively, previous to his voting at any such election; and every such person so appointed as aforesaid shall, immediately after such appointment, and before he shall take upon him to act under such appointment, take the following oath; (that is to say),

Persons so appointed to take the following

' I do swear, that I will faithfully and impartially administer the oaths of allegiance, supremacy, and abjuration, and the declaration of fidelity, and declaration or affirmation of the effect of the said oath of abjuration, to such persons as shall lawfully apply to me in that behalf, in order to qualify themselves to vote at this election; and that I will, on being thereunto requested, fairly and truly give to every such person, or any of them, who shall take such oaths, or subscribe such declaration of fidelity, and make such declaration or affirmation of the effect of the said oath of abjuration, or either of them, before me, a certificate thereof,

Oath.

according

according to the direction of an act of parliament, made in the *thirty-fourth* year of the reign of his majesty king *George* the *third*, intituled, [*Here set forth the title of the act*], and that I will not give such certificate to any person before he shall have taken such oath or oaths, or made or subscribed such declaration or declarations, affirmation or affirmations, as shall be mentioned in such certificate, before me and in my presence:'

Which oath to be taken by the respective persons so to be appointed, the returning officer or officers at every such election, and his or their deputy and deputies, or any of them, is and are hereby authorized and required to administer.

<small>Electors to apply to such persons before voting, who shall administer the oaths of allegiance, &c. and give certificates thereof.</small>

II. And be it further enacted by the authority aforesaid, that after the persons so appointed shall have taken such oath, so required to be taken by them respectively as aforesaid, any person or persons claiming to vote at any such election as aforesaid may at any time, before he or they shall give his or their vote or votes at such election, apply to any one of the persons so appointed and sworn as aforesaid, to take the said oaths of allegiance and supremacy, and abjuration, or any of them, or to subscribe the said declaration of fidelity, and make the said declaration or affirmation of the effect of the said oath of abjuration, or either of them, and the person to whom such application shall be made

shall

shall accordingly administer the same to such person or persons so claiming a right to vote, and shall immediately upon such oaths being taken, or declarations or affirmations respectively being subscribed or made, sign and deliver a certificate thereof to such person who shall have taken such oaths, or made or subscribed such declarations or affirmations respectively, which certificate shall contain the name, addition, and place of abode, of the person to whom the same shall be so given; and in case of persons taking the said oaths, shall be in the terms following; (that is to say)

A. B. [*naming the person taking the oath*] of [*naming the place of such person's abode, and his addition or occupation*] has taken the oath [*or oaths*] of [*naming the said oath or oaths so administered*] before me this
day of

Form of certificate of taking oaths,

And in case of Quakers subscribing the said declaration of fidelity, or taking their affirmation of the effect of the said oath of abjuration, shall be in the form following; (that is to say)

A. B. [*naming the person subscribing or affirming*] of [*naming the place of such person's abode, and his addition or occupation*] has made and subscribed the declaration of fidelity, and affirmed the effect of the oath of abjuration [*or if only one of those acts has been done, then naming such one act only*] before me, this
day of

Or of making affirmation.

And

Production of certificate to intitle to vote.

And every such person to whom such certificate shall be so given, and having a right to vote at such election, shall, on producing such certificate to the returning officer or officers, or other person or persons lawfully taking the poll at such election, be permitted to poll, and his vote shall be taken and received in like manner as if such respective oaths, declarations, or affirmations, mentioned and expressed in such respective certificates, had been administered by, and made, subscribed, or taken before, the returning officer or officers at such election.

Persons offering to vote without producing certificate, to withdraw and take the oaths.

III. And be it further enacted by the authority aforesaid, that when any person or persons offering to vote at any such election, without producing such certificate as aforesaid, shall be lawfully required to take the said oaths of allegiance, supremacy, and abjuration, or any of them, or to subscribe the said declaration of fidelity, and make the said declaration or affirmation of the effect of the said oath of abjuration, or either of them; then such oaths, subscription, declarations, or affirmations, or any of them, shall not be administered by the returning officer or officers, or other person or persons taking the poll, but the elector or electors so required to take such oaths, or to subscribe or make such declarations or affirmations respectively, shall immediately withdraw, and shall take the said oaths, or subscribe and make the said declarations or affirmations respectively,

spectively, before one of the persons appointed and sworn as aforesaid, in manner herein-before mentioned.

IV. And be it further enacted by the authority aforesaid, that if at any time during the poll at any such election it shall be found that the number of persons so appointed as aforesaid is insufficient for the purposes aforesaid, and that the poll is delayed for want of a sufficient number of persons to administer such oaths, declarations, and affirmations as aforesaid, then and in every such case the returning officer or officers at such election may, and he or they is and are hereby impowered and required, at the instance and request in writing of any candidate then present, to retain, nominate, and appoint, such further number of persons, for the purpose of administering the said oaths, declarations, and affirmations as aforesaid, and of granting such certificates as aforesaid, as shall be necessary to prevent such delay; and the persons so nominated and appointed shall take the like oath, which shall be administered to them respectively in like manner as is herein-before directed with respect to the persons first appointed for the purposes aforesaid.

If the number of persons so appointed should be insufficient, more may be appointed.

V. And be it further enacted by the authority aforesaid, that the returning officer or returning officers at every such election shall, and is and are hereby required to appoint, find, and provide, a proper place for every such person,

Returning officers to appoint proper places for taking the oaths, &c.

so appointed as aforesaid, to execute the duty hereby imposed upon such person, to which place the respective electors may have free access, without interrupting the poll, and so as to enable the persons so appointed to act separately without interfering with each other in the execution of their office; and that each of the said places so appointed shall be open, and attended by the person or persons appointed to act there, during all such times as the poll at any such election shall be kept open, and continue at least eight hours in every day, between the hours of eight in the morning and eight in the evening, until the final close of the poll; and that the said oaths, and the said declarations or affirmations of the effect of the said oath of abjuration, shall respectively be administered to as many of the electors, being ready, and desiring to take or make the same respectively, as can conveniently take or make the same together, not exceeding the number of twelve at one time; and such returning officers shall also find, provide, and deliver to each person, who shall be appointed by him or them in manner aforesaid, a sufficient number of printed forms of the declaration of fidelity required by law to be made and subscribed by *Quakers*, before they can be admitted to vote at such election, with blanks therein for the names of the persons offering to make and subscribe the same to be inserted therein, one of which forms shall

shall be filled up with the name of, and subscribed by, the persons desiring to make and subscribe the declaration of fidelity; and such returning officer or returning officers shall also find, provide, and deliver to each person who shall be so appointed by him or them as aforesaid, a sufficient number of printed certificates, agreeable to the form herein-before directed, to be filled up as occasion shall require, and deliver to each elector so taking the said oaths, or subscribing or affirming as aforesaid.

VI. And be it further enacted by the authority aforesaid, that in case the candidates, or any of them, shall, three days at the least before any such election, give or cause to be given notice in writing to the returning officer or officers to provide proper places for administering the said oaths, declarations, and affirmations as aforesaid, to the electors, then in every such case such proper places shall be prepared and provided, so as to be ready before and against the day of election; and in case there shall not be a sufficient number of fit and convenient places for that purpose, at the town or place where such election shall be had, which the returning officer or officers can conveniently and at a reasonable expence procure, then the said returning officer or officers shall, and is and are hereby required to cause such booths or temporary erections to be made, in convenient places in that behalf, as shall be necessary for the purpose,

The returning officer, on notice, to provide such places to be ready by the day of election.

> Expences to be defrayed by the candidates.

pose, the expence of which booths or places, and of the said printed forms, and also the allowance and compensation to be made to the several persons who shall be appointed to administer the said oaths, declarations, and affirmations as aforesaid, for their trouble and attendance, not exceeding one pound one shilling a day to every of them for each day of attendance, shall be defrayed and repaid by the candidates at such election, in equal proportions to the returning officer or returning officers who shall have incurred such expence, and shall and may be recovered by such returning officer or returning officers, in any of his majesty's courts of record at Westminster, by action of debt, or on the case, bill, suit, or information, wherein no essoin, protection, or wager of law, or more than one imparlance, shall be allowed.

A. D. 1794.

ANNO 34° GEORGII III. CAP. 83.

An Act to explain so much of an Act, made in the Twenty-eighth Year of His present Majesty's Reign, intituled, ' An Act for the further Regulation of the Trials of controverted Elections, or Returns of Members to serve in Parliament,' as relates to the Time of presenting certain renewed Petitions, and taking the same into Consideration.

> 28 Geo. III. cap. 52, recited.

WHEREAS, by an act, passed in the twenty-eighth year of his present majesty's reign,

reign, intituled, 'An act for the further regulation of the trials of controverted elections, or returns of members to serve in parliament,' it is enacted, that whenever any such select committee of the house of commons, as is therein mentioned, shall have reported to the house their judgment respecting the right of election of members to serve in parliament for any county, city, borough, or place, or of chusing, nominating, or appointing, the returning officer or returning officers, who is or are to make return of such election, it shall be lawful for any person or persons, at any time within twelve calendar months, after the day on which such report shall have been made to the house, or within fourteen days after the day of the commencement of the next session of parliament after that in which such report shall have been made to the house, to petition the house to be admitted as parties to oppose the right which has been deemed valid in the judgment of such committee; and that when such petition shall be so presented, a day shall be appointed by the house for taking the same into consideration, so that the space of forty days at the least shall always intervene between the day of presenting such petition and the day appointed by the house for taking the same into consideration: and whereas the said provision which directs that the said space of forty days shall intervene between the day of presenting such petition

tition and the day appointed by the house for taking the same into consideration, hath been construed to extend to petitions which are renewed in any session or sessions of parliament, subsequent to that in which such petition was originally presented to the house, which proceeding hath been found to be inconvenient; for remedy thereof, be it enacted by the king's most excellent majesty, by and with the advice and consent of the lords spiritual and temporal, and commons, in this present parliament assembled, and by the authority of the same, that every petition, so renewed as aforesaid, shall be presented to the house within fourteen days after the day of the commencement of any such subsequent session or sessions of parliament, and not otherwise; and that whenever any such renewed petition shall be so presented, a day and hour, at not less than fourteen days distance, shall be appointed by the house for taking the same into consideration; any thing in the said act to the contrary thereof notwithstanding.

Time of presenting and hearing renewed petitions of persons praying to be admitted as parties, to oppose the right of election reported by committees.

II. And be it further enacted, that if any such petition shall not, from time to time, and in every session of parliament, until the same shall be taken into consideration, be so renewed within the time above limited for renewing the same, the judgment of such committee on such question or questions shall be held and taken to be final and conclusive in all subsequent elections of members of parliament for that place to which

If such petitions be not renewed, the judgment of committees to be final.

A. D. 1794.

ANNO 36° GEORGII III. CAP. 59.

An Act for the more effectual Execution of several Acts of Parliament, made for the Trials of controverted Elections, or Returns of Members to serve in Parliament.

WHEREAS by an act, passed in the tenth year of the reign of his present majesty, intituled, 'An act to regulate the trials of controverted elections, or returns of members to serve in parliament,' it is enacted, that at the time appointed for taking any petition, complaining of an undue election or return of a member or members to serve in parliament, into consideration, and previous to the reading the order of the day for that purpose, the house shall be counted, and that if there be less than one hundred members present, the order for taking such petition into consideration shall be immediately adjourned to a particular hour on the following day, as therein mentioned, and the house shall then adjourn to the said day; and that on the said following day the house shall proceed in the same manner; and so from day to day till there be an attendance of one hundred members at the reading the order of the day to take such petition into consideration:

10 Geo. III. recited.

And

And whereas by an act, passed in the eleventh year of the reign of his present majesty, for explaining and amending the said act, it is enacted, that if at the time of drawing by lot the names of the members, in manner prescribed by the said former act, the number of forty-nine members, not set aside nor excused, cannot be completed, the house shall proceed in the manner they are directed by the said former act to proceed, in case there be less than one hundred members present at the time therein prescribed for counting the house; and so from day to day, as often as the case shall happen:

11 Geo. III. recited.

And whereas by an act, passed in the twenty-fifth year of the reign of his present majesty, intituled, ' An act to limit the duration of polls and scrutinies, and for making other regulations touching the election of members to serve in parliament for places within *England* and *Wales*, and for *Berwick upon Tweed*, and also for removing difficulties which may arise for want of returns being made of members to serve in parliament;' and by one other act, made in the twenty-eighth year of the reign of his present majesty, intituled, ' An act for the further regulation of the trials of controverted elections, or returns of members to serve in parliament,' it is enacted, that petitions complaining of the omission, or of the insufficiency of a return to any writ issued for the election of any member or members to serve in parliament, and also the petitions

25 Geo. III. recited.

28 Geo. III. recited.

petitions of any perfon or perfons defiring to oppofe any right of election, or the right of chufing, nominating, or appointing, any returning officer or returning officers, which fhall have been deemed valid by the determination of any felect committee, fhall be taken into confideration, tried, and determined, in the fame manner as petitions complaining of undue elections and returns are directed to be taken into confideration, tried, and determined, by the faid acts paffed in the tenth and eleventh years of the reign of his prefent majefty:

And whereas it is expedient that further provifion fhould be made for preventing delay in the appointment of any fuch felect committee, to be appointed for the purpofes aforefaid, any or either of them: be it enacted by the king's moft excellent majefty, by and with the advice and confent of the lords fpiritual and temporal, and commons, in this prefent parliament affembled, and by the authority of the fame, that *if, after counting of the houfe in the manner before mentioned, there be lefs than one hundred members prefent,* or if the forty-nine members, not fet afide nor excufed, cannot be completed, *it fhall and may be lawful* for the houfe, (after the order or orders for taking any fuch petition or petitions into confideration, fhall have been adjourned to a particular hour, on the following or fuch other day as in the faid acts is directed), *to proceed* (in like manner as they might have

proceeded

proceeded if there had been no order or orders for taking any such petition or petitions into consideration on that day) *upon any order of the day for the call of the house*, which shall have been previously fixed for that day, and to direct that the house, in pursuance of such order, be then called over, if they shall so think fit, or to direct that such order of the day for a call of the house shall be adjourned to such future day as they shall appoint, and in either of such cases to come to such resolutions, and to make such orders relating thereto, as are usually at any time made in such cases, or as to them shall seem meet; and in case no order of the day for a call of the house shall have been previously fixed for that day, then that it shall and may be lawful for the house *to order that the house shall be called over on such future day* as they shall appoint, and to make such orders relating thereto as they shall think necessary, and in any case to make such orders as to them shall seem expedient *for enforcing the attendance* of the members on the business of the house; and that the house shall then adjourn to the same day to which such order or orders shall have been adjourned, and so from time to time, as occasion shall require; and in case no such proceedings with respect to any call of the house, or other the matters before mentioned shall take place, or if in the course of those proceedings the house shall be adjourned for want of members, the house shall be be deemed and taken, and shall be declared to be adjourned to the same day to which such order or orders shall have been adjourned: provided always, that in case the forty-nine members, not set aside nor excused, cannot be completed, it shall not be lawful for the house to proceed upon any of the matters before mentioned, until the door of the house is unlocked, and the parties, their counsel and agents, are withdrawn from the bar.

Provided also and be it enacted, that the house shall not, on any day when any such petition or petitions shall be ordered to be taken into consideration, proceed to any other business (other than such as may, by virtue of any act of parliament, be proceeded on previous to the reading of the order of the day for taking any such petition or petitions into consideration) until there be an attendance of one hundred members, or until the number of forty-nine members, not set aside nor excused, shall be completed, other than and except to the calling over the house, adjourning such call, or ordering a call of the house on a future day, and making such orders relative thereto as they shall think fit, or such other order, as to them shall seem expedient for enforcing the attendance of the members on the business of the house, in the manner before mentioned.

A. D. 1796.

APPENDIX.

APPENDIX.

The Appendix is divided into three parts.

PART THE FIRST

Is a collection of all the orders of the house of commons now in force relating to writs, the elections of members, and proceedings before select committees, extracted from the journals and classed under the following heads, *viz.*

Issuing the writ, and delivery thereof, to the proper officer	page ii
Interference at elections, and qualifications of electors	iii
Bribery	v
Evidence at the poll and before the house	vii
Qualification of candidates	ix
Jurisdiction of the house	xi
Petition, proceedings on petition, and soliciting the attendance of members	xii
Exchange of lists	xxi
False evidence and tampering with witnesses	xxi
Amending returns	xxii

PART THE SECOND

Contains the acts respecting the elections of peers and members for Scotland subsequent to the union. xxiii

PART THE THIRD

Is a list of all the controverted elections that have been determined before select committees, as well upon the *right of election* as otherwise, with references to the journals of the house.

PART I.

Issuing the Writ, and Delivery thereof, to the proper Officer.

Ordered,

22 Nov. 1661.
THAT for the future when any writ shall be delivered for a new election of any member to serve in parliament, the party that doth receive the writ, shall deliver, or cause the same forthwith to be sent and delivered to the proper officer of the place for which the election is to be made.

Vol. viii. p. 317.

Ordered,

13 Feb. 1662.
THAT the lord chancellor be desired by Mr. *Speaker* to take care, that when any writ shall be sealed for a new election of any member to serve in parliament, that such writ be forthwith sent and delivered to the proper officer of the place for which the election is to be made. Vol. viii. p. 436.

Ordered,

13 April, 1675.
THAT Mr. *Speaker* do give order to the clerk of the crown, to take care that the writs for elections of new members be delivered to the sheriff, or proper officer. Vol. ix. p. 316.

Ordered,

Ordered,

THAT Mr. *Speaker* be defired to give notice to the clerk of the crown, to take care that the writs for the new elections be delivered to the hands of the high fheriffs of the refpective counties: and that the houfe do expect an account thereof. Vol. ix. p. 517.

21 Oct. 1678.

Refolved,

THAT all writs for the electing of members to ferve in parliament be immediately fent to the proper officers for execution thereof, with all convenient fpeed. Vol. xi. p. 184.

7 Dec. 1694.

Interference at elections, and Qualifications of electors.

Refolved,

THAT this houfe doth declare and order, that all elections of any knight, citizen, or burgefs, to ferve in parliament, be made without interruption or moleftation by any commander, governor, officer, or foldier, that hath not in the county, city, or borough, refpectively, right of electing; and that this order be fent to *Reddinge* at the next election: and it is further ordered that this order be printed.
Vol. iv. p. 346.

17 Nov. 1645.

Refolved,

THAT the fending of warrants, or letters in the nature of warrants, or letters to high conftables,

18 Jan. 1670.

stables, or constables, or other officers, to be communicated to the freeholders or other electors, when a knight of the shire or other member is to be chosen to serve in parliament, or threatening the electors, is unparliamentary, and a violation of the right of elections.

Vol. ix. p. 191.

Resolved,

30 April, 1690. THAT *Quakers* having a freehold, and refusing to take the oath when tendered by the sheriff, are incapable of giving their votes for knights of the shire for that reason.

Vol. x. p. 396.

Resolved, Nem. Con.

22 Dec. 1698. THAT no alien (not being a denizen, or naturalized) hath any right to vote in elections of members to serve in parliament.

Vol. xii. p. 367.

Resolved,

8 Feb. 1705. THAT any person having a right to vote for two members to serve in parliament, who hath given a single vote, have not a right to come afterwards and give a second vote during the said election. Vol. xv. p. 135, 137.

Resolved,

22 Dec. 1741. THAT the presence of a regular body of armed soldiers at an election of members to serve in parliament, is an high infringement of the liberties of the subject, a manifest violation

of

of the freedom of elections, and an open defiance of the laws and constitution of this kingdom. Vol. xxiv. p. 37.

Resolved,

THAT it is highly criminal in any minister or ministers, or other servants under the crown of *Great Britain*, directly or indirectly, to use the powers of office in the election of representatives to serve in parliament; and an attempt at such influence will at all times be resented by this house, as aimed at its own honor, dignity and independency, as an infringement of the dearest rights of every subject throughout the empire, and tending to sap the basis of this free and happy constitution. Vol. xxxvii. p. 507.

10 Dec. 1779.

Resolved,

THAT no peer of this realm hath any right to give his vote in the election of any member to serve in parliament.

Resolved,

THAT it is a high infringement of the liberties and privileges of the commons of *Great Britain*, for any lord of parliament, or any lord lieutenant of any county, to concern themselves in the elections of members to serve for the commons in parliament.

Note,—The two last resolutions are made at the commencement of every session.

Bribery.

Resolved,

THAT if any person hereafter to be elected into

2 April, 1677.

into a place for to sit and serve in the house of commons for any county, city, town, port, or borough, after the teste or the issuing out of the writ or writs of election, upon the calling or summoning of any parliament hereafter; or, after any such place becomes vacant hereafter in the time of parliament, shall, by himself or by any other on his behalf or at his charge, at any time before the day of his election, give any person or persons having voice in any such elections, any meat or drink, exceeding in the true value ten pounds in the whole, in any place or places but in his own dwelling house or habitation, being the usual place of his abode for *six months* last past; or shall, before such election be made and declared, make any other present, gift, or reward, or any promise, obligation, or engagement to do the same, either to any such person or persons in particular, or to any such county, city, town, port, or borough in general, or to or for the use and benefit of them, or any of them, every such entertainment, present, gift, reward, promise, obligation, or engagement, is by this house declared to be bribery; and such entertainment, present, gift, reward, promise, obligation, or engagement being duly proved, is, and shall be a sufficient ground, cause and matter, to make every such election void as to the person so offending, and to render the person so elected, incapable to sit in parliament by such election: and hereof the committee of elections and privileges, is appointed to take especial notice and care, and to

act

act and determine matters coming before them accordingly.

Resolved,

THAT the said order against excessive drinking at elections, be a further instruction to the committee of elections, and that it be from time to time entered amongst the constant and standing powers and instructions given by the house of commons to the said committee.

Vol. ix. p. 411.

Resolved,

THAT the lending of money upon any security to a corporation which sends members to parliament, and remitting the interest of the same with intent to influence the election of such corporation, is an unlawful and dangerous practice. Vol. xiii. p. 410.

17 Mar. 1700-1.

Resolved,

THAT if it shall appear that any person hath procured himself to be elected or returned a member of this house, or endeavoured so to be, by bribery or any other corrupt practices, this house will proceed with the utmost severity against such person.

Note.—*This resolution is made at the commencement of every session.*

Evidence at the poll and before the house.

Resolved,

THAT evidence ought not to be admitted to disqualify an elector as no freeholder, who at the election swore himself to be a freeholder.

16 Jan. 1695.

Vol. xi. p. 394.

Ordered,

Ordered,

16 Jan. 1735. THAT the counsel at the bar of this house, or before the committee of privileges and elections, be restrained from offering evidence touching the legality of votes for members to serve in parliament for any county, shire, city, borough, cinque port, or place contrary to the last determination in the house of commons; which determination by an act passed in the 2d year of his present majesty's reign, intituled 'An act for the more effectual preventing bribery and corruption in the election of members to serve in parliament,' is made final to all intents and purposes whatsoever, any usage to the contrary notwithstanding. Vol. xxii. p. 498.

Resolved,

26 Feb. 1735. THAT the counsel for the petitioners be admitted to give parole evidence as to a person being no freeholder at the time of the election who swore himself then to be a freeholder.

Vol. xxii. p. 593.

Resolved,

4 March, 1735. THAT the counsel for the petitioners be admitted to give evidence as to what a voter confessed of his having no freehold, who at the time of the election swore he had.

Resolved,

THAT the counsel for the petitioners be admitted to give evidence as to a person having no freehold at all, to whom the petitioners objected in their list of objections that such person had not a freehold of 40s. per annum. Vol. xxii. p. 604.

Qualification

Resolved,

THAT no mayor can duly return himself a burgess to serve in parliament for the same borough of which he is a mayor at the time of the election.   Vol. ix. p. 725.   *2 June, 1685.*

Resolved,

THAT no mayor, bailiff, or other officer of a borough, who is the proper officer to whom the precept ought to be directed, is capable of being elected to serve in parliament for the same borough of which he is mayor, bailiff, or officer at the time of the election.   Vol. ix. p. 725.   *2 June, 1685.*

Resolved,

THAT notwithstanding the oath taken by any candidate at or after any election, his qualification may afterwards be examined into.
Vol. xviii. p. 629.   *21 Nov. 1717.*

Resolved,

THAT the person whose qualification is expressly objected to in any petition relating to his election, shall within *fifteen* days after the petition read, give to the clerk of the house of commons, a paper signed by himself, containing a rental or particular of the lands, tenements, and hereditaments, whereby he makes out his qualification, of which any person concerned may have a copy.   Vol. xviii. p. 629.   *21 Nov. 1717.*

Resolved,

THAT of such lands, tenements, and hereditaments, whereof the party hath not been in possession   *21 Nov. 1717.*

possession, for three years before the election, he shall also insert in the same paper from what person, and by what conveyance or act in law he claims and derives the same; and also the consideration if any paid; and the names and places of abode of the witnesses to such conveyance and payment. Vol. xviii. p. 629.

Resolved,

2 Nov. 1717.
THAT if any sitting member shall think fit to question the qualification of a petitioner, he shall within *fifteen* days after the petition read, leave notice thereof in writing, with the clerk of the house of commons; and the petitioner shall in such case within *fifteen* days after such notice, leave with the said clerk of the house, the like account in writing of his qualification, as is required from a sitting member.

Vol. xviii. p. 629.

Resolved,

16 April, 1728.
THAT a person petitioning, and thereby claiming a seat in this house for one place, is capable of being elected and returned for another place pending such petition. Vol. xxi. p. 136.

Resolved,

6 Feb. 1734.
THAT on the petition of any elector or electors for any county, city, or place, sending members to parliament, complaining of an undue election and return, and alledging, That some other person was duly elected and ought to have been returned; the sitting member so complained of, may demand and examine into the qualification of such person so alledged to be

duly

duly elected in the same manner as if such person had himself petitioned. Vol. xxii. p. 355.

Jurisdiction of the House.

Resolved,

THAT according to the known laws and usage of parliament, it is the sole right of the commons of *England* in parliament assembled, (except in cases otherwise provided for by act of parliament) to examine and determine all matters relating to the right of election of their own members.

26 Jan. 1703.

Resolved,

THAT according to the known laws and usage of parliament, neither the qualification of any elector, or the right of any person elected, is cognizable or determinable elsewhere than before the commons of *England* in parliament assembled, except in such cases as are specially provided for by act of parliament.

Resolved,

THAT the examining and determining the qualification or right of any elector, or any person elected to serve in parliament in any court of law or elsewhere than before the commons of *England* in parliament assembled (except in such cases as are specially provided for by act of parliament) will expose all mayors, bailiffs, and other officers who are obliged to take the poll, and make a return thereupon, to multiplicity of actions, vexatious suits, and insupportable expences, and will subject them to different and independent

dependent jurisdictions, and inconsistent determinations in the same case without relief.

Resolved,

THAT *Matthew Ashby* having, in contempt of the jurisdiction of this house, commenced and prosecuted an action at common law against *William White* and others, the constables of *Aylesbury,* for not receiving his vote at an election of burgesses to serve in parliament for the said borough of *Aylesbury,* is guilty of a breach of the privilege of this house.

Resolved,

THAT whoever shall presume to commence or prosecute any action, indictment, or information, which shall bring the right of the electors or persons elected to serve in parliament, to the determination of any other jurisdiction than that of the house of commons (except in cases specially provided for by act of parliament), such person and persons, and all attornies, solicitors, counsellors, and serjeants at law, soliciting, prosecuting, or pleading in any such case, are guilty of a high breach of the privilege of this house.

Vol. xiv. p. 308.

Petitions, Proceedings on Petitions, and soliciting the Attendance of Members.

Resolved,

18 March, 1727. THAT in all cases *on double returns* where the same shall be controverted either at the bar of this house, or in committees of privileges and elections, the counsel for such person who shall be first named in such double return, or whose

return shall be immediately annexed to the writ or precept, shall proceed in the first place,

Vol. xxi. p. 89.

Ordered,

THAT no person do presume to solicit the attendance of members of this house, when the matter of any petition, complaining of an undue election or return is ordered to be taken into consideration.   Vol. xxxiii. p. 726.

4 May, 1772.

Resolved,

THAT according to the true construction of the act of the 10th year of the reign of his present Majesty (Mr. *Grenville's* act), whenever a petition, complaining of an undue election or return of a member to serve in parliament shall be offered to be presented to the house, within the time limited by the order of the house for questioning the returns of members to serve in parliament, the said petition shall be delivered in at the table and read, without a question being put thereupon.   Vol. xxxv. p. 10.

6 Dec. 1774.

Resolved,

THAT whenever more than one petition, complaining of an undue election or return for the same or for different places, shall at the same time be offered to be presented to the house, Mr. *Speaker* shall direct such petitions to be all of them delivered in at the table; and the names of the counties, cities, boroughs, or places to which such petitions shall relate, shall be written on several pieces of paper of an equal size; and the same pieces of paper shall be then rolled up, and
put

clafs: And the names of the places to which such petitions (contained in the first clafs, if more than one) shall relate, shall in the first place be written on several pieces of paper of an equal size, and the same pieces of paper shall be then rolled up, and put by the clerk into a box or glafs, and then publicly drawn by the clerk; and the said petitions shall be read in the order in which the said names shall be drawn: And then the like method shall be observed with respect to the several petitions contained in the second, third, and fourth clafses respectively.

Vol. xl. p. 11.

Resolved,

1 Dec. 1790. THAT whenever several petitions, complaining of undue elections or returns of members to serve in parliament, shall at the same time be offered to be presented to the house, Mr. *Speaker* shall direct such petitions to be all of them delivered in at the table, where they shall be clafsed and read in the following order, viz.

Such petitions as complain that no return has been made of a member or members to serve in parliament, in the first clafs.

Such as complain of double returns, in the second clafs.

Such as complain of the election or return of members returned to serve for two or more places, in the third clafs.

Such as complain of returns only in the fourth clafs; and

The residue of the said petitions in the fifth class.

And the names of the places to which such petitions (contained in the first class, if more than one) shall relate, shall, in the first place, be written on several pieces of paper of an equal size, and the same pieces of paper shall be then rolled up, and put by a clerk into a box or glass, and then publicly drawn by the clerk; and the said petitions shall be read in the order in which the said names shall be drawn; and then the like method shall be observed with respect to the several petitions contained in the second, third, fourth and fifth classes respectively. Vol. xlvi. p. 13.

The last resolution being read;

Resolved,

THAT whenever several renewed petitions complaining of undue elections and returns of members to serve in parliament, shall at the same time be offered to be presented to the house, Mr. *Speaker* shall direct such petitions to be all of them delivered in at the table; and the said petitions shall be read in the order of the classes mentioned in the said resolution, and in each of the classes, in the order in which they were directed to be taken into consideration in the last session of parliament.

1 Feb. 1792.

Vol. xlvii. p. 10.

Resolved,

THAT whenever several petitions, complaining

14 Dec. 1792.

plaining of undue elections and returns shall be renewed in this session of parliament, and shall be delivered in together at the table, the said petitions shall be read in the order in which they were directed to be taken into consideration in the last session. Vol. xlviii. p. 9.

Ordered,

22 Jan. 1794. THAT all persons, who will question any returns of members to serve in parliament, by the renewal of petitions, which were depending before this house at the end of the last session of parliament, do question the same within the time limited for the forfeiture of the recognizances in case such petitions shall not be renewed as mentioned in an act, made in the 28th year of the reign of his present majesty, intituled, " An act for the further regulation of the trials " of controverted elections, or returns of mem- " bers to serve in parliament." And that all other persons, who will question any returns of members to serve in parliament, do question the same within *fourteen* days next, and so within fourteen days next after any new return shall be brought in, and that all members who are returned for two or more places do make their election by this day three weeks for which of the places they will serve, provided there be no question upon the return for that place; and, if any thing shall come in question touching the return or election of any member, he is to withdraw during the time the matter is in debate, and

and that all members returned upon double returns, do withdraw till their returns are determined. Vol. xlix. p. 17.

Ordered,

THAT all perfons who will queftion any returns of members to ferve in parliament, by the renewal of petitions which were depending before this houfe at the end of the laft feffion of parliament, do queftion the fame within the time limited for the forfeiture of the recognizances, in cafe fuch petitions fhall not be renewed, as mentioned in an act, made in the 28th year of the reign of his prefent majefty, intituled, " An act for the further regulation " of the trials of controverted elections, or re- " turns of members to ferve in parliament;" and that all perfons, who will queftion the judgment of any felect committee refpecting the right of election, or of appointing returning officers by the renewal of petitions which were depending before this houfe at the end of the laft feffion of parliament, do queftion the fame within *fourteen* days after the commencement of the prefent feffion of parliament, according to the directions of an act paffed for that purpofe, in the 34th year of the reign of his prefent majefty; and that all other perfons, who will queftion any returns of members to ferve in parliament do queftion the fame within *fourteen* days next, and fo within *fourteen* days next after any new return fhall be brought in; and that

all

N. B.
14 Dec. 1792.
Vol. xlviii. p. 8.
the fame.

31 Dec. 1794.
N. B.
30 Oct. 1795.
the fame.

all members who are returned for two or more places, do make their election by this day *three weeks* for which of the places they will serve, provided there be no question upon the return for that place; and if any thing shall come in question, touching the return or election of any member, he is to withdraw during the time the matter is in debate; and that all members returned upon double returns do withdraw till their returns are determined.

Ordered,

THAT all persons, who will question any returns of members to serve in parliament, *(by the renewal of petitions which were depending before the house at the end of the last session of parliament, do question the same within the time limited for the forfeiture of the recognizances in case such petitions shall not be renewed as mentioned in the said act**, and that all other persons who will question any returns of members to serve in parliament,)* do question the same within *fourteen* days next, and *so within* fourteen *days next after any new return shall be brought in*; and that all members who are returned for two or more places do make their election by this day *three weeks* for which of the places they will serve, provided there be no question upon the return for that place; and if any thing shall come in question touching the return or election of any member, he is to withdraw during the time the matter is in debate; and that all members returned upon double re-

turns,

* Act 18 Geo. III. cap. 52.

turns, do withdraw till their returns are determined.

> *Note.—This order is made at the commencement of every session, (except the words printed in italicks, which are inserted on particular occasions.)*

Exchange of Lists.

Resolved,

THAT in all cases of controverted elections, for counties in *England* and *Wales*, the petitioners do, by themselves or by their agents, within a convenient time to be appointed by the house, deliver to the sitting members or their agents lists of the persons, intended by the petitioners to be objected to, who voted for the sitting members, giving in the said lists the several heads of objection, and distinguishing the same against the names of the voters excepted to; and that the sitting members do, by themselves or by their agents, within the same time, deliver the like lists on their part to the petitioners or their agents.

> *Note.—This resolution is made at the commencement of every session.*

False Evidence and tampering with Witnesses.

Resolved,

THAT if it shall appear that any person hath been tampering with any witness, in respect of
his

his evidence to be given to this houfe, or any committee thereof, or directly or indirectly hath endeavoured to deter or hinder any perfon from appearing or giving evidence, the fame is declared to be a high crime and mifdemeanour, and this houfe will proceed with the utmoft feverity againft fuch offender.

Refolved,

THAT if it fhall appear that any perfon hath given falfe evidence, in any cafe, before this houfe or any committee thereof, this houfe will proceed with the utmoft feverity againft fuch offender.

Note.—*Thefe two laft refolutions are made at the commencement of every feffion.*

Amending Returns.

20 July, 1660.   THIS houfe doth *declare* it to be the fundamental order of this houfe that the proper officer, except only in cafes of impotency and ficknefs, ought to amend in the houfe all returns of elections where, upon an error committed in the return, the houfe fhall fee caufe to order an amendment.   Vol. viii. p. 95.

Refolved,

12 April, 1690.   THAT after a return made into the crown office of members to ferve in parliament, the fame fhall not be altered by the fheriff or the clerk of the crown, or any other but by this houfe.   Vol. x. p. 377.

PART

ELECTIONS FOR *SCOTLAND*.

ANNÆ REGINÆ, SESS. 4. CAP. 8.

Act settling the Manner of electing the Sixteen Peers and Forty-five Commoners, to represent Scotland *in the Parliament of Great Britain.*

OUR sovereign lady considering, that, by the twenty-second article of the treaty of union, as the same is ratified by an act passed in this session of parliament, upon the sixteenth of January last, it is provided, That by virtue of the said treaty, of the peers of *Scotland*, at the time of the union, sixteen shall be the number to sit and vote in the house of lords, and forty-five the number of the representatives of *Scotland*, in the house of commons of the parliament of Great Britain, and that the said sixteen peers, and forty-five members in the house of commons be named and chosen in such manner, as by a subsequent act in this present session of parliament in *Scotland* shall be settled; which act is thereby declared to be as valid as if it were a part of, and

22d article of union.

ingrossed

ingrossed in the said treaty: Therefore, her majesty, with advice and consent of the estates of parliament, statutes, enacts, and ordains, That the said sixteen peers, who shall have right to sit in the house of peers in the parliament of Great Britain, on the part of *Scotland*, by virtue of this treaty, shall be named by the said peers of *Scotland*, whom they represent, their heirs or successors to their dignities and honours, out of their own number, and that by open election, and plurality of voices of the peers present, and of the proxies for such as shall be absent, the said proxies being peers, and producing a mandate in writing, duly signed before witnesses, and both the constituent and proxy being qualified according to law; declaring also That such peers as are absent, being qualified as aforesaid, may send to all such meetings lists of the peers whom they judge fittest, validly signed by the said absent peers, which shall be reckoned in the same manner as if the parties had been present, and given in the said list; and, in case of the death, or legal incapacity of any of the said sixteen peers, That the aforesaid peers of *Scotland* shall nominate another of their own number in place of the said peer or peers, in manner before and after-mentioned; and That of the said forty-five representatives of *Scotland* in the house of commons, in the parliament of Great Britain, thirty shall be chosen by the shires or stewartries, and fifteen by the royal boroughs, as follows, viz. one for every shire and stewartry; excepting the shires of Bute and Caithness, which shall choose one by turns,

Sixteen peers for Scotland to sit in the parliament of Great Britain, to be named by the peers of Scotland out of their own number.

Absents may vote by proxies.

Or send signed lists.

In case of death, or incapacity of any peer elected, another to be elected in his place in the same manner.

Of the forty-five commissioners for Scotland, thirty to be chosen by the shires, &c. and fifteen by the boroughs, each shire and stewartry to have one.

Exception.

Bute

Bute having the first election; the shires of Nairn and Cromarty, which shall also choose by turns, Nairn having the first election; and in like manner the shires of Clackmannan and Kinross shall choose by turns, Clackmannan having the first election. And in case of the death, or legal incapacity of any of the said members, from the respective shires or stewartries above-mentioned to sit in the house of commons, it is enacted and ordained, That the shire or stewartry who elected the said member shall elect another member in his place; and that the said fifteen representatives for the royal boroughs be chosen as follows, viz. that the town of Edinburgh shall have right to elect and send one member to the parliament of Great Britain; and that each of the other burghs shall elect a commissioner in the same manner as they are now in use to elect commissioners to the parliament of *Scotland*; which commissioners and burghs (Edinburgh excepted) being divided in fourteen classes or districts, shall meet at such time and place, within their respective districts, as her majesty, her heirs or successors shall appoint, and elect one for each district, viz. the burghs of Kirkwall, Wick, Dornork, Dingwall, and Tayne, one; the burghs of Fortrose, Inverness, Nairn, and Forress, one; the burghs of Elgin, Cullen, Banff, Inverury, and Kintore, one; the burghs of Aberdeen, Inverbervy, Montrose, Aberbrothock, and Brechin, one; the burghs of Forfar, Perth, Dundee, Cowper, and St. Andrews, one; the burghs of Crail, Kilrennie, Anstruther Easter, Anstruther Wester, and Pittenweem, one; the burghs of Dysart, Kirkcaldie,

In case of death or incapacity of any member, another to be chosen by the shire, &c. in his place.

Edinburgh to have one.

And fourteen to be chosen by the commissioners of the other boroughs, who are divided into fourteen districts.

caldie, Kinghorn, and Burntisland, one; the burghs of Inverkeithing, Dumferling, Queensferry, Culross, and Stirling, one; the burghs of Glasgow, Renfrew, Rutherglen, and Dumbarton, one; the burghs of Haddingtoun, Dunbar, North Berwick, Lawder, and Jedburgh, one; the burghs of Selkirk, Peebles, Linlithgow, and Lanerk, one; the burghs of Dumfries, Sanquhar, Annan, Lochmaban, and Kircudbright, one; the burghs of Wigtoun, Newgalloway, Stranrawer, and Whitehorn, one; and the burghs of Air, Irvine, Rothesay, Campbletown, and Inverary, one. And it is hereby declared and ordained, That where the votes of the commissioners for the said burghs met to choose representatives from the several districts to the parliament of Great Britain, shall be equal, in that case the president of the meeting shall have a casting or decisive vote, and that by and attour his vote as a commissioner from the burgh from which he is sent; the commissioner from the eldest burgh presiding in the first meeting, and the commissioners from the other burghs, in their respective districts, presiding afterwards, by turns, in the order as the said burghs, are now called in rolls of the parliament of *Scotland*; and in case that any of the said fifteen commissioners from the burghs, shall decease, or become legally incapable to sit in the house of commons, then the town of Edinburgh, or the district which choosed the said member, shall elect a member in his or their place. It is always hereby expressly provided and declared, That none

[margin: Where the voters at elections are equal, the president to have the casting vote, besides his own.]

[margin: In case of death, or incapacity, another to be chosen by the town of Edinburgh, or the district.]

none shall be capable to elect, or be elected, for any of the said estates, but such as are twenty-one years of age compleat, and protestant, excluding all papists, or such, who being suspected of popery, and required, refuse to swear and subscribe the *formula*, contained in the third act made in the eighth and ninth sessions of king William's parliament, intituled, "Act for preventing the growth of popery:" And also declaring, That none shall be capable to elect, or be elected, to represent a shire or burgh in the parliament of Great Britain, for this part of the united kingdom, except such as are now capable, by the laws of this kingdom, to elect, or to be elected as commissioners for shires or burghs to the parliament of *Scotland*. And further, her majesty with advice and consent aforesaid, for the effectual and orderly election of the persons to be chosen to sit, vote, and serve, in the respective houses of the parliament of Great Britain, when her majesty, her heirs and successors shall declare her or their pleasure for holding the first, or any subsequent parliament of Great Britain, and when for that effect a writ shall be issued out under the great seal of the united kingdom, directed to the privy council of *Scotland*, conform to the said twenty-second article, statutes, enacts, and ordains, That until the parliament of Great Britain shall make further provision therein, the said writ shall contain a warrant and command to the said privy council to issue out a proclamation in her majesty's name, requiring the peers of *Scotland* for the time, to meet and assemble at such time and place,

[marginalia: None but those of 21 years of age, and protestants, and who make the formula, *if required, capable to vote, or to be elected for any of the estates.]*

[marginalia: None to be a commoner for any place in Scotland, but such as were capable to be elected to the parliament of Scotland.]

[marginalia: Upon calling a parliament, writs shall be directed to the privy council of Scotland.]

[marginalia: Who are to issue a proclamation for electing sixteen peers for Scotland.]

place, within *Scotland*, as her majesty and royal successors shall think fit to make election of the said sixteen peers, and requiring the lord clerk register, or two of the clerks of session, to attend all such meetings, and to administer the oaths that are or shall be by law required, and to ask the votes, and having made up the lists in presence of the meeting, to return the names of the sixteen peers chosen (certified under the subscription of the said lord clerk register, clerk, or clerks of session attending) to the clerk of the privy council of *Scotland*; and sicklike requiring and ordaining the several freeholders in the respective shires and stewartries, to meet and convene at the head burghs of their several shires and stewartries, to elect their commissioners conform to the order above set down; and ordaining the clerks of the said meetings immediately after the said elections are over, respectively, to return the names of the persons elected to the clerks of the privy council; and lastly, ordaining the city of *Edinburgh* to elect their commissioner and the other royal boroughs to elect each of them a commissioner, as they have been in use to elect commissioners to the parliament, and to send the said respective commissioners, at such times, to such burghs, within their respective districts as her majesty and successors by such proclamation shall appoint, requiring and ordaining the common clerk of the respective burghs, where such elections shall be appointed to be made, to attend the said meetings, and immediately after the election, to return the names of the persons

so

so elected (certified under his hand) to the clerk of privy council, to the end that the names of the sixteen peers, thirty commissioners for shires, and fifteen commissioners for burghs, being so returned to the privy council, may be returned to the court from whence the writ did issue under the great seal of the united kingdom, conform to the said twenty-second article: And whereas by the said twenty-second article it is agreed, That, if her majesty shall, on or before the first day of May next, declare, That it is expedient the lords and commons of the present parliament of England, should be the members of the respective houses of the first parliament of Great Britain, for and on the part of England, they shall accordingly be the members of the said respective houses, for and on the part of England; her majesty, with advice and consent aforesaid, in that case only, doth hereby statute and ordain, That the sixteen peers, and forty-five commissioners for shires and burghs, who shall be chosen by the peers, barons, and burghs respectively in this present session of parliament, and out of the members thereof in the same manner as committees of parliament are usually now chosen, shall be the members of the respective houses of the said first parliament of Great Britain, for, and on the part of *Scotland*, which nomination and election being certified by a writ under the lord clerk register's hand, the person so nominated and elected shall have right to sit and vote in the house of lords, and in the house of commons, of the said first parliament of Great Britain.

[Marginal notes: The names of the sixteen peers, and forty-five commissioners to be returned by the privy council. Manner of electing the peers and commoners for Scotland to the first parliament of Great Britain in case the present members for England be continued.]

A. D. 1707.

ANNO

ANNO 6° ANNÆ REGINÆ, CAP. 6.

An Act for rendering the Union of the Two Kingdoms more entire and complete.

In what manner the 45 representatives of Scotland shall be elected.

5. AND for the more uniform and express method of electing and returning members of parliament, be it likewise further enacted by the authority aforesaid, That when any parliament shall at any time hereafter be summoned or called, the forty-five representatives of *Scotland* in the house of commons of the parliament of Great Britain, shall be elected and chosen by authority of the queen's writs under the great seal of Great Britain, directed to the several sheriffs and stewarts of the respective shires and stewartries; and the said several sheriffs and stewarts shall, on receipt of such receipts, forthwith give notice of the time of election for the knights or commissioners for their respective shires or stewartries, and at such time of election the several freeholders in the respective shires and stewartries shall meet and convene at the head burghs of their several shires and stewartries, and proceed to the election of their respective commissioners or knights for the shire or stewartry; and the clerks of the said meetings, immediately after the said elections are over, shall respectively return the names of the persons elected to the sheriff or stewart of the shire or stewartry, who shall annex it to his writ, and return it with the same into the court out of which the writ issued:

And as to the manner of election of the fifteen representatives of the royal boroughs, the sheriffs of the shire of Edinburgh shall, on the receipt of the writ directed to him, forthwith direct his precept to the lord provost of Edinburgh, to cause a burgess to be elected for that city; and on receipt of such precept, the city of Edinburgh shall elect their member, and their common clerk shall certify his name to the sheriff of Edinburgh, who shall annex it to his writ, and return it with the same into the court from whence the writ issued: and as to the other royal burghs, divided into fourteen classes or districts, the sheriffs or stewarts of the several shires and stewartries, shall on the receipt of their several writs, forthwith direct their several precepts to every royal borough within their respective shires or stewartries, reciting therein the contents of the writ, and the date thereof, and commanding them forthwith to elect each of them a commissioner as they used formerly to elect commissioners to the parliament of *Scotland*, and to order the said respective commissioners to meet at the presiding borough of their respective district (naming the said presiding borough) upon the thirtieth day after the day of the teste of the writ, unless it be upon the *Lord's-day*, commonly called *Sunday*, and then the next day after, and then to choose their burgess for the parliament; and the common clerk of the then presiding borough shall immediately after the election, return the name of the person so elected to the sheriff or stewart of the shire or stewartry wherein such presiding borough is, who shall

shall annex it to his writ, and return it with the same into the court from whence the writ issued: And in case a vacancy shall happen in time of parliament, by the decease or legal incapacity of any member, a new member shall be elected in his room, conformable to the method herein-before appointed; and in case such vacancy be of a representative for any one of the said fourteen classes, or districts of the said royal boroughs, that borough which presided at the election of the deceased or disabled member, shall be the presiding borough at such new election.

How vacancies happening in time of parliament shall be supplied.

6. Provided always, That upon the issuing of writs of summons for the electing of a parliament, if any shire or stewartry wherein a royal borough is, hath not then a turn, or right to elect a commissioner, or knight of the shire or stewartry for that parliament, That then it shall be omitted out of the writ directed to such sheriff or stewart, to cause a knight, or commissioner for that shire or stewartry to be elected for that parliament.

Shire or Stewartry, &c. not having a turn to elect, to be omitted out of the writ, &c.

ANNO 6° ANNÆ REGINÆ, CAP. 23.

An Act to make further Provision for electing and summoning Sixteen Peers of Scotland, to sit in the House of Peers in the Parliament of Great Britain, and for trying Peers for Offences committed in Scotland; and for the further regulating of Voters in Election of Members to serve in Parliament.

5 Ann. c. 8.

'WHEREAS by the two and twentieth article of the treaty of union, for uniting the

two

two kingdoms of England and *Scotland*, ratified and confirmed by the respective parliaments of each kingdom, it was amongst other things provided, That when her majesty, her heirs or successors, should declare their pleasure for holding the first, or any subsequent parliament of Great Britain, until the parliament of Great Britain should make further provision therein, writs should issue under the Great seal of the united kingdom of Great Britain, directed to the privy council of *Scotland*, commanding them to cause sixteen peers, who were to sit in the house of lords, to be summoned to parliament, in such manner as by an act of the then present session of parliament of *Scotland*, was or should be settled; in which session of the parliament in *Scotland* an act was accordingly passed for that purpose, intituled, 'An act settling the manner of electing the sixteen peers, and forty-five members to represent *Scotland* in the parliament of Great Britain, which act was afterwards confirmed by the parliament of England, and declared to be as valid as if the same had been part of and ingrossed in, the said articles of union; by which act it is, amongst other things, provided and enacted, That the sixteen peers who should have a right to sit in the house of peers in the parliament of Great Britain on the part of *Scotland*, by virtue of the said treaty, should be named by the said peers of *Scotland*, whom they represent, their heirs or successors to their dignities and honours out of their own number, and that by open election and plurality of voices of the peers present, and of the proxies for such as should be absent, the said proxies being

ing peers, and producing a mandate in writing duly signed before witnesses, and both the constituent and the proxy being qualified according to law; and that such peers as were absent being qualified as aforesaid, might send to all such meetings, a list of the peers whom they judged fittest, validly signed by the said absent peers, which should be reckoned in the same manner as if the parties had been present and given in the said list; and in case of the death, or legal incapacity, of any of the said sixteen peers, that the aforesaid peers of *Scotland*, should nominate another of their own number in place of the said peer or peers, in manner as therein is mentioned; and it was thereby further enacted, That until the parliament of Great Britain should make further provision therein, the said writs so to be issued, should contain a warrant and command, to command the said privy council to issue out a proclamation in her majesty's name, requiring the peers of *Scotland* for the time, to meet and assemble at such time and place within *Scotland*, as her majesty and her royal successors should think fit, to make election of the said sixteen peers, and requiring the lord clerk register, or two of the clerks of session, to attend all such meetings, and to administer the oaths as were, or should be, by law required, and to ask the votes, and having made up the list in presence of the meeting, to return the names of the sixteen peers chosen, certified under the subscription of the said lord clerk register, clerk, or clerks of session, attending, to the clerk of the privy council of *Scotland*, to the end

end that the names of the sixteen peers being so returned to the privy council, might be returned to the court from whence the writ did issue, under the great seal of the united kingdom, conform to the said twenty-second article; And whereas by an act of this present session, intituled, 'An act for rendering the union of the two kingdoms more entire and compleat,' it is declared and enacted, That from and after the first day of May, 1708, the privy council of *Scotland* shall cease and determine, whereby it is become necessary that some further provision should be made for the electing and returning the said sixteen peers, that are to sit in the house of peers in the parliament of Great Britain, pursuant to the said treaty: Be it therefore enacted by the queen's most excellent majesty, by and with the advice and consent of the lords spiritual and temporal and commons in parliament assembled, and by the authority of the same, That at all times hereafter, when her majesty, her heirs and successors shall declare her or their pleasure for summoning and holding any parliament of Great Britain, in order to the electing and summoning the sixteen peers of *Scotland*, a proclamation shall be issued under the great seal of Great Britain, commanding all the peers of *Scotland* to assemble and meet at Edinburgh, or in such other place in *Scotland*, and at such time as shall be appointed in the said proclamation, to elect by open election, the sixteen peers to sit and vote in the house of peers in the parliament

marginalia: 6 Annæ, c. 6.

marginalia: Proclamation to be issued for electing 16 peers of Scotland to sit in the parliament of Great Britain.

of Great Britain, in such manner as by the before-recited act and herein-after is appointed.

and published at Edinburgh, &c. 25 days before election.

2. And be it further enacted by the authority aforesaid, That every proclamation issued for the purpose aforesaid, shall be duly published at the market cross at Edinburgh, and in all the county towns of *Scotland*, five and twenty days at the least before the time thereby appointed for the meeting of the peers to proceed to such election.

All the peers present to take the oaths.

3. And be it further enacted by the authority aforesaid, That all the peers who meet on such proclamation, shall, before they proceed to the election, and in the presence of all the peers assembled for such election, take the respective oaths, *videlicet*:

Oaths.

" I, A. B. do sincerely promise and swear, That I will be faithful, and bear true allegiance to her majesty queen Anne,
So help me God.
A. B."

" I, A. B. do swear, That I do from my heart abhor, detest, and abjure, as impious and heretical, that damnable doctrine and position, That princes, excommunicated or deprived by the Pope or any authority of the See of Rome, may be deposed or murdered by their subjects or any other whatsoever: And I do declare, That no foreign prince, person, prelate, state, or potentate, hath or ought to have any jurisdiction, power, superiority, pre-eminence, or authority, ecclesiastical or spiritual within this realm,
So help me God."

And also make, repeat, and subscribe the declaration following, *videlicet:*

And subscribe the declaration.

"I, A. B. do solemnly and sincerely, in the presence of God, profess, testify, and declare, That I do believe that in the sacrament of the Lord's supper, there is not any transubstantiation of the elements of bread and wine into the body and blood of Christ, at or after the consecration thereof by any person whatsoever, and that the invocation or adoration of the Virgin Mary or any other saint, and the sacrifice of the mass, as they are now used in the church of Rome, are superstitious and idolatrous. And I do solemnly, in the presence of God, profess, testify, and declare, That I do make this declaration and every part thereof, in the plain and ordinary sense of the words read unto me, as they are commonly understood by English protestants, without any evasion, equivocation, or mental reservation whatsoever, and without any dispensation already granted me for this purpose by the Pope, or any other authority or person, or without any hope of any such dispensation from any person or authority whatsoever, or without thinking that I am, or can be, acquitted before God or man, or absolved of this declaration or any part thereof, although the Pope, or any other person or persons, or power whatsoever, should dispense with, or annul the same, or declare that it was null and void from the beginning."

And also take and subscribe the following oath, *videlicet:*

"I,

And also take the following oath.

"I, A. B. do truly and sincerely acknowledge, profess, testify, and declare, in my conscience before God and the world, that our sovereign lady queen Anne, is lawful and rightful queen of this realm, and of all other her majesty's dominions and countries thereunto belonging: And I do solemnly and sincerely declare, That I do believe in my conscience, the person pretended to be prince of Wales during the life of the late king James, and, since his decease, pretending to be, and taking upon himself the stile and title of, king of England by the name of James the Third, or of *Scotland* by the name of James the Eighth, or the stile and title of king of Great Britain, hath not any right or title whatsoever to the crown of this realm, or any other the dominions thereunto belonging, and I do renounce, refuse, and abjure any allegiance or obedience to him: And I do swear, That I will bear faith and true allegiance to her majesty queen Anne, and her will defend, to the utmost of my power, against all traiterous conspiracies which I shall know to be against her person, crown, or dignity: And I will do my utmost endeavour to disclose and make known to her majesty and her successors, all treasons, traiterous conspiracies, which I shall know to be against her or any of them: And I do faithfully promise to the utmost of my power, to support, maintain, and defend the succession of the crown against him the said James, and all other persons whatsoever, as the same is and stands settled by an act, (intituled, An act declaring the rights and liberties of the subject, and settling the succession of the crown to her present majesty and the heirs of her body, being protestants,) and as the same by one other act, intituled, (An act for the further limitation of the crown, and better securing the rights and liberties of the subject,) is and stands settled and entailed after the decease of her majesty, and for default of issue of her majesty, to the princess Sophia, electress and dutchess dowager of Hanover, and the heirs of her body being protestants: And all these things I do plainly and sincerely acknowledge and swear according to these express words by me spoken, and according to the plain and common sense and understanding of the same words, without any equivocation, mental evasion, or secret reservation whatsoever. And I do make this recognition, acknowledgement, abjuration, renunciation, and promise heartily, willingly, and truly, upon the true faith of a christian.

So help me God."

4. And that such peers that live in *Scotland*, but shall not be present at such meeting so appointed, may take the said oaths, and make and subscribe the said declaration in any sheriff's court in *Scotland*, and every sheriff or his deputy before whom such oaths, and such declaration shall be so made, subscribed and repeated, shall and is hereby required to return the original subscription of such oath and declaration, signed by the peer who took the same, and make a return in writing under his hand and seal to the peers so assembled, of such peers taking the said oaths,

[Marginal note: How peers living in Scotland or residing in England, not present at election, may take the oaths, &c.]

oaths, and making and subscribing the said oath and declaration, and such peer shall be thereby enabled and qualified to make a proxy, or to send a signed list containing the names of sixteen peers of *Scotland*, for whom he giveth his vote, and such of the peers of *Scotland*, as at the time of issuing such proclamation reside in England, may take and subscribe the said oaths, and make, repeat, and subscribe the said declaration in her majesty's high court of chancery in England, her majesty's court of queen's bench, common pleas, or court of exchequer in England, which being certified by writ to the peers in Scotland at their meeting, under the seal of the court where such oath and declaration shall be made, repeated, and subscribed, shall be sufficient to entitle such peer to make his proxy, and to send a signed list, as aforesaid; and in case any of the said peers of *Scotland*, who at any time before the issuing of such proclamation, have taken the said oaths and made and subscribed the said declaration in England or *Scotland*, to be certified as aforesaid, and if taken in parliament, to be certified under the great seal of Great Britain, shall at the time of issuing such proclamation be absent in the service of her majesty, her heirs or successors, such peer may make his proxy or send a signed list.

and be thereby qualified to make a proxy, &c.

How proxies shall be signed.

5. Provided always and be it enacted by the authority aforesaid, That such peers of *Scotland*, as are also peers of England, shall sign their proxies and lists by the title of their peerage in *Scotland*.

6. And

6. And be it further enacted by the authority aforesaid, That no peer shall be capable of having more than two proxies at one time.

No peer to have more than two proxies.

7. And be it further enacted by the authority aforesaid, That at such meeting of the peers, they shall all give in the names of the persons by them nominated to sit and vote in the house of peers in the parliament of Great Britain, and the lord clerk register, or two of the principal clerks of the session appointed by him to officiate in his name, shall, after the election is made and duly examined, certify the names of the sixteen peers so elected, and sign and attest the same in the presence of the peers, which certificate, so signed and attested, shall, by the lord clerk register, or two of the principal clerks of the session, be returned into her majesty's high court of chancery of Great Britain before the time appointed for the meeting of the parliament.

After election, lord clerk register to certify the names of the 16 peers elected.

8. And be it further enacted by the authority aforesaid, That the peers should come to such meetings with their ordinary attendants only, according to, and under the several penalties inflicted by, the several laws and statutes now in force in *Scotland*, which prescribe and direct with what number and attendants the subjects there may repair to the public courts of justice.

How peers shall come attended to elections.

9. And be it further enacted by the authority aforesaid, That it shall not be lawful for the peers so assembled and met together for the electing fixteen peers to sit and vote in the house of peers in the parliament of Great Britain, to act, propose, debate, or treat of any other matter or thing

And not debate or treat of any matter, &c. except only the election.

thing whatsoever, except only the election of the said sixteen peers, and that every peer who shall at such meeting presume to propose, debate, or treat of any other matter or thing contrary to the direction of this act, shall incur the penalty of *premunire*, expressed in the statute of the 16th year of king Richard the Second.

Confirmation of the act of parliament of Scotland.

10. And be it further declared by the authority aforesaid, That all and every matter and things for, or concerning, the election of sixteen peers of *Scotland*, to sit and vote in the house of peers in the parliament of Great Britain, directed and appointed to be observed and done by the articles of union, and the said recited act of parliament in *Scotland*, intituled, ' An act settling the manner of electing the sixteen peers and forty-five members to represent *Scotland* in the parliament of Great Britain,' which act, by an act of parliament in England, in the 5th year of her majesty's reign, intituled, " An act for the union of the two kingdoms of England and *Scotland*," was declared to be as valid as if the same had been part of, and ingrossed in, the articles of union thereby ratified and approved, shall be observed and performed, except only wherein this act has further declared and provided.

5 Annæ, c. 8.

Exception.

In case of death or disability of peers elected, proclamation to issue for electing another.

11. And be it further enacted by the authority aforesaid, That, in case any of the sixteen peers so chosen shall die, or become otherwise legally disabled to sit in the house of peers of the parliament of Great Britain, her majesty, her heirs and successors, shall forthwith, after such death or disability, issue a proclamation under the great

great seal of Great Britain, for electing another peer of *Scotland* to sit in the house of peers of the parliament of Great Britain in the room of such peer deceased or otherwise legally disabled; which proclamation shall be published at such time and places as is herein enacted, touching proclamation issued upon summoning a parliament of Great Britain; and the peers of *Scotland* being qualified as hereby directed, shall proceed to elect a peer of *Scotland* to sit in the house of peers of the parliament of Great Britain, in the room of such peer deceased or otherwise legally disabled, in such manner and under such restriction and regulations as are by this act directed to be observed, upon the electing sixteen peers of *Scotland* to sit in the house of peers of the parliament of Great Britain.

12. And be it further enacted by the authority aforesaid, That for the more effectual trial of any peer of Great Britain that hath committed, or shall commit any high treason, petit treason, misprision of treason, murder, or other felonies, in *Scotland*, commission or commissions may issue under the great seal of Great Britain to be directed to such person and persons as shall be therein named, constituting them, and such a number of them as shall be therein mentioned, justices of the queen, her heirs and successors, to enquire, by the oaths of good and lawful men of such county and counties of *Scotland* as shall be named therein, of all treasons, misprisions of treason, murders, and other felonies,

How peers shall be tried for treason, murder, &c. committed in Scotland.

nies, committed in such county by a peer or peers of Great Britain, which inquisition shall be taken and made in the same manner as the indictments found and taken before justices of oyer and terminer of any county of England, and shall be of the same effect, and proceeded upon in the same method as any inquisition found before justices of oyer and terminer in England, whereby any peer is indicted for any such offence, and such justices shall issue mandates or precepts to the sheriffs of the respective counties of *Scotland* to return to them at such day and place as they shall appoint, such and so many good and lawful men of the same county, as may be sufficient to enquire of the offences aforesaid, and twelve or more of them so returned being sworn, shall be sufficient to make such enquiry, and find any indictment; and if the sheriff of such county shall not summon a sufficient number of men to make such inquisition, the justices that do proceed upon such commission may impose a fine upon such sheriff which shall be levied by process, out of the exchequer; and if any of the persons summoned by the sheriff to enquire as aforesaid, shall not appear, the justices may, in like manner, impose a fine upon such person so making default to be levied in manner aforesaid.

<small>Persons refusing to take the oath, or Quaker to make affirmation, &c. un-</small>

13. And be it further enacted by the authority aforesaid, That every person who shall refuse to take the oath last herein-before recited, or, being a *Quaker*, shall refuse to declare the effect thereof upon his solemn affirmation as directed

rected by an act of parliament made in the 7th year of the reign of his late majesty, king William, intituled, "An act that the solemn affirmation and declaration of the people called *Quakers*, shall be accepted instead of an oath in usual form" (which oath or declaration the sheriff president of the meeting, or chief officer taking the poll at any election of members to serve in the house of commons for any place in Great Britain, or commissioners for chusing burgesses for any place in *Scotland*, at the request of any candidate or other person present at such election, are hereby impowered and required to administer) shall not be capable of giving any vote for the election of any such member to serve in the house of commons for any place in Great Britain or commissioner to chuse a burgess for any place in *Scotland*.

capable of voting for election of member, &c.

7 & 8 W. 3. c. 34.

14. Provided always, and be it enacted by the authority aforesaid, That if any person, being a *Quaker*, shall refuse to take the said oath, being tendered to him in pursuance of an act made in this present session of parliament, intituled, "An act for the better security of her majesty's person and government," but shall instead thereof declare the effect of the said oath, upon his solemn affirmation, as directed by an act of parliament made in the 7th year of the reign of his late majesty, king William the Third, intituled, "An act that the solemn affirmation and declaration of the people called *Quakers*, shall be accepted instead of an oath in usual form," which affirmation shall

Quakers declaring on their affirmation not liable to penalties, by 6 Ann. c. 14.

7 & 8 W. 3. c. 34.

See 1. Geo. 1. st. 2. 4. 6.

be

6 Ann. c 14.

be administered to such *Quaker* instead of the said oath, such *Quaker* shall not be liable to any the penalties or forfeitures for refusing the said oath when tendered to him, contained or mentioned in the said act, intituled, " An act for the better security of her majesty's person and government."

A. D. 1707.

ANNO 12° ANNÆ, CAP. 6.

An Act for the better Regulating the Elections of Members to serve in Parliament for that part of Great Britain called Scotland.

After the end of the parliament no conveyance whereon infeoffment is not taken, and seizin registered, a year before the teste of the writ, shall entitle to vote or be elected in Scotland; nor if any election happen during the continuance of a parliament.

'WHEREAS of late several conveyances of estates have been made in trust or redeemable for elusory sums, no ways adequate to the true value of the lands, on purpose to create and multiply votes in elections of members to serve in parliament for that part of Great Britain called *Scotland*, contrary to the true intent and meaning of the laws in that behalf.' Be it therefore enacted by the queen's most excellent majesty, by and with the advice and consent of the lords spiritual and temporal and commons in this present parliament assembled, and by the authority of the same, That from and after the determination of this present parliament, no conveyance or right whatsoever whereupon infeoffment is not taken and seizin registrated, one year before the teste

teste of the writs for calling a new parliament, shall upon objection made in that behalf, entitle the person or persons so infeoft, to vote or to be elected at that election in any shire or stewartry in that part of Great Britain called *Scotland*; and in case any election happen during the continuance of a parliament, no conveyance or right whatsoever, whereupon infeoffment is not taken one year before the date of the warrant for making out a new writ for such election, shall, upon objection made in that behalf, entitle the person or persons so infeoft to vote or be elected at that election; and that from and after the said day, it shall and may be lawful to or for any of the electors present, suspecting any person or persons to have his or their estates in trust and for the behoof of another, to require the preses of the meeting to tender the following oath to any elector; and the said preses is hereby impowered and required to administer the same in the following words, *videlicet*:

<small>Any elector may require the preses to tender an oath to one whom he suspects to have an estate in trust.</small>

"I, A. B. do, in the presence of God, declare and swear, that the lands and estate of   for which I claim to give my vote in this election, are not conveyed to me in trust, or for the behoof of any other person whatsoever; and I do swear before God, that neither I, nor any person to my knowledge, in my name, or by my allowance, hath given, or intends to give, any promise, obligation, bond, back-bond, or other security, for re-disponing or re-conveying the said lands and estate, any manner of way whatsoever;

<small>The oath.</small>

and

and this is the truth, as I shall answer to God."

Refusing, shall not vote. And in case such elector refuse to swear, and also to subscribe the said oath, such person or persons shall not be capable of voting, or being elected at such election.

Other objections as allowable by law. 2. Provided always, That notwithstanding such oath taken, it shall be lawful to make such other objections as are allowed by the laws of *Scotland* against such electors.

No infeoffment on any redeemable right (except proper wadsetts, &c.) shall entitle to vote or be elected. And persons not inrolled at former elections, shall not vote without producing a right. 3. And be it further enacted and declared by the authority aforesaid, That no infeoffment taken upon any redeemable right whatsoever (except proper wadsetts, adjudications, or apprisings allowed by the act of parliament relating to elections in 1681) shall entitle the person so infeoft to vote or be elected at any election in any shire or stewartry; and that no person or persons, who have not been inrolled and voted at former elections, shall, upon any pretence whatsoever, be inrolled or admitted to vote at any election, except he or they first produce a sufficient right or title to qualify him or them to vote at that election, to the satisfaction of the freeholders formerly inrolled, or the majority of them present; and the returning officers are hereby ordained to make their returns of the

This clause is in part repealed by 16 Geo. 2. cap. 11. persons elected by the majority of the freeholders inrolled, and those admitted by them, reserving always the liberty of objecting against the persons admitted to, or excluded from the roll, as formerly.

4. And

4. And be it further enacted by the authority aforesaid, That all sheriffs of shires, and stewarts and stewartries, shall be obliged, under the pain of fifty pounds sterling, one moiety whereof shall be to the queen's most excellent majesty, her heirs and successors, and the other moiety to the person or persons who shall sue for the same, to be recovered before the court of session, by any action summarily, without abiding the course of the roll, to make the public intimations required by the laws of *Scotland*, at the several parish churches within their respective jurisdictions, at least three days before the dyet of elections.

<small>Sheriffs, &c. shall on penalty of 50l. make public intimations three days before the day of election.</small>

5. Provided always, That the right of apparent heirs in voting at elections by virtue of their predecessors' infeoffments, and the right of husbands, by virtue of their wives' infeoffments, be and is hereby reserved to them, as formerly; any thing in this act contained to the contrary notwithstanding.

<small>Saving the rights of heirs and husbands.</small>

6. Provided also, That any conveyance of right, which by the laws of *Scotland* is sufficient to qualify any person to vote in the elections of members to serve in parliament for shires or stewartries, and whereupon infeoffment is taken, on or before the first day of June, in the year of our Lord 1713, shall entitle the person or persons so infeoft, to vote at the elections of members to serve in the next ensuing parliament; any thing herein contained to the contrary notwithstanding.

<small>Any right whereon infeoffment is taken before 1st of June, 1713, shall entitle to vote for members of parliament.</small>

7. Provided always, and it is hereby declared to be the true intent and meaning of this act, That no husbands shall vote at any ensuing election

<small>Husbands not to vote by virtue</small>

of their wives' infeoffments, unless they are heiresses, &c. election by virtue of their wives' infeoffments, who are not heiresses, or have not right to the property of the lands on account whereof such vote shall be claimed.

A. D. 1713.

ANNO I° GEORGII, CAP. 13.

An Act for the security of his Majesty's Person and Government, and the Succession of the Crown in the Heirs of the late Princess Sophia, being Protestants, and for extinguishing the hopes of the pretended Prince of Wales, and his open and secret Abettors.

4. AND whereas certain doubts and scruples have arisen concerning the sense and meaning of the clause following, contained in an act made in the 6th year of her late majesty queen Anne, intituled, An Act to make further provision for electing and summoning sixteen peers of *Scotland*, to sit in the house of peers in the parliament of Great Britain; and for trying peers for offences committed in *Scotland*; and for the further regulating of voters in elections of members to serve in parliament; whereby it is enacted, That every person who shall refuse to take the oath last therein-before recited, or being a *Quaker*, shall refuse to declare the effect thereof upon his solemn affirmation, as directed by an act of parliament made in the 7th year of the reign of his

6 Ann. c. 23.

7 & 8 W. 3. c. 34.

late majesty king William, intituled, An act that the solemn affirmation and declaration of the people called *Quakers*, shall be accepted instead of an oath in the usual form, (which oath or declaration, the sheriff, president of the meeting, or chief officer taking the poll at any election of members to serve in the house of commons for any place in Great Britain, or commissioners for chusing burgesses for any place in *Scotland*, at the request of any candidate, or other person present at such election, are hereby impowered and required to administer) shall not be capable of giving any vote for the election of any such member to serve in the house of commons for any place in Great Britain, or commissioners to chuse a burgess for any place in *Scotland*; on account of which words, some have pretended to vote in the meetings of free elections in *Scotland*, at the chusing of the president and clerk of the meeting, without taking the oath mentioned in the last recited act, whereby it has happened that rolls of electors have been unduly made up, and wrong returns made: And also, whereas divers of his majesty's good subjects, who have given convincing marks of their loyalty to his royal person and government, have scrupled to take the said oath, apprehending that the reference in the said oath may be construed in some respects to be inconsistent with the establishment of the church in *Scotland* according to law, and to a clause concerning oaths to be imposed in *Scotland* after the union, contained in an act made in the parliament of *Scotland* in the year 1707, intituled, An act for securing the protestant religion, and presbyterian church government; which act is declared to be a fundamental and essential condition of the treaty of union. To the end therefore that the said scruples, and all mistakes and divisions on account of the same may cease, be it further enacted and declared by the authority aforesaid, That every person who shall refuse to take the aforesaid oath of abjuration, or being a *Quaker*, shall refuse to declare the effect thereof upon his solemn affirmation, in manner aforesaid (which oath and declaration the member last elected for any county or stewartry in *Scotland*, or in his absence the sheriff or stewart's clerk, until a person be chosen to proceed (*a*) in the said meeting, according to the directions contained in the twenty-first act of the third parliament of king Charles the Second, held in *Scotland*, intituled, Act concerning the election of commissioners for shires, and after such choice the person so chosen to proceed, or any person chosen to proceed in any meeting of any county or stewartry there, in which rolls for elections shall happen to be made up, is hereby authorized and required to administer, at the request of any candidate or other person present at such meeting for election, before or after the chusing of the president of the meeting, or making up of the rolls) shall not be capable of giving any vote for the election of a president of the meeting, making up of the rolls, or of any member to serve in the house of commons for any place in *Scotland*, or commissioner to chuse a burgess

Marginal notes:
Persons in Scotland refusing to take the abjuration, incapacitated to vote at elections.

(*a*) Examined with the record.

a burgess for any place there; and further, that by no words in the said oath or oaths, formerly imposed, contained, it is or was meant to oblige his majesty's said subjects to any act or acts any ways inconsistent with the establishment of the church of *Scotland* according to law.

A. D. 1714.

ANNO 7° GEORGII II. CAP. 16.

An Act for the better regulating the Election of Members to serve in the House of Commons, for that part of Great Britain called Scotland; *and for incapacitating the Judges of the Court of Session, Court of Justiciary, and Barons of the Court of Exchequer in* Scotland, *to be elected, or to sit or vote as Members of the House of Commons.*

WHEREAS doubts may arise, whether the acts of parliament made in England for preventing false and undue returns of members to serve in parliament, extend to that part of Great Britain called *Scotland*: And whereas several questions have arisen concerning the election of commoners to serve in parliament for that part of Great Britain: Therefore, to obviate such doubts, disputes, and questions for the future, and for the more effectually preventing returning officers, in that part of Great Britain called *Scotland*, making false and undue returns: May it please your majesty that it may be enacted, and be it enacted by the king's most excellent majesty, by and with the advice and consent of the lords spiritual and temporal and commons in this present parliament assembled, and by the authority of the same, That if the clerk of any meeting of freeholders for the election of a commissioner to serve in parliament for any shire or stewartry in *Scotland*, after the first day of May, 1734, shall wilfully return to the sheriff or stewart any person, other than him who shall be duly elected, or if any other person pretending to be clerk, though not duly elected, shall presume to act as clerk, and wilfully to return to the sheriff any person as elected, who shall not be duly elected by the major part of such meeting, the party so offending shall for every such offence forfeit the sum of five hundred pounds sterling, to be recovered by the candidate so elected, to whose prejudice such false return is made, in such manner as is herein-after directed.

<small>After 1 May, 1734, 500l. penalty on every false return.</small>

2. And be it further enacted, That every freeholder who shall claim to vote at any election of a member to serve in parliament for any lands or estate in any county or stewartry in *Scotland*, or who shall have right to vote in adjusting the rolls of freeholders, instead of the oath appointed to be taken by an act made in the 12th year of her late majesty Queen Anne, intituled, An act for the better regulating elections of members to serve in parliament for that part of Great Britain called *Scotland*, shall, upon the request of any freeholder formerly inrolled, before he proceed to vote in the choice of a member, or on adjusting the rolls, take and subscribe, upon a roll of parchment to be provided and kept by the sheriff, or stewart clerk for that purpose,

<small>Freeholders on request, to subscribe the following oath instead of that appointed by the act 12 Annæ.</small>

the

the oath following, which the prefes or clerk to the meeting, either for the inrollment or election, is hereby impowered and required to adminifter; that is to fay,

'I, A. B. do, in the prefence of God, declare and fwear, That the lands and eftate of for which I claim a right to vote in the election of a member to ferve in parliament for this county or ftewartry, is actually in my poffeffion, and do really and truly belong to me, and is my own proper eftate, and is not conveyed to me in truft, or for or in behalf of any other perfon whatfoever; and that neither I, nor any perfon to my knowledge, in my name, or on my account, or by my allowance, hath given, or intends to give, any promife, obligation, bond, back-bond, or other fecurity whatfoever, other than appears from the tenour and contents of the title, upon which I now claim a right to vote, directly or indirectly, for redifponing or reconveying the faid lands and eftate in any manner of way whatfoever, or for making the rents or profits thereof forthcoming to the ufe or benefit of the perfon from whom I have acquired the faid eftate, or any other perfon whatfoever; and that my title to the faid lands and eftate is not nominal or fictitious, created or referved in me, in order to enable me to vote for a member to ferve in parliament; but that the fame is a true and real eftate in me, for my own ufe and benefit, and for the ufe of no other perfon whatfoever; and that is the truth, as I fhall anfwer to God.'

3. And

In case of refusal, vote not to be admitted, and name erased out of the roll.

3. And that in case he shall refuse, if required, to take and subscribe the oath aforesaid, his vote shall not be admitted or allowed, and his name shall forthwith be erased out of the roll of freeholders; and in case any person shall pre-

Penalty on falsely swearing or subscribing.

sume wilfully and falsely to swear and subscribe the said oath, and shall be thereof lawfully convicted, he shall incur the pains and punishment of perjury, and be prosecuted for the same according to the laws and forms in use in *Scotland*.

Judges of session, justiciary, or exchequer, uncapable to be elected.

4. And be it further enacted, That no judge of the court of session, or justiciary, or baron of the court of exchequer in *Scotland*, shall be capable of being elected, or of sitting or voting as a member of the house of commons in any parliament which shall be hereafter summoned and holden.

Sheriffs 4 days after receipt of the writs to issue precepts for chusing delegates,

5. And be it further enacted by the authority aforesaid, That the several sheriffs and stewarts in *Scotland* shall, within the space of four days after the writ shall come to their hand, issue their precepts to the several boroughs within their jurisdiction to elect their delegates, and shall cause the same to be delivered to the chief magistrate of such borough resiant in the borough for the time being; and that such chief magistrate, to

And chief magistrate two days after to summon the council of the borough.

whom such precept shall be delivered, shall within two days after his receipt of the same, call and summon the council of the borough together, by giving notice personally, or leaving notice at the dwelling place of every counsellor

Council to appoint a day for electing delegates.

then resiant in such borough, which council shall then appoint a peremptory day for the election of

the

the delegate; but two free days shall intervene betwixt the meeting of the council which appoints the day of election of the delegate, and the day on which the election of the delegate is to be made.

6. And to prevent double elections of magistrates in boroughs, which frequently occasion double commissions to delegates, be it enacted by the authority aforesaid, That at the annual election of magistrates and counsellors for boroughs, no magistrate or counsellors, or any number of magistrates or counsellors, shall, for the future, upon any pretence whatever, take upon or them to separate from the majority of the magistrates and counsellors, who have been such for the year preceeding, and to appoint or elect separate magistrates or counsellors, but shall submit to the election made, and to the magistrates and counsellors elected and appointed by the majority of the town council assembled; and if, contrary to the direction of this act, any number of magistrates or counsellors shall, in opposition to the majority, take upon them to make a distinct and separate election of magistrates or counsellors, their act and election shall be *ipso facto* void, and every magistrate or counsellor, who concurred therein, shall forfeit and lose the sum of one hundred pounds sterling, to be recovered by the magistrates and counsellors, from whom they separated, in manner herein-after directed.

100l. penalty on every counsellor or magistrate separating from the majority at the annual election for boroughs.

7. Provided

Magistrates or counsellors of boroughs may bring their action in eight weeks after the election.

7. Provided always, and it is hereby declared and enacted, That it shall and may be lawful to and for any magistrate or counsellor of the borough, who apprehends any wrong was done at any annual election, to bring his action before the court of session in *Scotland*, for rectifying such abuse, or for making void the whole election (if illegal) only within the space of eight weeks after such election is over; and the lords of session shall, and they are hereby expressly authorized and required to hear and determine the cause summarily, and to allow to the party that shall prevail their full costs of suit.

500l. penalty on neglecting to return the person duly elected.

8. And be it further enacted, That every sheriff or stewart in *Scotland*, who shall wilfully annex to the writ any false or undue return, and every common clerk of any presiding borough, who shall wilfully return to the sheriff or stewart any person, other than the person elected, or who shall neglect or refuse to return the person duly elected, shall forfeit the sum of five hundred pounds sterling to the person entitled to have been returned, and not returned, to be recovered from the said sheriff, stewart, or common clerk, their heirs, executors, or administrators respectively,

To be recovered in a summary way.

in a summary way, by action, petition, or summary complaint, before the said court of session, upon service of such summons, or of a copy of such petition or summary complaint, on fifteen days notice or warning, without abiding the course of any rolls, or further delay whatsoever; which action, petition, or complaint, the judges of the said court are hereby required to judge of, and

and determine with all convenient speed: Provided always, That such action, petition, or complaint be commenced, presented, or made within the space of six months after the return is made. And in case the person duly elected, and not returned, shall neglect or omit to sue for the said penalty within the time before mentioned, then any freeholder within the shire or stewartry, or any magistrate or person bearing office in any of the boroughs of the district for which the return is unduly made, may sue for and recover the same to his own use, by such action, petition, or complaint, and in such manner as is before mentioned, with double costs of suit; provided always, that such freeholder, magistrate, or person bearing office, shall commence or bring such action within the space of twelve months after the return is made.

<small>Complaints of undue returns to be commenced in six months after return.</small>

<small>Who may sue for such penalty,</small>

<small>And in what time.</small>

9. And be it enacted by the authority aforesaid, That every penalty by this act imposed, with respect to the recovery of which no particular provision is herein-before made, shall and may be sued for and recovered by way of summary complaint before the court of session in *Scotland*, upon fifteen days notice to the person complained of, without abiding the course of any roll; which said complaint the court of session is hereby authorized and required to determine with all convenient speed.

<small>Penalties how to be recovered.</small>

10. And be it further enacted, That every freeholder in *Scotland* shall, before he be either inrolled or admitted to vote at any future election, or meeting for inrollment, in any question

<small>Freeholders, if required, to take the oaths at the election of a clerk, &c.</small>

for

for the choice of clerk or prefes, or other question whatsoever (if required by any freeholder present) be obliged to take and subscribe the oaths appointed by law to be taken by electors of members to serve in parliament, when required so to do; which oath the prefes or clerk of the meeting is hereby impowered and required to administer.

<small>Method of presiding at elections.</small>

11. And whereas there have been some mistakes in the district of the boroughs of Wigtoun, Whithorn, New Galloway, and Stranraver, in relation to their presiding at elections of members of parliament for that district, which may occasion disputes at future elections: For remedying thereof, be it enacted, That the boroughs continue to preside in the course they are now in, and that the other borough of Wigtoun shall preside at the election of a member to represent that district in the next parliament, and that the other boroughs of the district preside afterwards in the method prescribed by the act of parliament of *Scotland*, made in the fourth session of the first parliament of queen Anne, intituled, An act for settling the manner of electing the sixteen peers, and forty-five commoners, to represent *Scotland* in the parliament of Great Britain.

A. D. 1734.

ANNO 16° GEORGII II. CAP. 11.

An Act to explain and amend the Laws touching the Elections of Members to serve for the Commons in Parliament, for that Part of Great Britain called Scotland; and to restrain the Partiality, and regulate the Conduct, of Returning Officers at such Elections.

WHEREAS many returning officers of members to serve for the commons in parliament for that part of Great Britain called *Scotland*, have of late presumed to act in a most partial and arbitrary manner, sometimes upon false pretences, that the rolls of electors of commissioners for shires were not regularly made up, or that the commissioners for the several boroughs intituled to vote in the choice of a member for the respective districts of boroughs were not duly elected, or were not authorized by proper commissions, and sometimes without any pretence at all, encouraged thereto from hopes of impunity, by reason that the laws in being have either provided no sufficient punishment for such offences; or where penalties are provided, it has been found by experience to be extremely difficult, and scarcely possible to recover them: For remedy thereof, be it enacted by the king's most excellent majesty, by and with the advice and consent of the lords spiritual and temporal and commons in this present parliament assembled, and by

Part of the act 12 Ann. st. 1. c. 6. § 3. repealed.

by the authority of the same, That so much of an act of parliament made in the 12th year of the reign of her late majesty queen Anne, intituled, 'An act for the better regulating the elections of members to serve in parliament for that part of Great Britain called *Scotland*,' as enacts, That no person or persons, who have not been inrolled, and voted at former elections, shall, upon any pretence whatsoever, be inrolled, or admitted to vote at any election, except he or they first produce a sufficient right or title to qualify him or them to vote at that election, to the satisfaction of the freeholders formerly inrolled, or the majority of them present, and ordains the returning officers to make their returns of the persons elected, by the majority of the freeholders inrolled, and those admitted by them, reserving always the liberty of objecting against the persons admitted to, or excluded from, the roll as formerly, shall be and is hereby repealed.

2. And whereas the rolls of electors of commissioners to serve in parliament for the several shires and stewartries within that part of Great Britain called *Scotland*, have not, in every one of the said shires, and stewartries, been made up every year, at the Michaelmas head courts, pursuant to the directions of an act of parliament made in that part of Great Britain called *Scotland*, in the year 1681, intituled, 'An act concerning the election of commissioners for shires: For remedy thereof, and the more effectually to carry the good intentions of the said act into execution;

cution; be it enacted and declared by the authority aforesaid, That such persons as stand upon the roll last made up by the freeholders, whether at the Michaelmas meeting, or at the last election of a member to serve in parliament, shall be the original constituent members at their next Michaelmas meeting, or meeting for election, to revise the said roll. *Act made in Scotland 1681, strengthened.*

3. Provided always, and be it enacted by the authority aforesaid, That it shall and may be lawful for any freeholder standing upon the roll, to object to the title of any person who stands at present upon the roll last made up, and for that purpose to apply at any time before the first day of December, which shall be in the year of our Lord 1743, by summary complaint to the court of session, who shall grant a warrant for summoning such persons upon thirty days notice to answer, and shall proceed in a summary way, to hear and determine upon such complaint; and if no such complaint shall be exhibited within the time aforesaid, then and in that case no freeholder, who at present stands upon the rolls last made up in the said counties and stewartries respectively, shall be struck off or left out of the roll, except upon sufficient objections arising from the alteration of that right or title, in respect of which he was inrolled, sustained by the other freeholders standing upon the said roll. *Freeholders may object.*

4. And be it enacted by the authority aforesaid, That if at any Michaelmas meeting, or meeting for election, any person claiming to be inrolled, shall by judgement of the freeholders be refused *Manner of acting, when a person claims to be inrolled.*

refused to be admitted, or if any person who stood upon the roll shall by like judgement be struck off, or left out of the roll; it shall and may be lawful for him or them who is so refused to be admitted, or whose name is so struck off or left out of the roll, to apply (so as such application be made within four kalendar months after their being so refused, struck off, or left out) by summary complaint to the court of session, who shall grant a warrant for summoning the person or persons upon whose objection or objections he was refused to be admitted, or was struck off or left out as aforesaid, upon thirty days notice to answer, and shall proceed to hear and determine in a summary way on such complaint; and if any person shall be inrolled, whose title shall be thought liable to objection, it shall and may be lawful for any freeholder standing upon the said roll (whether such freeholder was present at the meeting or not) who apprehends that such person had not a right to be inrolled, to apply in like manner by complaint to the court of session, so as such application be made within four kalendar months after such inrollment; and the said court, after service of such complaint, on thirty days notice, upon the person said to be wrongfully admitted to the roll, shall in manner aforesaid hear and determine; and if no such complaint shall be exhibited within the time aforesaid, the freeholder inrolled shall stand and continue upon the roll until an alteration of his circumstances be allowed by the freeholders at a subsequent Michaelmas meeting, or meeting for election, as a sufficient cause

If any freeholder objects, appeal may be made to the court of session.

cause for striking or leaving him out of the roll.

5. And be it enacted by the authority aforesaid, That if, in any of the aforesaid cases, the judgement of the court of session shall alter or reverse the determination of the meeting of the freeholders, by directing that any person shall be added to, or expunged from, the roll of election, the sheriff or steward's clerk shall, upon presenting to him the extract of such judgement, forthwith make the alteration thereby directed in the books that are kept by him; and in case of his refusal or delay, he shall forfeit the sum of one hundred pounds sterling to the person in whose favour the judgement of the court of session is given, to be recovered by him or his executors in the manner herein-after directed. *Penalty on officers not obeying the court of session.*

6. And be it further enacted by the authority aforesaid, That if the judgement of the freeholders refusing to admit, or striking off any person from the said roll shall be affirmed by the court of session, the person so complaining shall forfeit to the objector the sum of thirty pounds sterling, with full costs of suit. *Penalty on appellant, if the court of session affirm the freeholders order.*

7. And be it enacted by the authority aforesaid, That to prevent all surprise, at the Michaelmas meetings, every freeholder who intends to claim to be inrolled at any subsequent Michaelmas meeting of the freeholders, shall, for the space of two kalendar months at least before the said Michaelmas meeting, leave with the sheriff or steward's clerk a copy of his claim, setting forth the names of his lands, and his titles thereto, *Manner of acting to prevent surprise, on freeholder's claiming to be inrolled;*

and dates thereof, with the old extent or valuation, upon which he defires to be inrolled, and in cafe of his neglect to leave his claim as aforefaid, he fhall not be inrolled at fuch Michaelmas meet-

or on making objections to others already inrolled.

ing; and in like manner, whoever intends to object to any freeholder who ftands upon the roll, on account of the alteration of his circumftances, fhall, at leaft two kalendar months before the Michaelmas meeting, leave his objections in writing with the fheriff or fteward's clerk as aforefaid, who is hereby required, upon receipt of the aforefaid claim or objections, to indorfe on the back thereof the day he received the fame, and alfo to give a copy of the aforefaid claim or objections, to any perfon who fhall demand the fame, upon paying the legal fee of an ordinary extract of the fame length.

8. And whereas great difficulties have occurred in making up the rolls of electors of commiffioners for fhires, by perfons claiming to be inrolled, in refpect of the old extent of their lands, where the old extent does not appear from proper evidence, and votes have been unduly multiplied by fplitting and dividing the old extent of lands, fince the fixteenth day of September, 1681: for

Divifion of the old extent of lands, to multiply electors, prohibited.

remedy thereof, be it enacted and declared by the authority aforefaid, That no perfon is or fhall be entitled to vote for a commiffioner to ferve in parliament, for any fhire or ftewartry in that part of Great Britain called *Scotland*, or to be inrolled in the roll of electors, in refpect of the old extent of his lands, holden of the king or prince, unlefs fuch old extent is proved by a retour of the lands

of

of a date prior to the sixteenth day of September, 1681, and that no division of the old extent, made since the aforesaid sixteenth day of September, 1681, or to be made in time coming, by retour or any other way, is or shall be sustained as sufficient evidence of the old extent.

9. Provided always, That lands holden of the king or prince, liable in public burdens for four hundred pounds *Scots* of valued rent, shall in all cases be a sufficient qualification, whatever be the old extent of the said lands; any law or practice to the contrary notwithstanding. Proviso.

10. And be it further enacted by the authority aforesaid, That no purchaser, or singular successor, shall be inrolled till he be publicly infeoft, and his seisin registered, or charter of confirmation be expede where confirmation is necessary, one year before the inrollment; and that no heir apparent shall be inrolled, until his predecessor's titles are produced, and allowed by the freeholders, as a sufficient qualification for his voting for a member of parliament; and that any person may be inrolled, though absent at the time of such inrollment, provided the titles and vouchers of his qualification are produced, and laid before the freeholders; and if any person shall be chosen a member to serve in parliament for any shire or stewartry within that part of Great Britain called *Scotland*, who shall not be present at the meeting of election; be it enacted by the authority aforesaid, That the member to serve in parliament so elected, before he takes his seat in parliament, shall take the oath appointed to be taken by every freeholder, How a purchaser shall act before he is inrolled; also an heir-apparent. Persons may send their vouchers, and be inrolled, though absent. Every one chosen in his absence, to serve in parliament, shall take the freeholder's oath, before he takes his seat.

freeholder, who shall claim to vote at any election of a member to serve in parliament, by the act of the 7th year of his present majesty, intituled, 'An act for the better regulating the election of members to serve in the house of commons, for that part of Great Britain called *Scotland*; and for incapacitating the judges of the court of session, court of justiciary, and barons of the court of Exchequer in *Scotland*, to be elected, or to sit or vote as members of the house of commons, before the lord steward of his majesty's houshold, or any person or persons authorized by him for that effect, which he or they are hereby impowered and required to administer; and if a member to serve in parliament, so elected, shall neglect or refuse to take the aforesaid oath, such election shall be void.

7 Geo. 2. c. 16.

On refusing the oath, the election declared void.

11. And be it further enacted by the authority aforesaid, That at the annual meetings of the freeholders at Michaelmas, the original constituent members shall be such persons only as shall stand upon the roll, that shall have been last made up, whether at a Michaelmas meeting, or at a meeting for an election of a member to serve in parliament, and that a copy signed and extracted of the roll made up by the freeholders at their Michaelmas meetings, or meetings for elections, together with the minutes of their proceedings at their said meetings, shall, by the respective clerks of such meetings, be forthwith delivered to the sheriff or steward's clerk *gratis*, and shall be inserted in books to be kept by the said sheriff or steward's clerk for that purpose, who shall forthwith

Who are to be original constituent members.

Minutes of proceedings to be entered in books kept by the sheriff or steward's clerk.

with deliver copies of the same, extracted and signed, to any freeholder who shall desire the same, paying the legal fee for an ordinary extract of the same length, and shall at every subsequent meeting at Michaelmas, or meeting for any election, produce the said books, for the use of the freeholders; and in case such sheriff or steward's clerk shall neglect or refuse to enter the aforesaid rolls of election, or minutes of proceedings, into books so to be kept for that purpose as aforesaid, or shall neglect or refuse to give copies thereof, extracted and signed, or shall omit to produce the books at any subsequent meeting as aforesaid, he shall for every such offence forfeit the sum of one hundred pounds sterling, to be recovered by any freeholder, within such shire or stewartry, who shall sue for the same, in such manner as is hereafter directed; and if the aforesaid principal books, containing the rolls and minutes as aforesaid, shall not be produced at the Michaelmas meetings, or meetings for election, a copy of the said roll and minutes, extracted and signed by the sheriff or steward's clerk, shall be sufficient; and if the sheriff or steward's clerk shall give out false copies of the said roll or minutes, extracted and signed by him, he shall for every such offence forfeit the sum of one hundred pounds sterling to the person to whom the false copy is given, to be recovered by him or his executors, in the manner hereinafter directed, and shall be for ever after incapable of holding or enjoying his said office.

Minute-books to be produced at public meetings.

Penalty on refusal.

Penalty on giving false copies of the minutes.

12. And

The roll of electors laſt made up, ſhall be uſed at the next election.

12. And be it further enacted by the authority aforeſaid, That at every election of a commiſſioner to ſerve in parliament for any ſhire or ſtewartry, within that part of Great Britain called *Scotland*, the roll of electors which ſhall be laſt made up by freeholders, whether at the Michaelmas meeting, or at the laſt election of a member to ſerve in parliament, ſhall be the roll to be called over by the commiſſioner laſt elected, or in his abſence by the ſheriff or ſteward's clerk, in order to the election of preſes and clerk, as alſo by the preſes after he is choſen, for the choice of the member to ſerve in parliament, and for the determination of all the queſtions that ſhall ariſe in the adjuſting the roll, and in the courſe of the election, excepting ſo far as the ſaid roll ſhall, after the meeting is duly conſtituted by the choice of preſes and clerk, be altered by judgement of the majority of the freeholders ſtanding on that roll, by leaving out thoſe whoſe circumſtances are altered, and by adding others, who produce proper titles.

Penalty for taking falſe votes.

13. And be it further enacted by the authority aforeſaid, That at every meeting for an election of a commiſſioner to ſerve in parliament, if the commiſſioner laſt elected, or in his abſence the ſheriff or ſteward's clerk, ſhall, in the choice of preſes or clerk, receive the vote of any perſon that does not ſtand upon the ſaid roll, he ſhall, for every ſuch offence, forfeit the ſum of three hundred pounds ſterling to every candidate for the office of preſes or clerk

clerk respectively, for whom such person shall not have given his vote, to be recovered by him or them, his or their executors respectively, in manner herein-after directed; or if the commissioner last elected, or in his absence the sheriff or steward's clerk, shall, in the choice of preses or clerk, not call for, or shall refuse the vote of any person whose name is upon the said roll, he shall, for every such offence, forfeit the like sum of three hundred pounds sterling to the person whose name shall not be called for, or whose vote shall be refused, to be recovered by him, or his executors in the manner herein-after directed; and if the preses after he is chosen shall, in the election of the member to serve in parliament, receive the vote of any person who does not stand upon the roll duly made up by the said meeting, he shall, for every such offence, forfeit the sum of two hundred pounds sterling to every candidate for whom such person shall not have given his vote, to be recovered by him, or his executors, in the manner herein-after directed; or if the preses after he is chosen shall, in the election of the member to serve in parliament, not call for, or shall refuse the vote of any person whose name is upon the said roll so made up, as aforesaid, he shall, for every such offence, forfeit the like sum of two hundred pounds sterling to the person whose name shall not be called for, or whose vote shall be refused, to be recovered by him or his executors, in the manner herein-after directed: and it is hereby declared, That in case of equality of votes in the choice of preses or clerk, the commissioner

Penalty on refusing good votes.

On equality of votes, in chusing a clerk, who shall have the casting vote.

missioner last elected, and in his absence any freeholder present who last represented the shire or stewartry in any former parliament; and if no such person is present, the freeholder present who presided last at any meeting for any election, and in his absence the freeholder who last presided at any Michaelmas meeting; and if none of the said persons shall be present, the freeholder present who stands first on the roll, shall, besides their own votes as freeholders, have the casting and determining vote, and that the preses chosen, shall, after his election, in the choice of the commissioner to serve in parliament, and all other questions, where the votes are equal, in like manner, besides his own vote as a freeholder, have the casting and determining vote.

14. And be it further enacted by the authority aforesaid, That the persons chosen to be preses and clerk, by the majority of the freeholders present, standing on the said roll, shall be preses and clerk of the meeting for such election; and it shall not be lawful for any number of freeholders to separate from the majority of the persons present, who stand upon the said roll, and set up any person as preses or clerk, other than those who shall be chosen by the majority of the freeholders present, standing on the said roll, and that it shall not be lawful for any person to act as preses or clerk at any such election, unless they are chosen by the majority of persons standing on the said roll; and every freeholder who shall so separate from the majority of the freeholders on the roll, and set up any

The preses and clerk being chosen by the majority of freeholders, no separated party shall chuse another.

Penalty on separating from the freeholders.

person

person as preses or clerk, other than those who shall be chosen by the majority, as aforesaid, he shall for every such offence forfeit the sum of fifty pounds sterling, to the candidate who shall be chosen by the majority of the freeholders from whom such separation was made; to be recovered by him, or his executors, in the manner herein-after directed: and if any person presume to act as preses or clerk, who is not chosen by the majority of the freeholders present standing on the said roll, he shall, for every such offence, forfeit the sum of two hundred pounds sterling to the candidate who shall be chosen by the majority of the freeholders, as aforesaid, to be recovered by him, or his executors, as herein-after directed.

Penalty on acting a preses or clerk, without any authority.

15. And be it further enacted by the authority aforesaid, That the commissioner last elected, or in his absence the sheriff or steward's clerk, shall sign the minutes of the election of preses and clerk, and deliver the same to the clerk chosen by the majority of the freeholders, as aforesaid; and if the commissioner last elected, or in his absence, the sheriff or steward's clerk, shall neglect or refuse to sign the aforesaid minutes of election of preses and clerk, and deliver the same to the clerk chosen, as aforesaid, or shall sign false minutes thereof, he shall, for every such offence, forfeit the sum of one hundred pounds sterling to the person elected preses, as aforesaid, to be recovered by him, or his executors, in the manner hereafter directed.

Minutes of election of clerk to be signed, and delivered to the clerk chosen.

Penalty on refusing to sign, or on signing false minutes.

16. And

Clerk to make a true return.

16. And be it further enacted by the authority aforesaid, That the clerk chosen by the majority of the freeholders on the aforesaid roll, shall return to the sheriff or steward such person as shall be elected by the majority of the freeholders on the roll made up at the meeting for election, in the manner aforesaid; and if the clerk chosen, as aforesaid, shall refuse or neglect to return the person elected by the majority of the freeholders on the roll, made up at the meeting for election, or shall return any person other than him who shall be elected by the majority of the freeholders, as aforesaid, he shall, for every such offence, instead of the penalty or forfeiture to which he is made liable by the aforesaid act made in the *Penalty on refusing, or making a false one.* 7th of his present majesty, forfeit the sum of five hundred pounds sterling to the candidate chosen by the majority of the freeholders on the aforesaid roll; to be recovered by him, or his executors, in the manner herein-after directed.

The return to be annexed to the writ.

17. And be it further enacted by the authority aforesaid, That every sheriff or steward, of any shire or stewartry, within that part of Great Britain called *Scotland*, upon producing to him a copy of the aforesaid roll last made up by the freeholders at the last Michaelmas meeting, or at the last election of a member to serve in parliament, extracted and signed by the sheriff or steward's clerk, and upon producing and shewing to him the original minutes of the election of preses and clerk signed by the commissioner last elected, or in his absence, by the sheriff or steward's clerk,

clerk, shall annex to the writ the return made by the clerk chosen by the majority of the freeholders on the aforesaid roll; and if any such sheriff or steward shall neglect or refuse to annex to the writ such return, or if he shall annex to the writ the return made by any other person pretending to be clerk to the election; he shall for every such offence, instead of the penalty or forfeiture to which he is made liable by the aforesaid act made in the 7th year of his present majesty, forfeit the sum of five hundred pounds sterling, to the person returned by the clerk, and chosen by the majority of the freeholders on the aforesaid roll, to be recovered by him or his executors, in the manner herein-after directed.

Penalty.

18. And be it further enacted by the authority aforesaid, That every sheriff or steward of any shire or stewartry, within that part of Great Britain called *Scotland*, shall hold the Michaelmas head court in all time to come, on the day on which it shall appear to him to have been most usually held in times past; and to prevent all uncertainty in time coming, every sheriff or steward shall, at least fourteen days before Michaelmas next, appoint a precise day for holding his Michaelmas head court, in the year 1743; and shall cause intimate the day of holding his court at all the parish churches within his said shire or stewartry upon a *Sunday*, at least eight days preceding the next Michaelmas head court: And it is hereby declared, That the days so to be appointed by the said sheriff or steward before Michaelmas next, shall be the anniversary for holding

When the Michaelmas head court shall be held.

To be intimated in parish churches eight days before.

ing the Michaelmas head court of the said shire or stewartry in all time coming.

<small>Usage of the shire of Sutherland.</small>

19. And whereas by the constitution of the shire of *Sutherland*, and by constant usage, the small barons of the said shire have been represented in parliament, not only by the immediate vassals of the king and prince, but also by those who held their lands of the earls of *Sutherland*, or of other subject superiors, and such vassals holding their lands of subject superiors, have been in use to vote at the election of the commissioners for the said shire of *Sutherland*, as well as the vassals of the king and prince, and that without any restriction as to the *quota* of the old extent, or of the valued rent of the lands, in respect whereof a right to vote at such elections, or to be elected commissioner for the said shire was claimed, and thereby votes have been unduly multiplied, and several persons have claimed a vote in respect of the superiority and property of the same lands, whereby great confusions are likely to ensue in future elections; for remedy thereof, be it further enacted by the authority aforesaid, That from and after the first day of September, which shall be in the year of our Lord 1745, no

<small>Qualification of candidates and electors.</small>

person shall be capable to be elected commissioner for the said shire, or shall have right to vote at such election, unless he be infeoft, and in possession of lands liable to his majesty's supplies, and other public burthens, at the rate of two hundred pound *Scots* valued rent.

20. And be it further enacted by the authority aforesaid, That one person, and no more, shall

shall be intitled to vote at such elections, or to be elected, in respect of the same lands; and that where lands are now holden by any baron, or other freeholder, immediately of the king or prince, such baron or freeholder shall be capable to be elected, and shall be entitled to vote for those lands; and no vassal, or sub-vassal of the said baron or freeholder, shall have right to vote, or to be elected in respect thereof; and that where lands are now holden, or shall at any time hereafter be holden of the king or prince, by a peer or other person, or body politic or corporate, who by law are disabled to be a member of the house of commons, or to vote in such elections; in such case the proprietor and owner of such lands, and not any of his superiors, shall be entitled to vote, or to be elected, in respect of the same lands; and that no alienation of the superiority to be made by such peer, or other person, or body politic, incapable to elect or to be elected, shall deprive the proprietor and owner of the lands of his right to vote in the elections for the said shire, or his capacity to be elected; nor entitle the purchaser of the said superiority to vote, or to be elected; and that the property of lands, of the valuation aforesaid, holden in part immediately of the king or prince, and in part of a peer, or other person, or body politic incapable to elect, or to be elected, shall be a sufficient qualification to the proprietor and owner of such lands, and shall entitle such proprietor to vote, and to be elected for the said shire; any law or usage to the contrary notwithstanding.

Candidates and electors to hold their lands immediately from the king or prince.

In what cases the proprietors only shall vote.

Lands held part of the king, and part of a peer, &c. shall qualify the owner to elect or be elected.

21. And

When freeholders in Sutherland shall meet and make a roll.

21. And be it enacted by the authority aforesaid, That the freeholders and proprietors, having right to elect, or to be elected a commissioner for the shire of *Sutherland*, shall meet at the head borough of the said shire, at the Michaelmas head court, which shall be in the year of our Lord 1745, and shall make up a roll of the electors having right to vote in the choice of a commissioner, in the terms of this present act, and of the other acts of parliament, made touching the election of commissioners for shires in *Scotland*; and which roll, so made up, shall be revised yearly at the Michaelmas meetings, at and after elections, according to the rules prescribed in this act, and in other acts made for regulating the elections of commissioners for shires in that part of Great Britain called *Scotland*: And it is hereby declared, That the said acts of parliament do extend to the shire of *Sutherland* as well as to the other shires in *Scotland*, except in so far as it is otherwise provided by this present act.

At annual elections the minority shall not separate from the majority.

22. And whereas at the election of members to serve in parliament for the districts of boroughs in that part of Great Britain called *Scotland*, it often happens that more persons than one claim to be admitted to vote as commissioners for the same borough, which furnishes pretences to the clerks of the presiding boroughs for partially making false and undue returns: For remedy thereof, be it enacted by the authority aforesaid, That at the annual election of magistrates and counsellors, and in all the proceedings previous

to the election of the magistrates and counsellors for the succeeding year, it shall not be lawful for the minority of any meeting for election, either of magistrates or counsellors, or deacons, or other persons, who by the constitution of the respective boroughs may have votes in the election of magistrates or counsellors, to separate from the majority of those having right to act by the constitution of the burgh at such meetings, upon any pretext whatsoever; nor to make any separate election of magistrates, counsellors or electors; but the minority shall in all cases submit to the election made by the majority in all the parts of election; and if any person elected by the minority of any such meeting, shall presume to vote in the election of magistrates or counsellors, or in leeting the magistrates or counsellors, or in any other step of the election, he shall forfeit the sum of one hundred pounds sterling to any one of the majority of such meeting, to be recovered by him in the manner hereafter directed. *Penalty on offenders.*

23. And be it further enacted by the authority aforesaid, That no person elected to be a magistrate or counsellor by a minority of those having right to vote in elections of the magistrates and counsellors, shall, upon any pretext whatsoever, presume to act as magistrate or counsellor, and if any person shall notwithstanding presume to act as magistrate or counsellor, he shall, for every such offence, forfeit the sum of one hundred pounds sterling, to the magistrates or counsellors elected by the majority, or to any of them who shall sue for the same, to be recovered by him or them in the manner herein-after directed. *No person elected by the minority, shall have a right to act.* *Penalty on acting when so elected.*

Wrongs done by the majority, may be redressed by the court of session.

24. Provided always, and it is hereby declared and enacted, That it shall and may be lawful to and for any constituent member at any meeting for election of magistrates or counsellors, or of any meeting previous to that for the election of magistrates and counsellors respectively, who shall apprehend any wrong to have been done by the majority of such meeting, to apply to the said court of session, by a summary complaint for rectifying such abuse, or for making void the whole election made by the said majority, or for declaring and ascertaining the election made by the minority, so as such complaint be presented to the said court of session within two kalendar months after the annual election of the magistrates and counsellors; and the said court shall thereupon grant a warrant for summoning the magistrates and counsellors elected by the majority, upon thirty days notice, and shall hear and determine the said complaint summarily, without abiding the course of any roll, and shall allow to the party who shall prevail, their full costs of suit.

25. And whereas the magistrates and counsellors of the royal boroughs in that part of Great Britain called *Scotland*, by virtue of several laws now in force, are bound to take and subscribe the oath of allegiance, subscribe the assurance, and to take and sign the oath of abjuration, for and on account of their election into their respective offices; and that in his majesty's courts of session, justiciary or exchequer at Edinburgh, or at the quarter sessions of the respective shires and stewarties,

tries, within which the royal boroughs are situate, which has been found by experience to be attended with great trouble and expence to the said magistrates and counsellors: For remedy thereof, be it enacted by the authority aforesaid, That it shall and may be lawful to the said magistrates and counsellors to take and subscribe the oath of allegiance, subscribe the assurance, and take and sign the oath of abjuration, before the council of their respective boroughs; and which oaths the chief magistrate, or any other magistrate of the said boroughs respectively, is hereby impowered and required to administer; and the oaths so taken, shall be equal in all respects as if they had been taken in the courts, and before the judges directed by the several acts of parliament above referred to.

Manner of the magistrates and counsellors taking the several oaths.

26. And be it enacted by the authority aforesaid, That at every election of commissioners for chusing burgesses for any district of boroughs in that part of Great Britain called *Scotland*, the common clerk of each borough within the said district, shall make out a commission to the person chosen commissioner by the major part of the magistrates and town council assembled for that purpose; which magistrates and town council shall take the oath of allegiance, and sign the same with the assurance, and shall take all the other oaths appointed to be taken at such election, by this or any former act, if required; and the said clerk shall affix the common seal of the borough thereto, and sign such com-

The clerk to sign the commission, and fix the seal of the borough.

F F   mission

mission, and shall not on any pretence whatsoever make out a commission for any person as commissioner, other than him who is chosen by the majority as aforesaid; and if any common clerk of any borough shall neglect or refuse duly to make out and sign a commission to the commissioner elected by the majority as aforesaid, and affix the seal of the borough thereto; or if he shall make out and sign a commission to any other person who is not chosen by the majority, or affix the common seal of the borough thereto; he shall, for every such offence, forfeit the sum of five hundred pounds sterling to the person elected commissioner for the said borough as aforesaid, to be recovered by him or his executors in the manner herein after directed, and shall also suffer imprisonment for the space of six kalendar months, and be for ever after disabled to hold or enjoy the said office of common clerk of the said borough, as effectually as if he was naturally dead.

Penalty on any person acting as clerk, and making out wrongful commissions.

27. And be it further enacted by the authority aforesaid, That if any other person who is not the common clerk of the borough, shall take upon himself to act as such in any election of a commissioner for chusing a burgess for any district of boroughs in that part of Great Britain called *Scotland*, and shall make out a commission for any other person as commissioner, other than the person who was chosen by the majority as aforesaid, and shall sign or affix the common seal of the borough thereto; he shall, for every such offence, forfeit the sum of five hundred pounds sterling, to the person elected commissioner for

the

the said borough as aforesaid, to be recovered by him or his executors in the manner herein-after directed.

28. And whereas by an act passed in that part of Great Britain called *Scotland*, the fifth day of February, in the year 1707, intituled, 'Act settling the manner of electing the sixteen peers, and forty-five commoners, to represent *Scotland* in the parliament of Great Britain;' it is amongst other things enacted, That where the votes of the commissioners for the said boroughs met to chuse representatives from their several districts to the parliament of Great Britain, shall be equal; in that case, the president of the meeting shall have a casting or decisive vote, and that by and attour his vote as a commissioner from the borough from which he is sent; but no provision is made in case of the absence of the commissioner from the presiding borough, or of his refusing to vote at such election: For remedy thereof, be it enacted by the authority aforesaid, That if the commissioner from the presiding borough shall be absent from the meeting of commissioners for chusing burgesses to serve in parliament, or shall refuse to vote at such election, the commissioner from the borough which was the presiding borough at the last election; and if he also be absent, or shall refuse to vote as aforesaid, the commissioner from the borough which was the presiding borough at the election immediately preceding the last; and in case he shall be likewise absent, or shall refuse to vote as aforesaid, the commissioner from the borough which was the last presiding borough but two,

[Marginal note: Who shall act in absence of the presiding commissioners.]

two, shall have in the aforesaid respective cases, besides his own vote, the casting or decisive vote.

<small>No objection against non-residents, &c.</small>

29. And be it further declared by the authority aforesaid, That it is no objection to any commissioner for chusing a burgess, that he is not a residenter within the borough bearing all portable charges with his neighbours, or that he is no trafficking merchant therein, or that he is not in possession of any burgage lands or houses holding of the said borough, and that such qualifications need not be engrossed in his commission; any law, custom or usage to the contrary notstanding.

<small>What votes shall be allowed.</small>

30. And be it further enacted by the authority aforesaid, That at all meetings of commissioners for chusing burgesses to serve in parliament, the common clerk of the presiding borough shall allow the votes of such persons only who produce commissions authenticated by the subscription of the common clerk, and the common seal of the respective boroughs within the district, and shall return to the sheriff or steward the person elected by the major part of the commissioners assembled, whose commissions are authenticated as aforesaid; and if he neglect or refuse to return such persons so elected to the sheriff or steward, or if he shall return to the sheriff or steward any person other than him who is so elected, he shall, for every such offence, instead of the penalty or forfeiture to which he is made liable by the aforesaid act made in the 7th year of his present majesty, forfeit the

<small>Penalty.</small>

sum of five hundred pounds sterling, to the candidate

didate elected by the majority of the commiſſioners aſſembled, whoſe commiſſions are authenticated as aforeſaid, to be recovered by him or his executors, in the manner herein-after directed, and he ſhall alſo ſuffer impriſonment for the ſpace of ſix kalendar months, and be for ever after diſabled to hold or enjoy his ſaid office of common clerk of the ſaid preſiding borough as if he was naturally dead.

31. And be it enacted by the authority aforeſaid, That every ſheriff or ſteward in that part of Great Britain called *Scotland*, ſhall annex to the writ the return made by the aforeſaid clerk of the preſiding borough; and if any ſuch ſheriff or ſteward neglect or refuſe to annex to the writ ſuch return, or if he ſhall annex to the writ any return made by any other perſon, he ſhall, for every ſuch offence, inſtead of the penalty or forfeiture to which he is made liable by the aforeſaid act made in the 7th year of his preſent majeſty, forfeit the ſum of five hundred pounds ſterling to the candidate returned by the aforeſaid clerk of the preſiding borough, to be recovered by him, or his executors, in the manner hereinafter directed. *Writ and return to be annexed.* *Penalty.*

32. Provided always, That if any perſon to whom no commiſſion is made out, as aforeſaid, ſhall inſiſt that he was duly elected the commiſſioner from any royal borough, the perſon ſo claiming ſhall be admitted to the meeting of the commiſſioners for chuſing burgeſſes to ſerve in parliament, and may at the ſaid meeting make offer of taking all the oaths required by law, and *Proviſo.*

declare

declare for whom he would have voted, had he been duly commiffioned, which oaths the clerk of the prefiding borough is hereby required and impowered to adminifter; and the faid clerk fhall alfo fet down in the minutes of proceedings, the declaration of fuch perfon as to the candidate for whom he would have voted, had he been duly commiffioned; but the faid clerk fhall upon no pretence whatfoever receive or confider fuch perfon as a legal voter, or fuch declaration as a legal vote, at fuch election.

Act 2 Geo. 2. c. 24. extended to elections of delegates.

33. And whereas doubts have arifen, whether the act of parliament made in the 2d year of the reign of his prefent majefty, intituled, An Act for the more effectual preventing bribery and corruption in the election of members to ferve in parliament, extends to the electors of commiffioners for chufing burgeffes: Be it hereby enacted by the authority aforefaid, That the electors of commiffioners for any royal borough, within that part of Great Britain called *Scotland*, for chufing burgeffes to parliament, are within the true intent and meaning of the faid act, to be confidered as electors of the member to ferve in parliament, and fhall be fo deemed and adjudged to all intents and purpofes whatfoever, and fhall be liable to all the provifions, forfeitures, and incapacities, to which perfons voting or claiming to vote for any member to ferve in parliament are made liable by the faid act.

34. And be it further enacted by the authority aforefaid, That at every election of commiffioners

for chusing burgesses for the several districts of boroughs in that part of Great Britain called *Scotland*, and at the election of a burgess to serve in parliament for the city of Edinburgh, every magistrate, town counsellor, or person having or claiming to have a right to vote at such election, instead of the oath prescribed to be taken by the said act, before he is admitted to vote at the same election, shall take the following oath, in case the same shall be demanded by any one of the electors; and which oath any of the magistrates, or, in their absence, any of the town council, are hereby impowered and required to administer;

'I, A. B. do solemnly swear, That I have not directly or indirectly, by way of loan or other device whatsoever, received any sum or sums of money, office, place, employment, gratuity, or reward, or any bond, bill, or note, or any promise of any sum or sums of money, office, place, employment, or gratuity whatsoever, either by myself or any other, to my use or benefit, or advantage, or to the use, benefit, or advantage of the city or borough of which I am magistrate, counsellor, or burgess, in order to give my vote at this election.

So help me God.'

Oath to be taken by the magistrate, at the election of a burgess, &c.

35. And be it further enacted by the authority aforesaid, That in all elections of commissioners for chusing burgesses, and before they proceed to election, the common clerk of each borough shall take and subscribe the oath following, which any of the magistrates, or, in their absence, any

two of the town council are hereby impowered and required to administer:

<small>Oath to be taken by the common clerk, before the election of commissioners to chuse burgesses.</small>

' I, A. B. do solemnly swear, That I have not directly, or indirectly, by way of loan or other device whatsoever, received any sum or sums of money, office, place, employment, gratuity or reward, or any bond, bill, or note, or any promise of any sum, or sums of money, office, place, employment, or gratuity whatsoever, either by myself or any other, to my use, or benefit, or advantage, to make out any commission for a commissioner for chusing a burgess: and that I will duly make out a commission to the commissioner who shall be chosen by the majority of the town council assembled, and to no other person.

So help me God.'

And that at all meetings of the commissioners for chusing burgesses to serve in parliament, and before they proceed to the election, the clerk of the presiding borough shall take and subscribe the following oath, which the commissioner for the presiding borough, or in his absence any other of the commissioners, is hereby required and impowered to administer.

<small>Oath of the clerk of the presiding borough before election.</small>

' I, A. B. do solemnly swear that I have not directly or indirectly, by way of loan, or other device whatsoever, received any sum or sums of money, office, place, employment, gratuity, or reward, or any bond, bill, or note, or any promise of any sum or sums of money, office, place, employment, or gratuity whatsoever, either by myself,

myself, or any other to my use, or benefit, or advantage, to make any return at this election of a member to serve in parliament; and that I will return to the sheriff or steward the person elected by the major part of the commissioners assembled, whose commissions are authenticated by the subscription of the common clerk, and common seal of the respective boroughs of this district.

So help me God.'

36. And be it further enacted by the authority aforesaid, That if the clerk of the presiding borough shall neglect or refuse to take the oath aforesaid, such clerk, so refusing or neglecting, shall be incapable to act as clerk to the said meeting; and it shall be lawful to and for the said commissioners, and they are hereby impowered and required to chuse another clerk to the meeting for the election, and who shall have all the powers and authorities in the said meeting, and in the returning the member chosen by them, that by law are competent to the clerk of the presiding borough.

Penalty on the clerk of the presiding borough's neglect.

37. And be it further enacted by the authority aforesaid, That at all the elections of a member to serve in parliament for any county or stewartry in that part of Great Britain called *Scotland*, the clerk chosen by the majority of such persons as stand upon the said roll last made up by the freeholders, whether at the Michaelmas court, or at the last election of a member to serve in parliament, shall immediately after his election take and subscribe the following oath, which the

preses

preses of the meeting is hereby required and impowered to administer:

<small>Oath of the clerk at election of members.</small>

'I, A. B. do solemnly swear, That I have not directly, or indirectly, by way of loan or other device whatsoever, received any sum or sums of money, office, place, or employment, gratuity, or reward, or any bond, bill, or note, or any promise of any sum or sums of money, office, place, employment, or gratuity whatsoever, by myself, or any other, to my use, or benefit, or advantage, to make any return at the present election of a member to serve in parliament; and that I will return to the sheriff or steward the person elected by the majority of the freeholders upon the roll made up at this election, and who shall be present and vote at this meeting. So help me God.'

38. And whereas by the said act of parliament made in the 2d year of the reign of his present majesty, it is enacted, That every sheriff, mayor, bailiff, headborough, or other person being the returning officer of any member to serve in parliament, shall immediately after reading the writ or precept for the election of such members, take and subscribe the oath contained in the aforesaid act; be it enacted by the authority aforesaid, That so much of the said act as requires the said oath to be taken by any returning officer within that part of Great Britain called *Scotland*, shall be and is hereby repealed.

<small>Repeal of part of the act 2 Geo. 2. c. 24. as to *Scotland*.</small>

39. And be it further enacted by the authority aforesaid, That if any person shall presume wilfully and falsely to swear and subscribe any of the oaths

<small>Penalties of perjury.</small>

oaths required to be taken by this act, and shall thereof be lawfully convicted, he shall incur the pains and punishments of perjury, and be profecuted for the fame according to the laws and forms in ufe in *Scotland*.

40. And be it further enacted by the authority aforefaid, That when any new parliament shall at any time hereafter be fummoned or called, the lord chancellor, lord keeper, or lords commiffioners of the great feal for the time being, shall iffue out the writs for election of members to ferve in parliament for that part of Great Britain called *Scotland*, with as much expedition as the fame may be done; and that as well upon the calling or fummoning any new parliament, as alfo in cafe of any vacancy during this prefent or any future parliament, the feveral writs shall be delivered to the sheriff or steward to whom the execution thereof does belong or appertain, and to no other perfon whatfoever; and that every fuch sheriff or steward, upon the receipt of the writ, shall upon the back thereof endorfe the day he received the fame, and shall forthwith, upon receipt of the writ, at leaft within the fpace of four days after the receipt thereof, make out a precept to each borough within his jurifdiction, to elect a commiffioner for chufing a burgefs to to ferve in parliament, and shall caufe the fame to be delivered to the chief magiftrate of fuch borough refiant in the borough for the time being; and in cafe fuch sheriff or steward shall neglect to endorfe on the back of the writ the day he

Writs of fummons for calling a new parliament, to be made out immediately.

he received the same, or shall neglect to make out his precept, and to deliver the same to the chief magistrate within the time, and in the manner above directed, he shall, for every such offence, forfeit the sum of one hundred pounds sterling, to any magistrate of the borough to which the precept is not timously delivered, who shall sue for the same, to be recovered in manner herein-after directed.

<small>Penalty on sheriff's delaying the precepts.</small>

41. And be it further enacted by the authority aforesaid, That such chief magistrate to whom the precept shall be delivered in manner above directed, upon the receipt thereof, shall upon the back of the precept endorse the day he received the same, and shall, within two days after his receipt of the precept, call and summon the council of the borough together, by giving notice personally, or leaving notice at the dwelling-place of every counsellor then resiant in that borough, which council shall then appoint a peremptory day for the election of a commissioner for chusing a burgess to serve in parliament.

<small>When the council shall be called for setting a day to chuse a commissioner for electing a burgess.</small>

42. Provided always, That two free days shall intervene betwixt the meeting of the council which appoints the day of election of the said commissioner, and the day on which the election of the commissioner is to be made; and in case such chief magistrate shall neglect to endorse the day he received the precept on the back thereof, or to summon the council within the time and in the manner above directed, he shall, for every such offence, forfeit the sum of one hundred pounds

<small>Two days to be allowed between the council meeting and the day of election.</small>

<small>Chief magistrate to endorse the day he received the precept.</small>

<small>Penalty.</small>

pounds sterling, to any magistrate or counsellor of the said borough who shall sue for the same, to be recovered in manner herein-after directed.

43. And be it further enacted by the authority aforesaid, That every penalty or forfeiture by this act imposed, in that part of Great Britain called *Scotland*, shall and may be sued for and recovered by way of summary complaint, before the court of session, upon thirty days notice to the person complained of, without abiding the course of any roll; which said complaint the court of session is hereby authorized and required to determine; as also to declare the disabilities and incapacities, and to direct the imprisonments, as herein provided.

Manner of recovering penalties.

44. Provided always, and it is hereby declared and enacted by the authority aforesaid, That no person shall be made liable to any incapacity, disability, forfeiture, or penalty by this act imposed, in that part of Great Britain called *Scotland*, unless prosecution be commenced within one year after such incapacity, disability, forfeiture, or penalty shall be incurred.

Limitation of action.

A. D. 1743.

ANNO 14° GEORGII III. CAP. 81.

An Act for altering and amending an Act, made in the 16th Year of his late Majesty's Reign, intituled, An Act to explain and amend the Laws touching the Election of Members to serve for the Commons in Parliament, for that Part of Great Britain

Britain called Scotland; *and to restrain the Partiality, and regulate the Conduct, of returning Officers at such Elections, by altering the Time of Notice, ordered by the said Act to be given, in the Service of Complaints to the Court of Session, of Wrongs done in Elections, and by regulating the Manner, and settling the Place, of Election of a Burgess to serve in Parliament for a District of Boroughs in* Scotland, *when the Election of the Magistrates and Council of a Borough, which ought in Course to be the presiding Borough at an Election, happens to be reduced, and made void, by a Decree of the Court of Session, and not revived by the Crown, when such Election is made.*

Act 16. Geo. 2.

WHEREAS by an act, made in the 16th year of his late majesty's reign, (intituled, An act to explain and amend the laws touching the elections of members to serve for the commons in parliament, for that part of Great Britain called *Scotland*, and to restrain the partiality, and regulate the conduct, of returning officers, at such elections) complaints to the court of session, for redress of wrongs committed by the inrolling, or refusing to inrol persons claiming to be inrolled in the roll of freeholders, or in the annual elections of royal boroughs, are ordered to be served upon thirty days notice; And whereas it is found by experience, so long notice is unnecessary, and occasions delay in the summary determination of such complaints, agreeable to the intendment of the said act: May it there-

therefore please your majesty that it may be enacted, and be it enacted by the king's most excellent majesty, by and with the advice and consent of the lords spiritual and temporal, and commons in this present parliament assembled, and by the authority of the same, That from and after the twelfth day of June, in the year of our Lord 1774 the court of session shall grant warrants for the service of all such complaints as aforesaid, upon fifteen days notice.

2. And whereas the elections of magistrates and counsellors of royal boroughs in *Scotland* have sometimes been reduced and made void, by decrees of the court of session, in actions or complaints brought before the said court for that purpose, by which the corporate powers of such boroughs are in effect in a state of nonexistence, until restored by the justice and favour of the crown; and whereas no provision is made in the aforesaid act of the 16th year of the reign of his late majesty, or any other act now in being, for regulating the manner, and settling the place of election of a burgess to serve in parliament for a district of boroughs in *Scotland*, when the election of magistrates and council of a borough, which ought in course to have been the presiding borough at the election, happens to be reduced, and not revived when the election is made. For remedying thereof, be it enacted by the authority aforesaid, That in every election of a burgess to serve in parliament for a district of boroughs in *Scotland*, when it shall happen that the election of the magistrates and council of the borough, which

ought

ought to have been the prefiding borough at fuch election, is reduced and not revived, the next borough intitled to prefide in turn fhall be the prefiding borough, and the election fhall be made at that borough; and the commiffioner for that borough fhall be the prefident of the meeting of commiffioners for the election, and have a cafting and decifive vote, befides his own, as commiffioner, where the votes of the commiffioners are equal; and the common clerk of that borough fhall be clerk to the election; and every matter and thing concerning the election fhall be proceeded in as if that borough had been the prefiding borough, in the ordinary courfe of roration.

The prefiding borough of the diftrict how to be afcertained.

3. And be it further enacted by the authority aforefaid, That the borough which would have been the prefiding borough at the election, if the election of the magiftrates and counfellors of fuch borough had not been reduced, fhall, when revived by the juftice and favour of the crown, have no right or title to be a prefiding borough in the election of a burgefs to ferve in parliament for the diftrict of boroughs of which it is one, until the other boroughs of the diftrict, each in their turn, have fucceffively provided, and that the right devolves upon fuch borough in the ordinary courfe of rotation.

A. D. 1774.

ANNO 35° GEORGII III. CAP. 65.

An Act to prevent unnecessary Delay in the Execution of Writs, for the Election of Members to serve in Parliament for that Part of Great Britain *called* Scotland.

WHEREAS the execution of writs of election of members to serve for the commons in parliament for that part of *Great Britain* called *Scotland*, has often been improperly delayed; for remedy whereof, may it please your majesty that it may be enacted; and be it enacted by the king's most excellent majesty, by and with the advice and consent of the lords spiritual and temporal, and commons, in this present parliament assembled, and by the authority of the same, that the sheriff or stewart depute or substitute of any county or stewartry in that part of *Great Britain* called *Scotland*, shall, within *six free days* after receiving the writ or writs for the election of members to serve in parliament, direct the notices required by law to be given as to the time and place of election of a member for such county or stewartry; and that the day of election appointed by the sheriff shall not be *sooner* than six free days, nor *later* than fifteen days after the day of publication at the church doors.

Preamble.

Sheriffs deputes or substitutes, &c. to direct, within six days after receiving the writs, the notices required to be given for elections of members, &c.

II. And

None but sheriff's deputes, &c. or in their absence their substitutes, to receive and execute writs for elections.

II. And whereas doubts have been entertained by whom the writs for election of members to serve for the commons in parliament for that part of *Great Britain* called *Scotland*, should be received and executed when there happens to be a principal or high sheriff or stewart appointed by his majesty in any county or stewartry as well as a sheriff depute or stewart depute, whose commission is also derived from the crown, and is *ad vitam aut culpam*, in respect that, by an act, passed in the twentieth year of his late majesty, for taking away and abolishing the heritable jurisdictions, these offices, and the powers and authorities belonging to them, were essentially changed; for remedy thereof, and to remove such doubts, be it enacted, that, upon issuing of any writ or writs for the election of a member or members to serve in parliament for that part of *Great Britain* called *Scotland*, the said writ or writs shall be forthwith forwarded and delivered to the sheriff depute, or stewart depute, or to the substitute of each, and the principal or high sheriff, or stewart, shall not officiate either in receiving or in executing the writ, the whole of this duty being entrusted to the sheriff depute, or stewart depute, or, in case of absence, to the substitute of each, and to no other person whatsoever.

Penalty on sheriff's deputes, &c. for neglect of duty;

III. And be it enacted by the authority aforesaid, that if any sheriff or stewart depute or substitute shall wilfully refuse, neglect, or delay, to do

or

or perform what is hereby required of him in any of the particulars aforesaid, he shall, for every offence, forfeit and pay the sum of five hundred pounds sterling, one half to the person who shall sue for the same, and the other half to his majesty, to be sued for and recovered in the manner directed by an act of the sixteenth year of the reign of his late majesty king George the Second, intituled, 'An act to explain and amend the laws touching the election of members to serve for the commons in parliament for that part of *Great Britain* called *Scotland*; and to restrain the partiality, and regulate the conduct, of returning officers at such elections.' 16 Geo. II. recited.

IV. And be it enacted by the authority aforesaid, that if any principal or high sheriff or stewart, or any person, other than the sheriff or stewart depute, or the substitute of each, shall presume in any respect to interfere or take upon himself the execution of writs of election of members to serve in parliament for that part of *Great Britain* called *Scotland*, every such person so offending in any particular, shall, for every offence, forfeit and pay the sum of one thousand pounds sterling, one half to the person who shall sue for the same, and the other half to his majesty, his heirs and successors, to be sued for and recovered in the manner directed by an act of the sixteenth year of the reign of his late majesty king George the Second, intituled, 'An act to explain and amend and on high sheriffs, &c. for interfering in the execution of writs.

16 Geo. II recited.

amend the laws touching the election of members to serve for the commons in parliament for that part of *Great Britain* called *Scotland*; and to restrain the partiality, and regulate the conduct, of returning officers at such elections;' and further, the person convicted on any suit shall thereby become disabled and incapable of ever bearing or executing any office or place of trust whatsoever under his majesty, his heirs and successors.

Limitation of actions.

V. Provided always, and be it further enacted by the authority aforesaid, that every action or suit for any offence against this act, shall be commenced within twelve months after commission of the fact on which the same is grounded, or within twelve months after the conclusion of any proceedings in the house of commons relating to such election.

Writs for the election of members for Orkney and Zetland where to be published.

VI. And whereas the several parish churches in the stewartry of *Orkney* and *Zetland* are situated upon islands, detached and difficult of access; be it therefore enacted, that the writ for the election of a member to serve in parliament for the said stewartry shall be published at the town of *Kirkwall*, and the twelve parish churches in the island of *Pomona*, or the main land of *Orkney* only.

PART III.
CONTROVERTED ELECTIONS
DETERMINED BY SELECT COMMITTEES.

N. B. *The Letters D. P. L. and F. denote that the Case is to be found in the Reports by Mr. Douglas, Mr. Peckwell, Mr. Luders, or Mr. Fraser; and the Figures shew the Volume.—Where there is neither of these Letters the Case has not been reported.*

SESSIONS.	PLACES.	PETITIONERS.	SITTING MEMBERS.	IN WHOSE FAVOUR DETERMINED.	DATES.		
					PETITION PRESENTED.	COMMITTEE APPOINTED.	REPORT MADE.
1770-1,	Jedburgh, &c.	Charles Ogilvy,	Patrick Warrender,	Patrick Warrender,	19 March,	16 April,	19 April.
	New Shoreham,	Thomas Rumbold,	John Purling,	Thomas Rumbold,	3 Decem.	11 Decem.	17 Dec.
	Scarborough,	Sir Ja. Pennyman,	Ralph Bell, Sir Ja. Pennyman,	Double Return.—Petition of Sir James Pennyman withdrawn, 27th Nov.—Return amended in favour of Mr. Bell, 28th Nov.			

SESSIONS.	PLACES.	PETITIONERS.	SITTING MEMBERS.	IN WHOSE FAVOUR DETERMINED.	DATES.		
					PETITION PRESENTED.	COMMITTEE APPOINTED.	REPORT MADE.
1772,	Callington,	James Buller,	William Skrine,	*Petitioner died.—Order for hearing discharged,* 17 Feb.			
	Milborne Port,	George Prescott,	Richard Combe,	George Prescott,	15 April,	6 May,	22 May.
	Saltath,	Thomas Bradshaw,	John Williams,	Thomas Bradshaw,	15 May,	5 June,	8 June.
1774,	Worcester City,	Sir Watkin Lewes, Electors,	Thomas Bates Rous,	Declared void,	20 Jan.	2 Feb.	8 Feb.
1774-5, D. 1.	Abingdon,	Nathaniel Bayly,	John Mayor,	Declared void,	6 Decem.	3 March,	6 March.
D. 2.	Bedford Borough,	Samuel Whitbread, John Howard, Electors,	Sir William Wake, Robert Sparrow,	Sir William Wake, Samuel Whitbread,	6 Decem.	14 March,	23 March.
D. 1.	Bristol,	Matthew Brickdale, Freeholders,	Henry Cruger, Edmund Burke,	Henry Cruger, Edmund Burke,	6 Decem.	10 Feb.	20 Feb.

SESSIONS.	PLACES.	PETITIONERS.	SITTING MEMBERS.	IN WHOSE FAVOUR DETERMINED.	DATES.			REPORT MADE.
					PETITION PRESENTED.	COMMITTEE APPOINTED.		
1774-5 D. 2.	Clackmannan,	Ja. Fran. Erskine,	Ralph Abercrombie,	Ralph Abercrombie,	7 Dec.	5 April,		7 April.
D. 1.	Cricklade,	John Dewar, Samuel Peach,	Double Return,	Declared void,	19 Jan.	14 Feb.		21 Feb.
D. 1.	Dorchester,	Anthony Chapman,	John Damer, William Ewer,	John Damer, William Ewer,	6 Dec.	21 Feb.		23 Feb.
D. 1.	Downton,	Sir Philip Hales, John Cooper, Freeholders,	Thomas Duncombe, Thomas Dummer,	Sir Philip Hales, John Cooper,	6 Dec.	3 Feb.		14 Feb.
D. 2.	Haslemere,	William Burke, Henry Kelly, Voters,	Tho. More Molyneux, Sir Merrick Burrell,	Tho. More Molyneux, Sir Merrick Burrell.	6 Dec.	31 March,		9 May.
D. 2.	Helstone,	Philip Yorke, Francis Cuff, Freemen,	Marq. of Carnarthen, Francis Owen,	Philip Yorke, Francis Cuff,	6 Dec.	10 March,		14 March.

SESSIONS.	PLACES.	PETITIONERS.	SITTING MEMBERS.	IN WHOSE FAVOUR DETERMINED.	DATES.		
					PETITION PRESENTED.	COMMITTEE APPOINTED.	REPORT MADE.
1774-5 D. 1.	Hindon,	James Calthorpe, Richard Beckford,	Richard Smith, Tho. Brand Hollis,	Declared void,	6 Dec.	31 Jan.	14 Feb.
D. 2.	Ives, Saint,	Samuel Stephens, Electors.	William Praed, Adam Drummond,	Adam Drummond, [*other Seat void.*]	7 Dec.	28 April,	8 May.
D. 2.	Lanark, County,	Daniel Campbell,	Andrew Stuart,	Andrew Stuart,	7 Dec.	7 April,	10 April.
D. 1.	Milborne Port,	Edward Walter, Isaac H. Browne, Temple Luttrell, Charles Wolseley, Inhabitants,	Double Return,	Temple Luttrell, Charles Wolseley,	6 Dec.	20 Jan.	10 Feb.
D. 1.	Morpeth,	Hon. Will. Byron, Electors,	Francis Eyre,	Hon. Will. Byron,	6 Dec.	24 Jan.	27 Jan.
D. 1.	New Radnor,	Edward Lewes,	John Lewes,	Edward Lewes,	6 Dec.	17 Feb.	20 Feb.
D. 2.	North Berwick, &c. Burghs,	Sir A. Gilmour, Burgesses,	Hon. John Maitland,	Hon. John Maitland,	7 Dec.	2 May,	8 May.

SESSIONS.	PLACES.	PETITIONERS.	SITTING MEMBERS.	IN WHOSE FAVOUR DETERMINED.	DATES.		
					PETITION PRESENTED.	COMMITTEE APPOINTED.	REPORT MADE.
1774-5 D. 1.	Pontefract,	Hon. Charles James Fox, James Hare, Electors,	Sir John Goodricke, Cha. Mellish,	Sir John Goodricke, Charles Mellish,	6 Dec.	28 Feb.	3 March.
D. 2.	Poole,	Hon. Charles James Fox, John Williams, Electors,	Sir Eyre Coote, Joshua Mauger,	Sir Eyre Coote, Joshua Mauger,	6 Dec.	24 March,	29 March.
D. 2.	Shaftesbury,	Hans W. Mortimer,	Francis Sykes, Tho. Rumbold,	Hans W. Mortimer,	6 Dec.	28 March,	25 April.
D. 1.	Shrewsbury,	William Pulteney, Voters,	Lord Clive, Charlton Leighton,	William Pulteney, Lord Clive,	6 Dec.	7 March,	8 March.
D. 2.	Sudbury,	Sir Walden Hanmer, Sir Pat. Blake, Elector,	Tho. Fonnereau, P. C. Crespigny,	Sir Walden Hanmer, Sir Patrick Blake,	6 Dec.	17 March,	22 March.

SESSIONS.	PLACES.	PETITIONERS.	SITTING MEMBERS.	IN WHOSE FAVOUR DETERMINED.	DATES.		
					PETITION PRES. NT.D	COMMITTEE APPOINTED.	REPORT MADE.
1774-5 D. 1.	Taunton,	Alexander Popham, John Halliday, Electors,	Edward Stratford, Nathaniel Webb,	Alex. Popham, John Halliday,	6 Dec.	24 Feb.	16 March.
D. 1.	Westminster,	Lord Mountmorres, and several Electors,	Earl Percy, Lord T. P. Clinton,	Earl Percy, Lord T. P. Clinton.	12 Dec.	25 Jan.	27 Jan.
D. 2.	Wigton, &c.	Hen. Watkin Dashwood,	Wm. Norton,	H. W. Dashwood,	6 Dec.	21 March,	23 March.
1775-6 D. 3.	Cardigan, Borough,	Thomas Johnes, jun. Burgesses,	Sir Robert Smyth,	Thomas Johnes, jun.	31 October,	28 Nov.	7 Dec.
D. 4.	Cricklade,	John Dewar, Electors,	Samuel Peach,	John Dewar,	31 October,	7 Feb.	19 Feb.
D. 3.	Derby, Borough,	Dan. Parker Coke, Electors,	John Gisborne,	Dan. P. Coke,	31 October,	31 Jan.	9 Feb.
D. 4.	Fife, County,	John Henderson,	James Oswald,	James Oswald,	12 Feb.	19 March,	22 March.

SESSIONS.	PLACES.	PETITIONERS.	SITTING MEMBERS.	IN WHOSE FAVOUR DETERMINED.	DATES.		
					PETITION PRESENTED.	COMMITTEE APPOINTED.	REPORT MADE.
1775-6 D. 3.	Ivelchester,	Richard Brown, Inigo Wm. Jones, Voters,	Peregrine Cuft, William Innes,	Declared void,	31 Oct.	24 Nov.	4 Dec.
D. 4.	Ivelchester,	Richard Brown, Inigo Wm. Jones,	Nathaniel Webb, Owen S. Brereton,	Nathaniel Webb, Owen S. Brereton,	21 Dec.	19 Feb.	19 Feb.
D. 3.	Peterborough,	James Phipps,	Mat. Wyldbore,	Mat. Wyldbore,	31 Oct.	22 Nov.	27 Nov.
D. 3.	Petersfield,	Hon. J. Luttrell,	Sir Abr. Hume, William Jolliffe,	Sir Ab. Hume, William Jolliffe,	31 Oct.	15 Nov.	16 Nov.
D. 3.	Seaford,	Stephen Sayre, John Chetwood,	Lord Gage, George Medley,	Lord Gage, George Medley,	31 Oct.	17 Nov.	22 Nov.
D. 4.	Southampton, Town,	Electors,	John Flemming,	John Flemming,	9 Nov.	9 Feb.	12 Feb.
D. 3.	Worcester City,	Sir Watkin Lewes,	John Walsh, Tho. Bates Rous,	John Walsh, Tho. Bates Rous,	31 Oct.	29 Jan.	19 April.

SESSIONS.	PLACES.	PETITIONERS.	SITTING MEMBERS.	IN WHOSE FAVOUR DETERMINED.	DATES.		
					PETITION PRESENTED.	COMMITTEE APPOINTED.	REPORT MADE.
1776-7	Gloucester, County,	Hon. G. C. Berkeley,	Wm. B. Chester,	Wm. B. Chester,	8 Nov.	4 Feb.	29 April.
	Hindon,	Richard Beckford, Voters,	Richard Smith,	Declared void,	1 Nov.	27 Jan.	29 Jan.
	Newcastle,	A. R. Bowes, Electors,	Sir J. Trevelyan,	Sir John Trevelyan,	27 March,	25 April,	2 May.
	Shaftesbury,	Hon. B. Bouverie, Inhabitants,	George Rous,	George Rous,	6 Nov.	28 Jan.	18 Feb.
1776-7	Callingdon,	John Morshead,	George Stratton,	Declared void,	16 Dec.	8 Feb.	15 Feb.
1779-80	Downton,	Robert Shaftoe, Voters,	Hon. B. Bouverie,	Robert Shaftoe,	23 Dec.	15 Feb.	21 Feb.
	Fife, County,	John Henderson,	General Skene,	John Henderson,	9 Dec.	1 Feb.	7 Feb.
1780-1	Abingdon,	T. Wooldridge, Electors,	John Mayor,	John Mayor,	7} 20} Nov.	2 Feb.	6 Feb.

SESSIONS.	PLACES.	PETITIONERS.	SITTING MEMBERS.	IN WHOSE FAVOUR DETERMINED.	DATES.		
					PETITION PRESENTED.	COMMITTEE APPOINTED.	REPORT MADE.
1780-1 P.	Arundel,	Hon. Percy Wyndham.	Sir P. Cranford, Thomas Fitzherbert,	Thomas Fitzherbert, [*Void with respect to one Burgess.*]	7 Nov.	6 March,	12 March.
	Ayr County,	Sir Adam Ferguson,	Hugh Montgomery,	Sir A. Ferguson,	7 Nov.	23 March,	2 April.
	Berwick County,	Sir John Paterson,	Hugh Scott,	Declared void,	7 Nov.	2 March.	8 March.
	Bridgewater,	John Acland, Inhabitants, Electors,	Benjamin Allen, Hon. Anne Poulett,	John Acland, Hon. Anne Poulett,	7 } Nov. 20 }	20 Feb.	2 March.
	Clithero,	Asheton Curzon, Electors,	John Parker, Thomas Lister,	John Parker, Thomas Lister,	7 } Nov. 18 }	13 March,	26 March.
	Coventry,	Edward Roe Yeo, Lord Sheffield, Voters,	Sir T. Hallifax, Thomas Rogers,	Edward Roe Yeo, Lord Sheffield,	23 Jan.	15 Feb.	27 Feb.

SESSIONS.	PLACES.	PETITIONERS.	SITTING MEMBERS.	IN WHOSE FAVOUR DETERMINED.	DATES.		REPORT MADE.
					PETITION PRESENTED.	COMMITTEE APPOINTED.	
1780-1	Downton,	John Saunders, Alexander Hume, Freeholders,	Hon. H. S. Conway, Robert Shafto,	Hon. H. S. Conway, Robert Shafto,	7} Nov. 16	9 March,	13 March.
	Dumbarton County,	Hon. G. K. Elphinstone, Freeholders,	Lord F. Campbell,	Hon. G. K. Elphinstone,	7} Nov. 10	13 Feb.	14 Feb.
	Edinburgh City,	Sir L. Dundas, Lord Provost, &c. Electors,	William Miller,	Sir L. Dundas,	7} Nov. 13 19	16 March,	22 March.
	Hellston,	Philip Yorke*, Freemen, Lord Hyde, William Evelyn }	Double Return,	Philip Yorke, Jocelyn Dean,	7} Nov. 10 16	9 Feb.	19 Feb.
	Honiton,	Lawrence Cox †, Electors,	Alexander Macleod,	Declared void,	7} Nov. 20	20 March,	27 March.

* Mr. Dean was dead.
† This petition withdrawn.

SESSIONS.	PLACES.	PETITIONERS.	SITTING MEMBERS.	IN WHOSE FAVOUR DETERMINED.	DATES.		
					PETITION PRESENTED.	COMMITTEE APPOINTED.	REPORT MADE.
1780-1	Kirkcudbright,	John Gordon, Freeholders,	Peter Johnstone,	Declared void,	7 Nov.	23 Feb.	5 March.
	Lyme Regis,	Henry Harford, Lionel Darell, Electors, Hon. H. Fane, David R. Michel, Burgesses,	Double Return,	Declared void,	7 Nov. 20	24 Nov.	4 Decem.
P.	Lyme Regis,	Henry Harford, Lionel Darell, Electors,	Hon. Henry Fane, David Rob. Michel,	Hon. H. Fane, David Rob. Michel,	23 Jan.	28 Feb.	8 March
P.	Milborne Port,	Hon. T. Luttrell, Lect rs,	Tho. H. Medlycott, J. Townson,	Tho. H. Medlycott, J. Townson,	9 Nov.	27 April,	7 May
	New Salmor,	John Lewis, Edward Lewis,	Double Return,	Edward Lewis,	7 Nov.	27 Jan.	31 Jan

SESSIONS.	PLACES.	PETITIONERS.	SITTING MEMBERS.	IN WHOSE FAVOUR DETERMINED.	DATES.		
					PETITION PRESENTED.	COMMITTEE APPOINTED.	REPORT MADE.
1780-1	Orkney and Zetland,	Cha. Dundas, Freeholders,	Robert Backie,	Charles Dundas,	7} 15} Nov.	16 Feb.	23 Feb.
	Plymouth,	John Culme, Voters,	Geo. Darby, Sir F. L. Rogers,	George Darby, Sir F. L. Rogers,	9 Nov.	3 April,	5 April.
	Preston,	John Fenton, Electors,	John Burgoyne,	John Burgoyne,	7} 18} Nov.	27 March,	10 April.
	Shaftesbury,	Sir Geo Collier, Hans W. Mortimer, Inhabitants.	Sir Tho. Rumbold, Francis Sykes,	Francis Sykes, Hans W. Mortimer,	7} 16} Nov.	27 Feb.	2 April.
P.	Sudbury,	Sir James Marriott,	Sir P. Blake, P. C. Crespigny,	Sir P. Blake, Sir James Marriott,	9 Nov.	2 April,	24 April.
	Worcester City,	Sir W. Lewes, Freemen,	Hon. Wm. Ward,	Hon. Wm. Ward,	20 Nov.	6 Feb.	15 Feb.

SESSIONS.	PLACES.	PETITIONERS.	SITTING MEMBERS.	IN WHOSE FAVOUR DETERMINED.	DATES.		
					PETITION PRESENTED.	COMMITTEE APPOINTED.	REPORT MADE.
1781-2	Colchester,	Free Burgesses, on behalf of Edmund Affleck,	Christopher Potter,	Edmund Affleck,	30 Nov.	5 Feb.	4 March.
	Cricklade,	Samuel Petrie,	Paul Benfield, John Macpherson,	Paul Benfield, [Void with respect to one Burgess,]	30 Nov.	24 Jan.	1 Feb.
	Forfar County,	Sir David Carnegie,	Archibald Douglas,	Archibald Douglas,	6 March,	16 April,	23 April.
	Honiton,	Alexander Macleod, Electors,	Jacob Wilkinson,	Jacob Wilkinson,	30 Nov.	12 Feb.	18 Feb.
	Kirkcudbright,	Peter Johnston,	John Gordon,	Peter Johnston,	30 Nov.	1 Feb.	6 Feb.
	Newcastle upon Tyne,	Thomas Delaval, Electors *,	Andrew Robinson Bowes,	Andrew Robinson Bowes,	3 Dec. 12	18 Feb.	19 Feb.

* This petition withdrawn.

SESSIONS.	PLACES.	PETITIONERS.	SITTING MEMBERS.	IN WHOSE FAVOUR DETERMINED.	DATES.		
					PETITION PRESENTED	COMMITTEE APPOINTED.	REPORT MADE.
1781-2	Poole,	Joshua Mauger, Electors,	Joseph Gulston, Will. Morton Pitt,	Joseph Gulston, William M. Pitt,	30 Nov.	29 Jan.	4 Feb.
	Saltash,	John Buller, Freeholders,	Charles Jenkinson, Sir G. Cooper,	Charles Jenkinson, Sir G. Cooper,	30 Nov.	25 Jan.	4 Feb.
1782-3	Pontefract,	John Smyth, Electors,	Nathaniel Smith,	John Smyth,	29 Feb.	8 April,	11 April.
	Saltash,	John Buller, Freeholders,	Sir G. Cooper,	Sir G. Cooper,	16 April,	9 May,	20 May.
1784 L. 1.	Bedford County,	Lord Ongley,	Hon. St. Andrew St. John,	Lord Ongley,	25 May,	22 June,	1 July.
L. 1.	Colchester,	Sir Robert Smyth,	Christopher Potter,	Declared void,	25 May,	1 July,	5 July.

SESSIONS.	PLACES.	PETITIONERS.	SITTING MEMBERS.	IN WHOSE FAVOUR DETERMINED.	DATES.		REPORT MADE.
					PETITION PRESENTED.	COMMITTEE APPOINTED.	
1794 L. 1.	Downton,	Hon. Henry S. Conway, Robert Shafto, Freeholders, Hon. E. Bouverie, William Scott,	Double Return,	Robert Shafto, [*Void with respect to one Burgess,*]	25 May, 26 May, 27 May, 3 June,	17 June,	19 July.
L. 1.	Ipswich,	Charles Alexander Crickitt,	John Cator,	Declared void,	23 May,	11 June,	19 June.
L. 1.	Ivelchester,	John Harcourt. Sir Samuel Hannay, Electors,	Peregrine Cuft, Benj. B. Hopkins,	Peregrine Cuft, Benj. B. Hopkins,	23 May,	29 June,	21 July.
L. 1.	Midhall,	Roger Wilbraham, Christopher Hawkins,	Double Return,	Christopher Hawkins,	25 May,	15 June,	21 June.

SESSIONS.	PLACES.	PETITIONERS.	SITTING MEMBERS.	IN WHOSE FAVOUR DETERMINED.	DATES.		
					PETITION PRESENTED.	COMMITTEE APPOINTED.	REPORT MADE.
1784 L. 1.	Pontefract,	Hon. William Cockayne, John Walfh, Electors,	John Smyth, Will. Southeron,	John Smyth, William Southeron,	25 May,	8 June,	11 June.
1785 L. 2.	Bedford County,	Hon. St. Andrew St. John,	Lord Ongley,	Hon. St. Andrew St. John,	1 Feb.	18 March,	19 May.
L. 2.	Bucks County,	Earl Verney, Freeholders,	John Aubrey,	John Aubrey,	1 Feb.	4 April,	11 April.
L. 2.	Colchester,	Samuel Tyffen, Electors,	Sir Rob. Smyth,	Sir Rob. Smyth,	28 Jan.	3 March,	15 March.
L. 2.	Cricklade,	John Walker Heneage, Robert Nicholas, Voters,	Robert Adamfon, Charles Wetiley Coxe,	John Walker Heneage, Robert Nicholas,	25 Jan.	14 Feb.	4 April.

SESSIONS.	PLACES.	PETITIONERS.	SITTING MEMBERS.	IN WHOSE FAVOUR DETERMINED.	DATES.		
					PETITION PRESENTED.	COMMITTEE APPOINTED.	REPORT MADE.
1785,	Downton,	Four Petitions of Freeholders,	Hon. W. S. Conway, Hon. Ed. Bouverie, [Double return]	Hon. W. S. Conway,	28 Jan.	17 Feb.	9 March.
	Elgin and Forres,	Alex. P. Cumming, Freeholders,	Earl Fife,	Earl Fife,	28 Jan.	5 April.	8 April.
	Kirkwall, &c.	John Sinclair,	Right Hon. Charles James Fox,	Right Hon. Charles James Fox,	28 Jan.	12 April.	18 April.
L. 2.	Lyme Regis,	Robert Wood, John Cator, Freemen,	Hon. Hen. Fane, Hon. Tho. Fane,	Hon. Henry Fane, Hon. Thomas Fane,	28 Jan.	15 Feb.	21 Feb.
	Newport,	John Barrington,	Edw. Rushworth,	Edward Rushworth,	28 Jan.	22 Feb.	24 Feb.
L. 2.	Okehampton,	Humphry Minchin, Electors,	John Luxmoore, Thomas Wiggins,	Humphry Minchin, Lord Malden,	28 Jan.	26 April.	27 April.
	Penryn,	Joshua Smith, George Jackson,	Sir Francis Baffett, Sir John St. Aubyn,	Sir Francis Baffett, Sir John St. Aubyn,	28 Jan.	24 Feb.	18 March.

* * *

SESSIONS.	PLACES.	PETITIONERS.	SITTING MEMBERS.	IN WHOSE FAVOUR DETERMINED.	DATES.		
					PETITION PRESENTED.	COMMITTEE APPOINTED.	REPORT MADE.
1785 *L. 2.*	Preston,	Mich. A. Taylor, Ralph Clayton, Electors,	Sir Henry Hoghton, John Burgoyne,	Sir Henry Hoghton, John Burgoyne,	28 Jan.	20 April,	22 April.
	Saltash,	Lord Strathaven, John Curtis,	Right Hon. Charles Jenkinson, Charles Ambler,	Right Hon. Charles Jenkinson, Charles Ambler,	28 Jan.	14 April,	25 April.
	Seaford,	Electors, Hon. Lewis T. Watson,	Henry Neville, Sir Peter Parker,	Declared void,	8 } Feb. 9	15 March,	21 March.
	Southwark,	Sir Rich. Hotham, Electors,	Paul Le Mesurier,	Paul Le Mesurier,	28 Jan.	3 March,	4 April.
	Wigton, &c. Burghs,	Geo. Johnstone,	Will. Dalrymple,	Will. Dalrymple,	28 Jan.	7 April,	18 April.
	Wootton Bassett,	Geo. Tierney,	Hon. G. A. North, Hon. R. S. Conway,	Hon. G. A. North, Hon. R. S. Conway,	28 Jan.	21 April,	25 April.

SESSIONS.	PLACES.	PETITIONERS.	SITTING MEMBERS.	IN WHOSE FAVOUR DETERMINED.	DATES.			REPORT MADE.
					PETITION PRESENTED.	COMMITTEE APPOINTED.		
1786	Bristol,	Geo. Daubeny, Electors,	Henry Cruger,	Henry Cruger,	7 Feb.	16 March,		24 March.
	Carlisle,	John Christian, Voters,	John Lowther,	John Christian,	1 } May, 3	23 May,		31 May.
	Honiton,	Electors,	Sir Geo. Yonge, Sir Geo. Collier,	Sir Geo. Yonge, Sir Geo. Collier,	27 Jan.	15 Feb.		24 Feb.
	Ilchester,	Geo. Johnstone, Electors,	John Harcourt,	George Johnstone,	27 Jan.	16 Feb.		20 Feb.
	Lancaster Borough,	John Lowther, Freemen,	Abram Rawlinson, Francis Reynolds,	Abram Rawlinson, Francis Reynolds,	8 Feb.	23 Feb.		27 Feb.
	Nairn County,	Freeholders on behalf of George Campbell,	Alexander Brodie,	Alexander Brodie,	27 Jan.	29 March,		3 April.

SESSIONS.	PLACES.	PETITIONERS.	SITTING MEMBERS.	IN WHOSE FAVOUR DETERMINED.	DATES.		
					PETITION PRESENTED.	COMMITTEE APPOINTED.	REPORT MADE.
1786	Seaford,	Sir Godf. Webster, Thomas Alves, Electors, Henry Flood, Lawrence Farsons, Electors,	Sir Peter Parker, Sir J. Henderson,	Declared void,	27 Jan.	22 Feb.	13 March.
	Seaford,	R. H. Henry Flood, Sir Godf. Webster,	Sir Peter Parker, Sir J. Henderson,	R. H. Henry Flood, Sir Godfrey Webster,	27 March,	25 April,	26 April.
1787	Carlisle,	Rowld. Stephenson, Freemen,	Edward Knubley,	Rowland Stephenson,	26 Jan.	15 Feb.	26 Feb.
	Norwich,	Sir Thomas Beevor, Electors,	Hon. Henry Hobart,	Declared void,	26 Jan.	15 Feb.	9 March.

SESSIONS.	PLACES.	PETITIONERS.	SITTING MEMBERS.	IN WHOSE FAVOUR DETERMINED.	DATES.		
					PETITION PRESENTED	COMMITTEE APPOINTED.	REPORT MADE.
1787	Norwich,	Electors on behalf of Sir Thomas Beevor,	Hon. Henry Hobart,	Hon. Henry Hobart,	5 April,	2 May,	8 May.
1798-9	Saltash,	John Lemon,	Earl of Mornington,	John Lemon,	7 Feb.	24 April,	7 May.
	Colchester,	Geo. Tierney, Geo. Jackson,	Special Return,	Geo. Tierney,	7 & 10 Feb.	26 Feb.	6 April.
	Westminster,	Lord Hood, Electors,	Lord J. Townshend,	Lord J. Townshend,	17 Feb.	3 April,	6 July.
1790-1	Barnstaple,	Richard Wilson,	John Cleveland,	John Cleveland,	1 Dec.	9 March,	16 March.
	Bodmin,	Sir Ja. Laroche, John Sullivan, Electors,	Sir John Morshead, Roger Wilbraham,	Sir John Morshead, Roger Wilbraham,	14 Dec.	17 Feb.	21 Feb.

SESSIONS.	PLACES.	PETITIONERS.	SITTING MEMBERS.	IN WHOSE FAVOUR DETERMINED.	DATES.		REPORT MADE.
					PETITION PRESENTED.	COMMITTEE APPOINTED.	
1790-1	Carlisle,	John Christian Curwen, Wilson Braddyll, Freemen and Citizens,	James Clarke Satterthwaite, Edward Knubley,	John Christian Curwen, Wilson Braddyll,	1 } Dec. 3	22 Feb.	3 March.
F. 1.	Colchester,	George Tierney,	George Jackson, Robert Thornton,	George Jackson, Robert Thornton,	1 Dec.	31 March,	4 April.
	Dorchester,	Hon. Cropley Ashley, Electors,	Hon. Geo. Damer,	Hon. Cropley Ashley,	3 Dec.	7 April,	14 April.
	Downton,	Will. Wrightson, Freeholders,	Bartw. Bouverie, Sir William Scott,	Bartw. Bouverie, Sir William Scott,	3 } Dec. 14	7 April,	17 May.
	Dumfries, &c. Burghs,	Sir Ja. Johnstone,	Patrick Millar, Jun.	Patrick Millar, Jun.	1 } Dec. 9	25 March,	1 April.
	Exeter,	Freemen and Electors,	John Baring,	John Baring,	1 Dec.	4 March,	23 March.

SESSIONS.	PLACES.	PETITIONERS.	SITTING MEMBERS.	IN WHOSE FAVOUR DETERMINED.	DATES.		
					PETITION PRESENTED.	COMMITTEE APPOINTED.	REPORT MADE.
1790-1	Fowey,	Lord Valletort, Philip Rashleigh, Lord Shuldham, Sir Ralph Payne, Electors in favour of Lord Valletort and Mr. Rashleigh,	Double Return,	Lord Valletort, Philip Rashleigh,	3 } 9 } Dec. 14	8 Feb.	7 March.
	Haddington, &c. Burghs,	William Fullarton,	Hon. T. Maitland,	Hon. Tho. Maitland,	1 Dec.	21 March,	23 March.
F. 1.	Hellston,	Mayor & Freemen, Ja. Bland Burges, Charles Abbot, Sir Gilbert Elliot, Step. Luthington, Richard Penhall,	Double Return,	Sir Gilbert Elliot, Stephen Luthington,	1 } Dec. 3	16 Dec.	23 Dec.

SESSIONS.	PLACES.	PETITIONERS.	SITTING MEMBERS.	IN WHOSE FAVOUR DETERMINED.	DATES.		
					PETITION PRESENTED.	COMMITTEE APPOINTED.	REPORT MADE.
1790-1	Leominster,	Richard Beckford, Electors,	John Sawyer,	Richard Beckford,	1 Dec.	15 March,	28 March.
	Luggershall,	John Drummond, Rob. Drummond, Electors, Hon. John Tho. Townshend—*to defend the seat of Mr. Selwyn*,	George Augustus Selwyn—*deceased*, Will. Atheton Harbord,	George Augustus Selwyn, William Atheton Harbord,	1 Dec. 16 Feb.	29 March,	15 April.
F.1.	Newark,	William Paxton, Electors,	William Crosbie, J. Manners Sutton,	William Crosbie, John Manners Sutton,	1 13 } Dec.	10 March,	22 March.

SESSIONS.	PLACES.	PETITIONERS.	SITTING MEMBERS.	IN WHOSE FAVOUR DETERMINED.	DATES.			REPORT MADE.
					PETITION PRESENTED.	COMMITTEE APPOINTED.		
1790-1 F. 1.	Okehampton,	John St. Leger, Robert Ladbroke, J. Will. Anderton, John Townfon, Mr. Luxmoore, &c. in favour of Mr. St. Leger & Mr Ladbroke, Electors in favour of Mr. Anderton & Mr. Townfon.	Double Return,	John St. Leger, Robert Ladbroke,	3⎫ 6⎬Dec. 9⎪ 13⎭		3 Feb.	28 Feb.
F. 1.	Orkney and Zetland,	Colonel T. Dundas, Freeholders,	John Balfour,	John Balfour,	3⎫Dec. 8⎭		15 April,	21 April.
F. 1.	Pontefract,	Charles Mellith, John Anftruther, Freeholders of Burgage Tenure,	John Smyth, William Sotheron,	John Smyth, William Sotheron,	1 Dec.		1 March,	9 March.

* * * *

SESSIONS	PLACES.	PETITIONERS.	SITTING MEMBERS.	IN WHOSE FAVOUR DETERMINED.	DATES.		
					PETITION PRESENTED.	COMMITTEE APPOINTED.	REPORT MADE.
1790-1	Poole,	Michael Angelo Taylor, Rob. Kingsmill, Lord Hadlo, Lord Daer, Inhabitants and Houfeholders, paying Scot and Lot, Burgeffes in favour of Taylor and Kingsmill,	Benjamin Lester, Charles Stuart,	Benjamin Lester, Michael Angelo Taylor,	3 Dec.	10 Feb.	25 Feb.
F. 2.	Steyning,	Sir J. Honywood, John Curtis,	Ja. Martin Lloyd, Henry Howard,	Sir John Honywood, John Curtis,	4 Dec.	15 Feb.	7 March.
	Stirling County,	Freeholders, Sir Alex. Campbell,	Sir Tho. Dundas,	Sir Thomas Dundas,	1 Dec.	25 Feb.	14 March.

SESSIONS.	PLACES.	PETITIONERS.	SITTING MEMBERS.	IN WHOSE FAVOUR DETERMINED.	DATES.		
					PETITION PRESENTED.	COMMITTEE APPOINTED.	REPORT MADE.
1790-1	Westminster,	John Horne Tooke,	Right Hon. Charles James Fox, Lord Hood,	Right Hon. Charles James Fox, Lord Hood,	9 Dec.	4 Feb.	7 Feb.
1792	Bedford Borough,	John Payne,	Samuel Whitbread,	Samuel Whitbread,	1 Feb.	7 March,	12 March.
F. 2.	Cirencester,	Robert Preston,	Richard Master,	Robert Preston,	1 Feb.	5 March,	10 May.
F. 2.	Honiton,	James Frafer,	George Templar,	George Templar,	3 Feb.	21 March,	22 March.
F. 2.	Horsham,	Lord Will. Gordon, James Baillie, Electors,	Timothy Shelley, Wilson Braddyll,	Lord William Gordon, James Baillie,	1 Feb.	16 Feb.	10 March.
	Newcastle under Lyne,	Thomas Fletcher, Clement Kynnersley,	J. Leveson Gower, Sir Archibald Macdonald,	John Leveson Gower, Sir Archibald Macdonald,	1 Feb.	23 Feb.	21 March.

SESSIONS.	PLACES.	PETITIONERS.	SITTING MEMBERS.	IN WHOSE FAVOUR DETERMINED.	DATES. PETITION PRESENTED.	DATES. COMMITTEE APPOINTED.	REPORT MADE.
1792	Plymouth,	John Macbride, Freemen,	Sir Frederick Leman Rogers,	Sir Frederick Leman Rogers,	1 Feb.	23 Feb.	27 Feb.
F. 2.	Roxburgh County,	John Rutherfurd,	Sir George Douglas,	Sir George Douglas,	3 Feb.	26 March,	30 March.
F. 2.	Seaford,	Sir Godfrey Webster, John Tarleton,	John Sargent, Jun. Rich. Paul Jodrell,	John Sargent, John Tarleton,	1 Feb.	28 Feb.	19 March.
F. 2.	Steyning,	Samuel Whitbread, Electors,	Ja. Martin Lloyd,	Samuel Whitbread,	1 Feb.	20 April,	7 May.
F. 2.	Sutherland County,	Robert Home Gordon, Robert Bruce Ancas Macleod,	Gen. James Grant,	Lieut. General James Grant,	1 } 6 } Feb.	9 March,	13 March.

SESSIONS.	PLACES.	PETITIONERS.	SITTING MEMBERS.	IN WHOSE FAVOUR DETERMINED.	DATES.		
					PETITION PRESENTED.	COMMITTEE APPOINTED.	REPORT MADE.
1792-3	Clifton Dartmouth Hardness,	John Seale,	Right Hon. John Charles Villiers, Edmund Bastard,	Edmund Bastard, Rt. Hon. John Charles Villiers,	15 Dec.	20 Feb.	26 Feb.
	Cricklade,	Samuel Petric, Inhabitants,	Thomas Estcourt, J. Walker Heneage,	Thomas Estcourt, J. Walker Heneage,	19 Dec.	12 March,	22 March.
	Great Grimsby,	Hon. Will. Welley Pole, Robert Wood, Electors,	John Harrison, Dudley Long North,	Void Election,	18 Dec.	7 March,	11 April.
	Ludgershall,	Nath. Newnham,	Samuel Smith,	Samuel Smith,	14 Dec.	19 March,	20 March.
	Pontefract,	John Walsh,	John Smyth,	John Smyth,	19 Dec.	12 March,	13 March.
	Poole,	Lord Daer,	Benjamin Lester,	Benjamin Lester,	18 Dec.	12 March,	13 March.
	Shaftesbury,	William Bryant, Hans Wintop Mortimer,	Charles Duncombe, William Grant,	Charles Duncombe, William Grant,	17 Dec.	7 March,	11 March.

SESSIONS.	PLACES.	PETITIONERS.	SITTING MEM-BERS.	IN WHOSE FAVOUR DETERMINED.	DATES.		
					PETITION PRESENTED.	COMMITTEE APPOINTED.	REPORT MADE.
1792-3	Stockbridge,	Jof. Fofter Barham, George Porter, Electors,	John Cator, John Scott,	Jofeph Fofter Barham, George Porter,	14 Dec.	11 Feb.	22 Feb.
	Sudbury,	William Smith,	J. Coxe Hippifley,	John Coxe Hippifley,	18 Dec.	20 March,	21 March.
	Warwick Borough,	Voters,	Hon. Geo. Villiers,	Hon. George Villiers,	17 Dec.	11 Feb.	18 Feb.

RIGHTS OF ELECTION

DETERMINED BY SELECT COMMITTEES.

RIGHTS OF ELECTION

DETERMINED BY SELECT COMMITTEES.

SESSIONS.	PLACES.	PETITIONERS.	WHEN REPORTED.	DETERMINATION.	DATES.		
					PETITION PRESENTED.	COMMITTEE APPOINTED.	REPORT MADE.
1792	Fowey,	John Coryton and others to oppose, Sir Ralph Payne and Wm. Morthead to defend,	The right of choosing the returning officer for Fowey, reported to the House the 7th day of Mar. 1791,	Reversed the decision of the former committee,	1 Feb. 12 Mar.	15 March,	21 March.
	Steyning,	Ja. Martin Lloyd and others to oppose, Electors to defend,	The right of election reported to the House the 7th day of Mar. 1791,	Reversed the decision of the former committee,	1 Feb. 8	13 March,	4 April.

SESSIONS.	PLACES.	PETITIONERS.	WHEN REPORTED.	DETERMINATION.	DATES.		
					PETITION PRESENTED	COMMITTEE APPOINTED.	REPORT MADE.
1792-3	Pontefract,	John Walsh, Electors to oppose, John Smyth and Wm. Sotheron to defend,	The right of election reported to the House the 9th day of March, 1791,	Confirmed the decision of the former committee,	15 Dec. 4 Jan.	18 Feb.	27 Feb.
1794-5	Carlisle,	Citizens to oppose, J. Christian Curwen and Wilson Braddyll, Freemen and Citizens to defend,	The right of election reported to the House the 3d day of March, 1791,	Confirmed the decision of the former committee,	12 Jan. 13 Feb.	3 March,	12 March.
	Seaford,	Electors to oppose, Inhabitants and Housekeepers paying Scot and Lot to defend,	The right of election reported to the House the 10th day of Mar. 1792,	Confirmed the decision of the former committee, with explanation,	2 Jan. 12	13 Feb.	19 Feb.

* * * *

SESSIONS.	PLACES.	PETITIONERS.	WHEN REPORTED.	DETERMINATION.	DATES.		REPORT MADE.
					PETITION PRESENTED.	COMMITTEE APPOINTED.	
1795	Westminster,	Electors to oppose. Inhabitants and Householders paying Scot and Lot to defend,	The right of election reported to the House the 6th day of July, 1789,	Reversed the decision of the former committee,	13 Jan. 16 Feb.	16 March,	19 March.

F I N I S.

INDEX.

A.

                                                PAGE.

ABSENCE—confequence of member's abfence from parliament, - 20
———— confequence of member's abfence from felect committees, - - - - 187
Action againft privileged perfons in the intervals of parliament, - - - - 61, 125
Adjournment of county poll, - - 53
——————— ———— court, - - 118
——————— of committee, - - 186, 197
——————— of houfe for want of fufficient number of members, - - - - 286
——————— of the order of the day for taking petitions into confideration for want of members - 325, 327
Admiffion of freemen—how to compel infpection of, 206
Amercement of abfentees, - - - 1
—————————— of fheriffs for omiffions in returns, - ib.
Annuities and rent charges—act to regulate the right of voting under, - - - - 170
Attendance of members required on ballot, 179, 323

B.

Bailiff to return precept where there is no mayor, under penalty, - - - 17
Ballot—how to proceed in, - - 180, 196, 325
Bank directors, not difqualified, - - - 133

6 *   *Bedfordfhire*,

Bedfordshire—act to authorize the then committee to proceed, though they may be reduced to eleven in number, - - - - - 262
Booths—expence, number, and clerks of booths, and regulations concerning them, - - - 144
——— for *Coventry*, where to be erected, - 238
Bribery—penalty and remedy, - - 112, 123
——— at *Shoreham*, act to prevent, - - 200
——— at *Cricklade*, act to prevent, - - 242
——— See Appendix. - - - - v

C.

Chairman of committee—how to be chosen, - 185
Checkbook to be allowed, - - - 145
——————— in cities and towns, counties of themselves, - - - - 157
Cheshire—how poll to be taken, - - 90
Chester, to send members to parliament for the county and city of, - - - - 23
Cinque ports—the nomination of members by the *Lord Warden* illegal, - - - - 39
Cities and towns, counties of themselves—qualification of voters, - - - - 130
——— and towns counties of themselves, act to regulate elections for, - - - 149
Clerks of county elections, - - - 52
Clerk of the crown. See Return.
Commissioners of any office not to be increased, - 73
Committee—mode of forming them, - 183, 197
———— their power, - - - 186
———— as to their adjournment, - 186, 197
———— member of, consequence of absence, - 187
———— authorized to proceed on the *Bedford* petition, though they may be reduced to eleven in number, - - - - 262
———— to proceed on petition though there be no return, or undue return, and regulations, - 271

Committee,

INDEX.

PAGE.

Committee—may report on days appointed for taking petitions into consideration, - - - 287
——— proceedings, in case the number of them be reduced, - - - - 290
——— how to report, - - - 291
——— in what case to report right of election, 295
——— not to be dissolved on prorogation of Parliament, - - - - - 299
Controverted elections—acts to regulate, 178, 195, 206, 277, 321
Contractors—what contractors are incapable of being elected, or sitting in Parliament, - - 250
Conveyances to multiply votes, void, - - 55
——— colourably made to qualify electors, their effect and consequences, - - - 86
Copyholders disabled under penalty, - - 161
Costs—in what case incurred, and how to be ascertained, 293
——— recovered, 294
Coventry—act to regulate elections for, - - 233
——— mode of admitting freemen, and register of indentures, - - - - - 234
——— oath of electors, - - - 236
——— penalty in returning officers admitting persons not sworn, - - - - 237
——— on town clerk for fraudulent entries of freemen, - - - - - 238
——— booths, where to be erected, - - 239
County Court, for the election of county members, when and where to be held - - - 51
——— of *Yore*, where to be held, - 56
——— of *Southampton* may be adjourned from *Winchester* to *Newport*, - - ib.
——— concerning the adjournment of, 113, 146
County Election—acts concerning form and manner of, 3, 13, 137, 266, 301
——— what time of day it shall be, - 17
——— when to be, - - 265

INDEX.

	PAGE.
County Election—oath to freeholders,	9, 52, 88, 109, 138, 267
——————— See Writ, Poll, Return, &c.	
Cricklade—act to prevent bribery at,	242
——————— right of voting extended,	ib.
——————— qualification of new voters, and oath,	ib.
——————— returning officers duty,	245
Customs—commissioners and officers of, disqualified, and penalty	65

D.

Days excepted for proceeding of committee,	286
Death of a member in recess—how warrant for writ shall issue,	257
——————— petitioned against or returned, on double return what notice shall be given,	279
——————— how to be certified to obtain *Speaker's* warrant,	192
——————— of *Speaker*, respecting the issuing the warrant,	259
Defence of member petitioned against, abandoned—what notice thereof to be given,	280
Demise of the crown, not to dissolve the parliament,	69
——————— how parliament shall meet and proceed, and of dissolution of lords justices,	71
Determination of committee—mode of,	189
Discoverer of Bribery indemnified,	113
Disqualification. See Qualification.	
Dissolution—parliament not to be dissolved by the demise of the crown,	69
Dower—qualification by means of,	226
Durham—to send members for the county and city, who shall be electors, and how return shall be made,	29

E.

	PAGE
Elections for counties—what clause shall be in writs,	3
———————— what time of day it shall be,	17
———————— when and where to be held,	51
———————— borough and city, as to precept, return, and penalty,	15
———————— cities and towns, counties of themselves, proceedings in,	157
———————— *Scotland* within what time to be after receipt of the writ. See Appendix	xcvii
———————— See Precept, Poll, Return, &c.	
———————— controverted; see further Appendix.	
Electors for counties—residence not necessary,	206
———————— no person under 21 years of age shall be admitted to vote,	55
———————— See qualification.	
Evidence at the poll, and before the house; see Appendix,	vii
———————— false; see Appendix,	xxi
Excise officers shall not interfere in elections and penalty,	41
———————— disqualified,	59
———————— no persons belonging to, shall intermeddle in elections,	81
Exchange of lists; see Appendix,	xxi
Excused from ballot—who shall be,	181

F.

False evidence and disobedience of the authority of the committee,	289
Fee to clerk of the crown for filing return,	57
—- for administering oath to candidate, certificate, and filing,	79
—- for inspection and copies of land tax assessments,	142, 227
—- the like for cities and towns, counties of themselves,	155
—- for inspection and copy of minutes of admission of freemen,	167
—- for entering certificate and memorial of rent charge, searching, and copies,	175

Free-

	PAGE.
Freeholders to be sworn, and oath,	9, 52, 67
Freemen—act to regulate the qualification of,	166
———, how to compel admission, and inspection of admission,	205

I.

Interference at elections—persons concerned in collecting revenues not to interfere at elections,	84
——————————, See further Appendix,	iii
Jurisdiction of the house; see Appendix,	ib.

L.

Land tax assessments—where to be kept,	142
——————— fees for inspection and copies,	ib.
——————— for cities and towns counties of themselves, where to be kept, inspection and copies,	155
——————— qualification in respect of,	217, 303
——————— how to be made,	218
——————— appeal against and how to be amended,	220, 225
——————— penalty on assessor for neglect to deliver duplicate of,	221
——————— fine on constable and assessor in default of delivering duplicates and remedy,	ib.
——————— how far duplicates are evidence,	228
Last determination of the house—votes according to, are legal,	111
London—act to regulate elections for,	98

M.

Mandamus by freemen, to compel admission,	205
Minor not admitted to vote,	55
——— return of, void,	ib.
——— penalty on him for sitting in parliament,	55

Monmouth

	PAGE.
Monmouth to elect members,	21
Mortgage—qualification by means of,	54, 77

N.

Nominees—as to the naming them and how excused, 192, 198
Norwich—act to regulate elections at, - 115
Notice of petition to be given by the *Speaker*, when
 and to whom, - - - 179, 196
—— of the time and place of election - - 310
—— in *Scotland*. See Appendix, - - xcvii

O.

Oath to county electors, perjury and subornation, 9, 52, 88
 109, 138, 267
—— of allegiance and supremacy, and declaration
 against popery—consequence of refusing, - 34
—— of candidates qualification and by whom to be administered, - - - - 78
————————————— to be certified under penalty, - - - - ib
—— fee for administering, - - - 79
—— of liverymen—perjury and subornation, - 101
—— of returning officer, - - - 111
—— of electors in cities and towns, counties of them
 selves—by whom to be administered, and consequence
 of perjury, - - - 150
—— to be taken by members, - - 163
—— before committee, by whom to be administered, 190
—— of electors for *Shoreham*, and perjury, - 20
————————— *Cricklade* voters and perjury 243
—— in what case may be administered on scrutiny, 268
—— to poll clerks and perjury, - - 269
Oaths—returning officer may appoint persons to administer the oaths (or affirmation) at elections, and give
 certificates - - - - 312
—— places to be provided for taking the oaths - 317
—— expences of providing places for administering the
 oaths how to be defrayed - - - 320

Occasional

INDEX.

	PAGE.
Occasional freemen—act concerning,	166
Occasionalty—act to prevent,	275

Order of the day—in what cases the House may proceed previous to the order of the day for taking election petitions into consideration, - - 308

——————— in what respect the House may proceed to business notwithstanding there may not be sufficient members for a ballot, - - 323, 324

P.

Papists disabled from sitting in parliament, or voting for members, and other disabilities, - - 32
——— penalty for offence against the act disabling them, 35
Parliament, triennial, - - - 41
——————— septennial, - - - 96
Peers, *Speaker's* warrant may issue on member becoming, 212
——— member becoming peer in recess, how warrant for writ shall issue, - - - 257
——— what notice shall be given in case a member returned on double return becoming a peer, - 280
Penalty on sheriff, for undue return, - 4, 9, 16
——————— levying more wages than assessed, 12
——————— neglect of duty, - - 54
——— on returning officer for false return, - 17
——————— neglect of duty, - 58
——————— not certifying candidates oath, - - - - 78
——————— obstructing the election of his successor, - - - - 83
——————— refusing oath to electors, 110
——————— admitting persons to poll without taking the oath when demanded, - ib.
——————— disobedience under the act against bribery, - - - 114
——————— *Coventry*, for admitting persons to poll without being sworn, - - 237
——— on bailiff for not returning precept, - 17

Penalty

INDEX.

	PAGE.
Penalty on officer for taking more than his fee for candidates oath and certificate,	79
——— on presiding officer for *London*, for refusing oath to liverymen,	102
——— for offences against the act to regulate elections for *London*,	106
——— on officer witholding books of admission of freemen and remedy,	168
——— for offences against the act disabling papists,	35
——— for securing false or double return,	47
——— on clerk of the crown for neglecting to enter returns,	43
——— for bribery and remedy,	112
——— for neglect under the act respecting registering annuities and rent charges,	177
——— for refusing inspection and copies of admission of freemen,	206
——— on assessor of land tax assessments for neglect to deliver duplicate,	221
——— on clerk of the peace on refusing inspection of duplicates,	229
——— on town clerk of *Coventry* for making fraudulent entries of admission of freemen,	238
——— on persons voting under or making colourable conveyances to create votes,	87
———————— for county members not qualified,	143
———————— for cities and towns, counties of themselves, not being qualified,	131, 156
——— on copyholders voting, and remedy,	161
——— on freemen voting contrary to act,	167
——— on persons antedating the admission of freemen,	ib.
———————— voting being disabled under 22 G. 3. c. 41.	248
——— on minors sitting in parliament,	55
——— on incapacitated persons presuming to sit,	74
——— on persons sitting in parliament holding pensions,	98
——— on other disabled persons sitting in parliament,	136
——— on persons sitting disqualified by means of contract,	253

Penalty

	PAGE.
Penalty on contractors admitting members to share of contract,	253
—— on excise officers interfering in elections,	41, 81
—— on officers of customs,	66
—— on persons belonging to the post office,	80
—— on persons concerned in collecting certain revenues,	84
—— on sheriffs, deputes, &c. in *Scotland* for neglect of duty in executing the writ. See Appendix,	xcviii
—— on high sheriffs there, for interfering in the execution of writs. See Appendix,	xcix
Pensions—persons enjoying, incapable of being elected,	97
Perjury. See Oath.	
Petition—time to be fixed for considering, &c.	178
—— may be presented in case of no return or of undue return, and regulations concerning the same,	271
—— who may petition,	279
—— not to be withdrawn,	284
—— within what time petitioner must appear after the time appointed for his petition,	287
—— regulation for the trial of, where no party to oppose appears,	288
—— against the right of election, within what time to be presented, when to be heard and reported,	296
—— See Ballot, Committee, &c.	
—— time of presenting renewed petitions on the right of election, and taking the same into consideration,	322
—— proceedings on. See further Appendix,	xii
Placemen incapable of sitting in parliament,	135
—— See Customs, Excise, &c.	
Poll—by whom and how to be taken for counties,	51
—— in what case it may and may not be adjourned for counties,	ib.
—— for county—copy to be delivered,	54
—— how names of electors to be taken down,	89
—— books at county elections to be delivered to the clerk of the peace,	90
—— how to be taken for *Yorkshire* and *Cheshire*,	ib.

INDEX.

                                                                                  PAGE.

Poll—how to be taken for *London*, and proceedings therein, 100
—— act against bribery, to be read at - - 114
—— at election by freemen, act of 3 G. 3. c. 15. to be read - - - - - 169
—— and scrutiny, commencement and continuance thereof, - - - 263, 266
—— clerk's oath and perjury, - - 269
Popery—declaration against, to be made by members, 32
Post-office—no person belonging to, shall intermeddle in elections under penalty, - - 80
Precept to be delivered by the sheriff to the returning officer, - - - - - 15
——— to be returned, by whom and how, - 17
——— within what time to be delivered to the returning officer, - - - - 50
——— the like for the cinque ports, - - 58
Prevarication of witness—consequence of, - - 189
Privilege, respecting, - 60, 124, 192
——— peers and members subject to actions for breach of public trust, but not to arrest, - 67
——— of members from arrest, and consequence of non-appearance to action, - - - 194
Proclamation in counties, within what time to be made, 266
Prorogation of parliament not to dissolve election committees, - - - - - 299

Q.

Quaker's affirmation, and consequence of false affirmation, 91
Qualification of electors for counties, 8, 10, 87, 141, 217, 301
————————— *Wales* and *Monmouth*, - 27
————————— *Durham*, - 29
————————— Universities, - 76
————————— *London*, - 107
————————— cities and towns, counties of themselves, - - - 130, 154
————————— *Shoreham*, - 200

                                                              Qualification

Qualification of electors for *Cricklade*, - - 242
——————— by means of being heir apparent of a peer, &c. - - - 76
————————————————— a freeman, 167
——————— by trust or mortgage, - 54, 77
——————————— annuity or rent charge, - 171
————————————— ecclesiastical, and extra-parochial property, - - - - 93
————————————— dower, - - 226
————————————— scot and lot, - - 275
——————— of candidates for counties, - 5, 19, 75,
————————————— cities and boroughs, - 76
——————— Papists, } { 32
——————— Minors, 55
——————— Copyholders, 161
——————— Perjured persons, 112
——————— Pensioners, 97
——————— Collectors, *Salt*, } disqualified, { 38, 40
——————— ————— *Excise*, 59
——————— ————— *Customs*, 65
——————— certain officers, 72
——————— Placemen, 135
——————— Collectors, *Revenue*, 246
——————— Contractors, 250
——————— one person only for one tenement, 55
——————— of candidates to be sworn to, if required, and oath, - - - - - 77
——————— ————— See further, Appendix, - ix

R.

Recognizance to appear, to be entered into by petitioner, how, and consequence of neglect, - - 281
——————— time enlarged for John Macbride, Esq. and his sureties to enter into recognizance, - 305
Register of memorial, of annuity or rent charge to qualify voters, - - - - 173
Report of committee of complaint to the house, - 187

Report

INDEX.

	PAGE.
Report of committee may be received on days appointed for petitions,	287
——————— how to be made and its consequence,	291, 292
——————— of right of election, in what case,	295
Return of writ, to be made by the sheriff, and of returning officer's return,	16
——————— within what time to be made,	49, 57
——————— amercement of sheriffs for omissions in,	2
——————— false or undue, penalty on sheriff,	4, 9, 16, 94
——————— knight and sheriffs traverse on inquest,	7
——— of precept by mayor and bailiffs, how to be made,	17
——— false, prohibited,	46
——————— when contrary to last determination,	ib.
——— double; deemed false,	ib.
——— false by returning officer—penalty and remedy,	17, 46, 273
——— false or double—penalty for procuring the same,	47
——— to be entered by the clerk of the crown, and his book to be evidence,	ib.
——— clerk of the crown neglecting to enter, penalty,	48
——— of disabled persons is void,	74
——— death of member, returned on double return, what notice shall be given,	280
——— when to be made in case of no scrutiny,	264
——————— regulations concerning, in case of scrutiny,	265
——————— security given to procure return void,	47
——————— amended. See Appendix,	xxii
Returning officer to be annually elected,	82
——————— penalty on him for obstructing the election of his successors,	83
——————— See Return, Poll, &c.	

Residence. See Qualification.
Revenue officers. See Qualification.
———— penalty on disqualified persons voting, - 248
Right of election, in what case a statement to be delivered to the committee, - - - 295
Right of election, petition against the report of, when to be heard and determined, - - - 296
———— ———— time of presenting renewed petitions on the right of election, and taking same into consideration, - - - - 322

S.

Salt duty—persons concerned in collecting, disqualified, 38, 40
Scotland—acts relating to elections for, See App. xxiii to c
Scot and Lot—what inhabitancy required, - - 275
Secretary at War. See Soldiers.
Scrutiny for *London*—proceedings on, - - 104
———— how returning officer shall proceed in, 265
———— in what case returning officer may administer oath, - - - - - 268
Septennial parliament—act, - - - 96
Shaftesbury, *Speakers* warrant not to issue for a certain time, - - - - 213
Sheriff. See Return, Poll, &c.
———— penalty on high sheriff for interfering in the execution of writs for *Scotland*. See Appendix, - xcix
Shoreham—act to prevent bribery at elections for - 200
———— qualification of voters for - - ib.
———— how precept for, shall be indorsed, and election had, - - - - - - 202
Soldiers—of quartering them during elections, 119, 232, 240
Southampton—county court may be adjourned from *Winchester* to *Newport*, - - - 56
———— act for fixing a place for holding certain elections for the county of, - - - 213
———— when and where the same may be adjourned, 274
Speaker. See Warrant.

Splitting

INDEX.

	PAGE.
Splitting votes for counties—act to prevent,	86
Subornation. See oath.	
Summons to parliament,	1
———— of committee, consequence of disobedience,	189

T.

Tampering with witnesses. See Appendix.	xxi
Traverse of knights and sheriffs on inquest for false return,	7
Treating after the teste of the writ, prohibited, and election void,	43
Triennial parliament—act for,	41
Trust—qualification by means of,	54

U.

Universities to elect members,	76
Void—elections void for treating,	43
—— security given to procure false returns,	47
—— conveyances to multiply votes,	55
—— election of minors,	ib.
—— member accepting any office, his seat becomes,	74
—— election of persons not qualified shall be,	76
—— ———— of candidates on refusing oath to be,	79
—— securities given to defeat colourable conveyances,	85
—— return of placemen,	135
—— votes of copyholders,	161
—— members acting contrary to the act to regulate qualifications, their election,	165
—— freemen voting contrary to the act, their votes,	167
—— elections in favour of persons disqualified by means of contract,	253
—— what notice shall be given in case the house resolve the seat of a member petitioned against to be,	280

W.

Wages—how assessed and forfeited,	4, 9, 11, 12, 21, 25
Wales, to elect members,	21

INDEX.

	PAGE.
Wales, as to the levying and paying of the wages of the members,	25
——— and *Monmouth*, who are to be electors for	28
Warrant—in what case *Speaker* may issue, for new writ,	191, 212, 257, 259
Winchester Poll—when and where to the same may be adjourned,	274
Witness, prevaricating, or not attending summons—consequence of,	189
——— guilty of disobedience and false evidence,	289
Writs for county elections—what clause shall be inserted in,	3
—— to issue with expedition,	49
—— within what time to be returned,	ib.
—— to be delivered to the proper officer,	ib.
—— in what case *Speaker* to issue his warrant,	191, 212, 257, 259
—— by *whom* to be executed in *Scotland*. See Appendix,	xcvii, xcviii
—— for *Orkney* and *Zetland*, where to be published. See Appendix,	c
Writ—See further, Appendix,	ii, xcvii

Y.

York, county court—when to be held,	56
Yorkshire poll—how to be taken,	90

ERRATA.

Page		read	instead of
15	(*in margin*)	8 H. 6. c. 7.	6 H. 6. c. 7.
103	*line* 9	received any alms	received an alms
122	14	which notice	which writ
127	23	shall not be barred	shall not be bound
206	4	that the same	that the some
255	13	that no person	that person
301	(*title of act*)	cap. 35.	cap. *.